Wealth, Work, and Health

Wealth, Work, and Health

Innovations in Measurement in the Social Sciences

Essays in Honor of F. Thomas Juster

James P. Smith and Robert J. Willis, Editors

Ann Arbor

THE UNIVERSITY OF MICHIGAN PRESS

2002   2001   2000   1999   4   3   2   1

A CIP catalog record for this book is available from the British Library.

Library of Congress Cataloging-in-Publication Data

Wealth, work, and health : innovations in measurement in the social
    sciences : essays in honor of F. Thomas Juster / James P. Smith and
    Robert J. Willis, editors.
          p.   cm.
     A selection of 12 papers presented at a conference held in
    December 1996 at the Institute for Social Research (ISR) to
    honor Juster's contributions and mark his June 1997 retirement from
    ISR and the University of Michigan.
     Includes bibliographical references.
     ISBN 0-472-11026-8 (cloth : alk. paper)
     1. Social sciences — Research — Congresses.   2. Wealth — Research —
    Congresses.   3. Labor — Research — Congresses.   4. Health — Research —
    Congresses.   I. Juster, F. Thomas (Francis Thomas), 1926–   .
    II. Willis, Robert J. (Robert James), 1940–   .
    H62.W378   1999
    300'.7'2 — dc21   99-22997
                                                                          CIP

Contents

Introduction

James P. Smith and Robert J. Willis

In June 1997 F. Thomas Juster officially retired from the University of Michigan and the Institute for Social Research (ISR). To celebrate this occasion and to acknowledge the scientific contributions of his distinguished career, a conference was held in his honor at ISR in December 1996. The papers presented at this conference and included in this volume deal with some of the main themes highlighted in Tom Juster's forty years of scholarship.

Survey Measurement

From the very beginning, Tom has been interested in how to measure behavior by asking people questions about the objective and subjective circumstances of their lives. His interests, however, went beyond the tried and true survey practices of the day. He constantly asked (and continues to do so to this day) what respondents actually mean when they answer a question. He also took it as a personal challenge when told that you could not expect to measure something like consumer intentions, savings, wealth, or time allocation in conventional household surveys. To recognize his enduring concern with survey measurement, the first three papers in this volume deal directly with these issues.

In a paper written in 1966 that is now just receiving its due recognition, Juster argued and then demonstrated empirically that consumer intentions were better modeled and measured by subjective probability scales. These scales required respondents to numerically rank the probability of some future event. Until recently, this important idea had little impact, especially on the economics profession.

Jeff Dominitz and Charles F. Manski's essay, "The Several Cultures of Research on Subjective Expectations," deals with the changing attitudes of the research community toward the kind of subjective probability scales that Juster has long championed. Not only have opinions within disciplines changed considerably over time, the variation in attitudes across the social science disciplines is enormous.

But no discipline has been more hostile to measures of subjective belief than economics. No matter where they were trained, all economists were taught: "Don't trust what they say; see what they do." As Dominitz and Manski point out, this hostility persists despite the central role individual expectations play in most economic modeling. They trace this consensus professional distaste for subjective measurement to the findings of the Federal Reserve–appointed Smithies committee. This committee challenged the value of subjective expectations data in predicting subsequent individual outcomes. Although this negative assessment became the dominant professional opinion in economists, the principal investigators of many of the major economic surveys kept many of these subjective questions in their surveys. At best, an uneasy truce emerged between them and their professional colleagues in the leading economics departments. One unfortunate consequence was that the work of the survey collectors became increasingly divorced from the research of mainstream economic theorists and empiricists alike.

Dominitz and Manski argue that this negative professional judgment should have been limited to the particular qualitative form in which these subjective questions were asked. They argue that the quantitative subjective scales of the type favored by Juster more than thirty years ago offer far more promise. They believe that subjective probability scales more closely correspond to theoretical constructs and are more amenable to empirical hypothesis testing. Subjective probability scales are now routinely included in many ongoing household surveys and cover a wide spectrum of household behavior (mortality, job loss, income, fertility, and schooling to name a few). This is another reason why Juster's influence on his own discipline is so much greater at the end of his career than at any previous time. Of course, only time will tell, and even an intermediate verdict on how useful these probability scales will eventually become is probably a decade away.

N. Anders Klevmarken and Frank P. Stafford's essay, "Measuring Investment in Young Children with Time Diaries," deals with another idea that Tom Juster championed (once again often as a lonely voice) — the use of time diaries. While time diaries are potentially useful for many purposes, Klevmarken and Stafford's application concerns quantifying the time investments parents make in their young children. These investments are undervalued because they are often not measured in conventional surveys and do not enter national accounts.

In the aggregate, according to Klevmarken and Stafford, time investments in children are far from trivial. For example, they estimate that these investments are 22 percent of gross domestic product (GDP) for Sweden, larger than all investments in physical plant and equipment in that country. Nor is Sweden an exception to the general rule. In 1975, college educated U.S. mothers were spending 859 hours per year in child-related activities. One important difference does emerge between these two countries. In Sweden, the marginal effect of adding another child on total household work is actually negative, suggesting that the non-child-care activities are "outsourced" in Sweden.

Daniel Hill's essay, "Unfolding Bracket Method in the Measurement of Expenditures and Wealth," deals with a problem that Tom Juster has probably fretted over more than any other in recent years. On many issues, respondents may have difficulty answering because they have only a very fuzzy idea of what the correct answer is. Since they believe that the interviewer wants a precise answer, the end result may simply be high prevalence of item nonresponse. To alleviate this widespread problem, Juster helped develop another survey technique — unfolding brackets. When respondents did not know exact amounts (which occurred often), they would be asked a series of bracketing questions that would place the unknown value between a lower and an upper threshold.

Hill deals with two important applications of this general problem — out-of-pocket medical care expenditures and household wealth. Medical expenditures are among the most difficult items for respondents to remember, and, consequently, there has been little attempt to measure them in general-purpose surveys. The second wave of the Health and Retirement Study (HRS) contained a very brief set of questions aimed at estimating out-of-pocket and total medical expenditures over a two-year period. An assessment of the validity of these expenditure measures was derived by comparing them to measures obtained from a very detailed set of questions used in the National Medical Expenditure Survey (NMES — the so-called gold standard). Among the many complications raised in such comparisons across surveys, difference in reference periods can be among the most important. In this case, HRS relies on a two-year reference period while NMES uses only one year. Hill outlines a statistical modeling strategy that deals with these different reference periods.

His empirical results suggest considerable substantive similarities in the estimates obtained, once differences in the reference periods are taken into account. Low-level health expenditures do appear to be lower in HRS than in NMES, a finding Hill attributes to greater memory decay in the HRS survey.

Statistical models of the determinants (doctor visits, hospital nights) of medical care expenditures were also estimated for the two surveys. While differences emerge between the two surveys, they appear to be largely confined to modeling the incidence of expenditure (rather than the amount) and to goodness of fit. Not surprisingly, given that the HRS relies on a much noisier measure of expenditures, concerns arise regarding how to optimally select the bracket thresholds that are used in order to maximize their informational content. For example, it would make little sense to place all the bracket thresholds under $50,000 when a significant number of cases have values over $100,000. In his essay, Hill outlines a statistical procedure that selects the "optimal" thresholds. These thresholds are optimal in that they maximize how much of the variance can be explained (R^2) by a given set of thresholds. Based on this methodology, the baseline HRS wealth brackets were actually revised. In general, this revision placed more thresholds at very high values.

Hill deals with two other issues related to the bracket technology. The first, which he labels "contamination," concerns the potential problem that respondents who may have been willing to provide exact answers may be induced by the introduction of brackets to provide only categorical information instead. However, Hill's statistical results indicate that respondents who used brackets early in the HRS survey "learned" that very precise information was not required. Because of this learning, these respondents were actually more likely to provide exact information for items included later in the survey.

The final issue Hill addresses concerns "anchoring." Anchoring takes place when the wording of a question conveys information to the respondent about what the correct answer may be. For example, if entry points in the bracket sequence go from the highest to lowest values rather than the other way around, this may raise respondent estimates of the unknown values. Essentially, respondents may be picking up clues about what the "correct" answer is from the first entry value given by the interviewer. To test this possibility, HRS included in its third wave a question about the circumference of the earth. At least for this question, on which respondents' knowledge is quite poor, the evidence is that anchoring effects do indeed exist. For example, an initial entry point of ten thousand miles lowers the estimate of the circumference by more than nine thousand miles.

Household Wealth

Perhaps there is no more important contribution made by Juster to the ordinary professional practices of research economists than his thirty-year interest in obtaining better measures of household wealth. During his years at ISR, Tom Juster was principal investigator of the 1983 and 1989 Surveys of Consumer Finances (SCF). SCF continues to provide the most comprehensive and detailed measurement of the components of household wealth for a representative cross section of U.S. households. During the years of his leadership, a number of innovations were introduced into the SCF. One of the more important was the over-sampling of high-income households (where most wealth is concentrated) through tax records.

Tom's work on wealth culminated in the central role household wealth played in the HRS and Asset and Health Dynamics among the Oldest Old (AHEAD) studies. Tom was the original principal investigator for both studies. While anyone who knows Tom quickly realizes that he has strong opinions, he is also willing to try new methods and to change his mind when the evidence goes against him. In recognition of the importance of household wealth in Juster's career, four of the essays in this volume (Venti and Wise; Smith; Gustman, Mitchell, Samwick, and Steinmeier; and Wolff) focus on various aspects of the level and distribution of household wealth accumulation.

In their essay, "Lifetime Earnings, Savings Choices, and Wealth at Retirement," Steven F. Venti and David A. Wise address the central question of how much of the distribution of wealth is really the consequence of household choice about how much to save and how much to consume. Some observers believe that many households, particularly low-income and middle-income households, have just enough resources to get by on and, consequently, have little real choice in their savings decisions. The absence of any meaningful amounts of wealth *on average* for these low- and middle-income households compared to significant wealth accumulations among affluent households certainly contributes to the view that the options of those households at the bottom may be quite limited.

The fact that this is a commonly held belief has unfortunately not been matched by much empirical evidence either supporting or rejecting it. Venti and Wise tackle the question head-on by examining the amount of variation in wealth among households with the same lifetime incomes. Their ability to do so is based on another Justerian innovation in HRS — the matching of the detailed individual social security earnings records onto the household survey. Using these data they find that there exists a very wide dispersion in accumulated savings (wealth), even among families with the lowest lifetime incomes.

Holding lifetime incomes constant, the dispersion in wealth can only be described as enormous. For example, among those households in the median lifetime income deciles, the wealth of those at the 90th quantile is thirty-five times larger than the wealth of those at the 10th percentile. Similarly, even among those households at the lowest income decile the 90th percentile has $150,000 in household wealth. On the other side of the coin, many households with very high lifetime incomes have saved very little.

If households are able to save, why do so many decide not to do so while other households save so much? Within each lifetime income decile, Venti and Wise estimate a empirical model predicting household wealth. The covariates in this model include such "objective" circumstances as marital status, health, children, and the amount of inheritances received. Since these variables can explain little of the observed variation in wealth, Venti and Wise argue that only a small part of the dispersion in household wealth is explained by factors such as low income, children, marriage, and the lack of an inheritance that may constrain the ability to save. Instead, they conclude that most of dispersion in savings results from some households choosing to save while others decide to spend.

Better measures of household wealth in surveys such as HRS and AHEAD have encouraged economists to try again to elicit the underlying motives about why people and households save and accumulate wealth. There is no lack of competing models — life-cycle differences in the timing of income and consumption; precautionary reactions to uncertainty and risk; and bequests to name a few.

The relative importance of bequests and inheritances in wealth accumulation has been particularly hard to evaluate in part because those items are so difficult to measure in household surveys. Without a postdeath interview with relatives of the deceased respondent (extremely rare in household surveys), the existence and value of inheritances from the perspective of the donor are left unrecorded. Building on Juster's earlier insights about the potential power of subjective probabilities for measuring intentions, subjective probability measures of planned bequests were used in HRS and AHEAD. Respondents in both surveys were asked to rank on a scale of 0 to 100 the probability that they or their spouse would leave financial inheritances that exceeded certain thresholds (such as $10,000 or $100,000).

James P. Smith's essay, "Inheritance and Bequests," evaluates the usefulness of these subjective probabilities of bequests. Consistent with low prevalence rates of inheritances documented through estate records, Smith reports that large fractions of respondents in both HRS and AHEAD state that there is little chance of leaving an inheritance of any significant size. However, there is also a significant fraction of respondents who say that they fully intend to leave financial bequests, often of a considerable amount. Perhaps most important, there appears to be a strong trend toward higher fractions of households giving financial bequests. Far more households in their fifties (the HRS sample) state they will bequeath than do households over age sixty-nine (the AHEAD sample). Such data suggest that bequests motives may exist for a sizable and rising fraction of U.S. households.

Smith's essay also documents the important correlates of bequest intentions. Intentions to leave bequests are concentrated among the top third of the income, wealth, and education distribution; are higher among men than among women; and are stronger for those who are in good health and among those households with high levels of annuity incomes during their retirements. In contrast, family size or the number of children does not appear to be very important, as childless couples are little different than couples with children in their expectations of leaving bequests. Based on his analyses, Smith concludes with a generally positive assessment about the usefulness of subjective probability scales in helping researchers understand bequest leaving behavior.

Alan L. Gustman, Olivia S. Mitchell, Andrew A. Samwick, and Thomas L. Steinmeier's essay, "Pension and Social Security Wealth in the Health and Retirement Study," broadens the definition of household wealth to include the value of future pensions and future social security checks. Almost all households in their fifties anticipate some social security in their futures. These annuities can be discounted to give a present value of social security wealth. In a similar vein, private pensions, either directly in defined contribution plans or indirectly for defined benefit plans, are an important source of wealth for many households.

A contribution of this study is that it makes use of another Juster innovation imported into the HRS — the measurement of pension values from material collected directly from the firms that employ the respondents. Using a technology originally developed while Juster was principal investigator of the SCF, HRS respondents were asked to provide the names and addresses of their employers. After respondent permissions were granted, these employers were contacted and details of the firm pension plans were coded. The details of these plans permit a much more accurate calculation of pension wealth than could be obtained from respondents alone.

These additional components of wealth turn out to be extremely important. Combined, social security and pensions comprise roughly half of all household wealth. The impact of these two components on the distribution of wealth across households is, however, quite different. Social security has an equalizing impact on the distribution of wealth. In contrast, pension wealth is very unevenly distributed, accounting for 7 percent of the wealth of those in the bottom quarter of wealth holders compared to 31 percent of those households lying between the 75th and 95th percentiles.

Neglecting social security and pensions also distorts data on household income, although to a lesser extent. For example, the yearly accrual values of pensions and social security account for about 9 percent of total household income in this age group. This distortion of household income varies considerably among households. The distortion is particularly large for households with defined benefit plans in the year right before their retirement.

Edward N. Wolff's contribution to this volume, "The Size Distribution of Wealth in the United States: A Comparison among Recent Household Surveys," examines the wealth issue from another perspective. Unlike the other authors, who are relative newcomers to this subject, Ed Wolff has been studying the distribution of wealth for decades. Perhaps no one was better aware of the lack of attention paid to the measurement of wealth in household surveys. How different things are today! With the explosion of new wealth modules in recent household surveys (much of it due to Juster), there is now as Wolff says, "a wealth of wealth data."

But are the wealth data in these new surveys consistent, and do they paint similar portraits of U.S. society? These questions are the focus of Wolff's essay. He presents estimates of the distribution of wealth from alternative waves of three surveys: the 1983, 1989, and 1992 Surveys of Consumer Finances; the 1984, 1988, and 1983 Surveys of Income and Program Participation (SIPP); and the 1984, 1989, and 1994 Panel Studies of Income Dynamics. Combined, these data provide information about changes in wealth over time as well as on the differences obtained across alternative surveys fielded at roughly the same time.

There are some disquieting differences among the surveys not only in the levels of household wealth but also in the sign of the secular change in wealth, as well as in the precise timing of those changes. Whether means or medians are used, SIPP shows persistent *declines* in wealth from the mid-1980s to the mid-1990s. The fall in median wealth (presumably containing less measurement error) was over 2 percent per year. In remarkable contrast, over roughly the same period, the Panel Study of Income Dynamics (PSID) records a steady *increase* in median wealth of 2.8 percent per year. To add to the confusion, SCF claims a decline in median wealth while mean wealth was rising, with the peak levels occurring in 1989. A similar lack of consistency between the surveys emerges when the levels and distribution of wealth are examined. The highest wealth levels are obtained in the SCF, a consequence no doubt of their oversampling of high-income households. Even within-survey comparisons show major anomalies. For example, the SCF indicate a 35 percent decline in the value of corporate stock between 1989 and 1992, a period during which the Standard and Poor's 500 index increased by 29 percent.

Wolff is not able to provide a full resolution of why these differences between surveys exist, especially those that relate to time series trends. But he has pointed out a critical research problem that should be placed high on the research agenda. If we want to be able to track secular changes in wealth in the same way that we are accustomed to doing for wages and household income, the reasons why these surveys provide such different trends must be resolved.

Labor Force

With the indirect exception of his work on time budgets, Tom Juster has no entries on his vita that deal with labor supply or retirement. But his contribution on this subject will certainly be viewed as fundamental by future scholars. The reason, of course, is his leadership of the Health and Retirement Study. As we wait for enough HRS respondents to retire, most of the research coming out of HRS has been rightly in other substantive areas. Juster's durable contribution will lie in the state-of-the-art and innovative labor force modules contained in HRS.

HRS has set the international standard for other countries as they field surveys to deal with the impending retirement of their baby-boom generations. Indeed, one such example already exists as the Dutch have carried out their own survey that is in many ways comparable to the HRS. This comparability was no accident. Rich Burkhauser, an original member of the HRS design team, was spending a sabbatical leave at the University of Leiden. Once he heard of plans for a Dutch pre-retirement survey, Burkhauser alerted his Dutch colleagues to the ongoing HRS efforts. Jules Theeuwes then visited Juster and his colleagues at ISR, and ideas and codebooks were exchanged. While the Dutch survey (CERRA) is by no means just a replication of HRS, the two surveys share many similar modules. Two of the essays in this volume use some of the labor market innovations in the HRS and Dutch surveys.

Richard V. Burkhauser, Debra Dwyer, Maarten Lindeboom, Jules

Theeuwes, and Isolde Woittiez's essay, "Health, Work, and Economic Well-Being of Older Workers, Aged Fifty-One to Sixty-One: A Cross-National Comparison Using the U.S. HRS and the Netherlands CERRA Data Sets," compares the extent of work of men in their fifties in two countries — the United States and the Netherlands. Evaluated along this dimension, the countries are strikingly different. By the mid-1990s, little more than half of Dutch men in their fifties are in the labor market while 82 percent of U.S. men aged fifty-five are working. Although both countries have experienced declines in work effort across the last few decades, the drop in male labor force participation was much greater in the Netherlands than in the United States.

Why do Dutch men work less than their U.S. counterparts? Are Americans healthier or more ambitious, or do the Dutch like their leisure more? The authors conclude instead that institutional factors that affect the incentives to work are the main cause of these differences in work effort between the two countries. To provide income security during old age, the U.S. system relies on a combination of social security, private pensions, and private savings. The Netherlands has a very generous set of social welfare programs that include flat as well as means-tested benefits. The principal difference, however, is that the financial avenues out of work begin at much younger ages in the Netherlands than in the United States.

The most important of these avenues is that the Netherlands has an extremely generous and easily accessible disability system. When the data sets are compared, one-third of Dutch men aged sixty were receiving disability payments compared to only six percent of U.S. men of that age. At the same time, their study demonstrates that there appears to be very little difference in health of men in the two countries. Instead, they conclude that the Netherlands offers greater financial incentives to leaving the labor force at older working ages. The compensation is that these programs provide far more income stability in the Netherlands than is available in the United States.

Michael D. Hurd's essay, "Labor Market Transitions in the HRS: Effects of the Subjective Probability of Retirement and of Pension Eligibility," describes retirement transitions between the first two waves of the HRS. As part of the baseline survey, respondents were asked the probability that they would be working at ages sixty-two and sixty-five. One advantage of these subjective probability questions is that, unlike with mortality or bequests, some information on the actual outcomes is available as early as the second HRS wave. This research compares the actual retirement realizations of groups with their baseline subjective probabilities.

Hurd first describes labor force transitions as they are revealed in the HRS survey. For men, the dominant transition until age fifty-nine is from full-time work to full-time work (mostly reflecting continued work on the same job). After this age, the probability of remaining in a full-time job declines significantly, largely through transitions out of the labor force. Once out of the labor force, men tend to remain out. The patterns are similar among women, although the transitions from full-time work to out of the labor force begin at earlier ages. Finally, for both men and women, the hazards of moving out of the labor force (retirement) are strongly influenced by the presence of defined benefit (DB) pensions.

Hurd also reports that these baseline subjective probabilities do strongly correlate with actual labor market outcomes. In addition, the subjective probabilities generally also correlate in a sensible way with well-known determinants of labor force retirement such as pension eligibility. Perhaps Hurd's most important substantive conclusion is that subjective probabilities of retirement are inherently different from subjective probabilities of mortality. Unlike with mortality, a high subjective probability of retiring at age sixty-two or sixty-five (say due to the provision of DB plans) may say little about retirement probabilities at earlier ages (due also to the particular structure of a DB plan). If so, standard proportional hazard models widely applied to mortality issues may not be appropriate for modeling the retirement process.

Health and Intergenerational Exchange

Throughout most of his career, Tom Juster's substantive interests were quintessentially economic. With his leadership of the HRS and especially the AHEAD survey, his professional colleagues began to include many scholars who were not economists. This change was also no accident. The strict compartmentalization of subject matter and the nonoverlap of disciplinary expertise were becoming real constraints on scientific advancement. To use but one of many possible examples, all interested parties might agree that the interaction of health outcomes and socioeconomic status (SES) was critically important. In the last decade, health researchers had made significant progress on how to measure health outcomes, conditions, and utilizations while economists were making parallel advances in measuring economic resources. But no one was talking. The end result was that economic variables in the major health surveys and health variables in the principal economic surveys were both correctly viewed as deficient.

Another problem was that many surveys would treat respondents as if they lived in generational isolation. A survey of fifty year olds would contain many questions about the respondents' own lives but very few items concerning their interactions with their adult children or their elderly parents. This was very shortsighted as many of the behaviors of people at age fifty are heavily influenced by what is happening to their non-co-resident relatives. Theoretical models in sociology and economics were also increasingly emphasizing the importance of these exchanges across generations.

One of the real contributions of the HRS-AHEAD enterprise is that from the start a different model was followed. Multidisciplinary research teams were set up on many of the central research areas to be covered in the survey. Tom's open style and easy manner eased the tensions in the room, and trust gradually developed among scholars who began by thinking that their interests were very much opposed. Alongside the state-of-the-art economic measures used in HRS and AHEAD, modules were fielded that included health outcomes, health care utilization, and a variety of transfers made between the generations. Three of the essays in this volume make extensive use of these modules.

Linda A. Wray, A. Regula Herzog, Robert J. Willis, and Robert B. Wallace's essay, "The Impact of Education and Heart Attack on Smoking Cessation among Older Adults," focuses their research microscope on one particular pathway through which schooling can impact health outcomes. In their essay, they examine how education affects the cessation of smoking following a heart attack. That such a direct and important research question has not already been adequately answered may at first blush seem strange. But to answer this question, we need to have adequate samples of respondents who smoke and who also have experienced a nonfatal heart attack. Most social science surveys do not. We also have to be able to measure and control for all the other correlated factors that may contaminate the relation between smoking cessation and education. Most medical trials and surveys do not do this. Using the panel nature of HRS, these researchers were able to track changes in individual smoking behavior following a respondent's heart attack while at the same time controlling for other factors that are also associated with both smoking and education.

Wray et al. push this question an important step further by asking why schooling may affect smoking. There are a number of possible reasons. First, education may be correlated with the cognitive ability to digest and act on the body of information that has been provided on the harmful effects of smoking. Second, even among smokers, more educated respondents may be more future oriented (have higher time preference for the future) and thus see more harm from smoking. Third, environmental factors, proxied by whom the respondent associated with (nonsmoking spouse or professional colleagues), may be the underlying cause. Fourth, those respondents with more to lose (higher wealth) or with health insurance will more likely quit.

The empirical models do suggest that, among those smokers who experienced a heart attack between the first two waves of HRS, the more educated were more likely to quit. The magnitude of this effect is quite large. For example, among those smokers with only an eighth grade education, the probability of quitting was only .2, while among those with a college degree, this probability was .77. When the potential pathways through which this effect could operate were examined, Wray et al. found that neither environmental factors nor household resources appeared to be the central reasons. Instead, cognitive ability was crucial. However, cognitive ability does not by any means explain all of schooling's effect on smoking cessation.

Robert B. Wallace, Sara Nichols, and Michael D. Hurd's essay, "The Association of Influenza Vaccine Receipt with Health and Economic Expectations among Elders: The AHEAD Study," investigates another possible health enhancing choice — the use of preventive health behaviors among those who are at least seventy years old. The preventive behavior examined in their research involved having an influenza vaccine in the year prior to the administration of the baseline AHEAD survey. While influenza vaccines are of proven medical efficacy and are universally recommended for those over age sixty-five, utilization is far from complete. Reflecting the multidisciplinary nature of the research team and the AHEAD survey, the receipt of the vaccine is regressed against several demographic, health, economic, and personal expectations variables.

A number of intriguing results are reported in this essay. Although all the respondents are covered by Medicare, financial variables (higher wealth) were still associated with the increased receipt of an influenza vaccine. Those respondents who self-report themselves in poorer health or who had functional limitations were more likely to receive the vaccine, consistent with current medical recommendations. An intriguing finding is that those respondents who expect to live longer were less likely to be vaccinated, possibly reflecting a belief that they are less susceptible to health problems.

Beth J. Soldo, Douglas A. Wolf, and John C. Henretta's essay, "Intergenerational Transfers: Blood, Marriage, and Gender Effects on Household Decisions," looks at some of the exchange relationships that exist between older people and their younger relatives. These exchanges can take many forms — money and time transfers, frequent visits and phone calls, and in some cases co-residence between the generations. This research examines the probability of co-residence between married adult children in their fifties and their elderly unmarried mothers. An innovation of their research is that it recognizes that one of the competing options is that the unmarried mother of the other spouse may also want to co-reside.

The statistical results indicate that this potential competition between the two mothers for co-residence space is empirically unimportant. What mostly matters instead are the attributes of the unmarried mothers — their age, their functional ability, whether other children are available as substitute providers, and whether the HRS respondent is a daughter or son. Co-residence of elderly unmarried mothers and their adult children is dominated by situations in which the mother has difficulty taking care of herself. In addition, the mother-daughter bond trumps all other factors in determining who lives with whom. Even in cases in which the husband's mother is disabled, the odds are higher that the wife's mother co-resides in the household.

We close on a personal note. We both met Tom Juster for the first time when we were starting out as research associates at the National Bureau of Economic Research, where Tom was a vice president for research. Then as now, Tom was accessible and supportive and helped us both on our way. Our relationship grew closer and stronger with the onset of the HRS-AHEAD survey. In fact, we were both members of another research team that competed with Tom for the original HRS grant (we lost!). It speaks volumes about the kind of man he is that it was so easy for both of us to quickly sign on as members of his team. One of us has succeeded Tom as the principal investigator of HRS (Willis) while the other (Smith) is a frequent coauthor and golf partner (Smith wins!). We both count him as a dear friend. On behalf of all his friends, we wish Tom and Marie all good luck and much relaxation during their retirement. The early empirical evidence is that work effort hasn't changed all that much. Along with his other colleagues, we share some responsibility for we continue to seek his counsel and to coauthor papers. But happily their joint travel has increased, especially to far-off places, so that Justerian wisdom is now spreading around the globe.

The Several Cultures of Research on Subjective Expectations

Jeff Dominitz and Charles F. Manski

The nature of subjective expectations is a shared concern of researchers who study human behavior. Yet there is a wide spectrum of views on how expectations should be conceptualized and measured. Some time ago, the sharply different perspectives of social psychologists and economists were contrasted in Manski 1990, 1993. More recently, our joint empirical research exploring probabilistic elicitation of economic expectations has made us aware of multiple discordant perspectives within cognitive research (Dominitz and Manski 1997a).

Despite shared concerns, researchers in different disciplines rarely communicate. Their literatures are so separate as to suggest distinct cultures of research on subjective expectations. The long-term coexistence of several insular schools of thought is both troubling and fascinating. It is troubling that, for many years, the different strands of research on expectations have failed to confront one another. It is fascinating that researchers housed in the same universities, often in the same buildings, can pursue closely related research agendas and yet persistently ignore each other.

This essay critically examines the several cultures of research on subjective expectations. We do not "celebrate the differences" among research cultures, in the morally neutral fashion of modern multidisciplinary discourse. We have developed strong perceptions of what is right and wrong with current research practices and aim to say so clearly and directly. Our presentation draws in part on earlier discussions in Manski 1990, 1993 and Dominitz and Manski 1997a, 1997b.

First, the essay examines the prevailing practice in economics of inferring expectations from realizations data. As historical background, we also describe an early scientific controversy that soured economists on direct measurement of expectations. Second, the essay critiques

15

qualitative attitudinal research as commonly practiced by sociologists and social psychologists. Third, the history and present status of elicitation of subjective probabilities by economists and cognitive researchers are described. The last section of the essay draws conclusions.

Inference on Expectations from Realizations in Economics

Early in their careers, economics students are taught that a good economist believes only what people do, not what they say. Economists are skeptical of subjective statements of any kind. It is revealing that a 1984 National Academy of Sciences Panel on Survey Measurement of Subjective Phenomena had no economist as a member of the panel and cited almost no economics literature in its report (Turner and Martin 1984). Yet subjective phenomena—including preference orderings, perceived choice sets, perceived behavioral strategies of other agents, and expectations of prospective outcomes—are central to economic models of behavior.

Prevailing Practices

Economists attempt to infer expectations of prospective outcomes by combining data on realized experiences with assumptions about the process of expectations formation. To credibly infer expectations from realizations, researchers must somehow know (and be able to persuade others that they know) what information on realizations persons possess and how they use the available information to form their expectations. The available data on realizations, moreover, must be rich enough for the researchers to simulate the assumed processes of expectations formation. Economists seeking to infer expectations from realizations are generally unable to meet these requirements for credible inference. Instead, they can only make assumptions about expectations formation and hope that these assumptions approximate reality.

Economists have typically assumed that expectations formation is homogeneous; all persons condition their beliefs on the same variables and process their information in the same way. The hypothesized conditioning variables and information processing rule, however, vary considerably across studies.

Consider, for example, Hall and Mishkin (1982), Skinner (1988), Zeldes (1989), Caballero (1990), and Carroll (1992), all of whom are concerned with unconditional income expectations. These authors assume that persons use their own past incomes to forecast their future incomes. Perhaps so, but how do persons form expectations of future income conditional on past income? The authors assume that persons have *rational expectations;* that is, they know the actual stochastic process generating their income streams. Perhaps so, but what is this stochastic process? Each study a priori specifies the income process up to some parameters and uses available data on income realizations to estimate the parameters. The various authors differ, however, in their specifications of the income process.

Or consider Freeman (1971), Willis and Rosen (1979), and Manski and Wise (1983), all of whom are concerned with the returns to schooling. These authors do not assume that persons use their own past incomes to forecast their future incomes. Rather, their models of expectations invoke cohort comparisons of different types. Freeman (1971) assumes that expectations are myopic: each person believes that, should he or she obtain specified schooling, this will result in the mean income realized by the members of an earlier cohort who have the same schooling. Willis and Rosen (1979) assume rational expectations, each person somehow knowing the schooling-specific income distributions pertaining to his or her own cohort. In Manski and Wise 1983 (chap. 6), youth do not necessarily know either the outcomes realized by earlier cohorts or the actual process generating outcomes. Rather, they are assumed to believe that the returns to enrolling at a specific college are a function of the difference between their own SAT score and the average at the college.

Economists have lacked empirical evidence that any of the expectations assumptions made in the studies to date is correct. Nor have they had reason to think that misspecifying expectations is innocuous. To the contrary, misspecification of expectations can easily generate flawed interpretations of observed behavior. In Manski 1993, for example, a simple model is used to show that misspecification of the information on which youth condition in forming their expectations of the returns to schooling can lead to the mistaken conclusion that youth are unconcerned with the income returns to schooling.

Some History

If inference on expectations from realizations is so challenging, why do economists not collect and analyze data on expectations? The answer lies at least partly in the history of a scientific controversy that began in the 1940s and persisted until the 1960s.

In the 1940s, the Federal Reserve Board began to fund an annual

Survey of Consumer Finances, conducted by the University of Michigan Survey Research Center (SRC), that elicited qualitative assessments of expected household finances. A typical question took this form: "How about a year from now — do you think you people will be making more money or less money than you are now, or what do you expect?"

The usefulness of responses to such vaguely worded questions was controversial, and the Board of Governors appointed a committee to assess their value. The Federal Reserve Consultant Committee on Consumer Survey Statistics, known informally as the Smithies committee for Chair Arthur Smithies, issued findings that called into question that predictive value of subjective data, with the exception of purchase intentions (Federal Reserve Consultant Committee on Consumer Survey Statistics 1955). The conclusions were at odds with the views of SRC researchers, notably George Katona, a leading proponent of research on consumer attitudes and expectations.

A main bone of contention was the relevance of the "reinterview test," in which financial expectations data are evaluated by their ability to predict subsequent individual outcomes (e.g., durable goods expenditures) reported later in reinterviews. The Smithies committee argued that "reinterviews provide the only satisfactory way to test the usefulness or relevance of statistics on expectations and intentions." Katona (1957) argued that, although reinterviews provide one test, aggregate predictive tests are equally relevant. Katona reported that, once aggregated into his Index of Consumer Sentiment, data on consumer attitudes and expectations improve forecasts of aggregate consumer savings, aggregate consumer durables expenditures, and gross national product. Thus, Katona asserted that the data were useful in predicting aggregate consumer behavior even if they were not useful in predicting individual behavior.

Subsequently, qualitative expectations data continued to fail, or only marginally pass, the reinterview test, yet the SRC researchers stood their ground. See, for example, the work of SRC researcher Eva Mueller (1957, 1963), Smithies committee member James Tobin (1959), and the report of a contentious conference on expectations data at the National Bureau of Economic Research (1960). F. Thomas Juster closed this period of activity with an intensive study, drawing largely negative conclusions, of the usefulness of qualitative expectations data in predicting individual behavior (Juster 1964).

By the mid-1960s, opinion among mainstream economists was firmly negative. SRC has, however, continued to collect qualitative expectations data and to publish aggregate findings monthly in its Index of

Consumer Sentiment (see Curtin 1976; Patterson 1991). The SRC surveys are no longer funded by the Federal Reserve, but recent studies of aggregate consumer confidence have been published by economists working within the Federal Reserve system (e.g., Carroll, Fuhrer, and Wilcox 1991; Fuhrer 1988; Garner 1991; Throop 1992).

It is important to recognize that the SRC controversy only concerned the usefulness of a certain type of qualitative expectations data in predicting consumer behavior. Academic economists, however, appear to have drawn the broader conclusion that all expectations data are suspect.[1] Economists also failed to take note when Juster (1966) proposed elicitation of probabilistic expectations of consumer durable purchases and reported favorable empirical evidence. Exploration of Juster's idea had to wait a quarter century, as described in "General Considerations" under "Elicitation of Probabilistic Expectations."

Attitudinal Research on Expectations

In contrast to economists, attitudinal researchers in sociology and social psychology routinely collect and analyze subjective data of many kinds. We have sought to determine whether useful lessons can be extracted from these literatures. Unfortunately, the findings have been largely negative.

Prevailing Practices

The prevailing measurement practice is to interpret responses to loosely worded questionnaire items as indicators of expectations. Consider the way the returns to schooling are elicited. Berndt and Miller (1990), for example, ask a sample of junior high school students to respond, on a five-point scale, to the question, "How valuable do you think your education will be in getting the job you want?" Mickelson (1990) asks a sample of high school seniors to express their degree of agreement with the statement, "Studying in school rarely pays off later with good jobs." Most of the literature poses such vague questions.[2]

The looseness with which attitudinal researchers typically measure expectations is matched by looseness in their thinking about expectations formation. Attitudinal researchers tend to theorize verbally rather than mathematically. As a consequence, it is difficult to determine whether different researchers interpret the term *expectations* in a common, coherent fashion. There are, of course, some psychologists who interpret expectations in the same subjective probabilistic way as economists (e.g., Kahneman, Slovic, and Tversky 1982). Their work, however, seems to have had little impact on attitudinal research.

The influential Fishbein-Ajzen model of intentions provides a good example of the manner in which attitudinal researchers in social psychology connect theory and measurement. Fishbein and Ajzen (1975) propose that "intention" is a mental state that causally precedes behavior and that can be elicited through questionnaires or interviews. Intention is said to be an intermediate variable in a path model wherein (1) intentions are determined by attitudes and social norms and (2) behavior is determined by intentions alone.

According to Ajzen and Fishbein (1980), a person's "behavioral intention" is his or her subjective probability that the behavior of interest will occur. (They refer to the response to a yes/no intentions question as "choice intention.") It seems, however, that social psychologists do not use the term *subjective probability* as a statistician would. Ajzen and Fishbein (1980, 50) state: "[W]e are claiming that intentions should always predict behavior, provided that the measure of intention corresponds to the behavioral criterion and that the intention has not changed prior to performance of the behavior." In their well-known review of attitudinal research, Schuman and Johnson (1976, 172) write that the Fishbein-Ajzen model implies that "the correlation between behavioral intention and behavior should approach 1.0, provided that the focal behavior is the same in both cases and that nothing intervenes to alter the intention." It is difficult to reconcile these statements with the idea that behavioral intention is a subjective probability, unless that probability is always zero or one.

In practice, social psychologists typically measure intention on some nominal scale (e.g., Ajzen and Fishbein [1980] recommend a seven-point scale whose verbally described responses range from "likely" to "unlikely") and report the arithmetic correlation between this measure and the behavioral outcome. It is usually found that the correlation is positive but well below unity. See, for example, Schuman and Johnson 1976 and Davidson and Jaccard 1979. Social psychologists have reacted by generalizing the Fishbein-Ajzen model while maintaining its basic path structure. See, for example, Davidson and Jaccard 1979, Liska 1984, and Ritter 1988.

Attitudinal Research on Economic Expectations

The early economics tradition of collecting qualitative expectations data has persisted at SRC and at other survey organizations that report on "consumer confidence" or "consumer sentiment" to nonacademic audiences. While the substantive concerns are economic, the empirical work falls squarely within the tradition of attitudinal research.

When asked to consider the prospects for a given economic outcome, such as the loss of one's job, respondents are often asked to report whether they "think," "expect," or "are worried" that the event will occur. Sometimes they are asked to report the strength of this belief or worry by attaching one of a choice of modifiers, such as "very," "fairly," "not too," or "not at all" likely/worried that the event will occur. An example is this question appearing in the General Social Survey (GSS) (see Davis and Smith 1994): "Thinking about the next twelve months, how likely do you think it is that you will lose your job or be laid off — very likely, fairly likely, not too likely, or not at all likely?"

Perhaps the most basic problem concerns the interpersonal comparability of responses. Do different respondents interpret verbal phrases such as "fairly likely" in the same way? Empirical evidence reported in the cognitive research literature indicates that interpretations of qualitative expectations questions vary substantially between respondents (see Wallsten et al. 1986). Even if respondents identically interpret the phrases, the qualitative response options limit the information contained in the responses. It is of interest to learn how accurately individuals predict their future job experiences. An obvious way to address this question is to compare elicited expectations with subsequent realizations. The responses to the GSS question, however, permit only a coarse ordinal comparison. The most that one can do is to observe whether those who report "very likely" experience a higher frequency of job loss than those who report "fairly likely," and so on.

Concern about interpersonal comparability comes into even sharper focus when considering the outcomes about which respondents are asked. What does it mean to be "economically secure," as in this question from the *New York Times* (3 March 1996): "All in all, how economically secure do you feel? Very insecure, somewhat insecure . . . ?" How does the respondent reduce the many facets of economic security into one dimension? Do respondents interpret security as an absolute concept or as a relative one? If the concept is relative, to whom or to what time period does the respondent compare it?

Similar concerns about interpersonal comparability apply to SRC's forward-looking financial well-being question (Curtin 1982): "Now looking ahead — do you think that a year from now you (and your family living there) will be better off financially, or worse off, or just about the same as now?" Such questions are also asked by the Conference Board (Linden 1982) and by the Gallup Organization (Newport and Saad 1996), among others.

Elicitation of Probabilistic Expectations

General Considerations

Elicitation of probabilistic expectations has several a priori desirable features. Perhaps the most basic attraction is that probability provides a well-defined absolute numerical scale for responses. Hence there is some reason to think that responses may be interpersonally and intrapersonally comparable.

A second attraction is that some empirical assessment of the internal consistency and external accuracy of respondents' expectations is possible. A researcher can use the algebra of probability (Bayes theorem, the law of total probability, etc.) to examine the internal consistency of a respondent's elicited expectations about different events. In those cases where probability has a frequentist interpretation, a researcher can compare elicited subjective probabilities with known event frequencies and reach conclusions about the correspondence between subjective beliefs and frequentist realities.

A third consideration is the usefulness of elicited expectations in predicting prospective outcomes. Suppose that respondents have reasonably accurate expectations about the likelihood of future events. Then, as argued by Juster (1966) and Savage (1971), numerical responses to probability questions should have more predictive power than do categorical responses to qualitative expectations questions. For further discussion, see the "Some History in Economics" subsection, which follows.

From the perspective of economic research, another attraction is that probabilistic expectations provide empirical evidence in the form sought by modern economic theory. Economists analyzing decision making under uncertainty generally assume that individuals assign coherent subjective probabilities to future events. So economists can readily utilize probabilistic expectations data, whereas qualitative expectations data are difficult to interpret.

The a priori desirable features of probabilistic expectations data must be weighed against a set of potential problems. Perhaps the most basic concern is that there is no direct way to assess how well elicited subjective probabilities reflect respondents' thinking. Of course this concern is not specific to elicitation of probabilities. Interpretation of responses to subjective questions of any type runs up against the generic problem that a researcher cannot directly observe a respondent's thinking.

A specific concern in the elicitation of probabilities is that respondents may not think probabilistically about uncertain events. A large and diverse literature, ranging from Keynes 1921 through Ellsberg 1961 to Walley 1991 among many others, suggests that persons may think about uncertain events using less than the full structure of modern probability theory. For example, they may think in terms of upper and lower subjective probabilities (see Walley 1991 for an extensive review). If so, then questions eliciting precise probabilities force respondents to give point responses when only interval responses are meaningful.

Some cognitive researchers have posited behavioral models in which decisions are made by individuals who assign upper and lower probabilities to prospective outcomes, rather than the unique subjective probabilities implied by Savage's development of subjective expected utility (SEU) theory (Savage 1954). Work on these models (see Camerer and Weber 1992 for a review) has been motivated in part by observed violations of SEU theory, in particular by the Ellsberg paradox. To the extent that these behavioral models are accurate representations of actual decision making, they call into question not only the practice of probability elicitation but also the large body of economic research (see the earlier "Inference on Expectations from Realizations in Economics" section) that maintains SEU theory and attempts to infer subjective probabilities from data on realizations.

Some History in Economics

The idea that probabilistic elicitation of expectations might improve on the traditional qualitative approaches of attitudinal research appears to have originated with Juster (1966). Considering the case in which the behavior of interest is a binary purchase decision (buy or not buy), Juster considered how responses to traditional yes/no buying intentions questions should properly be interpreted. He wrote:

> Consumers reporting that they "intend to buy A within X months" can be thought of as saying that the probability of their purchasing A within X months is high enough so that some form of "yes" answer is more accurate than a "no" answer. (664)

Thus he hypothesized that a consumer facing a yes/no intentions question responds as would a statistician asked to make a best point prediction of a future event.[3]

Working from this hypothesis, Juster concluded that it would potentially be more informative to ask consumers for their purchase probabilities than for their buying intentions. He went on to collect data of the two types and to compare their predictive power. He found that stated purchase probabilities are better predictors of subsequent individual behavior than are yes/no intentions data.

Market researchers were attracted to Juster's proposal, and elicitation of purchase probabilities has since become a common practice in market research (see Morrison 1979; Urban and Hauser 1980; Jamieson and Bass 1989). The idea that expectations might be elicited probabilistically from survey respondents did not, however, draw the attention of economists or attitudinal researchers. By the time Juster's article was published, economists were preaching that empirical research on decision making should be based only on choice data as interpreted through revealed preference arguments and not on subjective data of any kind. We are not sure why attitudinal researchers failed to react to Juster's work.

In the late 1980s, one of us (Manski) became aware of Juster's 1966 article. Manski 1990 examines the relationship between stated yes/no intentions and subsequent behavior under the "best-case" hypothesis that individuals have rational expectations and that their responses to intentions questions are the best predictions of their future behavior. In the midst of this research, I learned that Juster had developed similar ideas twenty-five years earlier. Reading his article, I was taken aback by the proposal to elicit economic expectations probabilistically. The idea was so straightforward that it took me some time to grasp how it could have been ignored for so long.

Better late than never. Today a growing set of major household surveys is using probabilistic formats to elicit economic expectations, and with these surveys a new field of economic research on measurement of expectations is beginning to emerge. The surveys with currently available data include the following.

HRS/AHEAD: In 1992 SRC, with Juster as principal investigator, began two companion panel surveys of fifty-one to sixty-one-year-old and of over seventy-year-old Americans, the Health and Retirement Study (HRS) and the Asset and Health Dynamics among the Oldest Old (AHEAD) survey (see Juster and Suzman 1995). In addition to many questions on outcomes actually realized, respondents are asked a number of questions eliciting the subjective probability of living to age seventy-five/eighty-five, job loss, entering a nursing home, and medical expenses using up all savings, among other events. Thus far, analyses of these data have focused on expectations of one outcome at a time, such as mortality (Hurd and McGarry 1995a) or nursing home utilization (Holden, McBride, and Perozek 1995).

PSID: The 1994 administration of the Panel Study of Income Dynamics (PSID) contains a set of expectations questions similar to those appearing in the first wave of the HRS.

The Italian SHIW and Dutch VSB-Panel Surveys: Two European surveys include questions eliciting subjective probabilities of one-year-ahead growth rates in income. Responses to the Bank of Italy's 1989 Survey of Household Income and Wealth (SHIW) have been analyzed by Guiso, Jappelli, and Terlizzese (1992), who focus on the effect of income uncertainty on savings behavior. Responses to similar questions contained in the more recent continuing VSB-Panel survey conducted by the Center for Economic Research in Tilburg, the Netherlands, have been analyzed by Das and Donkers (1997).

The Survey of Economic Expectations: We have designed and implemented the Survey of Economic Expectations (SEE). SEE is an ongoing national survey initiated in an effort to learn how Americans perceive their near-term economic prospects. Probablistic questions are used to elicit expectations about income, employment, health insurance coverage, and crime victimization one year into the future. Data collection began in 1993, and, at present, approximately fifteen hundred interviews are conducted per year. SEE is administered as a periodic module in WISCON, a national continuous computer-assisted-telephone-interview (CATI) survey conducted by the University of Wisconsin Survey Center at the University of Wisconsin-Madison. Two analyses of SEE data have been completed to date. Dominitz and Manski (1977a) report empirical evidence on the one-year-ahead household income expectations of respondents as given to SEE in 1993. Dominitz and Manski (1997b) use SEE data on over two thousand labor force participants interviewed in 1994 and 1995 to describe how Americans in the labor force perceive the risk of near-term economic misfortune. Economic insecurity is measured through responses to questions eliciting subjective probabilities of three events in the year ahead: health insurance coverage, victimization by burglary, and job loss.

Expectations data from another major survey will be available soon. The new 1997 cohort of the National Longitudinal Survey of Youth (NLSY97) contains a set of questions eliciting risk perceptions and expectations about future schooling, labor supply, and fertility.

Some History in Cognitive Research

Elicitation of subjective probabilities has long been a topic of research in cognitive research. Respondents may be asked a general knowledge question and then asked to report the probability that they have given the correct response. Or they may be asked to report the probability that some given statement is true. Other times they are asked to report the probability that a specified prospective event will occur.

Calibration studies assess the accuracy of elicited expectations reports when the outcome is known. Lichtenstein, Fischhoff, and Phillips (1982) review findings from calibration studies dating back to 1906. McClelland and Bolger (1994) update the review with findings from 1980 through 1994. Whereas the older studies mostly examined the accuracy of experts (e.g., weather forecasters reported probabilities of precipitation), the more recent research typically analyzes the expectations of nonexperts, especially students situated in a cognitive laboratory.

Studies conducted prior to 1980 have been characterized by Lichtenstein, Fischhoff, and Phillips (1982) as "dust-bowl empiricism," almost completely lacking in psychological theory. The main findings pertain to the so-called overconfidence and hard-easy effects. The former concerns the tendency for respondents to overstate the probability of being correct, whereas the latter concerns the tendency for overconfidence to be more pronounced when problems are deemed to be difficult.

Studies after 1980 have sought to develop psychological theories to explain the observed empirical regularities. Koriat, Lichtenstein, and Fischhoff (1980), for example, argued that individuals tend to ignore disconfirming evidence when assessing the probability of being correct. They concluded that encouragement to consider such evidence should improve calibration. Kahneman, Slovic, and Tversky (1982) argued that individuals adopt simple rules or heuristics when engaging in cognitively difficult tasks, such as probabilistic reasoning. These rules, they asserted, generate the observed empirical regularities. Other researchers, however, have argued that the empirical regularities result not from the respondents' use of heuristics but from the tendency of researchers to pose selective and misleading questions (e.g., Gigerenzer 1991).

Within cognitive research, much of the controversy about probability elicitation concerns the way in which humans internally represent their beliefs and their ability and willingness to express their internal beliefs as numerical probabilities. Although Koriat, Lichtenstein, and Fischhoff (1980) and Ferrell and McGoey (1980) pose models in which individuals may have some difficulty expressing beliefs as numerical probabilities, both studies nevertheless conclude that elicitation of numerical subjective probabilities is feasible. Yet Zimmer (1983, 1984), who argues that humans internally process information using verbal rather than numerical modes of thinking, concludes that expectations should be elicited in verbal rather than numerical forms.

We are not aware of empirical research that directly supports Zimmer's argument or conclusion. Two recent studies report that a majority of respondents prefer to communicate their own beliefs verbally and to receive the beliefs of others in the form of numerical probabilities (Erev and Cohen 1990; Wallsten et al. 1993). This asymmetry is intriguing but only marginally relevant to the design of expectations questions. The relevant question is not what communication mode respondents prefer to use but rather what modes they are willing and able to use. Wallsten et al. report that virtually all of their respondents were willing to communicate their beliefs numerically, should the situation warrant it.

A related theme of cognitive research is to learn how individuals associate numerical probabilities and verbal phrases such as "very likely," "probable," or "rarely" (see Lichtenstein and Newman 1967; Beyth-Marom 1982; Wallsten et al. 1986). A central finding, noted earlier in the "Attitudinal Research on Economic Expectations" subsection of the "Attitudinal Research on Expectations" section, is that individuals vary considerably in the numerical probabilities that they associate with given verbal phrases. There is, however, controversy about the proper conclusion to be drawn. Should one conclude that individuals differ in their interpretation of verbal phrases, in their interpretation of numerical probabilities, or in their interpretation of both? The empirical findings are compatible with all of these conclusions.

Conclusion

Several years ago, frustration with the calcified state of economic and attitudinal research on expectations led us to initiate a program of empirical research using probabilistic modes of questioning to elicit the economic expectations of ordinary household members. We could not be sure whether probabilistic elicitation would be feasible or useful, but three considerations encouraged us to try.

First, we recognized that the prevalent approaches to measurement of expectations in economics and in attitudinal research are both deeply flawed, for reasons described in the "Inferences on Expectations from Realizations in Economics" and "Attitudinal Research on Expectations" sections. For reasons that we still do not fully understand, these flaws have long been tolerated or simply ignored.

Second, we knew that the widespread hostility of economists and attitudinal researchers to probabilistic elicitation has been grounded in anecdotes and casual introspection, not in scientific evidence. In particular, the SRC controversy of the 1950s should at most have led economists to conclude that collection of qualitative expectations data is not worthwhile. This narrowly focused controversy should not have led economists to reach the sweeping conclusion that collection and analysis of subjective data are generically without merit.

Third, we were aware that hostility to probability elicitation is far from universal among behavioral and social scientists. In contrast to economists and attitudinal researchers, many cognitive researchers have long been actively engaged in probability elicitation—albeit more typically from experts and from students in cognitive laboratories than from ordinary household members.

As our work on probability elicitation has progressed, the normal processes of scientific discourse—personal communications, seminar presentations, and journal review of submitted papers—have made us sensitive to the existence of several distinct cultures of research on subjective expectations. We do not want to speculate on the social processes that have enabled these separate cultures to coexist within the behavioral and social sciences, but we do think that the failure of researchers with different perspectives to confront one another has retarded scientific progress.

The near-term outlook for empirical research on the economic expectations of household members seems clear from our perspective. Studies using HRS and SEE data clearly establish that probability elicitation is feasible and that the responses are meaningful in various senses (see Hurd and McGarry 1995a, 1995b; Dominitz and Manski 1997a, 1997b; Dominitz 1998). While we believe that the credibility of probability elicitation has been established, we see much scope for improving the state of the art. Constructive interdisciplinary discourse, particularly between economists and cognitive researchers, might do much to enhance the progress that is now being made.

Over the longer term, we see the need to move from studies that focus on elicitation per se and toward the execution of research in which expectations data are utilized in empirical analyses of behavior. The HRS/AHEAD surveys initiated by Tom Juster offer the best currently available data for the conduct of such behavioral research. The HRS/AHEAD surveys collect data on probabilistic expectations, on realizations of outcomes, and on many behaviors that should be influenced by respondents' expectations. The inclusion of probabilistic expectations questions in other large-scale longitudinal surveys, such as the NLSY97, will open up additional research possibilities.

NOTES

1. An exception is Nerlove 1983.

2. Somewhat of an exception is the study of the income expectations of college seniors by Smith and Powell (1990). These authors ask respondents to make unconditional forecasts of their "anticipated annual income in ten years" and their "expected earnings" in the first year of their first job. They also ask respondents to provide similar forecasts for the average member of their class.

3. Earlier, Tobin (1959) and the Smithies committee offered similar interpretations of binary intentions data. They, however, do not appear to have suggested eliciting probabilities directly.

REFERENCES

Ajzen, I., and M. Fishbein. 1980. *Understanding Attitudes and Predicting Social Behavior.* Englewood Cliffs, NJ: Prentice-Hall.
Berndt, T., and K. Miller. 1990. "Expectancies, Values, and Achievement in Junior High School." *Journal of Educational Psychology* 82:319–26.
Beyth-Marom, R. 1982. "How Probable Is Probable? A Numerical Translation of Verbal Probability Expressions." *Journal of Forecasting* 1:257–69.
Caballero, R. 1990. "Consumption Puzzles and Precautionary Savings." *Journal of Monetary Economics* 25:113–36.
Camerer, C., and M. Weber. 1992. "Recent Developments in Modeling Preferences: Uncertainty and Ambiguity." *Journal of Risk and Uncertainty* 5: 325–70.
Carroll, C. 1992. "The Buffer-Stock Theory of Saving: Some Macroeconomic Evidence." *Brookings Papers on Economic Activity* 2:61–156.
Carroll, C., J. Fuhrer, and D. Wilcox. 1991. "Does Consumer Sentiment Affect Household Spending? If So, Why?" Finance and Economics Discussion Series, Federal Reserve Board, Washington, DC.
Curtin, R. 1976. "Survey Methods and Questionnaire." In R. Curtin, ed., *Surveys of Consumers: 1974–75.* Ann Arbor, MI: Institute for Social Research.
———. 1982. "Indicators of Consumer Behavior: The University of Michigan Surveys of Consumers." *Public Opinion Quarterly* 46:340–52.
Das, M., and B. Donkers. 1997. "How Certain Are Dutch Households about Future Income? An Empirical Analysis." Center for Economic Research discussion paper no. 9738, Tilburg University, the Netherlands.
Davidson, A., and J. Jaccard. 1979. "Variables That Moderate the Attitude-

Behavior Relation: Results of a Longitudinal Survey." *Journal of Personality and Social Psychology* 37:1364–76.

Davis, J., and T. Smith. 1994. *The General Social Surveys, 1972–1994, Cumulative File.* Chicago: National Opinion Research Center.

Dominitz, J. 1998. "Earnings Expectations, Revisions, and Realizations." *Review of Economics and Statistics* 80:374–88.

Dominitz, J., and C. Manski. 1997a. "Using Expectations Data to Study Subjective Income Expectations." *Journal of the American Statistical Association* 92:855–67.

———. 1997b. "Perceptions of Economic Insecurity: Evidence from the Survey of Economic Expectations." *Public Opinion Quarterly* 61:261–87.

Ellsberg, D. 1961. "Risk, Ambiguity, and the Savage Axioms." *Quarterly Journal of Economics* 75:643–69.

Erev, I., and B. Cohen. 1990. "Verbal versus Numerical Probabilities: Efficiency, Biases, and the Preference Paradox." *Organizational Behavior and Human Decision Processes* 45:1–18.

Federal Reserve Consultant Committee on Consumer Survey Statistics. 1955. "Smithies Committee Report." In *Reports of the Federal Reserve Consultant Committees on Economic Statistics: Hearings before the Subcommittee on Economic Statistics of the Joint Committee on the Economic Report.* 84th Cong.

Ferrell, W., and P. McGoey. 1980. "A Model of Calibration for Subjective Probabilities." *Organizational Behavior and Human Performance* 26:32–53.

Fishbein, M., and I. Ajzen. 1975. *Belief, Attitude, Intention, and Behavior: An Introduction to Theory and Research.* Reading, MA: Addison-Wesley.

Freeman, R. 1971. *The Market for College-Trained Manpower.* Cambridge, MA: Harvard University Press.

Fuhrer, J. C. 1988. "On the Information Content of Consumer Survey Expectations." *Review of Economics and Statistics* 70:140–44.

Garner, A. 1991. "Forecasting Consumer Spending: Should Economists Pay Attention to Consumer Confidence Surveys?" *Federal Reserve Bank of Kansas City Economic Review* (May/June): 57–71.

Gigerenzer, G. 1991. "How to Make Cognitive Illusions Disappear: Beyond Heuristics and Biases." *European Review of Social Psychology* 2:83–115.

Guiso, L., T. Jappelli, and D. Terlizzese. 1992. "Earnings Uncertainty and Precautionary Saving." *Journal of Monetary Economics* 30:307–37.

Hall, R., and F. Mishkin. 1982. "The Sensitivity of Consumption to Transitory Income: Estimates from Panel Data on Households." *Econometrica* 50: 461–77.

Holden, K., T. McBride, and M. Perozek. 1995. "Expectations of Nursing Home Use in the Health and Retirement Survey: The Role of Race, Health, and Family Structure." Paper presented at the Minority Perspectives in the Health and Retirement Survey Workshop, Institute for Social Research, Ann Arbor, MI.

Hurd, M., and K. McGarry. 1995a. "Evaluation of the Subjective Probabilities of Survival in the Health and Retirement Study." *Journal of Human Resources* 30:S268–92.

———. 1995b. "The Predictive Validity of the Subjective Probabilities of Survival in the Health and Retirement Study." Paper presented at the HRS Wave 2 Early Results Workshop, Institute for Social Research, Ann Arbor, MI.

Jamieson, L., and F. Bass. 1989. "Adjusting Stated Intentions Measures to Predict Trial Purchase of New Products: A Comparison of Models and Methods." *Journal of Marketing Research* 26:336–45.

Juster, T. 1964. *Anticipations and Purchases: An Analysis of Consumer Behavior.* Princeton, NJ: Princeton University Press.

———. 1966. "Consumer Buying Intentions and Purchase Probability: An Experiment in Survey Design." *Journal of the American Statistical Association* 61:658–96.

Juster, T., and R. Suzman. 1995. "An Overview of the Health and Retirement Study." *Journal of Human Resources* 30:S7–56.

Kahneman, D., P. Slovic, and A. Tversky, eds. 1982. *Judgment under Uncertainty: Heuristics and Biases.* New York: Cambridge University Press.

Katona, G. 1957. "Federal Reserve Board Committee Reports on Consumer Expectations and Savings Statistics." *Review of Economics and Statistics* 39:40–46.

Keynes, J. 1921. *A Treatise on Probability.* London: Macmillan.

Koriat, A., S. Lichtenstein, and B. Fischhoff. 1980. "Reasons for Confidence." *Journal of Experimental Psychology: Human Learning and Memory* 6: 107–18.

Lichtenstein, S., B. Fischhoff, and L. Phillips. 1982. "Calibration of Probabilities: The State of the Art to 1980." In D. Kahneman, P. Slovic, and A. Tversky, eds., *Judgment under Uncertainty: Heuristics and Biases.* New York: Cambridge University Press.

Lichtenstein, S., and R. Newman. 1967. "Empirical Scaling of Common Verbal Phrases Associated with Numerical Probabilities." *Psychonomic Science* 9:563–64.

Linden, F. 1982. "The Consumer as Forecaster." *Public Opinion Quarterly* 46:353–60.

Liska, A. 1984. "A Critical Examination of the Causal Structure of the Fishbein/Ajzen Attitude-Behavior Model." *Social Psychology Quarterly* 47:61–74.

Manski, C. 1990. "The Use of Intentions Data to Predict Behavior: A Best Case Analysis." *Journal of the American Statistical Association* 85:934–40.

———. 1993. "Adolescent Econometricians: How Do Youth Infer the Returns to Schooling?" In C. Clotfelter and M. Rothschild, eds., *Studies of Supply and Demand in Higher Education.* Chicago: University of Chicago Press.

Manski, C., and D. Wise. 1983. *College Choice in America.* Cambridge, MA: Harvard University Press.

McClelland, A., and F. Bolger. 1994. "The Calibration of Subjective Probabilities: Theories and Models 1980–94." In G. Wright and P. Ayton, eds., *Subjective Probability.* New York: Wiley.

Mickelson, R. 1990. "The Attitude-Achievement Paradox among Black Adolescents." *Sociology of Education* 63:44–61.

Morrison, D. 1979. "Purchase Intentions and Purchase Behavior." *Journal of Marketing* 43:65–74.

Mueller, E. 1957. "Effects of Consumer Attitudes on Purchases." *American Economic Review* 47 (December): 946–65.

———. 1963. "Ten Years of Consumer Attitude Surveys: Their Forecasting Record." *Journal of the American Statistical Association* 58:899–917.

National Bureau of Economic Research. 1960. *The Quality and Economic Significance of Anticipations Data.* Special Conference Series. Princeton, NJ: Princeton University Press.

Nerlove, M. 1983. "Expectations, Plans and Realizations in Theory and Practice." *Econometrica* 51:1251–79.

Newport, F., and L. Saad. 1996. "The Economy and the Election." *Public Perspective* (April/May): 1–4.

Patterson, G. 1991. "Consumer-Confidence Surveyor Has Become an Economic Guru." *Wall Street Journal,* 2 May.

Ritter, C. 1988. "Resources, Behavior Intentions, and Drug Use: A Ten-Year National Panel Analysis." *Social Psychology Quarterly* 51:250–64.

Savage, L. 1954. *The Foundations of Statistics.* New York: Wiley.

———. 1971. "Elicitation of Personal Probabilities and Expectations." *Journal of the American Statistical Association* 66:783–801.

Schuman, H., and M. Johnson. 1976. "Attitudes and Behavior." *Annual Review of Sociology* 2:161–207.

Skinner, J. 1988. "Risky Income, Life Cycle Consumption and Precautionary Savings." *Journal of Monetary Economics* 22:237–55.

Smith, H., and B. Powell. 1990. "Great Expectations: Variations in Income Expectations among College Seniors." *Sociology of Education* 63:194–207.

Throop, A. 1992. "Consumer Sentiment: Its Causes and Effects." *Federal Reserve Bank of San Francisco Economic Review* (winter).

Tobin, J. 1959. "On the Predictive Value of Consumer Intentions and Attitudes." *Review of Economics and Statistics* 41:1–11.

Turner, C., and E. Martin, eds. 1984. *Surveying Subjective Phenomena.* Vol. 1. New York: Russell Sage Foundation.

Urban, G., and J. Hauser. 1980. *Design and Marketing of New Products.* Englewood Cliffs, NJ: Prentice-Hall.

Walley, P. 1991. *Statistical Reasoning with Imprecise Probabilities.* London: Chapman and Hall.

Wallsten, T., D. Budescu, A. Rapoport, R. Zwick, and B. Forsyth. 1986. "Measuring the Vague Meanings of Probability Terms." *Journal of Experimental Psychology: General* 115 (4): 348–65.

Wallsten, T., D. Budescu, R. Zwick, and S. Kemp. 1993. "Preferences and Reasons for Communicating Probabilistic Information in Verbal or Numerical Terms." *Bulletin of the Psychonomic Society* 31:135–38.

Willis, R., and S. Rosen. 1979. "Education and Self-Selection." *Journal of Political Economy* 87:S7–36.

Zeldes, S. 1989. "Optimal Consumption with Stochastic Income: Deviations from Certainty Equivalence." *Quarterly Journal of Economics* 104:275–98.

Zimmer, A. 1983. "Verbal vs. Numerical Processing of Subjective Probabilities." In R. Scholz, ed., *Decision Making under Uncertainty.* Amsterdam: North-Holland.

———. 1984. "A Model for the Interpretation of Verbal Predictions." *International Journal of Man-Machine Studies* 20:121–34.

Measuring Investment in Young Children with Time Diaries

N. Anders Klevmarken and Frank P. Stafford

In the late 1970s Tom Juster became interested in using time diaries as part of a system of national accounts. The most comprehensive approach along these lines was sketched out in a framework where total social output is constrained by the available resources of capital and time (Juster, Courant, and Dow 1985). Time can be split into three broad uses: production of goods and services in the market; household production of nonmarket goods and services; and leisure, personal care, and biological maintenance. The aggregate of time available must be in these categories, and the allocation is driven by traditional efficiency motivations including the importance of social capital or "societal variables" and "contexts" that are not under the individual's own control but have various public good or externality elements. Intervening variables shaping these choices are market wage rates, the available technology, and preferences of individuals. The final outputs are Becker-Lancaster-like nonmarket basic commodities or characteristics (Becker 1965; Lancaster 1966) that are arguments in the individual's utility function.

Household activities combine with gross domestic product-type (GDP-type) goods used directly by households to produce tangible and intangible output. In this system measurement of a broader concept of investment was a key motivation. Further, the locus of any activity could shift between market and nonmarket sectors, so a less comprehensive measurement system would be vulnerable to technical shifts that alter the sectoral location of activity. To illustrate: "A new technology (television) can reduce market sector output (movie attendance) and increase nonmarket output (viewing movies at home) with the major net impact of reducing expenditures for transportation. Expanding publicly financed day-care facilities or nursery schools can increase government activity devoted to skill development of children, while simultaneously decreasing nonmarket investment of parental time devoted to child care, without having any impact at all on the aggregate level of skill development of children."

With respect to the more current emphasis on the rise of human skills as a rising share of the total capital stock (Tinbergen 1975) and school quality (Johnson and Stafford 1973, 1996), an important possibility is that there are shifts back toward the nonmarket sector (as in the television example) and that the greater resources in the form of market purchased inputs in the United States, 1950–90[1] have been matched by smaller or larger per pupil investments in nonmarket time by parents. One might expect larger investments by parents, particularly for very young children, if these early home investments provide a type of "enabling" capital of values and preferences that improves the ability to acquire additional human capital at higher levels of out-of-home schooling and to respond to changing environments throughout the life cycle (Gustafsson and Stafford 1997). This greater home investment could be all the more important if the home educational sector is characterized by the absence of productivity-enhancing technical change (Baumol, Batey-Blackman, and Wolff 1985). Then resources are absorbed in disproportionate share into this activity, just as more resources are claimed by the service sector or the R & D sector.

An estimate of child investment time (hours per week) by U.S. fathers and mothers for children ages 0–2, 3–4, and 5–17 was offered in a paper entitled "Investments of Time by Men and Women" (Juster 1985a). The estimates for 1975–76 were about 1 hour per week for men with preschool children and 4 hours per week, 2.5 hours, and 1 hour per week for women with children in the age ranges 0–2, 3–4, and 5–17, respectively. The investment definition was diary-based "time spent in helping children make or do things, in teaching them new skills, and providing for their health care plus .5 of the time spent caring for, reading to, talking to, playing with and being a chauffeur of one's children" (186). This definition implies about 250 hours per year of investment time by parents per very young child as of the mid-1970s. Suppose one knew that "teacher's" time (defined as out-of-home care by a non-relative) were another 150. This totals 400 hours per year of "investment time," but what is the value on a cost basis? The adult time has a possible wage cost, and, to illustrate, at $10 per hour, annual human investment would be $4,000.

Should we develop some accounting for the child's own time? This makes sense if the effort on the part of young children has increased, and there is evidence that across countries, the effort expected of children, even at the grade school level can differ substantially. As of 1981–

82, primary school children in the United States put in 27.0 hours of schoolwork (25.2 in school and 1.8 studying outside of school) while in Japan in 1986 primary school children put in 46.5 hours of school work (38.2 in school and 8.3 studying outside of school) (Juster and Stafford 1991). While a wage rate approach seems implausible (as the basis for a cost of investment approach) one might then ask if the study time leads to more skills that eventually are reflected in market wages (the value of market output approach). The latter approach has the obvious drawback that the market value of skills can shift through time (Freeman 1975; Johnson and Stafford 1996), but such issues of cost versus market value are familiar to those studying physical capital. For this reason one may simply want to keep investment hours to a child by each caregiver type (including "own"-child time) as separate, but including measures of cognitive development that in turn depend on the investment time would be very important from the perspective of investment.

In this essay we set out a more narrowly defined investment paradigm and sketch out the diverse kinds of inputs to the developmental process across different countries at selected time points. The observable inputs are time and goods and can arise both in the home and in formal care settings. These formal care settings can be purchased by the parents or provided as market goods but through the public sector (as with public schooling). While at a high level of aggregation one can think of out-of-home settings as a type of market good (purchased privately or by the public), there are important issues concerning the use of adult time and instructional style that produce learning in these out-of-home settings. In the educational literature there are studies of time-on-task within the classroom setting as measured by observational classroom diaries. The more microlevel issues of what time and goods inputs matter the most are not a topic that can be addressed in our essay. Indeed, this is the entire interdisciplinary field of child development research.

An Investment Paradigm

Overview

Most societies put a high priority on having children and on giving their children a better life than their parents. Older generations not only transfer material wealth to younger generations but also, and probably more importantly, human capital. By providing good care, good health, material wealth, and schooling, societies give young generations the knowledge and experiences of the older generations as well as the tools to develop this human capital further.

The care and schooling of children have been the topic of research in several disciplines using many different approaches. In economics child care and schooling are viewed as investment activities. Parents use their own time and purchased goods and services to give their children human capital in the form of knowledge, experiences, and good health. In some cultures parents get a return on their investments when their children later work in the market and contribute to family income, particularly when the parents get old. To have many children is thereby old age pension insurance in these cultures. In our modern Western societies this motive to invest in children has no longer the same importance.

It is still true that the working generations provide for the retired generations, but this is now done in collective forms and via market investments across families, and there is usually only a weak link (if any) between the child's human capital and the well-being of its parents. My pension is thus not decreased if I neglect my children and use all my resources on myself (it might even increase!) provided everyone does not act in the same way. From a collective point of view, however, it is of utmost importance that the parental generations invest in their children and that these investments generate economic growth. If not the parental generations will have a loss of well-being when they retire since there will be reduced output to support both the economically active and dependent populations. In a collectively responsible society there are compelling reasons to invest in children. This also suggests that we could measure the return on these investments by their contribution to economic growth, which at the individual level implies that the return on the investments made in one child could be measured by the child's contribution to the production of goods and services. The share of this contribution that goes to the market could thus be measured by the stream of lifetime earnings, while the measurement of the share that goes to the nonmarket sector is less obvious.

Quite independently of our self-interest (individually or collectively) when retiring, most people would probably acknowledge that it is important to have children and to give them a good start in life. Whether the desire to have children is explained as a natural instinct, an altruistic concern for one's children and future generations, or a selfish satisfaction derived from child-related consumption patterns, most people want children and enjoy having them. As shown by Juster (1985b) and Flood and Klevmarken (1990), playing with children and taking care of them are activities that give the highest "process benefit," to borrow Juster's terminology.

In work on the economics of the family Becker (1965, 1981) and Willis (1973) made the distinction between the number of children a couple may want and the skills, knowledge, and experiences, called quality, the parents wish to give their children. Using this distinction, these researchers were able to explain why rich parents do not necessarily want to have more children than do less well-to-do parents. Rather, they prefer children with more "quality." Thus, in this model both the quantity and the quality of children contribute to the satisfaction of the parents. If quality is more income elastic than quantity the interaction between quality and quantity can lead to an apparent negative income elasticity of demand for quantity. Utility is also a function of non-child-related consumption, and parents are assumed to make a choice between the number of children they want, the resources they want to allocate to the children, and other non-child-related consumption so as to maximize their joint utility subject to an intertemporal budget constraint and a time constraint.

The more children parents choose to have the less time they will have for market work and leisure activities, and the lower their (nonchild) consumption standard becomes. In Gronau's model (1973, 1986) there are two aggregate commodities that give utility, "child services" and a "consumption standard," but utility is independent of how these commodities are produced. The model does not accommodate Juster's idea that the investment process as such gives utility (process benefits), just that the result, "well-behaved children" does. The introduction of Juster's process benefits makes the distinction between investments and consumption fuzzy. If parents' efforts to bring up their children are solely motivated by the joy and satisfaction they get by doing so independently of the result, then what we would normally call investments in children are only consumption or produces *both* consumption and investment as outputs.

Parental Investment in Young Children

In this essay we will emphasize the investment aspects of having children rather than the consumption aspects. One starting point is the scheme laid out by Leibowitz (1974). The approach indicates how the parents' genetic endowment, socioeconomic background, living circumstances, and investments in their children determine the children's adult production ability and living standard. Leibowitz's figure is modified to include out of home early investments and is reproduced as figure 1. It shows that home investment consists of the quantity and quality of time inputs and the quantity and quality of goods inputs that, jointly with inherited ability, will determine the level of schooling that finally will influence

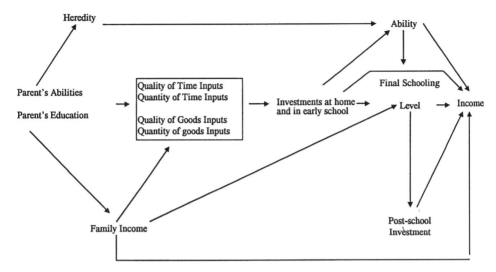

Fig. 1. Home investments in children. (Adapted from Liebowitz 1974.)

postschool investments and income. We may thus distinguish between home investments and investments outside the home and between time investments and goods investments.

Here we offer some brief remarks to explain the strong empirical relationship between parental education and child care time, a pattern observed in many countries. This is a simpified version of the models developed by Willis (1973) and Becker and Lewis (1973). The family has a utility function

$$U = U(N,C,Z) \tag{1}$$

where N is the number of children and C is child quality or home input received by each child. (Here we ignore interchild differences). All other goods are represented as Z. To simplify we assume C and Z are produced according to the following linearly homogeneous "household" production functions:

$$C = C(h_c, M_c) \tag{2}$$

$$Z = Z(h_z, M_z) \tag{3}$$

where $C = NQ$, with Q per child quality and h_i and M_i ($i = C,Z$) are, respectively, vectors of time and goods allocated to children and other pursuits. In the framework one can develop expressions for the parents' allocation of time to child care. Specifically, it can be shown that the compensated wage elasticity of child care time can be expressed as

$$\frac{\partial h_c}{\partial w} \cdot \frac{w}{h_c}\bigg|_F \equiv \epsilon = -(1 - \alpha_c)\gamma_c + (1 - k)\sigma(\alpha_z - \alpha_c) \tag{4}$$

where $\alpha_c = wh_c/\Pi_c C$ is the time intensity parameter for the production of $C = NQ$ (α_z is analogously defined for the production of Z); Π_c is the full price interim of time and money, γ_c is the elasticity of substitution between h_c and M_c in the production of C; k = share of the full budget (F) going to child care; and σ is elasticity of substitution in consumption between C and Z. The algebraic sign of the second term on the right hand side of (equation 4) depends on the difference in tie intensity parameters in the production of C and Z. It seems very plausible that, particularly in the preschool years, $\alpha_C > \alpha_Z$. An increase in market wage of the parent raises the marginal cost of both C and Z but raises it relatively more for the more time intensive commodity. For $\sigma > 0$ this will lead to a substitution away from C.

The explanation for greater time in child care for more educated parents rests on the underlying income elasticity for C. Further, as distinct from other household activities, the production of child care probably exhibits a very low elasticity of substitution between goods and time (γ_c) and accounts for a large fraction of the family's full budget.

Time Investments at Home

Time investments at home are predominantly, but not exclusively, by parents, who decrease their market and leisure time to care for their children. A few studies have pointed out that in addition to income forgone while a parent is at home taking care of children there is a dynamic shadow price of the forgone opportunity to invest in one's own human capital and build up future earnings. These estimates (Smith and Ward 1989; Joshi 1990, 1994; Calhoun and Espenshade 1988; Dankmeyer 1996; Stafford and Sundström 1997) indicate a substantial cost of this sort. In the Netherlands, this "time out" appears to be very costly for women with less schooling, since the market work experience is even more important for their careers (Dankmeyer 1996).

Time investments may also be made by the extended family and friends or by others who with or without compensation, for instance, baby-sit, give care, or provide lessons. One may even see socializing with family relatives and friends as an investment activity or the production of social capital (Coleman 1990) that shapes child development, notably including values and preferences of children. We might further wish to distinguish between different kinds of time inputs. One is the direct care of a child, an activity in which the child (children) is the primary target: for instance, feeding a child, dressing a child, reading to a child, or helping out with homework. People commonly do more than one activity at the same time (or in Juster's view switch back and forth between activities in a way that makes it hard to distinguish each separately). For instance, a mother might be cooking and helping with homework at the same time. The activity the mother considers to be her "primary activity" (in time-use studies) is classified as the primary activity and the other as a secondary activity.

Both primary and secondary activities could involve investments in children. There are also activities in which the child is not the primary target but in which the child is present when the activity is done. A family could, for instance, have a meal jointly, or they could be doing some kind of sports or outdoor activity together, or a child could simply be watching when an adult is doing something. These activities may also include investment aspects, that is, the child is learning while watching and doing. Finally, there are activities in which the child is not present but which are carried out to the benefit of the child: for instance, the child's dirty laundry is washed and ironed, or a meal is cooked for the child.

It is not obvious how one should go about assigning investment measures to these diverse forms of activity. Time-use studies give the time input of parents (and others) into direct child care and sometimes also data on other episodes during which children are present. Time use for the benefit of children without them being present can usually only be estimated indirectly (cf. "An Overview of Time and Goods: Incremental Housework and Child Care Time," which follows). Most current time-use studies only give estimates on the time use of the adult but not on how much time was spent on each child. Simply averaging by the number of children in the family will not do because in some activities a child might benefit as much from the activity by doing it jointly with other children as by doing it alone. Indeed, there are activities such as certain games that require more than one participant. Also, parents and school-based caregivers may provide unequal amounts of time to siblings. One apparent motivation is a type of intraschool or intrafamily equity (Brown and Saks 1975, Gustafsson and Stafford 1997). The literature on child investments also discusses the importance of the order of birth among siblings for the level of parents' time investments as well as the transmission of human capital between siblings. There are, for example, results indicating that the first and last child receive more attention from parents than do middle children (Hanushek 1992).

Ideally one would need child time diaries. Even for diaries of individual children in the same family there are questions of "scale economies" or public goods. In this case adult time for one child is not at the expense of the other children, and, as in the example of organizing a game, the value is from the team element. One view is that formal school settings consist heavily of those activities where there are scale economies or public goods for adult time in the learning process.

Measures of time input are not necessarily good measures on investments for at least two reasons. First, as noted previously, an activity might be done both for its investment contents and for its consumption benefits, and it is difficult to separate the two. Second, the quality of the input of hours and minutes might differ. Is one hour of TV viewing equivalent to one hour of homework? To what extent does the content of the TV show or homework matter? It might be possible to rank activities as to their investment contents and more or less arbitrarily weight the time use proportionally to this. If measures on the return on child investments were available these could be related to the time input in various activities, and one could in this way assess their relative importance. In the absence of return measures any such operation involves many ad hoc judgments.

An alternative approach to measuring investments is the "cost of time approach." That is, time inputs are converted into monetary inputs by using either a wage rate of the person doing the activity or, if there is a market alternative, what it would cost to purchase the service or good produced. This approach is easiest to defend when there are true opportunity costs or market alternatives; when this is not the case any monetary evaluation becomes rather arbitrary. If, for instance, a woman gives up her job to care for her children, then there is a recognizable opportunity cost, but if a housewife gives up some of her time to care for her children the opportunity cost is less well defined.

Time Inputs outside the Home

From an investment perspective the most important time input outside home is certainly time in preschool and school activities. Here, an underlying factor is the presence of greater scale economies in instruction and learning as children become more developed, and, as with in-home capital formation, there are quality differences between time on task at school, for instance, and leisure and break time. We might also believe that certain tasks at school have more investment content than others. Outside school there are also activities that contribute to the human capital of a child. There are more or less organized post school activities that aim at teaching the child certain skills, but also socializing among other children gives the child useful experiences about group behavior and how to establish relations with others. The playground is an important arena for investments in human capital! For most countries we currently lack measures of time inputs outside the home, except for a few classroom surveys, none of which are based on national samples. Time-use surveys only give data on the time adults interact with children. We need child time-use diaries for this purpose, particularly of the day at school or other out-of-home activities.

Estimates of the monetary value of these out-of-home investments would have to build on estimates of the value of adult time input, especially for young children, and the value of any goods input. In this way it might be possible to estimate, for instance, the investment value of preschool and school activities. Similarly, for a sports activity one might like to add the time cost of an adult coach and the rental value of the sports ground and any equipment. A problem in this case, though, is that one also might like to subtract something for the consumption benefit of sporting. For child activities that neither involve any adults nor any equipment there is no monetary estimate obtainable from the cost side. For children at older ages, their own time and its opportunity cost become more important. In higher school grades there are higher pupil/teacher ratios, so the active engagement of the child and forgone market earnings become important (Hansen 1963).

Goods Inputs

Considerations similar to those for the time input apply to the input of goods. For some goods it is possible to uniquely identify them with the children of a family, for instance, clothing for children (but not necessarily with individual children as younger siblings inherit from older siblings), while goods like furniture, TV sets, and the home in which the family lives are jointly consumed by all family members. One may buy a larger home, more furniture, and more than one TV set if there are children in the family, but it is not possible, for instance in a family expenditure survey, to unambiguously say that such and such a share should be viewed as used by or for the children. With some modeling it is possible to estimate the incremental consumption expenditures due to children.

Using such measures of incremental expenditures for the goods input as an investment implies that these expenditures on children are in fact investment expenditures. The child does not consume at all! A candy bar is probably consumption, but is a hamburger a nutritional investment? As a first approximation, the only way to proceed is to empirically relate such goods inputs to some intermediate (developmental) capital in the broad schematic of figure 1. The widely used HOME Scale (Baker and Mott 1989) includes rough indicators of physical resources available to young children.

Goods inputs outside the home involve purchases by someone other than the child's parents or other family members. For instance, scholarships and grants given to the child could be used to buy the services of a school. In most countries compulsory schooling is paid for by the public, and in some countries the public also covers most of the direct costs of both preschool and postcompulsory schooling. These public costs should be viewed as investment costs, but the question arises of the return on the investment. Otherwise, they may effectively be a type of transfer payment to the parents, possibly to support consumption.

In some countries the public also gives additional support to families with the intent that this support provide resources to children. These benefits may take the form of cash transfers to families with children of certain ages or to mothers (and fathers). If because of a subsidy the parents give up market work, do they allocate added time to child care? Are the subsidies also used to increase the expenditures on goods inputs to the children? For the labor supply substitution to child care, the investment cost (opportunity cost of not working) is usually shared between the parents and the public, with the public carrying the larger part, at least during the first year after a child is born. There are also housing benefits targeted for families with children. In some countries benefits are given in the form of income deductions before tax or as tax credits rather than in the form of cash benefits. In the case of maternity benefits and family allowances for parents who stay at home to care for their children the potential investment character is rather obvious, but less so for other benefits. If the housing benefits simply reduce the expenses that would otherwise have gone to housing, the net result is just somewhat greater family income, and the issue then becomes the size of the income elasticity of demand for child quality and the induced time and goods inputs that would make an incremental contribution toward investments in children. An interesting case is special health care expenditure for young children (Gustafsson and Stafford 1997). Here there is a tying-in of the benefits that may reduce the extent of such budgetary substitution.

An Overview of Time and Goods

Time Inputs at Home

To the extent measures are available, this section aims at assessing the total magnitude of time investments at home for selected countries and years. Table 1 gives time-use estimates in child care for a number of countries ranging in time from the beginning of the 1970s to the beginning of the 1990s. On average males provide about 0.2 hours per day for primary child care time and females 0.4–0.7 hours, depending on country and year. These estimates include all families whether they have own children or not. Time use in child care differs of course very much between families with children and families without. The age of the children is also important as shown by table 2. Families without children use little time in child care. Bulgarian females are an exception. It is likely that the extended family is more important for the upbringing of a child in this country than in most other Western countries. (The high estimates for Sweden and Married, aged 16–44, with no children are probably due to small sample size.) In families with small children (below seven) males spend on average 0.5–1.0 hours per day in child care and females between 1.5 and 3 hours. In families with older children the corresponding estimates are lower, 0.2 hours per day for men and between 0.2 and 0.7 for women. Considering the relatively high Swedish

TABLE 1. Average Child Primary Care Hours per Day by Adults at Home, by Country and Gender, Selected Years

Country/Year	Males	Females
Bulgaria, 1988	0.1	0.5
Finland, 1979	0.2	0.4
Finland, 1987	0.2	0.5
Hungary, 1976–77	0.2	0.5
Hungary, 1986	0.2	0.6
Norway, 1971–72	0.2	0.6
Norway, 1980–81	0.2	0.6
Sweden, 1984	0.2	0.5
Sweden, 1993	0.3	0.5
United States, 1975–76	0.2	0.7

Source: Kirjavainen et al. 1992; Barbarczy, Harsca and Paakonen 1991; Niemi Kiiski and Liikkanan 1979; Lingsom and Ellingsaeter 1983; the Time Budget Survey 1980–81 from the Central Bureau of Statistics of Norway, Oslo 1983; and own computations for Sweden using HUS-data (see Klevmarken and Olovsson 1993 and Flood and Olovsson 1997).

Note: This table gives averages for all individuals whether they live in families with or without children.

labor force participation rate it is interesting to note that Swedish women use less time in child care than women in the other countries.

Table 3 exhibits estimates for three Scandinavian countries of parents' time with their children including child care *and other activities* during which the child is present. The overall averages for males range

TABLE 2. **Average Primary Child Care Hours per Day by Marital Status and Gender, Selected Years**

Country/Year	Singles, 16–44, No Children	Singles with Children	Married, 16–44, No Children	Married, 45–74, No Children	Married with Children < 7	Married with Children 7–18
Males						
Bulgaria, 1988	0.0	0.2	0.1	0.1	0.5	0.2
Finland, 1979	0.0	0.3	0.0	0.0	0.9	0.2
Norway, 1971–72	0.0	0.1	—	0.0	0.5	0.2
Norway, 1980–81	0.0	0.4	—	—	1.0	0.2
Sweden, 1984	0.1	0.4	0.1	0.1	1.0	0.2
Sweden, 1993	0.0	0.1	0.1	0.1	0.9	0.2
Females						
Bulgaria, 1988	0.1	0.9	0.2	0.3	3.0	0.5
Finland, 1979	0.0	0.7	0.0	0.0	2.5	0.2
Norway, 1971–72	0.0	0.6	0.0	0.1	2.1	0.7
Norway, 1980–81	—	1.0	0.0	0.0	2.3	0.6
Sweden, 1984	0.0	0.5	0.6	0.1	1.8	0.3
Sweden, 1993	0.0	0.5	0.3	0.1	1.5	0.4

Source: Kirjavainen et al. 1992; Niemi, Kiiski, and Liikkanan 1979; Lingsom and Ellingsaeter 1983; the Time Budget Survey 1980–81 from the Central Bureau of Statistics of Norway, Oslo 1983; and our own computations for Sweden using HUS-data (see Klevmarken and Olovsson 1993 and Flood and Olovsson 1997).

TABLE 3. **Average Total Child Related Hours per Day with Own Children by Age of the Youngest Child and Gender of Parent**

	Males				Females			
Country/Year	0–6	7–12	13–18	All	0–6	7–12	13–18	All
Finland, 1979	5.3	5.3	6.1	5.5	9.2	7.1	7.4	8.1
Norway, 1980–81	5.3	4.5	4.2	4.8	9.1	6.9	5.1	7.4
Sweden, 1984	5.5	4.0	2.8	4.3	8.7	5.4	3.5	6.1
Sweden, 1993	5.1	4.3	3.0	4.1	7.8	5.2	3.7	5.7

Source: Use of Time in Finland 1979, Studies no. 65 (Helsinki: Central Statistical Office of Finland, 1981), 60–61. The Time Budget Survey 1980–81, table 59 (Central Bureau of Statistics of Norway, 1983), B378. Our own calculations using the Swedish HUS surveys 1984 and 1993.

Note: Time-use estimates include *both* active child care and other activities with children present.

from 4.1 hours per day to 5.5 hours per day depending on country and for females the estimates range between 5.7 hours and 8.1 hours. It is of course difficult to separate country effects from annual effects, but given the similarities between these Scandinavian countries, the lower estimates for Sweden, 1993, might suggest that parents now spend less time with their children than they used to. Table 3 also shows how time use depends on the age of the children. The younger the children the more time parents and, in particular, women spend with their children.

Comparing tables 1 and 2 with table 3 highlights the "joint products" problem in studying child care. Much child care takes place in conjunction with other activities. Is this joint activity less important? Is one-on-one child care a measure of something closer to "quality time"? Two approaches to resolving these questions are the "value" approach and the "cost" approach. In the value approach the weight for joint time versus one-on-one time can be determined by the relationship of joint versus one-on-one time to impacts on various developmental outcomes at later ages and then to longer term outcomes such as completed schooling and earnings. In the cost approach one would reduce the investment in time by allowing for the fact that multiple outputs are produced. The simplest method is to give joint time a lower investment weight. Regardless of how to best proceed here, it is evident that joint time is a large share of total child time, particularly for fathers.

Another drawback with these tables is that they do not tell us how much of the adult time each child gets. In countries with high fertility and large families average time for child care is likely to become higher than in countries with low fertility. But families with many children are likely to use adult time jointly, and we also know from other studies that the incremental time for an additional child levels off rather rapidly with increasing number of children. For these reasons we will also estimate incremental time use in child care and household work.

Incremental Housework and Child Care Time

Children's development involves some baseline maintenance efforts by the parents. In this view parents have a quartermaster function. While not thought of as the critical developmental input, resources are involved, as are interesting aspects of intrafamily decision making. It has been shown that allocation of time by the spouses to these activities appears to be related to relative wage rates of the spouses, but when sex of parent was added the predictive power of relative spousal wages was reduced dramatically (Juster and Hill 1985). It was further shown that drudge work time arising from the presence of young children cut into shared free time of the spouses and increased the probability of marital instability (Hill 1988).

Here we provide a selection of estimates of housework time and its relation to children in different age ranges. In table 4A we have incremental housework, including child care, based on reports of housework, including child care for the United States. For higher socioeconomic status (SES) families, children under six appear to be receiving on the order of 1–2 hours per day, based on time diary estimates, but, from table 4B, only on the order of 1 hour per day based on respondent reports of housework. In table 4C the child care and housework components are separated, based on the 1975–76 time diary study for the United States. For mothers with educational attainment of some college

TABLE 4A.   Annual per Child Hours of Mother's Care and Socioeconomic Status (SES), United States

		Measure	Groups		
Year	Study	Incremental Housework[a] (from diary)	High[b] SES	Middle SES	Low SES
1965	Time Use I	Children aged 0–2.99	741 (237)	352 (149)	494 (109)
		Children aged 3–4.99	489 (189)	508 (157)	−23 (104)
		Children aged 5–6.99	455 (229)	496 (144)	−158 (126)
		Children aged 7–17.99	164 (97)	198 (63)	−37 (39)

Source: Hill and Stafford 1974, table 2. Reprinted by permission of the University of Wisconsin Press.

[a]Housework includes child care.

[b]Socioeconomic status as measured by the Duncan Index.

TABLE 4B.   Annual per Child Hours of Mother's Care, United States

Year	Study	Incremental Housework[a] (respondent hours reports)	Low, Low[b]	Low, High	High, Low	High, High
1969	PSID	Children aged 0–6.99	156 (33)	299 (104)	343 (72)	434 (74)
		Children aged 7–17.99	49 (20)	119 (74)	45 (47)	128 (50)

Source: Hill and Stafford 1977. Reprinted by permission.

Note: The entries in tables 4A–4C are regression coefficients in a simple descriptive regression of mother's time use. Standard errors are in parentheses.

[a]Housework includes child care.

[b]Less than some college education, both head and wife.

TABLE 4C. Annual per Child Hours of Mother's Care, United States

Year	Study	Incremental Child Care (primary time from diary)	13+ Years ED	9–12 Years ED	<8 ED
1976	Time Use II	Children aged 0–2.99	485	383	386
			(37)	(38)	(81)
		Children aged 3–4.99	218	261	120
			(45)	(38)	(75)
		Children aged 5–12.99	142	77	42
			(19)	(16)	(29)
		Children aged 13–17.99	52	6	−3
			(23)	(26)	(43)
		Incremental Housework[a] (from diary)	13+ Years ED	9–12 Years ED	<8 ED
1976	Time Use II	Children aged 0–2.99	374	171	62
			(75)	(80)	(165)
		Children aged 3–4.99	389	328	−131
			(89)	(79)	(153)
		Children aged 5–6.99	150	120	−62
			(37)	(35)	(60)
		Children aged 7–17.99	164	233	−28
			(45)	(54)	(88)

Source: Hill and Stafford 1985.
Note: ED = education. Standard errors are in parentheses.
[a]Other than child care.

or more, we can see that the total incremental child care time of about 800 hours per year for children ages 0–2.99 (859 hours) is divided as 485 hours for direct child care and 374 hours of incremental housework. Children take time!

Tables 5A and 5B present incremental time for children based on Swedish time-use data. The United States and Sweden show noticeable differences! From table 5A we find that on average one-on-one incremental child care time is only about 100 hours per year in Sweden. The estimates of incremental household work other than child care are also low compared to the United States (table 5B). Males increase their household work by about 50 hours per year and child for very young children, and the corresponding estimate for women is about 200 hours.[2] The older the children the smaller these estimates become. Because there are clear birth cohort differences in the time allocation to household work, younger cohorts do less household work, a few birth cohort variables were added to the regression models. As previously mentioned, there are also differences in behavior related to schooling.

TABLE 5A. Incremental Child Care Estimates by Years of Schooling for Sweden (primary time from diary, hours/year)

	≤9	10–12	13+	All
		Years of Schooling		
1984	83 (7)	115 (12)	97 (14)	102 (6)
1993	72 (4)	130 (14)	96 (12)	111 (7)

Source: Own calculations using HUS-data (see Klevmarken and Olovsson 1993 and Flood and Olovsson 1997).

Note: The estimates were obtained by regressing primary time in child care on the number of children in the family including families with no children. Standard errors are in parentheses.

TABLE 5B. Estimates of Incremental Housework Other than Child Care by Gender and Years of Schooling, Sweden 1993 (primary time from diary, hours/year)

	Less than 13 Years of Schooling		At Least 13 Years of Schooling		All Levels of Schooling	
Males						
Birth cohort						
1929–38	587.6	(122.6)	409.0	(165.7)	543.5	(97.9)
1939–48	377.8	(119.7)	306.3	(150.9)	351.7	(93.7)
1949–58	411.8	(125.9)	308.3	(153.4)	377.1	(97.0)
1959–68	231.1	(126.0)	71.6	(153.2)	175.0	(97.3)
No. of siblings × the age of the youngest child						
0–2	48.7	(50.7)	43.5	(59.5)	49.2	(38.7)
3–4	16.0	(62.9)	46.1	(47.6)	28.6	(39.4)
5–12	6.9	(44.8)	−9.6	(42.5)	−1.3	(31.5)
13–17	38.9	(74.6)	−36.8	(68.1)	1.2	(51.4)
Constant	531.3	(103.8)	578.7	(133.6)	546.0	(81.8)
R^2	0.0534		0.0513		0.0513	
No. of observations	511		286		797	
Females						
Birth cohort						
1929–38	644.4	(120.7)	417.6	(188.1)	621.9	(99.3)
1939–48	608.7	(117.9)	426.4	(149.5)	544.2	(92.8)
1949–58	370.3	(131.5)	497.9	(162.6)	436.1	(101.8)
1959–68	129.2	(128.5)	191.4	(154.4)	138.9	(98.5)
No. of siblings × the age of the youngest child						
0–2	212.1	(53.0)	205.6	(69.6)	213.7	(41.7)
3–4	104.2	(50.3)	147.5	(62.9)	119.6	(39.1)
5–12	16.5	(48.6)	137.8	(55.8)	65.5	(36.5)
13–17	89.7	(89.1)	130.1	(76.3)	82.9	(56.9)
Constant	824.5	(102.1)	701.1	(129.7)	780.5	(80.5)
R^2	0.0943		0.1308		0.0918	
No. of observations	507		320		829	

Source: Own calculations using HUS-data; Flood and Olovsson 1997.

Note: Sample restricted to individuals born after 1928. The constant represents cohorts born after 1968 to which the older cohorts are compared. Standard errors are in parentheses.

Although the estimates for Sweden are not well determined, they indicate that more educated women use relatively more time in child-related household work if the youngest child is older than two years. For the youngest there is no difference due to schooling. The results for the United States are even more clear cut. Independently of the age of the children, women with more schooling use more time in child-related household work (tables 4B and 4C). Why is there more incremental housework by more educated women? Why weren't these activities more likely to be "outsourced" for those with higher market wage potential and a presumed higher value to career enhancing activities? Do more educated women have higher preferences for child quality as reflected in a higher income elasticity?

The analysis of the 1984 time-use study in Flood and Klevmarken (1989) provides additional details. Using a Tobit-type selection model they obtained only small and insignificant effects of children on household work other than child care in addition to the positive effect of household size. The marginal effect of household size was estimated to 127 hours per year for males and 204 hours for females, but only the latter estimate was significant. For child care activities the results were reversed; the effect of household size was small and insignificant while parents' time in child care increased for every child, in particular every young child. According to the point estimates, women increased their time use in child care by 214 hours for every child below four, and men increased their time by 138 hours. Flood and Klevmarken also showed that the increased time for child care and household work was compensated primarily by a reduction of market work, in particular when the kids were young, but also by a reduction of leisure time. Men also decreased their time for sleep and rest somewhat, while women with young children increased their time for sleep and rest. There are similar results for the United States. Hill and Stafford (1977, 1985) showed that for U.S. women, the incremental child care time and housework time associated with children was "financed" by reduced market work, passive leisure, and sleep.

In comparing the typical patterns of time-use for child care and child-related household work in the two countries we thus find that Swedish parents in the 1980s and 1990s spent slightly less time in these activities than did U.S. parents in the 1970s. Without further study it is currently only possible to speculate about what caused these differences between the two countries. It is conceivable that the difference in labor force participation between U.S. women and Swedish women could be an explanation. The Swedish female labor force participation rate was higher, which is at least partly explained by the supply of inexpensive public child care. It is also conceivable that, to some extent, care at home by parents has been substituted for care at public nurseries. The results from the study by Gustafsson and Kjullin (1994) confirm such a conclusion.

Swedish public policy may also have changed the intrafamily bargaining process compared to the United States (Rosen 1995; Sundström and Stafford 1992). As an interesting look at intrafamily child care decisions, table 6 shows time with and without children for Sweden in 1993. What seems quite surprising is the rather equal time by men and women, both in direct child care time and in other activities with children present. As of 1976, U.S. men spent very little time in child care, about 2.25 hours per week, and that was only for college-educated men with children under age five. Changing gender roles in the care of young children may have also taken place in the United States since 1976.

The differences across countries (Sweden and the United States) in "induced" housework time because of young children, combined with the joint child care estimates of table 3, highlight the need to measure a wide array of time inputs in order to quantify investments in children. The routine housework costs of children also raise the question of how to value such "inputs." From a cost perspective, things seem clear. The added housework is a cost, especially since these activities are rated as having the lowest intrinsic satisfaction or "process benefits" (Juster 1985b). From a value perspective, does one really expect more routine chore time to lead to better school performance? Will Swedish children have less success in school because of less drudge work by their parents?

The estimates in table 7 show a volatility that is hard to explain other than as the result of sampling variability, but the numbers indicate

TABLE 6. Time with and without Children, Sweden 1993 (minutes/day), by Gender and Age of the Youngest Child (families with children under 18)

	Child Care	Other Activities with Children	Sleep, Rest, Personal	Other Time Use without Children
Men				
Child aged <7	79.2	249.6	403.1	631.8
Child aged 7–12	14.6	240.8	447.9	711.1
Child aged 13–17	2.4	173.3	458.1	783.4
Women				
Child aged <7	89.7	374.5	437.9	445.0
Child aged 7–12	29.5	292.0	449.7	605.3
Child aged 13–17	3.8	225.2	443.0	702.1

Source: Own calculations using HUS-data; see Flood and Olovsson 1997.

TABLE 7. Consumption Expenditures per Child, Sweden, 1958–92 (in SEK)

	1958	1969	1978	1985	1988	1992
Singles						
With children	10,162	22,236	55,454	102,815	122,700	184,556
Without children	6,809	14,432	37,159	69,526	89,541	120,513
Incremental exp./child	2,395	5,202	13,068	23,778	23,685	42,695
Incremental exp./child in constant						
1992 SEK	20,908	31,238	36,969	35,928	31,145	42,695
Couples						
With children	14,213	31,025	84,346	162,568	206,080	272,848
Without children	11,920	24,025	64,970	131,157	166,567	230,045
Incremental exp./child	1,274	4,079	10,764	17,451	20,796	22,528
Incremental exp./child in constant						
1992 SEK	11,122	24,494	30,451	26,368	27,346	22,528

Source: Hushållsbudgetundersökningen (Family Expenditure Survey) 1978, pt. 3. Statistics Sweden, 1982. Hushållens utgifter 1985, 1988, and 1992, published by Statistics Sweden in 1987, 1990, and 1994.
Note: The average number of children for singles: 1.4, 1.5, 1.4, 1.4, 1.4, and 1.5; for couples: 1.8, 1.8, 1.8, 1.8, 1.9, and 1.9. Conversion into constant prices was made using the Consumer Price Index, total annual average.

that the average incremental expenditures per child and year were about 35,000 in 1992 Swedish kronor (SEK) for singles and about 25,000 for couples. Converted into U.S. dollars (USD) these estimates amounted to about 5,000 and 3,500 dollars. Table 8 shows that the incremental expenditure per child is highest for the first child and then levels off with increasing number of children, reflecting economy of scale.

Public Investments in Children

A few results from a Swedish study of public support to families with children in Europe (Wallberg, Medelberg, and Stromquist 1996) are reproduced in table 9 and supplemented with data for the United States. The table gives the sum of all benefits an average child gets from birth to the age of nineteen (finishing high school) as if the benefit levels in 1993 had applied all years. It also details by the benefit type. In table 9 the unit of measurement is GDP per capita.

There is a clear age profile in the public support of families with children and also clear differences between countries in addition to the general pattern shown in table 9. This can be seen in table 10. Most countries have a relatively generous support to families with newborn babies, but even by the first year child benefits drop rather precipitously,

TABLE 8. Consumption Expenditures per Child by Number of Children per Family, Sweden 1985, 1988, and 1992 (in SEK)

	Expenditure			Incremental Exp./ Child			Incremental Exp./ Child in Constant 1992		
	1985	1988	1992	1985	1988	1992	1985	1988	1992
Singles									
No children	71,129	94,626	123,686						
1 child	95,378	109,932	172,950	24,249	15,306	49,264	36,640	20,127	49,264
>1 child	118,385	145,839	203,389	17,698	27,620	23,415	26,742	36,320	23,415
Couples, Head <65									
No children	131,157	166,567	230,045						
1 child	152,179	190,149	260,117	21,022	23,582	30,072	31,764	31,010	30,072
2 children	166,214	212,823	275,564	14,035	22,674	15,447	21,207	29,816	15,447
>2 children	174,317	221,107	289,438	6,753	6,903	11,562	10,203	9,077	11,562

Source: Hushållens utgifter 1985, 1988, and 1992, published by Statistics Sweden in 1987, 1990, and 1994.

Note: The average number of children for singles with more than one child was 2.3 all three years. For couples with more than 2 children the average was 3.2. Conversion into constant SEK was done using the Consumer Price Index, total annual average.

TABLE 9. Public Support to Children 0–18 Years Old in 1993 by Country (support per child measured in GDP per capita)

	Country[a]								
Benefit	DK	SF	N	S	F	NL	GB	D	US
Child allowances	0.90	0.94	1.55	1.09	1.16	1.03	0.98	0.61	0.00
Parental leave	0.23	0.67	0.45	0.69	0.18	0.06	0.04	0.40	0.00
Alimonies (advance payments)	0.01	0.06	0.14	0.17	0.04	0.00	0.00	0.01	n/a
Housing allowances	0.18	0.31	0.11	0.41	0.41	0.11	0.42	1.10	0.00
Public child care	1.33	1.01	0.65	1.62	0.65	0.03	0.05	0.63	0.16[b]
Public schools	3.22	3.75	3.70	3.94	2.70	2.58	2.99	2.75	3.92[c]
Tax allowances	0.00	0.59	0.26	0.00	0.34	0.04	0.09	0.55	0.35[d]
Total	5.88	7.33	6.86	7.92	5.47	3.86	4.58	5.06	4.43

Note: n/a = not available.

[a]Country abbreviations are as follows: DK = Denmark, SF = Finland, N = Norway, S = Sweden, F = France, NL = The Netherlands, GB = Great Britain, D = Germany, and US = United States.

[b]Hofferth 1993, 210; Wallberg, Medelberg, and Stromquist 1996.

[c]Expenditures on Children in Primary and Secondary Public Schools, 1993, divided by 1993 GDP.

[d]Total of children under age 20 as of 1994 (74.955 million) and an assumed tax reduction of $300 per child (state and federal combined).

and in countries with little public child care, like the Netherlands and Great Britain, the level of public support is quite modest for 1 and 2 year olds. Public support rises later in two stages, once at the time primary school starts and then again at a second time when high school starts. Table 10 includes public support for parental leave and other programs. These payments may generally improve the opportunities parents have to provide resources to young children but do not necessarily measure the actual developmental inputs per se. Parents may use the public funds for their own consumption or may reduce their own child development efforts as the publicly provided care resources are increased. Research on Swedish parents with preschool children shows that for age of child ranges (0–2, 2–7) the hours per week of mother's active child care are 5.31 and 2.26 for those without daycare and 4.22 and 2.48 for those with day care (Gustafsson and Kjulin 1994, table 2). This suggests only a modest offset to parental time for publicly provided care—unless it is

TABLE 10.   Public Support to Children, 1993, by Age of Child and Country (SEK per child)

Age of Child	Country[a]							
	S	DK	SF	N	NL	GB	D	F
<1	101,869	54,650	84,179	107,408	18,576	21,230	60,207	59,646
1	45,048	46,068	50,706	36,719	8,138	13,898	25,889	35,311
2	56,889	47,861	59,947	42,694	9,176	13,898	12,764	44,638
3	57,198	47,861	44,697	46,624	11,091	18,365	35,664	47,492
4	56,915	47,861	44,697	46,624	30,142	18,365	58,564	47,492
5	56,673	47,861	44,697	46,624	30,142	46,737	58,564	47,492
6	56,506	47,861	44,697	46,624	36,952	46,737	40,968	45,210
7	77,280	58,770	59,633	67,070	36,952	46,737	40,968	45,210
8	77,080	58,770	57,361	67,070	36,952	46,737	40,968	45,210
9	76,954	58,770	57,361	67,070	36,952	46,737	40,968	45,210
10	76,775	58,770	57,361	63,139	36,952	46,737	56,766	46,710
11	64,240	49,089	56,002	63,139	36,952	60,170	56,766	64,543
12	63,827	49,089	56,002	61,927	49,711	60,170	55,549	64,543
13	73,448	73,941	57,197	77,243	49,711	60,170	55,549	64,543
14	73,448	73,941	57,197	77,243	49,711	60,170	55,549	64,543
15	73,448	73,941	57,197	77,243	49,711	60,170	55,549	66,273
16	83,756	78,707	88,005	105,363	49,781	46,051	56,696	66,308
17	82,155	69,042	76,494	99,347	47,575	34,757	58,056	63,747
18	57,181	69,184	66,319	86,852	43,552	14,428	51,515	48,434

Source: Wallberg, Medelberg, and Stromquist 1996.

[a]Country abbreviations are as follows: S = Sweden, DK = Denmark, SF = Finland, N = Norway, NL = The Netherlands, GB = Great Britain, D = Denmark, F = France.

believed that there is strong selection on unobservables in the decision to participate and get a space in public daycare.

The data in table 11 on school expenditures from the Organization for Economic Cooperation and Development (OECD) provide a somewhat different picture of public resources to children. At the primary and secondary levels, a point in development where we would expect child development to be the primary goal of the expenditure, we can see the OECD average running about $4,000–5,000 per student. There are some fairly large differences between countries; the expenditures for primary and secondary schools in Spain is 35 to 40 percent and in France 50 to 70 percent of those in the United States and Sweden. The effectiveness of school expenditures is a major question. What actually transpires in the classroom? Do greater expenditures partly go to the provision of extended postschool activities as is often the case for U.S. schools, or do the greater expenditures go to non-teaching-related activities, such as preventative health care, cooked meals, and special teaching activities, as is often the case in Sweden? In the U.S. experience parents may gain a better return on *their* human capital by more market time and career development from added expenditure (Johnson and Stafford 1996).

Total Magnitude of Child Investments

To get an idea of orders of magnitude we now put together estimates from the preceding tables for Sweden. Table 2 shows that a couple uses about 2.5 hours per day in direct child care, which corresponds to 912 hours in a year for children under age seven. If, on average, the couple

TABLE 11.   Public Support to Students, 1991, by Age of Child and Country (USD per child)

| School Level | Country[a] | | | | | | |
	S	DK	US	E	GB	F	OECD Total
Preschool[b]	2,501	4,376	4,014	1,777	2,233	2,163	3,125
Primary	5,470	4,397	5,177	1,861	2,794	2,591	3,969
Secondary	6,635	5,378	6,472	2,730	4,255	4,640	4,791
Primary and secondary	6,057	4,962	5,780	2,405	3,559	3,785	4,664
Higher	8,561	7,685	11,802	3,242	9,621	4,760	8,477
All levels combined	6,157	5,489	6,527	2,490	4,268	3,847	4,681

Source: Expenditure per student and by level, OECD. These are for public schools only.

[a]Country abbreviations are as follows: S = Sweden, DK = Denmark, US = United States, E = Spain, GB = Great Britain, F = France.

[b]The OECD data are not comparable for preschool expenditures.

has two children and each gets about half of this time, the annual care time totals 456 hours. For older children the corresponding estimate only amounts to 91 hours. The incremental estimates in table 4C for the United States are lower, and the companion estimates for Sweden are about half this size, so we assume that 300 hours is a reasonable per child estimate of primary child care time for children younger than seven years old, and 70 hours is a reasonable estimate for older children. The incremental estimates for household work is about 200 hours per couple per child younger than seven and about 70 hours for older children (table 5B).

The final time input component is other or "joint time" with children, which, from table 6, can be estimated to be on the order of 3,800 hours per year for children younger than seven and 2,860 hours for older children. From this amount we should subtract any incremental household work with the children present, say 100 and 10 hours respectively. (This could also include some public good elements, with joint time on multiple children. We disregard this.) In total, a couple would thus use about 4,200 hours per year on an average child less than seven years old and about 3,000 hours on an average child 7–17 years old. To compare with the input of goods and services we need to convert these hours into monetary units. In doing this we have quite arbitrarily assumed that household work only has 50 percent of the investment value of direct child care and other time with children has been multiplied by 0.5 and 0.2, respectively. Then we have used an average hourly wage rate (before tax) of 80 SEK. The result is displayed in table 12.

TABLE 12. Total Value of Child Investments, Time and Goods Average per Child with Two Parents, Sweden, 1993

	Children less than 7 years old		Children 7–17 years old	
	Hours per Year	SEK per Year	Hours per Year	SEK per year
Time input				
Direct child care	300	24,000	70	5,600
Household work	200	8,000	70	2,800
Time with children	3,700	59,200	2,850	45,600
Total	4,150	87,200	3,100	65,600
Family Goods Input		30,000		30,000
Publicly Provided Goods and Services Input		62,000		73,000
Total		183,200		157,000

These estimates indicate that Swedes on average invest between 150,000 and 200,000 SEK on a young child annually, which approximately corresponds to an investment of between 22,000 and 29,000 USD. Given our weighting of the time inputs, total time input makes up 50 percent of the total, private goods and services 16 percent, and publicly provided goods and services for young children 34 percent. For older children the corresponding shares are 34, 19, and 47 percent. The share for expenditures on goods and services should probably be somewhat lower for young children and somewhat higher for older children because older children usually cost more than younger children. In this case, we have used the same estimate of 30,000 SEK for everyone. There are also other shortcomings: health investments, other than publicly provided health care in schools and the small share of the costs for health care and medicine paid by parents,[3] are not included; the value of children's own time is not included; and we have neglected that a child who lives with a single parent probably gets less time input but more goods input (cf. tables 7 and 8).

Discussion and Conclusion

In this essay, we have attempted to piece together time-use and other data to provide an overview of the magnitude of investments in early human capital in Sweden, the United States, and selected countries. Our data have been primarily based on parental time. An alternative is to use data on children's own activities, classifying the activities in terms of learning and development potential. For Sweden the number of children under age eighteen in 1992 (1,914,616) times the 170,000 SEK gives the total of 325,485 million SEK, an amount equal to 22.7 percent of GDP. Gross fixed capital formation in 1992 was 17 percent of GDP in this year, so investment in children by adults (i.e., ignoring the own value of time for older children) is of greater magnitude than traditional economic investment.

To judge the developmental potential of the activities we can rely on estimates of the effectiveness of early time-use from panel data (Stafford 1987). This is not a simple task either. Parents appear to be equity seekers with regard to their children, and children with developmental limitations appear to "get more" (Barnett 1993). This seems at odds with the idea that parents could provide for children with limited human capital potential by simply transferring more financial wealth to them. In dissertation work by Dan Natali in the mid-1970s (Natali 1979), people in the Economic Behavior Program became familiar with the "compensation hypothesis": middle-class parents receiving feedback of lagging performance of their first graders were likely to spend more time to "compensate" for the deficit. To what extent are skill-equalizing investments important as ex ante income inequality reduction mechanisms? Will these grow in importance if public support for ex post income inequality reduction dwindles in the United States and Sweden?

Despite the difficulties in implementing an investment perspective on early human capital formation, it is now evident that there is a rising importance of human capital in the total capital stock of an economy. In the case of Sweden we can see a very modest decline in child care time by families over the period 1984 to 1993, but this was arguably offset by the extensive public day care, and cross-sectional evidence indicates that parents with children in the system reduce their child care time at home only modestly. This is an area that deserves further study.

Recent use of repeated cross-section surveys with more detailed disaggregation than in our table 1 for Norway and Finland indicate a modest upward drift in child care minutes per day (Harvey and Naugler-Haugen 1996). For Norway, in 1971–72, total family care was .30 hours per day, by 1980–81 it had risen to .37 hours, and by 1990–91 it had risen to .45 hours. For Finland the estimates were given under a somewhat different definition but rose from .17 hours in 1980–81 to .20 hours in 1990–91. In both these countries the number of young children in the family was stable or falling, so there was a modest rise in care time per child. These patterns are consistent with the human capital and "new home economics" models discussed in "Parental Investment in Young Children." Using such a framework combined with household time diary data it is possible to develop the types of accounting systems advocated by Tom Juster over twenty years ago. The promise is that our knowledge of capital formation and long run growth can be thereby improved greatly!

NOTES

1. The average real per pupil expenditure relative to the earnings of a forty-year-old male high school graduate has risen steadily from .060 in 1950 to .094 in 1970 and then to .189 in 1990 (Johnson and Stafford 1996).

2. The variable used in regressions of table 5B are interactions of the number of siblings and dummy variables for the age of the youngest child.

3. In Sweden a larger share is payed for through the social security system.

REFERENCES

Baker, Paula C., and Frank Mott. 1989. *National Longitudinal Survey of Youth Child Handbook 1989*. Athens: Center for Human Resource Research, Ohio State University. 51–56.

Barbarczy, A., I. Harcsa, and H. Paakkonen. 1991. *Time Use Trends in Finland and in Hungary.* Helsinki: Statistics Finland, Studies no. 180.

Barnett, W. Steven. 1993. "New Wine in Old Bottles: Increasing the Coherence of Early Childhood Care and Education Policy." *Early Childhood Research Quarterly* 8:519–58.

Baumol, William J., Sue Anne Batey-Blackman, and Edward J. Wolff. 1985. "Unbalanced Growth Revisited: Asymptotic Stagnancy and New Evidence." *American Economic Review* 75 (September): 806–17.

Becker, Gary S. 1965. "A Theory of the Allocation of Time." *Economic Journal* 75 (September): 493–517.

———. 1981. *A Treatise on the Economics of the Family.* Cambridge, MA: Harvard University Press.

Brown, Byron, and Daniel Saks. 1975. "The Production and Distribution of Cognitive Skills within Schools." *Journal of Political Economy* (June): 571–93.

Calhoun, C. A., and T. J. Espenshade. 1988. "Childbearing and Wives." *Population Studies* 44:41–60.

Coleman, James S. 1990. "Social Capital in the Creation of Human Capital," *American Journal of Sociology* 94 (supplement): S95–120.

Dankmeyer, Benjamin. 1996. "Long Run Opportunity Costs of Children According to the Education of the Mother." *Journal of Population Economics* 9:349–61.

Flood, Lennart, and N. Anders Klevmarken. 1987. "Tidsanvandningen i Sverige 1984" (Time-use in Sweden 1984). Memorandum no. 127, Department of Economics, Gothenburg University.

———. 1990. "Arbete och fritid: Svenska hushålls tidsanväding 1984." In *Tid och Råd. Om hushållens ekonomi,* ed. N. A. Klevmarken, 177–233. Stockholm: Industrial Institute for Economic and Social Research (IUI), Almquist & Wiksell International.

Flood, Lennart, and Paul Olovsson. 1997. *Household Market and Nonmarket Activities (HUS). Procedures and Codes.* Vols. 3–4. Uppsala: Department of Economics, Uppsala University.

Freeman, Richard B. 1975. "Overinvestment in College Training?" *Journal of Human Resources* 10, no. 3 (summer): 287–311.

Gronau, Reuben. 1973. "The Intrafamily Allocation of Time: The Value of the Housewives' Time." *American Economic Review* 63, no. 4: 634–51.

———. 1986. "Home Production—A Survey." In *Handbook of Labor Economics,* vol. 1, ed. Orley C. Ashenfelter and R. Layard, 273–304. Amsterdam: North-Holland.

Gustafsson, Björn, and Urban Kjulin. 1994. "Time Use in Child Care and Housework and the Total Cost of Children." *Journal of Population Economics* 7: 287–306.

Gustafsson, Siv, and Frank P. Stafford. 1994. "Three Regimes of Child Care: The United States, the Netherlands, and Sweden." In *Social Protection and Economic Flexibility: Is There a Tradeoff?* ed. Rebecca Blank. New York and Chicago: National Bureau of Economic Research and University of Chicago Press.

———. 1996. "Equity Efficiency and Externality in Early Childhood Care and Education." Working paper, Department of Economics, University of Amsterdam, February.

———. 1997. "Childcare, Human Capital and Economic Efficiency." In *Economics of the Family and Family Policies,* ed. Inga Persson and Christina Jonung. London and New York: Routledge.

Hansen, W. Lee. 1963. "Total and Private Rates of Return to Investment in Schooling." *Journal of Political Economy* 76 (April): 128–40.

Hanushek, E. A. 1992. "The Trade-off between Child Quantity and Quality." *Journal of Political Economy* 100, no. 1: 84–117.

Harvey, Andrew S., and Debbie Naugler-Haugen. 1996. "Children's Use of Time: Time for Growing." Manuscript, Time Use Research Program, Saint Mary's University, Halifax, Nova Scotia.

Hill, Russell C., and Frank P. Stafford. 1974. "Allocation of Time to Preschool Children and Educational Opportunity." *Journal of Human Resources* 9, no. 3: 323–41.

———. 1977. "Family Background and Lifetime Earnings." In *The Distribution of Economic Well-Being,* ed. F. T. Juster. New York National Bureau of Economic Research, 1977.

———. 1985. "Parental Care of Children: Time Diary Estimates of Quantity, Predictability, and Variety." In *Time Goods and Well-Being,* ed. F. Thomas Juster and Frank P. Stafford. Ann Arbor: Survey Research Center, Institute for Social Research, University of Michigan.

Hill, Martha. 1988. "Marital Stability and Spouses' Shared Time." *Journal of Family Issues* 9, no. 4 (December): 427–51.

Hofferth, Sandra L. 1993. "The 101st Congress; An Emerging Agenda for Children in Poverty." In *Child Poverty and Public Policy,* ed. Judith A. Chafel, 203–43. Washington, DC: Urban Institute.

Johnson, George E., and Frank P. Stafford. 1973. "Social Returns to Quantity and Quality of Schooling." *Journal of Human Resources* 8, no. 2 (spring): 139–55.

———. 1996. "On the Rate of Return to Schooling Quality." *Review of Economics and Statistics* 78, no. 4 (November): 686–91.

Joshi, Heather. 1990. "The Cash Alternative Costs of Childbearing: An Approach to Estimation Using British Data." *Population Studies* 44:41–60.

———. 1994. "The Foregone Earnings of Europe's Mothers." In *Standards of Living and Families: Observation and Analysis,* ed. O. Efert-Jaff. London: John Libbey.

Juster, F. Thomas. 1985a. "Investments of Time by Men and Women." In *Time Goods and Well-Being,* ed. F. Thomas Juster and Frank P. Stafford. Ann Arbor: Survey Research Center, Institute for Social Research, University of Michigan.

———. 1985b. "Preferences for Work and Leisure." In *Time Goods and Well-Being,* ed. F. Thomas Juster and Frank P. Stafford. Ann Arbor: Survey Research Center, Institute for Social Research, University of Michigan.

Juster, F. Thomas, and Frank P. Stafford. 1991. "The Allocation of Time: Empirical Findings, Behavioral Models and Problems of Measurement." *Journal of Economic Literature* 29 (June): 471–522.

Juster, F. Thomas, and Martha Hill. 1985. "Constraints and Complementarities in Time Use." In *Time Goods and Well-Being,* ed. F. Thomas Juster and Frank P. Stafford. Ann Arbor: Institute for Social Research, University of Michigan.

Juster, F. Thomas, Paul N. Courant, and Greg K. Dow. 1985. "A Conceptual Framework for the Analysis of Time Allocation Data." In *Time Goods and Well-Being,* ed. F. Thomas Juster and Frank P. Stafford. Ann Arbor: Survey Research Center, Institute for Social Research, University of Michigan.

Kirjavainen, L. M., B. Anachkova, S. Laaksonen, I. Niemi, H. Paakkonen, and Z. Staikov. 1992. *Housework Time in Bulgaria and Finland.* Helsinki: Statistics Finland, Studies no. 193.

Klevmarken, N. Anders, and Paul Olovsson. 1993. *Household Market and Nonmarket Activities. Procedures and Codes 1984–1991.* Vols. 1–2. Stockholm: Industrial Institute for Economic and Social Research, Almquist & Wiksell International.

Lancaster, K. J. 1966. "A New Approach to Consumer Theory." *Journal of Political Economy* 74:132–57.

Leibowitz, Arleen. 1974. "Home Investments in Children." *Journal of Political Economy* 82, no. 2, part 2 (March–April): S111–S131.

Lingsom, Susan, and A. L. Ellingsaeter. 1983. *Work, Leisure and Time Spent with Others: Changes in Time Use in the '70's.* Oslo: Central Bureau of Statistics of Norway, Statistiske Analyser 49.

Natali, Daniel Ernest. 1979. "A Methodological and Developmental Study of Maternal Time Use and Cognitive Abilities in Preschool and Early Elementary School Children." Ph.D. diss., Department of Psychology, University of Michigan.

Niemi, I., S. Kiiski, and M. Liikkanen. 1979. *Use of Time in Finland.* Helsinki: Statistics Finland, Studies no. 65.

OECD. 1993. "Education at a Glance. OECD Indicators." Paris: Centre for Educational Research and Innovation, OECD.

Rosen, Sherwin. 1995. "Public Employment and the Welfare State in Sweden." NBER/SNS Project Reforming the Welfare State, occasional paper no. 61, January.

Smith, James, and Michael Ward. 1989. "Women in the Labor Market and the Family." *Journal of Economic Perspectives* 3 (winter): 9–23.

Stafford, Frank P. 1987. "Women's Work, Sibling Competition and Children's School Performance." *American Economic Review* 7:972–80.

Stafford, Frank P., and Marianne Sundström. 1996. "Time Out for Childcare: Signalling and Earnings Rebound Effects for Men and Women." *Labour* 10, no. 3: 609–29.

Sundström, Marianne, and Frank P. Stafford. 1992. "Parental Leave and Female Labor Force Participation in Sweden." *European Journal of Population* 8:199–215.

Tinbergen, Jan. 1975. Income Distribution: Analysis and Policies. Amsterdam: Nort-Holland Publishing Company.

Wallberg, E., M. Medelberg, and S. Stromquist. 1996. "Samhallets stod till barnfamiljerna i Europa" (Public support to families with children in Europe). Report to ESO, Ds 1996:49. Stockholm: Ministry of Finance.

Willis, Robert. 1973. "A New Approach to the Economic Theory of Fertility Behavior." *Journal of Political Economy* 81 (March/April): S14–64.

Unfolding Bracket Method in the Measurement of Expenditures and Wealth

Daniel Hill

One of the most perplexing problems in survey measurement of economic variables such as income and wealth is the vast amount of missing data from item nonresponse one encounters. Many individuals who are willing to participate in surveys are either unable or unwilling to provide dollar amounts when asked about economic variables. They either say that they "don't know" the answer, or they refuse to give it. This sort of nonresponse is often so high as to seriously undermine the value of the data for analysis. Reports for the value of assets in the form of stocks, bonds, and trusts were missing for roughly a quarter of the respondents in the 1979 Retirement History Survey as well as in the 1984 Survey of Income and Program Participation.

Tom Juster's most recent contribution to measuring methods for economic variables is the testing, refinement, and popularization of the unfolding bracketing sequence for following up and greatly reducing item nonresponse in income, wealth, and expenditure data. Rather than simply leaving the dollar amount missing, the unfolding bracket method asks respondents who do not provide an answer a series of yes/no questions of the form "would it (the measure in question) amount to x dollars or more?" The genius of this technique is that by asking the respondent a few easily answered quick questions our uncertainty of the cardinal value can be reduced substantially. In wave 1 of the Health and Retirement Study (HRS), for instance, it reduced the amount of completely missing data on the value of farms and businesses from 32 percent to under 6 percent.

There are, however, a number of important scientific questions relating to the unfolding bracket method that need to be answered. First, is it possible with this method to obtain empirically useful measures for quantities about which respondents are highly uncertain or even largely ignorant? Second, can we design bracket sequences that maximize the informational content of the data—especially if the data are to be used for a variety of purposes? The third question is whether the entry point to a bracketing sequence can substantially influence the final measure. Finally, to what extent does the bracket method affect the quality of other measures in the survey?

To address the first of these questions, we first analyze medical expenditure data collected in the second wave of the HRS. Respondents are likely to be quite uncertain about these medical expenditures—especially total expenditures—because they often never see the full bill but only the portion they have to pay out of pocket. We compare these HRS data to benchmark data from the 1987 National Medical Expenditure Survey (NMES). In assessing the empirical validity of the HRS measures an adjustment must be made for the fact that the HRS reference period is two years whereas the NMES's is one year. This adjustment is complicated by the fact that medical expenditures are both episodic and stochastically spaced in time. In the next section, "Optimal Breakpoints," a method of designing unfolding brackets that maximize the informational content of the data is discussed. Since some potential users are interested in absolute measures whereas others are interested in proportionate measures, the question becomes, in part, whether a single set of questions can provide good data for both levels and log-levels. "Anchoring and Measurement Contamination" is concerned with the effects of exposure to bracketing on the quality of measures. Here we examine the question of whether the design of the bracket sequence has important effects on the measure in question—specifically whether the initial entry point to the sequence systematically affects the final measure in the survey. Such phenomena have come to be called "anchoring," and we are interested in understanding how serious anchoring might be. Finally, we address the question of whether the bracketing method used in one question contaminates subsequent measures. We do so by looking first at the effect of exposure to bracketing early in a given interview on the propensity of respondents to provide cardinal reports later in the interview. To provide another test of possible contamination, we also examine the effect of bracketing in one wave of the panel on bracketing in a subsequent wave.

Medical Expenditures

The second wave questionnaire for the HRS contained a section on health care utilization, expenditures, and insurance coverage. Each respondent was first asked about visits to the physician's office, nursing home stays, and hospitalizations over the two-year period between surveys. Respondents were then asked about the total costs associated with this health care, the extent to which it was covered by insurance, and the out-of-pocket costs.

Not surprisingly, many respondents are unable or unwilling to provide an exact report. For total medical expenditures nearly a third of the respondents (31.9 percent) initially claimed ignorance, in which case they were asked the series of bracketing questions. Almost all (94.3 percent) of these respondents provided answers to the bracket questions. These "unfolding" bracket questions have been found to be very effective tools in reducing item nonresponse in other measures as well (see, e.g., Heeringa, Hill, and Howell 1995; Juster and Smith 1997). In the case of health care expenditures, the nonrespondents were first asked if the total expenditure over the two-year period amounted to $5,000 or more. If they said "no" then they were asked if it amounted to $1,000 or more. Respondents who said the expenditure was $5,000 or more were next asked if it was in excess of $25,000 and, if so, whether it was more than $100,000.

The result of this measurement method is that for almost all respondents we obtain either a cardinal measure or an ordinal one corresponding to the $0, $1–$1,000, $1,001–$5,000, $5,001–$25,000, $25,001–$100,000, or $100,001+ intervals. These ordinal data have been used in a variety of ways. First, the data are used, to great effect, in the imputation phase of the data processing. Rather than using the entire set of cardinal respondents as the donor pool for the hot deck procedure, the donors can be limited to individuals whose medical expenditures were in the same broad interval as the nonrespondent. The partitioning itself accounts for 84 and 93 percent of the variance in total and out-of-pocket expenditures, respectively. This explanatory power is far greater than what can be explained using covariates. Bracket data also have been used directly in analysis. In this case, the data can either be analyzed as a set of ordinal limits or the brackets can be incorporated explicitly into the statistical model.

To judge how useful these HRS medical expenditures data are, Hill and Mathiowetz (1998) recently compared them with similar data from the 1987 National Medical Expenditures Survey. Before examining some of the results of those comparisons, it is necessary to mention some differences we *should* expect. First, HRS has a two-year reference period whereas the NMES had a one-year measurement period. This difference in time frame implies that we should expect proportionately more HRS than NMES respondents to have some positive amount of medical expenditures. To see why, consider the following, decidedly non-economic, model of expenditures. Assume that medical expenditures are the result of a series of discrete "contacts" or "encounters" with the medical system — where a contact is defined as any type of utilization such as a visit to a physician's office or being admitted to a hospital. Further assume that the incidence of these encounters is determined by one of the family of stochastic processes for which the probability of going t periods without any such expenditure-producing contact is

$$\text{Prob}(k = 0) = e^{-t\lambda} \tag{1}$$

where λ is a nonnegative intensity parameter. The family of processes for which this is true includes the Poisson, the Neyman A, the Polya-Aeppli, the Thomas, the Poisson-Pascal, and all the other discrete stochastic processes that are Poisson mixtures of other distributions.

The important thing to note about equation (1) is that it implies the proportion of observations with no encounters, and thereby no expenditures, will decline monotonically with the length of the reference period t. That is, HRS *should* have proportionately fewer cases with zero expenditures than NMES even if the underlying validity of the data is the same.

The picture becomes more complex when we consider out-of-pocket expenditures. Here the incidence of positive expenditures will be lower because insurance coverage will shield some people from the expenditures associated with encounters they have had. If P_c is the proportion of the population fully covered by medical insurance then the proportion of the population with no out-of-pocket expenditures will be

$$\text{Prob}(M_{OOP} = 0) = (1 - P_c)e^{-t\lambda} + P_c \tag{2}$$

where M_{OOP} is the level of out-of-pocket medical expenditures. Clearly, since P_c is bounded to the positive unit interval, the proportion of the population with no out-of-pocket medical expenditures will exceed that with no medical expenditures in total for all t and λ. It is less clear, but nevertheless true, that the effect of increasing the length of the reference period will be smaller for out-of-pocket expenditures. To see this, note first that the derivative of total expenditures with respect to t is

$$\partial P_{oTot}/\partial t = -\lambda e^{-t\lambda} \tag{3}$$

which, since λ is nonnegative, is always negative. For out-of-pocket expenditures, assuming (for the moment) that P_c is constant, the corresponding derivative is

$$\partial P_0/\partial t = -\lambda e^{-t\lambda}[1 - P_c].\tag{4}$$

Thus, since $1 - P_c$ is also confined to the unit interval, the probability of having no out-of-pocket expenditures is less sensitive to the length of the reference period than are total medical expenditures. If we allow P_c to be a function of time, this result becomes ambiguous but almost certainly still holds.

Finally, if one adds the assumption that individuals who only infrequently use medical services are healthier than frequent users, the model predicts that the longer the reference period the lower the expenditures, for those having them, will be.

The longer reference period of the HRS has clear implications for the differences we should expect between HRS and the NMES. Table 1 presents the estimated percentages of the fifty-three- to sixty-three-year-old population of the United States with and without medical expenditures during the reference periods. The incidence patterns are distinctly and significantly different between the studies, but the differences are completely consistent with the hypothesis that they are due to the differing length in the reference periods. As predicted, the proportion of the sample reporting no medical expenditures is nearly twice as high (23.3 percent vs. 12.4 percent) in the NMES as in the HRS. For out-of-pocket medical expenditures the difference, while still present, is not nearly so dramatic. Finally, as predicted, the incidence of out-of-pocket medical expenditures is lower than total, and the difference between the studies in incidence is substantially greater for total expenditures than for out of pocket.

TABLE 1. Medical Expenditure Incidence by Type of Expenditure and Study, Adults, ages 53–63 (design-corrected standard errors in parentheses)

	NMES		HRS	
	No Expenses	Some Expenses	No Expenses	Some Expenses
Total	23.3%	76.76%	12.4%	87.6%
	(0.86)		(0.42)	
Out-of-pocket	35.3%	64.7%	32.5%	67.5%
	(1.00)		(0.89)	

Source: HRS Wave 2 Gamma release file and NMES Public Use data file DA6247.

Note: Estimates for NMES are based on a one-year reference period; those for HRS are based on a two-year reference period.

Table 2 lists the percentages of cases falling in each of a set of categories defined by the breakpoints used in the HRS unfolding bracket sequence. For this table, the NMES expenditures have been multiplied by (1) the difference in the general level of medical prices between 1987 and 1993[1] and (2) the ratio of the average reference period in the HRS (twenty-three months) to that of the NMES (twelve months). The combination adjustment produced by these two factors is 2.91. These data demonstrate that HRS and NMES estimates of total medical expenditures are significantly different. The adjusted Wald statistic for the null hypothesis of no difference is 29.33 with 5 and 157 degrees of freedom. This is well over the critical value of 2.27. All of this difference, however, is concentrated at the bottom end of the distribution. If we compare only those respondents with positive expenditures, the adjusted Wald for the null hypothesis is only 0.85—this time with 4 and 157 degrees of freedom. As already noted, the proportion of HRS respondents with no medical expenditures is 10.9 percentage points lower than the corresponding proportion of NMES respondents. Interestingly, this HRS "deficit" is mostly made up for by the higher fraction of the sample in the lowest expenditure category $1–$1,000. While it is premature to conclude that the distributional differences are due solely to the effects of the longer HRS reference period on incidence, this conclusion is plausible. NMES, because of its more narrow observation period,

TABLE 2. Distribution of Medical Expenditures from the HRS and NMES (two-year dollar amounts)

	Total Expenditures		Out-of-Pocket Expenditures	
	NMES	HRS	NMES	HRS
None	23.3%	12.4%	35.3%	32.5%
	(0.86)	(0.42)	(1.02)	(0.89)
$1–$1,000	45.1%	52.5%	53.2%	58.7%
	(1.00)	(0.75)	(1.10)	(0.85)
$1,001–$5,000	18.1%	18.8%	9.5%	7.0%
	(0.91)	(0.42)	(0.68)	(0.31)
$5,001–$25,000	9.3%	11.6%	1.8%	1.4%
	(0.64)	(0.33)	(0.25)	(0.13)
$25,001–$100,000	3.5%	3.9%	0.2%	0.2%
	(0.40)	(0.20)	(0.08)	(0.06)
$100,000+	0.7%	0.9%	0.0%	0.0%
	(0.17)	(0.11)	(0.00)	(0.00)

Source: HRS Wave 2 Gamma release file and NMES Public Use data file DA6247.
Note: HRS: $N = 9,278$; NMES: $N = 2,958$.

misses more of the infrequent health care users. HRS captures them. Since they are infrequent and presumably healthier users they appear in the lower of the HRS expenditure categories.

The picture for out-of-pocket expenditures is slightly different in that there are significant differences between HRS and NMES in each of the bottom three expense categories. Indeed, the largest and most significant difference between the studies is in the fraction of respondents with positive out-of-pocket expenditures of less than \$1,001 per two-year period. The fraction of such respondents in the HRS is 5.5 percentage points higher than that in the NMES. This difference may reflect a real increase between 1987 and 1994 in co-pay provisions.

The next question concerns the impact of using the unfolding bracket data in estimating the parameters of more complex models— more specifically the relationship between health care utilization and expenditures. For example, the encounters model can be expanded by assuming that medical expenditures are driven by discrete encounters with the medical system that can be both episodic and stochastic in time. One stochastic process that is appropriate for this sort of behavior results in the Thomas distribution. In this case, there are two Poisson intensity parameters—one (λ) governing the incidence of episodes of expenditures and the other (θ) their average size. A "Thomas regression" model[2] of medical expenditures and utilization results when we specify these intensity parameters as functions of the individual's health care utilization. That is:

$$\lambda_i = \exp(X_i'\beta_\lambda)$$

$$\theta_i = \exp(X_i'\beta_\theta)$$

(5)

where X_i is a vector consisting of (1) the number of doctor office visits made by the ith individual during the reference period and (2) the number of nights he or she spent in the hospital. The β's are parameters relating these utilization measures to expenditures via the Thomas distribution.

Table 3 presents the maximum likelihood estimates of these coefficients for out-of-pocket and total medical expenditures. The estimated coefficients obtained from the two studies are roughly similar. Thus, the abbreviated HRS medical expenditure question sequence provides sufficient "signal" to mimic similar modeling obtained from the far more detailed set of questions contained in NMES. The similarity of the model estimates can be demonstrated by comparing model predicted expenditures by utilization as in table 4. Although the estimates for the HRS are a few hundred dollars higher than those for the NMES at low

TABLE 3. Maximum Likelihood Estimates of Effects of Health Care Utilization on Medical Expenditures, NMES and HRS: Thomas Regression (design-corrected standard errors in parentheses)

	Out-of-Pocket Medical Expenditures		Total Medical Expenditures	
	NMES	HRS	NMES	HRS
Expenditure Cluster Incidence				
Constant	−.20*	−.157*	.066*	.446*
	(.027)	(.022)	(.0241)	(.0133)
Doctor visits	.036*	.016*	.034*	.021*
	(.0042)	(.0012)	(.013)	(.0012)
Hospital nights	.021*	.010*	.057*	.042*
	(.0044)	(.0030)	(.0094)	(.0041)
Expenditure Cluster Level				
Constant	−.838*	−1.527*	−.471*	.146*
	(.095)	(.101)	(.161)	(.0399)
Doctor visits	.039*	.038*	.036*	.040*
	(.0095)	(.0048)	(0.347)	(.0009)
Hospital nights	.063*	.035*	.124*	.110*
	(.0064)	(.0074)	(.0379)	(.0015)
Pseudo-R^2	12.1%	5.3%	30.2%	18.0%
Log-likelihood	−5,643	−15,958	−7,031	−35,219
Number of observations	2,955	9,119	2,955	9,119

Source: HRS Wave 2 Gamma release file and NMES Public Use data file DA6247.
*Significant at the .01 level.

TABLE 4. Predicted Total Medical Expenditures by Utilization and Study (HRS estimates in parentheses)

Hospital Nights/ Doctor Visits	0	3	6	9	12	15
0 NMES	$1,319	$1,836	$2,645	$3,941	$6,057	$9,566
(HRS)	($1,685)	($2,312)	($3,255)	($4,689)	($6,893)	($10,303)
3	$1,524	$2,143	$3,118	$4,690	$7,270	$11,560
	($1,917)	($2,656)	($3,772)	($5,476)	($8,102)	($12,172)
6	$1,767	$2,509	$3,687	$5,597	$8,743	$13,994
	($2,189)	($3,061)	($4,384)	($6,411)	($9,542)	($14,405)
9	$2,054	$2,946	$4,372	$6,694	$10,537	$16,968
	($2,508)	($3,539)	($5,110)	($7,523)	($11,259)	($17,072)
12	$2,395	$3,469	$5,197	$8,026	$12,724	$20,606
	($2,884)	($4,105)	($5,917)	($8,847)	($13,308)	($20,259)
15	$2,801	$4,097	$6,194	$9,644	$15,392	$25,051
	($3,327)	($4,774)	($6,994)	($10,425)	($15,775)	($24,071)

Source: HRS Wave 2 Gamma release file and NMES Public Use data file DA6247.

levels of utilization, the overall pattern of the estimates is identical, rising from roughly fifteen hundred dollars per two years at low utilization levels to roughly twenty-five thousand dollars at the highest levels of utilization. The goodness of fit for the HRS is, however, significantly lower for both out-of-pocket and total expenditures—a finding consistent with there being relatively more noise in the HRS data.

In conclusion, the unfolding bracket method appears to produce empirically valid data for measures about which respondents are probably truly uncertain. There are differences between medical expenditure estimates based on the HRS and those based on the NMES, but for the most part, these differences are entirely consistent with the hypothesis that they are generated by differences in the length of the reference periods in the two studies. In the next section we will continue to examine the medical expenditure data but in this case with an eye toward developing a procedure for deriving optimal breakpoints.

Optimal Breakpoints

The second question about the unfolding bracket technique is whether it is possible to select bracket boundaries or breakpoints in such a manner as to maximize the informational content of the resulting data. How much of the information about the true measures the bracketed reports contain depends on the precise placement and number of breakpoints in the bracket sequence and on the empirical distribution of the true values. In this section, we will present a method of setting the breakpoints in such a way as to maximize their explanatory power. To see how optimal breakpoints can be constructed, assume there are N_e cardinal observations of the variable of interest y. The within group sum of squares (WSS) can be expressed as a function of the vector of breakpoints (β) defining a set of brackets as

$$\text{WSS} = \text{WSS}(\beta) = \sum_i \sum_j (y_{ij} - \bar{y}_{\beta_j})^2 \tag{6}$$

where $\bar{y}_{\beta_j}$ is the mean of the exact reports in the interval β_j to β_{j+1}. Assuming that the underlying distribution of the missing reports is the same as the exact reports, optimal breakpoints can, in principle, be obtained by setting them to minimize WSS.[3] Since WSS is not differentiable in the β (or even continuous), optimization requires a non-Newtonian computer intensive method such as the downhill simplex.

The issue of which metric to use for y will depend on the intended analytic uses of the final data. If variation at the top of the distribution is important, it is generally best to optimize equation (6) using levels of y, whereas if variation at the bottom of the distribution is more critical then log-levels may be the better choice. When there are many intended uses, we may want to choose a set of breakpoints that does a good job in explaining both levels and log-levels. The well-known Box-Cox transform provides a metric that lies between levels and log-levels. The transform can be expressed as

$$y_i^* = \frac{y_i^\lambda - 1}{\lambda} \tag{7}$$

where λ is the Box-Cox parameter. As λ approaches 0, y^* tends to $\ln(y)$, whereas as λ approaches 1, y^* approaches $y - 1$. If y^* is used in place of y in minimizing equation (6), λ can be varied to attain a set of breakpoints that yields an acceptable goodness of fit for both levels and log-levels. Unfortunately, in this case, equation (6) becomes quite unstable, and the downhill simplex can tend toward corner solutions. The reason is that the total sum of squares (TSS) is now a function of one of the parameters over which we are optimizing. A solution to the instability problem is to first scale equation (6) by the TSS and then to systematically search over λ until we find a value that yields acceptable R^2's in both metrics. This search is aided by the fact that (barring extreme clumping) if $R_x^2 < R_{\ln(x)}^2$ the overall performance can be improved by decreasing λ (i.e., by placing more emphasis on larger observations). This is illustrated graphically in figure 1, which presents the ANOVA R^2's (i.e., (TSS − WSS)/TSS) for the level of out-of-pocket medical expenditures and its logarithm as a function of λ. While the plots of these R^2's are neither smooth nor even monotonic (a result of finite clumpy data), apparently there is an overall trade-off between levels and log-levels. For small λ, the optimal bracket R^2's for log-levels are much larger than for raw levels. A small λ corresponds more closely to logarithms, and emphasis is then placed on variation at the bottom of the distribution. For large λ, on the other hand, the optimal bracket R^2's for levels exceed those for log-levels. In this case the Box-Cox transform is closer to levels, and the algorithm stresses variation at the top of the distribution.

Turning now from medical expenditures to asset amounts table 5 presents the R^2's obtained using the bracket breakpoints from the HRS wave 1 brackets and those that would have been obtained using the optimized breakpoints for four of the net-worth components in the HRS. In three of the four cases, the R^2's for levels were increased as a

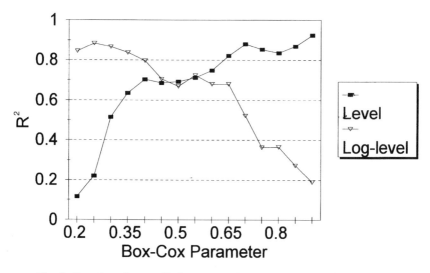

Fig. 1. Out-of-pocket medical costs: explanatory power of bracket partition. (From HRS Wave 2 Gamma release file.)

result of the optimization with only modest reductions in the R^2's for the log-level values. In the fourth case, the R^2's for *both* levels and log-levels were increased by the optimization. As was the case with medical expenditures, detailed examination of the breakpoints (not shown) reveals that most of the improvement for levels came about by increasing the uppermost breakpoint. A high upper breakpoint has the effect of isolating these few but important cases at the top of the distribution into the upper bracket. For levels, of course, it is just such cases that contribute the most to the variance.

In sum use of the Box-Cox transform and the downhill simplex algorithm provides a means of obtaining breakpoints that do a good job of capturing most of the variance in both levels and log-levels of asset

TABLE 5.   Goodness of Fit with Optimized Breakpoints (in percentages)

Net-Worth Component	Level Wave 1	Level Optimized	Log-Level Wave 1	Log-Level Optimized
IRA	55.4	87.3	87.2	82.7
CD	38.1	81.1	90.5	76.7
Other assets	14.0	53.0	76.2	68.2
Business	52.8	60.7	80.8	96.6

Source: HRS Wave 1 Gamma release file.

and expenditure data. The breakpoints used subsequent to wave 1 of the HRS are based on this type of optimization.

Anchoring and Measurement Contamination

The final two questions posed at the beginning of this essay dealt with the extent to which exposure to bracketing affects the quality of the data gathered after the respondents' initial exposure to the brackets. The first issue deals with some potentially immediate effects on the measure in question — the so-called anchoring effects. The second issue concerns the delayed effects on questions subsequent to the particular measure in question — that is, on variables obtained later in the interview or in subsequent waves of the study. These issues arise because exposure to bracketing questions may convey information to the respondent and taint responses. In the case of anchoring, for instance, the level of the initial breakpoint may affect the final bracket in which a respondent's answers may ultimately lie because it tells the respondent something about what is a "normal" or "acceptable" level of the construct. Alternatively, it may give the respondent some information about how inclusive the researchers want the respondent to be constructing the asset measure.[4]

Whether exposure to bracketing also affects the quality of measure subsequent to the specific measure in question depends in part on what it may suggest to respondents about the level of precision required. If the breakpoints presented are very precise (e.g., "Is it greater than $55,312?") the respondent may think that great precision is required in formulating answers. If, on the other hand, the breakpoints are set at very round numbers (e.g., "Is it more than $50,000?") the respondent may conclude that only very rough estimates are required.

Anchoring

A number of recent papers based on randomized entry point data from the Asset and Health Dynamics among the Oldest Old survey (AHEAD) have concluded that anchoring effects can be quite substantial (see, e.g., Hurd and McFadden 1997). Similar results were obtained from an experimental module included in wave 3 of the HRS. This experimental question asked respondents about the circumference of the earth. The purpose of the experiment was to evaluate the extent to which the accuracy of reports as measured by the mean-square error (MSE) was affected by (1) the level of the entry point (10,000, 25,000, or 50,000 miles) and (2) the wording of the comparison ("more than x", "x or more," "less than, about, or more than x"). The reason for using the circumference of the earth as the measure is that there is a single correct answer so that it is possible, in theory, to calculate the bias of the estimates. In addition, the circumference of the earth is a measure for which respondents are likely to be uncertain about the correct answer.

Our hypothesis with respect to the entry point issue is that people have a prior notion of the circumference of the earth that can be characterized by its mean and variance. The level of the entry point, however, provides the respondent with new information that can be used to update the prior before an answer is given. If the level differs from the mean of the prior, the respondent may adjust the prior mean by an amount related to (1) the magnitude difference, (2) the credibility of the entry point, and (3) the variance of the prior. The effect of the level of the entry point on the *variance* of the posterior prior is that it will be adjusted upward in proportion to the size of the difference of the entry from the mean of the prior. The variance may also be related to credibility of the prior, but this effect may not be monotonic. With respect to the wording of the comparisons, our hypothesis is that unbalanced wording will pull the mean of the posterior prior in the direction of the comparison (i.e., in our case upward). That is, if the question is worded as "greater than x" as opposed to "less than x," respondents' estimates will be higher in the first case compared to the second.

Let Y_i^* represent the mean of the respondents' prior distribution after the treatment (t_i) has been applied. We can represent it as

$$Y_i^*(t_i) = Y(t_i) + \epsilon_i(t_i) \tag{8}$$

where Y is the mean and ϵ_i is a random error with mean 0 and variance $\sigma^2(t_i)$. We do not observe Y_i^* directly but only whether it falls in one of four intervals defined by the breakpoints $10k$ miles, $25k$ miles, and $50k$ miles. That is, we observe

$$I_1 = 1 \quad \text{if } Y^* \leq 10k$$

$$I_2 = 1 \quad \text{if } 10k < Y^* \leq 25k$$

$$I_3 = 1 \quad \text{if } 25k < Y^* \leq 50k \tag{9}$$

$$I_4 = 1 \quad \text{if } 50k > Y^*.$$

If f is the pdf of the ϵ, then individual I's contribution to the likelihood function is

$$L_i = \sum_{i=1}^{4} \int_{b_{lo}}^{b_{hi}} I_i f(z) \, dz \tag{10}$$

where b_{lo} is the lower boundary of the bracket and b_{hi} is the upper. If the ϵ are normally distributed,

$$L_i = \sum_{i=1}^{4} I_i[\Phi\left((b_{ihi} - Y(t_i))/\sigma(t_i)\right) - \Phi((b_{ilo} - Y(t_i))/\sigma(t_i))]. \tag{11}$$

The likelihood function for the entire sample is obtained by multiplying out the individual contributions. This is a standard ordered-probit model. In our application, there is one slight complication — some respondents will say that the answer is equal to one of the breakpoints. In this case, under the normality assumption, their contribution to the likelihood function is

$$L_i = \phi((b_i - Y(t_i))/\sigma(t_i))/\sigma \, (t_i) \tag{12}$$

where b_i is the breakpoint value they say the answer is.

To estimate the effects of the experimental treatments on the mean and variance of the reports, it is useful to parameterize them into an overall estimate (y_1) and deviations from that associated with main effects $(y_2 \ldots y_5)$ and interaction effects $(y_6 \ldots y_9)$. Accordingly, the expected effects for each cell of the experimental matrix are as follows.

MATRIX 1. Treatment Effects by Cell of Design Matrix

	Enter at 10,000 Miles (y_2)	Enter at 25,000 Miles	Enter at 50,000 Miles (y_3)
Would it amount to x or more? (y_4)	$Y(t_{11}) = y_1 + y_2 + y_4 + y_6$	$Y(t_{21}) = y_1 + y_4$	$Y(t_{31}) = y_1 + y_3 + y_4 + y_8$
Would it be less than, about or more than x?	$Y(t_{12}) = y_1 + y_2$	$Y(t_{22}) = y_1$	$Y(t_{32}) = y_1 + y_3$
Would it be more than x? (y_5)	$Y(t_{13}) = y_1 + y_2 + y_5 + y_7$	$Y(t_{23}) = y_1 + y_5$	$Y(t_{33}) = y_1 + y_3 + y_5 + y_9$

The same parameterization is made for the variance using $y_{10} - y_{18}$.

Table 6 presents the maximum likelihood effects obtained.[5] The coefficients are interpretable in units of 10,000 miles. Thus, the 42.4

coefficient for the mean (y_1) implies that the average circumference estimate for individuals assigned to the balanced 25,000 mile treatment (t_{22}) is 42,400 miles for the circumference of the earth at the equator. Similarly, the −9.19658 coefficient on "Enter Low" (y_2) implies that the effect of being presented with 10,000 miles entry point is to lower the estimate by 9,196.58 miles from roughly 42,400 to 33,304 miles. The rest of the coefficients, including those for the dispersion (σ), have similar interpretations.

There are a couple of interesting patterns to note. First, the estimates overall and on average are highly biased. The overall mean estimate of the circumference of the earth of 42,000 miles is some 17,000 greater than the true value. While it may simply be that people believe the earth is bigger than it actually is, the upward bias in the reports here raises a more disturbing possibility that there is something about bracketing itself that leads to exaggerated reports. The second interesting pattern is that most of the treatment effects are confined to the main effects of entry point level. The wording of the comparisons has little systematic effect. This is especially true for the effects on the mean of the reports but also holds for their dispersion (σ).[6]

TABLE 6.   Circumference of the Earth Ordered Probit Estimates

1 Mean	42.40076**	s.e.	0.89272	BHHH T	47.49593
2 Enter Low	−9.19658**	s.e.	1.09445	BHHH T	−8.40289
3 Enter High	17.31534**	s.e.	1.34357	BHHH T	12.88760
4 "X or more"	3.88973**	s.e.	1.02292	BHHH T	3.80257
5 "More than X"	0.41132	s.e.	1.12694	BHHH T	0.36499
6 GE Low	−1.77437	s.e.	1.40925	BHHH T	−1.25909
7 Gt Low	1.81407	s.e.	1.86155	BHHH T	0.97450
8 GE High	−6.52039**	s.e.	1.62527	BHHH T	−4.01188
9 Gt High	−2.96112*	s.e.	1.22461	BHHH T	−2.41800
10 σ	19.41799**	s.e.	0.85762	BHHH T	22.64166
11 Enter Low	0.16291	s.e.	1.08605	BHHH T	0.15001
12 Enter High	7.87234**	s.e.	1.38993	BHHH T	−5.66384
13 "X or more" (GE)	−1.56057	s.e.	1.00220	BHHH T	−1.55715
14 "More than X" (Gt)	−0.52413	s.e.	1.20818	BHHH T	−0.43382
15 GE Low	1.65669	s.e.	1.43685	BHHH T	1.15300
16 Gt Low	3.21586*	s.e.	1.51913	BHHH T	2.11691
17 GE High	−3.39955*	s.e.	1.59243	BHHH T	−2.13482
18 Gt High	−2.75025*	s.e.	1.31649	BHHH T	−2.08907
Log-likelihood	−11,081.816				ncases = 7,772

Source: HRS Wave 3 Alpha release file.
*Significant at the .05 level.
**Significant at the .01 level.

Table 7 presents the means (in thousands of miles), squared biases, variances, and mean-square errors of the estimates by treatment group for the circumference of the earth experiment. For the low entry point treatments, variance dominates squared bias, whereas for the high entry point treatments the squared bias overwhelms variance — even though these latter groups also have substantially higher variances. In other words, to the extent that these results are generalizable, the worst possible thing to do in designing unfolding brackets is to enter the sequence from the very high side. Not only is the central tendency of the prior distribution pulled up, but the presentation of a very high entry point appears to increase the respondents' uncertainty as measured by the variance.

In conclusion anchoring can have a very big effect on the data accuracy as measured by the mean-squared error. It would appear that entering a bracketing sequence too high will increase not only the final estimates but also the variance. Further research is needed in this area if we are to attempt to remove anchoring bias from our imputation methods.

Response Contamination

The final question we raised at the beginning of the essay was whether exposure to the bracketing method for one measure affected the quality of responses for subsequent measures. We can imagine how such expo-

TABLE 7. **Circumference of the Earth Estimates and Squared Bias, Variance, and Mean-Squared Error by Treatment**

Treatments		Enter at 10,000 Miles	Enter at 25,000 Miles	Enter at 50,000 Miles
Would it amount to x or more?	Y (thousands)	35.32	46.29	57.09
	$(Y - \mu)^2$	108	458	1,036
	σ^2	357	319	499
	MSE	465	777	1,535
Less than, about, or more than x?	Y (thousands)	33.20	42.40	59.72
	$(Y - \mu)^2$	69	306	1,212
	σ^2	383	377	745
	MSE	452	683	1,957
Would it be more than x?	Y (thousands)	35.41	42.80	57.16
	$(Y - \mu)^2$	110	320	1,041
	σ^2	496	357	577
	MSE	606	677	1,618

Source: HRS Wave 3 Alpha release file.

sure might have counteracting effects. Exposure may reassure respondents that the interviewer will help out in future questions by giving brackets; consequently, they will be more comfortable with admitting that they don't know a particular amount. This would lead to an increased propensity to say "don't know" and to use the bracketing sequences later on. On the other hand, exposure in the survey may tell respondents that extreme accuracy is not necessary. If so, they may be more comfortable with providing rough cardinal reports. This would lead to reduced propensities to say "don't know" and, therefore, reduced propensities to fall into the bracket mode later on in the survey.

The empirical task of seeing which of these possible effects dominates is complicated by what we might call "heterogeneity in candor." The fact is that virtually no respondent is able to formulate a truly precise report for most items. But there are huge interpersonal differences in their underlying propensity to admit it or to let it get in their way of being responsive. Some people may be very hesitant to ever say they "don't know" an answer even when they don't have the foggiest notion, while others might prefer to say "don't know" when they are not certain about the last penny. The effect of such heterogeneity in assessing the impact of early exposure to brackets on later propensities is to impart a positive bias on the coefficient on the dummy variable measuring early exposure. That is, early exposure to brackets will appear to increase the chances of later bracketing simply because some respondents tend to get into bracketing more frequently than others.

Short of conducting true experiments, there are two ways of removing this heterogeneity bias from estimated effects of bracket exposure on bracket propensity. These involve formulating a structural model and (1) including controls for bracket propensity and (2) allowing for correlated unmeasured heterogeneity. Suppose there are two underlying latent propensities to provide responses that get respondents into a bracketing sequence — one for items early in the interview (B_e^*) and one for items late in the interview (B_l^*). Suppose that these propensities are composed of systematic and random components according to

$$B_{ei}^* = \beta_e' X_i + \epsilon_{ei}$$

$$B_{li}^* = \gamma B_{ei} + \beta_l' X_i + \epsilon_{li}$$

(13)

where X_i is a vector of individual I's characteristics, β_e and β_l are vectors of parameters relating these characteristics to the bracket propensities, ϵ_{ei} and ϵ_{li} are random components of the bracket propensities, B_e is a dummy variable equaling 1 if an early bracket situation occurred, and γ is a parameter that reflects the effect of early bracketing on the propensity of the respondent to provide a later bracket. The term γ is the primary parameter of interest. If it is positive, bracketing begets bracketing, while if it is negative bracketing changes respondents' quality standards such that they become less likely to get into bracketing situations.

If the ϵ_e and ϵ_l were uncorrelated, we could simply estimate the second equation in expression (13) and obtain and estimate of γ. Unmeasured heterogeneity, however, should lead to a positive correlation in these random components. Unless the estimation method is sensitive to this problem, the estimated coefficient for γ will be positively biased. Thus, we need to estimate both equations in expression (13) simultaneously and allow explicitly for the correlation (ρ) between ϵ_e and ϵ_l. We can do so by assuming the ϵ are drawn from the bivariate normal distribution and estimating the model as a bivariate probit.

Our empirical strategy limits attention to the financial respondent and concentrates on one of the last items in the HRS wave 1 questionnaire for which an unfolding bracket was used. To make the results most useful, we chose an asset item that most respondents had — checking, savings, and/or money market accounts (Accounts). Whether an unfolding bracket situation occurred for this item is used as the empirical realization of B_l. The measure of early bracket exposure we chose is whether an unfolding bracket was encountered prior to the "Accounts" question.

As background predictors of bracketing propensity, the number of "don't knows" (DKs) and refusals encountered in the Housing section of the questionnaire are used as well as a number of personal characteristics of the respondent. Since exposure to the range card in earlier sections of the survey will send the same type of messages to the respondent as exposure to the brackets in the Assets section, we also include whether any range card responses are recorded in the housing section as an additional control.

In order to provide some orientation, table 8 presents a simple

TABLE 8. Simple Bivariate Association of Early and Subsequent Bracketing

	Subsequent Not Bracketed	Subsequent Bracketed	Total
Early not bracketed	3,903	576	4,479
	66.2%	9.8%	76.0%
Early bracketed	717	699	1,416
	12.2%	11.9%	24.0%
Total	4,620	1,275	5,895
	78.4%	11.9%	100.0%

Source: HRS Wave 1 Gamma release file.
Note: χ^2 of independence = 845.8; df = 1.

cross-tabulation of the number of cases with bracketing early by late. The sample is limited to those financial respondents who had nonzero amounts in "Accounts." Given the marginal distributions in the table, under the null hypothesis of independence we would expect about 5.2 percent of the cases to have bracketed reports both prior to and in the "Accounts" item. In fact, 11.9 percent had such a pattern of reports, which suggests a positive simple association between the bracketing propensity. The χ^2 statistic of 845.8 means that this association is highly significant.

The question remains, however, as to what extent this association is structural or simply due to shared heterogeneity (either measured or unmeasured). Table 9 presents the results relevant to this question. The top panel of the table lists the parameter estimates for the "Early

TABLE 9.   Bivariate Probit Model, Effects of Bracketing Exposure on Subsequent Bracketing

Early Bracket Exposure Portion					
1 Early Constant	−1.21800**	s.e.	0.08900	BHHH T	−13.68610
2 #DKs Housing	0.31598**	s.e.	0.03185	BHHH T	9.92181
3 #Refusals Housing	0.23430**	s.e.	0.02943	BHHH T	7.96008
4 Income	−1.55650**	s.e.	0.38948	BHHH T	−3.99635
5 Education	0.11562*	s.e.	0.05507	BHHH T	2.09940
11 Understanding	−0.16723**	s.e.	0.02871	BHHH T	−5.82445
12 Cooperation	0.23696**	s.e.	0.02756	BHHH T	8.59925
13 Age/10	0.02675*	s.e.	0.01239	BHHH T	2.15889
14 Male	0.34064**	s.e.	0.04257	BHHH T	8.00168
15 Married	−0.11022	s.e.	0.11754	BHHH T	−0.93776
21 Range Card Housing	−0.28018**	s.e.	0.07599	BHHH T	−3.68723
Subsequent Bracket Portion					
6 Late Constant	−0.62325**	s.e.	0.08667	BHHH T	−7.19069
2 #DKs Housing	0.31598**	s.e.	0.03185	BHHH T	9.92181
3 #Refusals Housing	0.23430**	s.e.	0.02943	BHHH T	7.96008
8 Income	−4.82230**	s.e.	0.29933	BHHH T	−16.11037
9 Education	−0.01211	s.e.	0.05685	BHHH T	−0.21295
16 Understanding	−0.22095**	s.e.	0.02434	BHHH T	−9.07773
17 Cooperation	0.32353**	s.e.	0.02325	BHHH T	13.91306
18 Age/10	0.01268	s.e.	0.01162	BHHH T	1.09134
19 Male	0.26511**	s.e.	0.03964	BHHH T	6.68743
20 Married	0.01918	s.e.	0.11084	BHHH T	0.17301
22 Range Card Housing	−0.38905**	s.e.	0.07044	BHHH T	−5.52303
7 γ	−0.79847**	s.e.	0.03377	BHHH T	−23.64628
10 $f(\rho)$	4.14774**	s.e.	0.55371	BHHH T	7.49088
Log-likelihood	−5,584.931				ncases = 5,895

Source: HRS Wave 1 Gamma release file.

Bracket Exposure" portion of the model. The first thing to note about these estimates is that there exists a strong and highly significant effect of the numbers of DKs and refusals encountered in the Housing section on the propensity to become exposed to the brackets early on. Furthermore, there are very strong effects of (1) the interviewers' rating of respondent cooperation (uncooperative being more likely to bracket) and (2) gender (males being more likely to bracket as well).

The substantively more interesting results are contained in the bottom panel of table 9 and pertain to the "Subsequent Bracket" portion of the model. Here, the same general pattern of results holds, but additionally we obtain an estimate of γ of $-.79847$, which is hugely significant. This result (which is opposite to that implied by the simple association of table 9) is consistent with the hypothesis that *exposure to bracketing conveys the message to respondents that great precision is not required.* The reason this result is different from the simple association can be seen from examination of the coefficient for the stochastic dependence $f(\rho)$ shown as the last coefficient in the table. The fact that it is positive and highly significant suggests that much of the simple association of table 9 operated through unmeasured heterogeneity. For numerical reasons, we do not include ρ in the model directly but only the monotonic transform $f(\rho)$. The estimate of 4.14774 for this corresponds to a correlation coefficient of 96.8 percent—implying that from a stochastic point of view these two latent variables are virtually identical.

The results show that once one controls for the fact that some people tend to be the type who are prone to saying "I don't know" (i.e., unmeasured heterogeneity), exposure to the bracketing method in one question significantly lowers the propensity of respondents to say they don't know the answer to subsequent questions *within the same interview.*

Table 10 presents the results obtained with a slightly more parsimonious specification of the model applied to the effect of bracketing in one interview on the propensity to bracket in the next wave's interview. Identification is obtained now by including the number of items the respondent had that might lead to bracketing. This can be thought of as the size of the risk set. The interesting thing to note about the results of this cross-wave analysis is that while the correlation of the error terms remains positive and significant (i.e., unmeasured individual heterogeneity persists across waves), the structural effect of exposure to bracketing in one wave on the propensity to bracket in the next disappears. Thus, while there appears to be a strong negative effect of exposure to bracketing on bracket propensities within waves there is no evidence that it persists across waves.

TABLE 10. Effect of Wave 1 Bracketing on Wave 2

2 Wave1 Constant	−2.07206**	s.e.	0.19266 BHHH T	−10.75488
3 #W1 Items	0.11958**	s.e.	0.01260 BHHH T	9.49306
4 Income	−0.50322**	s.e.	0.16823 BHHH T	−2.99131
5 Net Worth	1.39300**	s.e.	0.12260 BHHH T	11.36255
6 Wave2 Constant	−1.54778**	s.e.	0.14611 BHHH T	−10.59292
7 #W2 Items	0.14171**	s.e.	0.01126 BHHH T	12.58918
8 Income	−0.23654	s.e.	0.14910 BHHH T	−1.58645
9 Net Worth	0.86200**	s.e.	0.09102 BHHH T	9.47069
10 γ	−0.12650	s.e.	0.09482 BHHH T	−1.33404
1 $f(\rho)$	0.97063**	s.e.	0.12644 BHHH T	7.67672
Log-likelihood	−6,882.508			$n$cases = 6,405

Source: HRS Waves 1 and 2 Gamma release file.

Conclusion

One of Tom Juster's most important recent innovations in survey measurement methods is the unfolding bracket technique. This technique is quite effective in reducing item nonresponse. In addition, the resulting data appear to be empirically useful for measures about which respondents are truly uncertain. This conclusion is based on our findings that medical expenditures collected using the method compare favorably with benchmark data from the NMES — both in terms of univariate comparisons and comparisons of the parameters of a simple structural model. There are significant differences between the NMES and the HRS in measure of health expenditures. But many of these differences are the result of differences in the lengths of the reference period. Based on the results reported in this essay, it is also possible to design the unfolding brackets so as to maximize the informational content of the data using more than one metric.

We were also interested in this essay in two questions regarding the effect of exposure to the unfolding bracket method on response quality — first for the quality of the measure in question and second for subsequent measures. The level of the entry point was found to have a major impact on the accuracy (as measured by its mean-square error) of the resulting data. This conclusion is based on experimental data using the circumference of the earth as the measure of interest. This measure was chosen because the true value is a known constant but one about which most respondents are quite uncertain. The experimental treatments were a combination of level of the entry point and three competing wordings of the comparisons presented in the unfolding. We found that the effects of comparison wording were relatively minor but that there were substantial effects of the level of the entry point. In terms of the mean-square error of the resulting data, and under the assumption of normally distributed errors, the worst data were obtained when the entry point was unreasonably high. Not only was the estimated mean report severely biased upward for the high entry point cases, but the variance was also greatly increased.

As for whether exposure to the bracketing method affected the quality of subsequent data, the answer is "yes" for measures obtained in subsequent questions of a given wave's interview and "no" for measures obtained in subsequent waves of the study. We found strong evidence of positively correlated heterogeneity in the propensity to bracket from time frame to time frame and strong evidence of a negative association of bracketing early in the interview on subsequent bracketing within the same interview. Evidently, exposure to bracketing gives the respondent the message that extreme precision is not necessary in the context of a given interview. While the correlated heterogeneity results persisted when the time frame was changed from within to between waves, the structural association vanished. Evidently, the effects of exposure to bracketing decay with elapsed time.

In conclusion, the unfolding bracket method for eliminating item nonresponse, something that Tom Juster has been instrumental in developing and popularizing, seems to be quite effective. It does, however, affect the quality of reports regarding the specific question where it is used and in subsequent questions (although not in subsequent interviews). Just how serious these effects are and, therefore, what the overall effect of the method is on data quality is an open question—one on which we are certain to be working for some time to come.

NOTES

1. We used the medical costs portion of the Consumer Price Index for this adjustment. This is not an entirely satisfactory series for our purposes because it is based solely on out-of-pocket costs and includes only the household's contributions to health insurance. It is particularly problematic for the purposes of adjusting for hospital cost inflation.

2. See Hill 1993 for an explanation of the Thomas regression model.

3. This assumption is equivalent to assuming that the data are coarsened at random (see Heitjan and Rubin 1991; Juster and Smith 1997). This assumption is not true for most financial items in the HRS—reports are more apt to be missing for wealthier respondents. Nevertheless, the Missing Completely at Random (MCAR) assumption may be a good first approximation for setting breakpoints.

4. There is an interesting and rapidly developing literature in cognitive psychology and econometrics on anchoring effects (see, e.g., Belli 1997; Hurd and McFadden 1997).

5. The model estimates presented here are based on the cases completed by December 6, 1996.

6. While there are a couple of significant interaction effects for the high entry point and question wording, these are of secondary importance relative to the main effects.

REFERENCES

Belli, R. 1997. "A Review of Anchoring Effects in the Psychological Literature." Paper presented at the HRS/AHEAD Anchoring Workshop, Ann Arbor, University of Michigan, October 17, 1997.

Heeringa, S. G., D. H. Hill, and D. A. Howell. 1995. *Unfolding Brackets for Reducing Item Nonresponse in Economic Survey.* Health and Retirement Study Working Paper Series, no. 94–029, Ann Arbor, Mich.

Heitjan, D. F., and D. B. Rubin. 1991. "Ignorability and Coarse Data." *Annals of Statistics* 19 (4): 2244–53.

Hill, D. 1993. "Response and Sequencing Errors in Surveys: A Discrete Contagious Regression Model." *Journal of the American Statistical Association,* 88, no. 423 (September): 775–81.

Hill, D., and N. Mathiowetz. 1998. "The Empirical Validity of the HRS Medical Expenditure Data: A Model to Account for Different Reference Periods. Working paper, Institute for Social Research, University of Michigan, Ann Arbor, MI.

Hurd, M., and D. McFadden. 1997. "Consumption and Savings Balances of the Elderly: Experimental Evidence on Survey Response Bias." Paper presented at the HRS/AHEAD Anchoring Workshop, Ann Arbor, University of Michigan, October 17, 1997.

Juster, F. T., and J. P. Smith. 1997. "Improving the Quality of Economic Data: Lessons from the HRS and AHEAD." *Journal of the American Statistical Association* 92, no. 440: 1268–78.

Lifetime Earnings, Saving Choices, and Wealth at Retirement

Steven F. Venti and David A. Wise

"People earn just enough to get by" is a phrase often used to explain the low personal saving rate in the United States. The implicit presumption is that households simply do not earn enough to pay for current "needs" and to save. We consider this explanation by examining the dispersion in wealth among households with the same lifetime earnings. Controlling for lifetime earnings, we weigh the relative importance of lifetime resources versus the choice to save from those resources as determinants of the wide variation in asset accumulation among U.S. households.

Thus the essay is about why some elderly households with similar past lifetime earnings have much more wealth than others. The accumulation of wealth has been widely studied and is understood to depend on many factors.[1] Some of these, such as special aptitudes and talents, may be determined by the "luck of the draw" at birth. During a lifetime many other "random" events not directly under the control of the household may affect the accumulation of wealth. These may include both unfavorable shocks to earning capacity — such as job loss or poor health — and positive shocks to income such as inheritances or shocks to spending, perhaps associated with child rearing or medical care. Collectively, we think of such events as due to chance.

In contrast to such "random" events, other determinants of the accumulation of wealth are more closely associated with choice than chance.[2] Such choices may include educational attainment, career decisions, and labor market effort. The decision to save is another and is the focus of this essay. We consider how much of the dispersion in the wealth of older households can be attributed to differences among families in the choice of how much to save (or how much to spend) over their lifetime versus differences in the resources out of which households could have saved. For persons in the *same lifetime earnings decile*, we do this by comparing the unconditional dispersion in wealth at retirement with the dispersion after controlling for chance events that may have affected lifetime resources out of which saving could have been drawn. A person's lifetime earnings decile is of course determined by educational and job related choices as well as by chance events that may have affected earnings capacity. So we are asking what proportion of the dispersion of wealth among persons similarly situated in these respects can be attributed to saving choice versus chance.

Whether accumulated wealth is attributable to the choice to save rather than to chance can have significant implications for government policy. Many policies impose ex post taxes on accumulated assets. For example, elderly Americans who have saved when young and thus have higher capital incomes when old pay higher taxes on Social Security benefits than other persons with the same lifetime earnings who did not save when young. Indeed, Shoven and Wise (1988) show that those who save too much in pension plans in particular face very large "success" tax penalties when pension benefits are withdrawn. Pension assets left as a bequest can be virtually confiscated through the tax system. The belief — perhaps unstated — that chance events determine the dispersion in wealth may weigh in favor of such "redistributive" taxes in the legislative voting that imposes them. If, on the other hand, the dispersion of wealth among the elderly reflects deliberate lifetime spending versus saving decisions — rather than differences in lifetime resources — these higher taxes may be harder to justify and appear to penalize savers who spend less when they are young. From an economic perspective, if wealth accumulation is random, taxing saving has no incentive effects. If wealth accumulation results from conscious decisions to save versus spend, however, penalizing savers may have substantial incentive effects, discouraging individuals from saving for their own retirement and limiting aggregate economic growth. It is important to keep in mind that this essay is about the dispersion in the accumulation of assets of persons with similar lifetime incomes. The issue raised here is not about progressive taxation but rather about differences in taxes imposed on persons who save for tomorrow versus those who spend today, given the same after-tax earnings.

It is surely true that some persons face hardships over an extended period of their lives or are hurt by sudden catastrophic events that leave them with limited financial resources when they are older. And of course individuals differ in their earning abilities. Yet in other developed countries the saving rate at all income levels is much higher than in the United States. Even in Canada — in many respects similar to the United States — the personal saving rate is almost twice as high as in the United States. Such international comparisons alone suggest that saving depends on much more than lifetime economic resources.

We try in this essay to understand how much of lifetime saving can be explained by simply choosing to save rather than spend and how much might be explained by individual circumstances that limit the accumulation of wealth over one's lifetime. We begin by controlling for lifetime earnings as reported in individual Social Security records. Given lifetime earnings we examine the distribution of wealth, finding a very wide dispersion in the distribution of accumulated saving, even among families with the lowest lifetime earnings. We then show that only a small fraction of the dispersion can be explained by individual circumstances that may have limited the ability to save out of income.

Thus we conclude that, among families with the same lifetime earnings, the bulk of the dispersion in wealth at retirement results from the choice of some families to save while other similarly situated families choose to spend. For the most part, controlling for lifetime earnings, persons with little saving on the eve of retirement have simply chosen to save less and spend more over their lifetimes. It is particularly striking that some households with very low lifetime resources accumulate a great deal of wealth and some households with very high lifetime resources accumulate little wealth. We find these saving disparities cannot be accounted for by adverse financial events such as poor health or by inheritances. While better control for individual circumstances that may limit resources could change somewhat the magnitudes that we obtain, we believe that the general thrust of the conclusions would not change.[3]

We then consider the wealth that would have been accumulated if families in our sample had followed specific saving plans throughout their working lives. This exercise shows that even families with modest lifetime incomes would have accumulated substantial wealth had they saved consistently and invested prudently over the course of their working lives.

There is one potentially important aspect of wealth accumulation that we have not attempted to address directly in this version of the essay: households with similar lifetime resources may invest in different assets that earn different rates of return. We might think of three groups: nonsavers, savers who invest conservatively and have low rates of return, and savers who invest in more risky assets and have higher rates of return. Persons who invest in bonds or bank savings accounts will have lower rates of return on average than those who invest in stocks. It seems clear that part of the wealth accumulation of savers is due to choice — conservative versus risky assets — and part is due to chance. Chance may play a particularly prominent role in housing investments. For example, a person who purchased a home in Boston twenty years ago likely benefited from large capital gains. On the other hand, a person who purchased in Houston may well have lost money. We will find, however, that the wide dispersion in accumulated wealth pertains to all forms of assets; dispersion is not peculiar to housing equity. There is of course a chance aspect to financial asset accumulation as well. Given the level of risk, some savers will be winners and have large returns while others will have lower returns. But unlike a random shock to financial resources due to illness, for example, this risk and associated distribution of shocks to accumulation might best be considered as chosen. If one considers the selection between conservative versus risky investment as a choice, then it is likely that — accounting for investment choices — most of the dispersion in accumulated assets would still be due to choice and only a small part due to chance. In this case, higher expected returns come at the expense of more risk when young, just as higher saving rates come at the expense of lower consumption when young. And, just as it may be harder to justify imposing higher taxes on older households who choose to consume less and save more while young, it may also be harder to justify imposing higher taxes on older households for assuming greater risk while young. In both cases, the higher taxes may discourage saving and limit economic growth. Again, the question raised here is about the taxing of persons who consume today versus the taxing of those who save today and consume tomorrow.

Another, although we believe much less important, potential determinant of asset accumulation is the age profile and the variance of lifetime earnings. We control for the *present value* of lifetime resources. Some explanations of saving, including precautionary and buffer stock motivations, suggest that either the age profile or the variance of lifetime earnings may also affect accumulated wealth. In this case, households with identical preferences facing the same lifetime resources may save different amounts, and our approach ascribes any such variation to choice rather than chance.

Finally, it may be useful to view our estimates in the context of the broader literature on saving and consumption.[4] Our focus is on the dispersion in saving among households with similar lifetime resources. The idea is to empirically isolate the portion of the dispersion in saving that might be attributed to individual choice, once differences in lifetime earnings are accounted for. In most standard consumption models, dispersion in saving arises primarily from differences in household incomes. Such models do not aim to explain the variation in wealth among families with the same lifetime incomes. Other authors, such as Attanasio et al. (1995) and Venti and Wise (1990), allow saving choices to depend on household characteristics like education and marital status. Another way to account for taste variation is to estimate a distribution of rates of time preference that "fits" the variation in saving, given income. This approach has been adopted by Samwick (1996). This approach equates taste with time preference but also does not aim to distinguish choice (taste) from chance. Still another — and quite different — explanation for saving variation among households with similar resources is provided by behavioral models in which households differ in the level of discipline or self-control required to commit to a saving plan (see Shefrin and Thaler 1988). The aim is to explain why households make different choices but not to isolate the effects of choice from chance events.

The Data

The analysis is based on household data collected in the baseline interview of the Health and Retirement Study (HRS). The household heads were aged fifty-one to sixty-one in 1992 when the baseline survey was conducted. The analysis relies on the wealth of households at the time of the survey and on lifetime earnings, which are measured by historical earnings reported to the Social Security Administration.[5] The Social Security earnings data are available for 8,257 of the 12,652 HRS respondents. Comparison of respondents for whom we do and do not have Social Security records suggests that they are very similar. Selected characteristics of the two groups are shown in table 1. The groups have almost the same household income, the same average age, and the same years of education; the same proportion are married; almost the same proportion are female. A slightly larger proportion of those for whom we have Social Security records are HRS primary respondents (64 percent versus 60 percent).

Our analysis is based on household rather than individual respondent data, however. Historical earnings for a single-person household

TABLE 1. Comparison of HRS Respondents for Whom Social Security Data Are and Are Not Available[a]

Characteristic	Persons without Social Security Records	Persons with Social Security Records
Mean household income	$54,252.64	$53,434.20
Percentage female	53.00	54.00
Mean age	55.57	55.40
Percentage nonwhite	15.00	13.00
Mean years of education	12.37	12.40
Percentage married	76.00	76.00
Percentage primary respondent	60.00	64.00

[a]Weighted estimates from the HRS wave 1.

required only that Social Security earnings records be available for that person. But for a two-person household, it was necessary to have historical earnings for both persons in the household if both had been in the labor force for a significant length of time. The HRS obtained such data for 1,625 single-person households and for 2,751 two-person households, together comprising 4,376 of the 7,607 HRS households. Two additional sample adjustments were made. First, we retained households in which one or both members reported never having worked, even if the household member was missing a Social Security earnings record. We assumed zero earnings for such persons. Second, we excluded from the sample all households that included any member who had zero Social Security earnings *and* reported working for any level of government for five (not necessarily consecutive) years. This latter restriction is intended to exclude households that have zero Social Security earnings due to gaps in coverage. The final sample includes 3,992 households.

The other important data component is wealth at the time of the survey. We need a complete accounting of assets, including personal retirement assets such as IRAs and 401(k) balances, other personal financial assets, employer-provided pension assets, home equity, and assets such as real estate and business equity. In most instances the value of these assets is reported directly. For nonpension assets the HRS survey reduces nonresponse considerably by adopting bracketing techniques for important wealth questions (for details, see Juster and Smith 1994; Smith 1995a).

In other cases asset values are not easily determined. The most important asset that is not directly reported is the value of benefits promised under employer-provided defined benefit pension plans. For persons who are retired and receiving benefits this value can be approximated by using life tables to determine the expected value of the future stream of benefits. But for persons covered by a defined benefit plan who are not retired — and for whom the benefit is not known — the value of future benefits can be only very imprecisely imputed. The imputation process relies on the respondent description of pension provisions and is described in detail in the appendix. The HRS also surveyed employers about the features of respondent pensions, but those data are not used in this analysis.

Lifetime Earnings and the Wealth of Households

Social Security earnings are a good measure of lifetime labor income for persons whose earnings are consistently below the Social Security earnings maximum and who have been in jobs covered by the Social Security system. Historically, the Social Security earnings maximum has been adjusted on an ad-hoc basis. The percentage of HRS respondents exceeding the maximum was at its highest in the early 1970s, peaking at 26.9 percent in 1971. The percentage has been below 10 percent since 1981 and was 4.8 percent in 1991.

For persons with incomes above the limit, reported Social Security earnings can significantly underestimate actual earnings. (In addition, as explained previously some persons may report zero Social Security covered earnings because they were employed in sectors not covered by the Social Security system, and we have excluded certain government employees from the sample.) Thus we do not rely directly on Social Security earnings to establish the level of lifetime earnings, but rather we use reported Social Security earnings to *rank* families by lifetime earnings. Then we group families into Social Security earnings deciles, which hereafter we refer to as lifetime earnings deciles. We believe that the ranking by Social Security earnings represents a good approximation to a ranking based on actual total earnings, and thus the deciles are a good approximation to actual lifetime earnings deciles. However, the problems caused by the earnings maximum and by "zeros" may make results based on the lowest and highest deciles less reliable than results based on the other deciles.

The mean present value of lifetime Social Security earnings within each decile is shown in table 2. To obtain lifetime Social Security income the Consumer Price Index (CPI) was used to convert past earnings to 1992 dollars. The means range from about $36,000 in the lowest decile to

TABLE 2.   Present Value of Social Security Earnings by Lifetime Earnings Decile

Lifetime Earnings Decile	Present Value of Social Security Earnings
1st	35,848
2nd	193,664
3rd	372,534
4th	567,931
5th	741,587
6th	905,506
7th	1,055,782
8th	1,186,931
9th	1,333,162
10th	1,637,428

Source: Weighted estimates based on sample of 3,992 households as described in the "Data" section of the text.

just over $1,600,000 in the highest decile. (Within the deciles the medians are essentially the same as the means.)

The medians of assets (other than Social Security wealth) are shown in table 3. The median of total wealth ranges from $3,000 for families in the lowest lifetime earnings decile to almost $400,000 for families in the top lifetime earnings decile. Many assets are held by fewer than 50 percent of households—indicated by zero medians. The 5th and 6th earnings deciles span the median of lifetime earnings, and the median of total wealth in these earnings deciles is $105,166 and $126,082 respectively. Fewer than half of the families in these deciles have IRA or 401(k) accounts. Fewer than half have business equity or real estate. And the value of other assets is small. The median of firm pension assets is $4,000 for the 5th and $14,035 for the 6th lifetime income decile, not much higher than the median value of vehicles—$6,000 and $8,000 respectively. The median level of financial assets is only $3,000 and $5,000 respectively. The largest component of the wealth of these families is home equity; the medians are $30,000 and $35,000 for the 5th and 6th lifetime earnings deciles respectively.

The means of assets by lifetime earnings decile are shown in table 4. Comparison of the means and medians foretells the wide dispersion in

TABLE 3.   Median Level of Assets by Lifetime Earnings Decile and by Asset Category

Category	Lifetime Earnings Decile									
	1st	2nd	3rd	4th	5th	6th	7th	8th	9th	10th
Financial	0	0	100	1,800	3,000	5,000	10,000	17,000	24,600	36,500
Per retirement	0	0	0	0	0	0	4,500	10,000	22,000	40,000
IRA	0	0	0	0	0	0	2,000	5,000	12,000	21,000
401(k)	0	0	0	0	0	0	0	0	0	0
Firm pension	0	0	0	0	4,000	14,035	34,295	40,000	57,542	83,087
DB	0	0	0	0	0	0	0	1,497	3,598	22,337
DC (excluding 401k)	0	0	0	0	0	0	0	0	0	0
PV benefits	0	0	0	0	0	0	0	0	0	0
Vehicles	0	1,500	3,000	5,000	6,000	8,000	10,000	10,000	12,000	15,000
Business equity	0	0	0	0	0	0	0	0	0	0
Real estate	0	0	0	0	0	0	0	0	0	3,000
Home equity	0	3,000	16,000	21,000	30,000	35,000	52,000	60,000	70,000	76,000
Home value	0	8,000	30,000	35,000	45,000	63,000	75,000	85,000	100,000	120,000
Mortgage	0	0	0	0	0	7,000	7,000	8,000	15,500	20,000
Total wealth	3,000	28,800	47,025	72,504	105,166	126,082	195,000	224,000	305,536	380,115

Source: Weighted estimates from the HRS Wave 1.

assets, even among families with similar lifetime earnings. The means are typically much higher than the medians, and in some lifetime earnings deciles the mean of financial assets is over ten times as large as the median.

The Distribution of Wealth for Given Lifetime Earnings

We discuss first the distribution of wealth within lifetime earnings deciles, and then we consider how much of the dispersion can be accounted for by personal circumstances — like health status or children — that might be expected to limit the accumulation of savings.

The Same Lifetime Earnings but Very Different Saving

The dispersion in total accumulated wealth by lifetime earnings decile is shown in figure 1A. For each earnings decile, the figure shows five quantiles: the 10th, 30th, 50th, 70th, and 90th. The median is the 50th quantile. Ten percent of families have wealth below the 10th quantile, 30 percent have wealth below the 30th quantile, and so forth. Several features of the data stand out. Perhaps not surprisingly, a noticeable

TABLE 4. Mean Level of Assets by Lifetime Earnings Decile and by Asset Category

Category	\multicolumn{10}{c}{Lifetime Earnings Decile}									
	1st	2nd	3rd	4th	5th	6th	7th	8th	9th	10th
Financial	20,663	14,315	18,999	30,416	32,927	31,510	52,544	54,108	110,725	87,746
Per retirement	4,384	5,002	5,584	10,351	10,396	14,823	27,410	39,196	64,711	75,540
IRA	3,416	3,697	3,723	6,974	8,287	9,567	17,823	24,420	38,633	52,406
401(k)	969	1,306	1,862	3,376	2,109	5,256	9,587	14,776	26,028	23,134
Firm pension	10,036	17,000	21,025	29,822	39,905	53,308	79,108	91,140	132,644	143,335
DB	6,029	8,694	11,249	14,278	19,714	26,871	37,421	50,861	73,472	91,024
DC (excluding 401(k))	19	1,642	1,736	5,156	2,808	4,521	10,830	12,714	22,424	18,364
PV benefits	3,987	6,664	8,040	10,388	17,383	21,916	30,857	27,565	36,748	33,947
Vehicles	2,440	4,727	5,996	8,626	10,962	12,254	18,392	15,936	16,215	19,489
Business equity	81	2,370	3,588	23,643	22,339	42,030	48,323	31,325	75,634	54,659
Real estate	18,038	12,790	16,782	41,328	31,777	53,139	50,750	56,473	56,468	79,349
Home equity	17,365	29,724	32,473	38,283	43,175	53,402	65,646	71,488	92,335	97,030
Home value	23,163	40,645	44,919	56,588	60,493	76,276	100,781	100,383	127,967	137,012
Mortgage	5,798	10,921	12,446	18,304	17,318	22,874	35,135	28,895	35,632	39,982
Total wealth	72,977	85,927	104,437	18,246	191,480	260,466	342,156	359,666	548,731	557,148

Source: Weighted estimates from the HRS Wave 1.

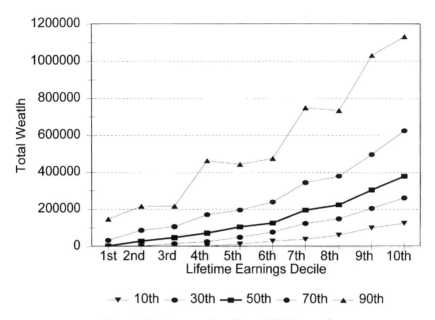

Fig. 1A. Wealth quantiles. (From HRS Wave 1.)

proportion of households in the lowest lifetime earnings deciles have accumulated almost no wealth by the time they have attained ages fifty-one to sixty-one. Half of those in the lowest earnings decile have less than $5,000 in wealth, and so do 30 percent of those in the 2nd decile, 20 percent of those in the 3rd, and 10 percent of households in the 4th earnings decile. But even among households with the highest lifetime earnings, some households have very limited wealth. For example, 10 percent of households in the 6th earnings decile have less than $30,000 in assets, and 10 percent of those in the ninth earnings decile have less than $100,000.

To address the principal question of this essay, it is the dispersion of wealth that is the most critical, and here the data are striking. Even controlling for lifetime earnings, the range of wealth is enormous. In the 5th lifetime earnings decile, the 90th quantile is 35 times as large as the 10th quantile. The range is less extreme in higher earnings deciles but still very wide: 16, 19, 12, 10, and 9 in the 6th through the 10th lifetime earnings deciles respectively.

While many families with low lifetime earnings have very limited wealth — as do some who earned the most — the wide dispersion in accumulated wealth is evident among those with low and high lifetime earn-

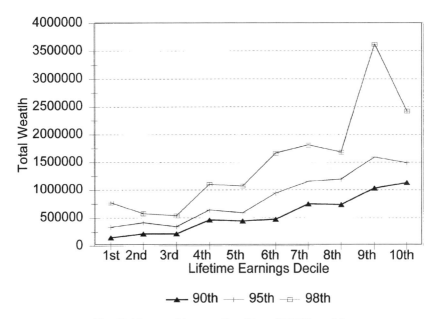

Fig. 1B. Top wealth quantiles. (From HRS Wave 1.)

ings alike. Thus some families with the lowest lifetime earnings have accumulated noticeable wealth. For example, the 90th quantile is approximately $150,000 for the lowest decile and is well above $200,000 for the 2nd and 3rd deciles.

The dispersion at the highest levels of wealth accumulation is itself substantial and is presented separately in figure 1B, which shows the 90th, 95th, and 98th quantiles by lifetime earnings decile. The 98th quantile is typically two and a half to three times as large as the 90th quantile. Overall there is enormous variation in wealth accumulation among households whose members had similar earnings over their lifetimes. The wide variation in wealth will not be new to many readers. Not so widely appreciated is the vast variation in wealth among households with similar lifetime earnings.

Figure 2A shows the dispersion of personal financial assets (excluding personal retirement assets such as IRA and 401(k) accounts). That most people do not save much is not new. That many of those with high incomes save so little is, however, striking. The 10th quantile is negative or close to zero for every lifetime earnings decile! The same is true for the 30th quantile, with the exception of the highest earnings decile for which the 30th quantile is a paltry $6,400. The medians range from zero

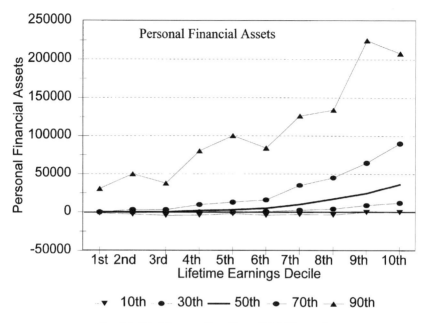

Fig. 2A. Wealth quantiles. (From HRS Wave 1.)

for the lowest three deciles, to $3,000 and $5,800 for the 5th and 6th deciles, to $10,000 for the 7th to $36,500 for the highest earnings decile. Like the dispersion in total wealth the range of personal financial assets from the 10th to the 90th quantiles is extremely broad, and the dispersion is even greater when the very top quantiles are considered, as in figure 2B.

Almost all of the HRS respondents have had the opportunity to contribute to either an Individual Retirement Account (IRA) or a 401(k) plan. Before considering wealth accumulated in these plans, we briefly review the expansion of these programs and their prominence in aggregate personal saving. The two saving programs introduced in the early 1980s were motivated by the low U.S. saving rate, as well as by the concern that many Americans reached retirement with little personal saving. IRAs became available to all employees as part of the Economic Recovery Tax Act of 1981. Any employee could contribute $2,000 per year to an IRA account, and a nonworking spouse could contribute $250. The contribution was tax deductible. Annual contributions grew from about $5 billion in 1981 to about $38 billion in 1986, approximately 30 percent of total personal saving. The Tax Reform Act of 1986 limited the tax advantages of IRAs for higher income persons, and contribu-

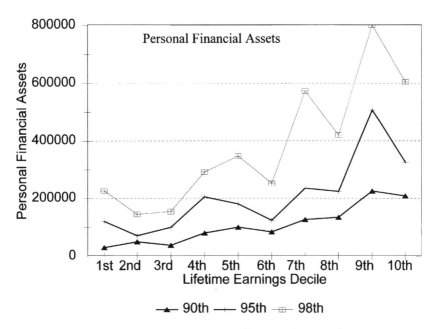

Fig. 2B. Top wealth quantiles. (From HRS Wave 1.)

tions declined precipitously thereafter. By 1994, only $7.7 billion was contributed to IRAs, and while over 15 percent of tax filers contributed in 1986, less than 4 percent contributed in 1994.

The other program introduced in the early 1980s was the 401(k) plan.[6] Thereafter, 401(k) saving grew continuously, with contributions increasing from virtually zero at the beginning of the decade to over $64 billion by 1992, when over 25 percent of families contributed to a 401(k). Contributions to 401(k) accounts are also tax deductible, and the return on the contributions accrues tax free; taxes are paid upon withdrawal. But these plans are available only to employees of firms that offer such plans. Prior to 1987 the employee contribution limit was $30,000, but the Tax Reform Act of 1986 reduced the limit to $7,000 and indexed this limit for inflation in subsequent years.

By 1986, contributions to all personal retirement saving plans exceeded contributions to traditional employer-provided pension plans. Although contributions to IRAs declined precipitously after 1986, 401(k) contributions continued to grow, and now saving through these plans far exceeds saving through traditional employer-provided defined benefit plans. Contributions to all personal retirement saving plans totaled $81 billion, and contributions to traditional employer-provided defined benefit and defined contribution plans totaled $64 billion in 1992. Saving for retirement through employer-provided and personal pension plans together now accounts for a very large proportion of personal saving. Over the past several years retirement saving has accounted for between 70 and 80 percent of personal saving as defined in the National Income and Product Accounts.

It is not surprising then, that personal retirement saving has become an important component of the wealth of some HRS households. Quantiles of personal retirement saving assets by lifetime earnings decile are shown in figure 3A. Although personal retirement accounts are now an important form of personal saving, only about half of HRS households have such accounts. Most households in the highest lifetime earnings deciles have such accounts, but households in the lowest deciles do not. Like the dispersion in personal financial saving and in total wealth, even for households with similar lifetime earnings the variation in personal retirement assets is very large. Again, substantial variation is observed in the top quantiles as shown in figure 3B. Although we have no way of knowing how much the IRA and 401(k) — as well as Keogh — limits constrained the personal retirement saving of HRS households, it is likely that many households at the top quantiles were constrained by the limits.

Individual Circumstances Do Not Account for Much

We want to obtain a rough indication of how much of the dispersion in saving can be attributed to differences in the simple choice of persons to save — the "taste" for saving. We have already considered the variation in saving controlling for lifetime earnings, surely the single most important determinant of how much a person might reasonably be able to save. But there are other circumstances as well. Here we do not want to control for education, ethnic group, and other attributes that might be correlates of the taste for saving. Rather we want to consider individual circumstances that may enhance or limit the available income out of which saving is made. We consider inheritances and gifts, health status, age, children, and marital status. That inheritances and gifts might ease the burden of saving seems clear. Poor health and associated health expenditures may also increase the burden of saving. Health status may also affect lifetime earnings and thus the earnings decile of households. The question here is whether given earnings, health status may affect the resources out of which households might plausibly save. Unfortunately, we have only limited indications of health status and know little about health over a person's lifetime. Thus we use health status at the time of

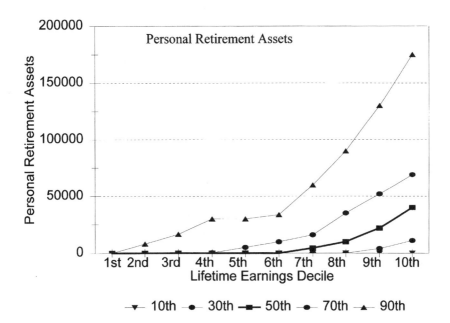

Fig. 3A. Wealth quantiles. (From HRS Wave 1.)

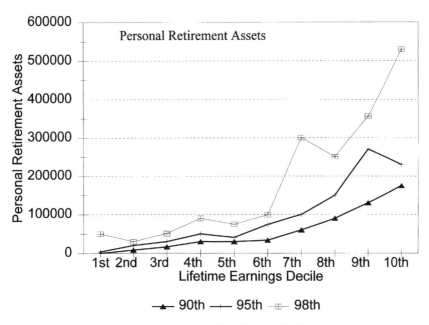

Fig. 3B. Top wealth quantiles. (From HRS Wave 1.)

the survey as an imperfect control for medical circumstances. It is likely that expenses associated with children draw from resources that could be saved. Indeed, under some circumstances children could be a substitute for saving for retirement. Finally, marital status, if only because of economies of scale, may be a determinant of resources out of which saving could plausibly be drawn. We have not controlled for how savings were invested or for rates of return on housing equity, which may have varied appreciably among geographic regions.

Within each lifetime earnings decile, we predict wealth with a simple specification of the form

$$
\begin{aligned}
\text{Wealth} = {} & \text{Constant} \\
& + \beta_1\,(\text{Married}) + \beta_2\,(\text{Never Married}) \\
& + \beta_3\,(\text{Widowed, Divorced, or Separated}) \\
& + \beta_4\,(\text{No Children}) + \beta_5\,(\text{Number of Children if} > 0) \\
& + \beta_5\,(\text{Age}) \\
& + \beta_6\,(\text{Poor Health Single Person}) + \beta_7\,(\text{Poor Health} \\
& \quad \text{1 of 2 in family}) \\
& + \beta_8\,(\text{Poor Health 2 of 2 in family}) \\
& + \beta_9\,(\text{No Inheritances}) + \beta_{10}\,(\text{Amount of Inheritances} \\
& \quad \text{Received} < 1980) \\
& + \beta_{11}\,(\text{Amount of Inheritances Received 1980 to 1988}) \\
& + \beta_{12}\,(\text{Amount of Inheritances Received} > 1988)
\end{aligned}
\tag{1}
$$

with appropriate normalizing restrictions for the indicator variables. From this equation, we obtain predicted wealth. Then within each earnings decile adjusted wealth is determined by

$$
\begin{aligned}
\text{Adjusted Wealth} = {} & (\text{Unadjusted Wealth}) - (\text{Predicted Wealth}) \\
& + (\text{Mean of Wealth})
\end{aligned}
\tag{2}
$$

which gives distributions of adjusted and unadjusted (observed) wealth with the same means.

We emphasize the effect of these adjustments on the distribution of wealth within lifetime earnings deciles, and thus the exposition is necessarily graphical for the most part. Figure 4 shows graphs of the adjusted compared to the unadjusted quantiles for each lifetime earnings decile. Overall, the adjustment for individual circumstances does not have much effect on the dispersion of wealth. Thus we conclude that for the most part within decile differences in saving can be attributed to differences in the amount of income that households choose to save; some choose to save a good deal, many choose to save very little. As men-

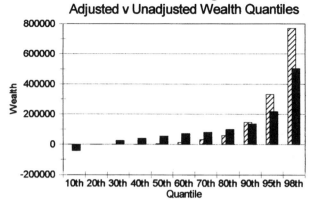

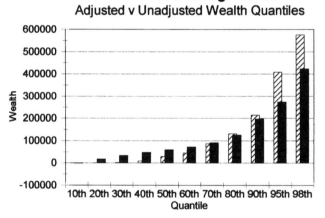

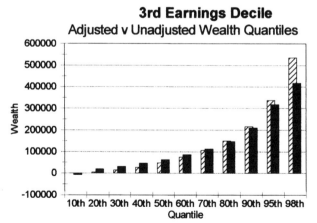

Unadjusted   Adjusted

Fig. 4. Adjusted vs. unadjusted quantiles for each lifetime earnings decile. (From HRS Wave 1.)

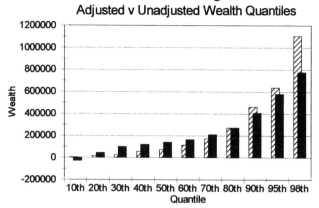

4th Earnings Decile

Adjusted v Unadjusted Wealth Quantiles

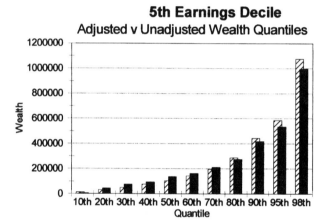

5th Earnings Decile

Adjusted v Unadjusted Wealth Quantiles

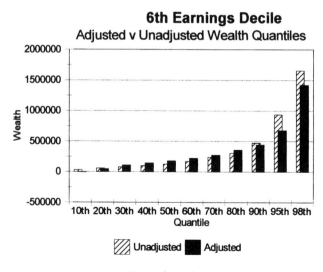

6th Earnings Decile

Adjusted v Unadjusted Wealth Quantiles

Unadjusted   Adjusted

Fig. 4. (*cont.*)

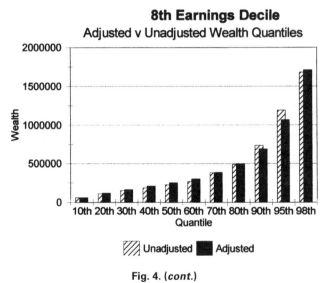

Fig. 4. (*cont.*)

tioned previously, we have not accounted for how financial assets are invested, and this could account for some portion of the variation in accumulated wealth but — for reasons discussed earlier — we believe that most of this variation can be attributed to saving choice. Housing values, however, have increased much more in some parts of the country than in others, and this may account for some portion of the variance and might be attributed more to chance than to saving choice.

The comparison of adjusted and unadjusted distributions, however,

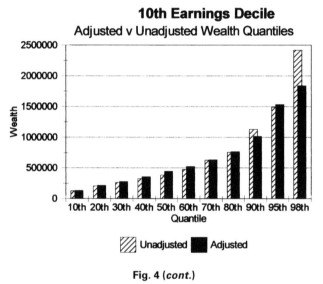

Fig. 4 (*cont.*)

does reveal some systematic patterns. First, the 95th and 98th quantiles are reduced in almost every decile, and the reduction in the 98th quantile is especially noticeable. Second, for the 5th to the 10th deciles, the adjustment has very little effect on all but the extreme quantiles. Modest leveling occurs within the 3rd and 4th deciles, with the 90th quantile reduced a bit and the lower quantiles raised a bit. Third, the greatest leveling occurs in the 1st and 2nd lifetime earnings deciles, in which the highest quantiles are reduced and the lowest quantiles raised. Still, in all deciles an enormous dispersion in assets remains.

For comparison, more traditional measures of unconditional versus conditional variance (controlling for individual circumstances) are shown in table 5. The unconditional standard deviation of total wealth over the entire sample is 23.82 million. Controlling for lifetime earnings decile, the standard deviation is reduced by 5.92 percent. When lifetime earnings decile and the individual attributes are controlled for (with complete interaction of earnings decile and attributes) the reduction is 9.77 percent. Thus by this conventional measure, only a small proportion of the dispersion in wealth can be attributed to either income or to these selected additional attributes. The effect of controlling for the individual attributes within earnings decile is shown in the second panel of table 5.

TABLE 5. Unconditional versus Conditional Standard Deviations, Controlling for Individual Circumstances

Total Sample		
Control	Standard Deviation (in millions)	Percentage Reduction versus Unconditional Standard Deviation
Unconditional	23.82	—
Controlling for lifetime earnings decile	22.41	5.92
Controlling for lifetime earnings decile plus other attributes	21.70	9.77

By Lifetime Earnings Decile		
Decile	Unconditional Variance	Conditional Variance	Percentage Reduction
1st	12.07	11.10	8.04
2nd	7.73	5.86	24.19
3rd	10.80	10.61	1.76
4th	16.23	11.93	26.49
5th	13.29	12.84	3.39
6th	25.85	24.47	5.34
7th	23.51	21.19	9.87
8th	23.35	22.80	2.36
9th	43.45	42.64	1.86
10th	29.44	28.23	4.11

Source: Weighted estimates from the HRS Wave 1.

The conditional standard deviation is typically only a few percentage points lower than the unconditional standard deviation (although as high as 27 percent in the second and fourth deciles), and thus within earnings deciles little of the dispersion can be ascribed to these attributes. Although consistent with the graphical information, these measures provide no detail on how the distribution of wealth may be affected by the individual attributes, and that is what we wish to emphasize.

Finally, controlling for education and ethnic group, which are typically found to be related to saving and presumably influence the "taste" for saving, has only a very modest effect on the distributions. By way of illustration, figure 5 shows the quantiles for the 7th earnings decile when these variables are added. The principal effect of the addition of these "taste" variables is to increase a bit the lower quantiles. Nonetheless, the major dispersion remains: some people choose to save and others do not.

We have focused here on the dispersion of total wealth. Within lifetime earnings deciles, wide dispersion characterizes all asset categories, and little of the dispersion can be attributed to individual household circumstances. For example, figure 6 shows adjusted and unadjusted quantiles for personal financial assets plus IRA assets for households in the 8th lifetime earnings decile. Although the top adjusted quantiles are lower than the unadjusted quantiles, overall the adjustment has only a modest effect on the dispersion.

The Wealth That Consistent Saving Would Have Produced

We see that a large fraction of households on the eve of retirement have meager financial asset saving and indeed limited total wealth. Given the promise of Social Security benefits, it may be that many households rationally choose to save little. Preliminary evidence gathered through an experimental survey of 10 percent of HRS households brings into question the extent to which this is true, however. When asked if they thought they had saved enough for retirement, 75 percent of respondents said they had not. Only 25 percent said they had saved enough, and virtually none said they had saved too much.

We now ask what the wealth of HRS respondents might have been had they saved consistently for retirement throughout their working lives. The answer to this question can only be illustrative, because it requires a choice of saving rate out of income and a choice of rate of return. We make calculations based on several different saving rates and

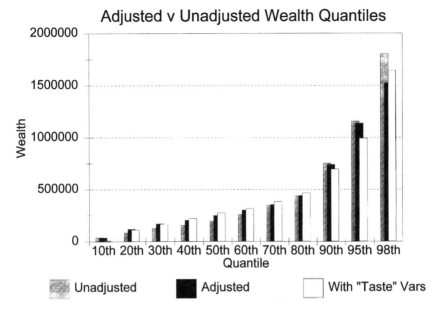

Fig. 5. Quantiles for the 7th earning decile with "taste" variables. (From HRS Wave 1.)

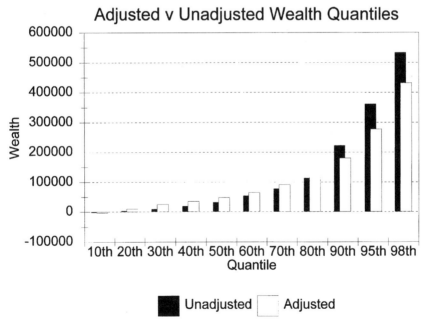

Fig. 6. Adjusted vs. unadjusted quantiles for personal financial assets plus IRA assets for households in the 8th income decile. (From HRS Wave 1.)

rate of return values. Basically, we ask what if a proportion s of earnings had been saved each year and each year this saving had been invested in assets earning a rate of return r.[7] Using a given s and a given r, we calculate the resulting asset accumulation of our sample. There is one important limitation to this method: historical earnings are reported only up to the Social Security earnings limit, as emphasized previously. Actual earnings in these deciles may be substantially higher than Social Security reported earnings.

Because of this limitation of the Social Security data, we also make calculations based on the annual March Current Population Survey (CPS), which reports earnings well above the Social Security maximum.[8] We follow this procedure: (1) We identify lifetime earnings deciles, as described previously, using the Social Security earnings histories of each family in the HRS. (2) Using the annual March CPS we calculate earnings deciles by age for the years 1964–91. Using published data on median earnings prior to 1964, we extrapolate this series back to 1955. Thus we obtain CPS earnings histories by decile for the years 1955 to 1991. (3) To compare the Social Security data with the analogous CPS data we assign each HRS household to a CPS decile according to the household Social Security earnings decile. The CPS earnings histories begin at age twenty-five, and a given household is assumed to have been in the same decile since age twenty-five. (4) Using this earnings profile and saving and rate of return values, we calculate accumulated wealth up to the age of the respondent at the time of the survey in 1992.

Results for several saving rates (s) and nominal investment returns (r) are shown in table 6. For each combination of s and r, the first column presents results using only the Social Security earnings data. The second column shows the results of the alternative calculation based on the CPS earnings data. Calculations are made for three values of s (5, 10, and 15 percent) and two values of r (6 and 12.5 percent). The assumed values of s reflect what we believe to be "reasonable" rates of saving for households. Indeed, if saving is broadly defined to include investments in housing, businesses, pensions, and vehicles, then a rate of even 15 percent may be conservative. The rates of return of 6 percent and 12.5 percent and the mean annual returns for long-term corporate bonds and the Standard and Poor's index (S&P 500), respectively, between 1926 and 1995.

For the most part the Social Security earnings histories and the CPS constructed histories yield rather similar results, although the CPS histories are associated with larger wealth accumulation. The greatest differences occur at the top earnings deciles and are typically larger for large saving rates and rates of return. The actual assets with which these

TABLE 6. Assets at the Time of the HRS Survey if Respondents had Saved Throughout Their Working Lives

Earnings Decile	s = .05, r = 6%		s = .05, r = 12.5%		s = .10, r = 6%		s = .10, r = 12.5%		s = .15, r = 6%		s = .15, r = 12.5%	
	SS	CPS	SS	CPS	SS	CPS	SS	CPS	SS	CPS	SS	CPS
1st	1,608	34	4,329	137	3,216	69	8,658	275	4,824	103	12,987	412
2nd	9,178	11,402	24,887	38,066	18,356	22,804	49,773	76,133	27,534	34,207	74,660	144,199
3rd	18,321	23,738	50,004	73,290	36,642	47,475	100,008	146,580	54,962	71,213	150,012	219,870
4th	28,236	33,627	78,897	100,608	56,472	67,253	157,794	201,216	84,708	100,880	236,690	301,825
5th	37,083	42,606	105,962	124,198	74,166	85,212	211,925	248,395	111,249	127,819	317,887	372,593
6th	45,490	51,079	125,965	144,557	90,981	102,158	251,930	289,113	136,471	153,237	377,896	433,670
7th	53,617	61,056	150,462	173,856	107,234	122,112	300,923	347,712	160,851	183,168	451,385	521,567
8th	60,073	71,689	163,745	199,094	120,147	143,378	327,490	398,189	180,220	215,068	491,236	597,283
9th	67,457	88,701	183,935	251,229	134,914	177,401	367,869	502,459	202,370	266,102	551,804	753,688
10th	83,810	125,418	226,230	354,536	167,620	250,835	452,460	709,072	251,430	376,153	678,690	1,063,609
All	40,487	50,935	111,442	145,957	80,975	101,870	222,883	291,914	121,462	152,805	334,325	437,872

Source: Weighted estimates from the HRS Wave 1.
Note: Saving Rate = s and Rate of Return = r.

accumulations should be compared is unclear. We are inclined to compare these values to all financial assets that might be used for support in retirement — that is, personal retirement assets, firm pension assets, and other personal financial assets. For convenience the medians of these assets are shown by lifetime earnings decile in the first column of table 7. Since housing equity is typically not used to finance retirement spending, at least not until advanced ages, it is convenient to make comparisons excluding housing equity, which is the largest asset of the majority of households. In any case, total wealth is also shown in the second column of table 7. (The comparison should be with the actual median, and not the mean, because the same saving and rates of return are assigned to all households. In addition, within a decile, the same CPS earnings are assigned to all households.)

Saving rates of 10 percent would typically yield much larger assets than the median of actual total financial assets. Consider the 6th lifetime earnings decile, for example. Actual median total financial assets in this decile are $46,882. With a rate of return of 6 percent, a saving rate of 10 percent would have produced median assets of about $100,000 at the time of the survey. At the average rate of return for the S&P 500, the accumulation would have been between $250,000 and $300,000. The actual median of total (financial and nonfinancial) wealth in the 6th decile is $126,082. In all earnings deciles, the "as if" accumulation of financial assets is much larger than the actual accumulation of financial assets. Indeed, for saving rates of 10 percent and the S&P 500 rate of return the "as if" potential accumulation is much larger than total actual wealth. The average age of the HRS respondents is only fifty-six, how-

TABLE 7.   Actual Median Total Financial Assets (personal retirement, firm pension, and other financial) and Total Wealth, by Lifetime Earnings Decile

Lifetime Earnings Decile	Total Financial Assets	Total Wealth
1st	0	3,000
2nd	431	28,800
3rd	6,770	47,025
4th	22,000	72,504
5th	35,668	105,166
6th	46,882	126,082
7th	86,000	195,000
8th	111,465	224,000
9th	162,825	305,536
10th	213,855	380,115

Source: Weighted estimates from the HRS Wave 1.

ever, so assets projected to age sixty-five could easily be more than double those reported in table 7. Nonetheless these potential saving accumulations are in stark contrast with the actual saving of these families. With the illustrative lifetime saving rates and investment returns, families in all but the lowest decile would have accumulated sizable wealth by the time of the HRS survey.[9]

Saving rates like those used in these illustrative calculations are likely to be increasingly common with the continuing spread of 401(k) plans. For example, if current trends continue, it would not be unusual for a person to contribute 10 percent of income to a 401(k) and to invest in an S&P 500 index mutual fund. It is easy to see that consistent lifetime saving, perhaps through a 401(k) plan, could yield large asset accumulations for a very substantial fraction of households.

Discussion and Conclusion

It is often asserted that after taking care of current needs, people just do not have enough left to save. Yet it is not only households with low incomes that save little. A significant proportion of high-income households also save very little. And, not all low-income households are nonsavers. Indeed a substantial proportion of low-income households save a great deal. In this essay we have considered the extent to which differences in household lifetime financial resources explain the wide dispersion in the wealth of families approaching retirement. We find there is an enormous dispersion in wealth even among households with similar lifetime earnings, as measured by Social Security earnings records. Very little of this dispersion can be explained by differences in individual circumstances that might limit the resources from which saving might plausibly be made. The choices vary enormously across households. Some choose to save more and spend less over their working lives while others choose to save little and spend more. These choices — together with the choice between conservative versus more risky investments — lead to vastly different asset accumulations by the time retirement age approaches. Thus we conclude that the bulk of the wealth dispersion among families with similar lifetime earnings must be attributed to differences in the amounts that households choose to save.

Perhaps based on the presumption that differences in wealth can be attributed more to differences across households in adverse circumstances that limit saving, rather than to explicit individual choices, government policy often penalizes persons who have saved over their lifetimes. For example, persons with *the same lifetime earnings* will face very different tax rates on Social Security benefits: those who saved will pay higher taxes while those who did not will pay lower taxes. Given the same lifetime earnings, however, one may question whether savers should be penalized when they are older rather than simply reaping the benefits of their thrift while younger.

Although the distribution of the tax burden will inevitably be based on many factors, most observers believe that the extent to which older persons with more assets are taxed more should depend in part on how they acquired the assets. If they did so by choosing to consume less when young while others chose to consume more, many would argue that they should not be doubly penalized when they are old because they consumed less while young. As emphasized at the outset, this essay is about the dispersion in the accumulation of assets of persons with *similar lifetime earnings*. Thus the issue raised here is not about progressive taxation, but rather — given the same after-tax earnings — about differences in the tax imposed on persons who save today in order to spend more tomorrow versus those who spend all today. Our analysis shows that a very large proportion of the variation in the wealth of older households can be attributed to household saving choices while younger rather than limitations on lifetime resources.

APPENDIX

The Sample

The analysis is based on the first wave of the Health and Retirement Study (HRS), which sampled families with heads aged age fifty-one to sixty-one in 1992. This wave of the HRS includes 12,652 respondents in 7,702 households. For two reasons our analysis was based on only 3,992 households.

First, in 379 married or partnered households one of the respondents did not respond to the survey. Because the pension wealth of both members is a critical component of the analysis, we have deleted these households from the sample.

Second, the analysis relies heavily on lifetime income as measured by Social Security earnings records. These records are available for only 8,257 of the 12,652 HRS respondents. The analysis is based on household rather than individual respondent data. Historical earnings for a single-person household required only that Social Security earnings records be available for that person. But for a two-person household, it was necessary to have historical earnings for both persons in the household if both had been in the labor force for a significant length of time. The HRS obtained such data for 1,625 single-person households and for 2,751 two-person households, together comprising 4,376 of the 7,607 HRS households.

Two related sample adjustments were made. First, we retained households in which one or both members reported never having worked, even if the household member was missing a Social Security earnings record. We assumed zero earnings for such persons. Second, we excluded from the sample all households that included any member who had zero Social Security earnings *and* reported working for any level of government for five (not necessarily consecutive) years. This latter restriction is intended to exclude households that have zero Social Security earnings due to gaps in Social Security coverage. The final sample includes 3,992 households.

Wealth

Total wealth is comprised of the following broad categories.

> *Financial Assets:* stocks, mutual funds, investment trusts, checking or saving account balances, money market funds, CDs, government saving bonds, treasury bills, bonds, bond funds, and other savings or assets, less unsecured debt.
>
> *Personal Retirement Assets:* IRA, Keogh, and 401(k) balances.
>
> *Firm Pension Assets:* defined contribution plan balances (other than 401(k)) and the present value of promised defined benefit plan benefits. (See the following for details.)
>
> *Net Vehicle Equity*
>
> *Net Business Equity*
>
> *Real Estate:* real estate other than main home, net of debt
>
> *Home Equity:* value of primary residence less outstanding balances on all mortgages, home equity loans, and lines of credit used.

Pension Wealth

Imputation of Key Missing Data

It is particularly difficult to produce a measure of pension wealth for this sample.[10] Many respondents were missing key pieces of data needed to construct pension wealth. For some types of pensions less than half of the respondents provided data complete enough to directly calculate pension wealth. Here is a brief overview of the procedures used to impute these missing data.

In the HRS, the information required to construct pension wealth comes from three sources: the pension on the current job for persons still working, the pension on the last job for persons no longer working, and pension income by source for persons receiving benefits.[11]

All currently employed workers were asked if they were "included" in a pension plan "through your work" (if self-employed) or if they were "included" in a pension plan "sponsored by your employer or union" (if not self-employed).

Each respondent could list up to three plans. About 76 percent of the respondents listed a single plan, 21 percent listed two plans, and the remaining 3 percent of the respondents listed three plans. Respondents were most likely to cite a defined benefit (DB) plan as their first plan. Of the first plans reported, 61 percent were DB and 34 percent were defined contribution (DC) plans. Of the second plans reported, only 16 percent were DB; 81 percent were DC. Most of the third plans reported were DC.

For each of the three plans, if the reported plan type was DB "both," or "don't know," then the respondent was first asked the expected age of retirement, then asked to give an estimate of the pension benefit at retirement. The benefit could be expressed as a percentage of final salary or as an amount (in dollars) per unit of time (month, quarter, year, etc.), or as a lump sum at retirement. Most respondents (44 percent) gave an amount per unit of time, and we have converted these to annual pension benefits. For those providing a percent of final salary (15 percent) we have also computed an annual pension benefit using an assumed (see the following) annual rate of growth of earnings until the expected date of retirement. Still, there is a great deal of data missing; the remaining 41 percent of the plans require imputation. To impute pension benefits we first divide the sample by the number of plans (three could be listed), type of response (DB, DC, or both), and ten wage and salary earnings deciles. We then used a hotdeck imputation procedure using these ninety cells.[12]

If the reported plan type is "DC" or "both," then the survey asks for the balance accumulated in the plan. The difficulty caused by missing data, although still a problem, is not as severe as for DB plans: for 71 percent of DC plans an account balance is reported. If the plan type is DC then further details on the type of plan are asked. Responses to these detailed questions are used to categorize DC contributions as contributions to either "401(k) plans" or to "traditional DC plans." Our definition of "401(k) plans" broadly includes the HRS response categories "401(k)/403(b)/SRA," "thrift or savings," "tax shelter," "IRA/SEP," "SEPP," or any response combination that includes these (i.e., some respondents indicated that their plan was a combination of a 401(k) and a thrift plan). The category "traditional DC plans" covers the remaining types of DC plans, including ESOPs and money purchase plans. If a respondent indicated plan type "both," then no detailed questions about plan type were asked. For these plans the entire balance is assumed to be in a "traditional DC plan," thus perhaps underestimating 401(k) balances. For plans known to be DC, but for which the balance is unknown, the hotdeck imputation method is again used, based on plan number, plan type (traditional DC and 401(k)), and ten wage and salary earnings deciles.

Persons not currently employed are asked about their most recent job. As before, they can specify four pension types: DB, DC, both, and don't know (DK). However, each respondent could provide information on only one plan. In general, the follow-up questions parallel the questions asked for the current job discussed previously. We will only note the differences here. First, persons covered by DB plans are asked about expected future benefits, benefits currently being received, and benefits already distributed as a lump sum. We disregard all but the former because benefits currently received are picked up elsewhere in the survey (the income section, see the following) and benefits already paid out will show up as IRA balances if rolled over (and do not represent pension wealth if not). If the respondent is covered by a DC plan, the balance is only included if "left to accumulate" with the former employer. DC balances rolled over into an IRA, converted to an annuity, or withdrawn are not included. Finally, respondents who indicated coverage by "both" plan types were asked, "How much money was in your account when you left that employer?" The survey does not ask how much remains in the account as of the survey date. Based on the proportion of DC balances remaining with the employer to accumulate, we randomly include the balances of one-third of these respondents. Again, missing DB benefits and DC data are imputed by the hotdeck method described earlier. Unfortunately, there is no way to distinguish between 401(k) balances and traditional DC plan balances acquired on prior jobs. Thus all DC balances are assumed to be from traditional DC plans.

The final source of information on pension wealth is from income currently being received. We use income streams from pensions, annuities, and veterans' benefits. There is no way to distinguish between DC and DB sources, so we report these data as a separate category, "PV benefits," in tables 3 and 4.

Constructing Pension Wealth
For DC type pensions the reported balance is our measure of pension wealth. For persons expecting DB pension benefits and persons currently receiving pension income, we compute the present value of the benefit stream using the following assumptions. Mortality data are based on population averages by gender, age, and birth cohort provided by the Social Security Administration. See Mitchell, Olson, and Steinmeier 1996 for a discussion of these data. For discounting and earnings growth we use the "intermediate" interest rate assumptions used by the Social Security Administration (see Board of Trustees 1995). Public pensions are assumed to be fully indexed, again using the "intermediate" projections of the Social Security Administration (see Board of Trustees 1995). Private sector pension benefits are not indexed.

Respondents were asked to provide the expected pension benefit at their expected date of retirement. If benefits are not currently being received, they are assumed to commence at the expected age of retirement (the mean is sixty-two). The average age of HRS respondents is fifty-five. Thus for the typical HRS respondent, retirement benefits do not begin for another seven years. We have assumed that their responses to the expected pension benefit question are denominated in future (date of retirement) dollars. Moreover, we have assumed that the benefit amount is a single survivor benefit. Accordingly, we use individual survival probabilities in the computation of the present value. If instead we assumed the responses represented joint survivor benefits, calculated pension wealth would be somewhat higher.

We further assume that when respondents report expected pension benefits they do not anticipate separating from their employer prior to retirement. This assumption allows us to calculate the present value of retirement wealth conditional on continued years of service until retirement. The component of this wealth "earned" as of the survey date is this present value multiplied by the ratio of years of service at the survey date to years of service at the expected date of retirement. This adjustment is necessary to make the present value of DB benefits comparable to the accumulated balance in a DC plan at the date of the survey.

NOTES

This research was supported by the National Institute on Aging. We benefited from the comments of Matthew Eichner, Annamaria Lusardi, and Jim Poterba on an earlier draft of the essay. We are also grateful to the Unicon Research Corporation for providing a copy of their CPS Utilities data and software.

1. Although our work is distinguished by the data available to us, there are many related papers. See, for example, Smith 1980, Davies 1982, Kessler and Masson 1998, and Wolff 1987.

2. Friedman 1953 provides a more detailed discussion of the distinction between choice and chance and how they may affect the realized distribution of wealth.

3. These results are consistent with the findings of Smith (1995a, 1995b) although he does not consider lifetime earnings and more generally our approach is rather different from his. In the first analysis he finds that even after controlling for current income and other covariates, significant wealth disparities persist between racial and ethnic groups. In the second analysis Smith finds that "income explains a significant part, but certainly not all of wealth disparities that exist, especially among the poor."

4. Recently surveyed by Browning and Lusardi (1996).

5. See Juster and Suzman 1995 for a discussion of the structure and content of the HRS. Mitchell, Olson, and Steinmeier (1996) describe the attached Social Security earnings file.

6. Although formally created in 1978, 401(k)s were not used much until after 1981, when the Treasury Department issued clarifying regulations that made it possible for employers to establish these plans.

7. These calculations assume a constant rate of saving as a person ages.

8. The ratio of the CPS maximum to the Social Security maximum has ranged from a low of just under 2 in 1981 to a high of over 20 in 1964. In 1991 the CPS reported earnings up to a maximum of $200,000; the Social Security maximum was $53,400 in that year.

9. In the CPS data families in the lowest Social Security earnings decile are assumed to have been in the lowest earnings decile in all years. Thus in most years these families are assumed to be zero earners.

10. Our estimates of pension wealth are based on the respondent's report of the provisions of employer-sponsored pension plans. The HRS also conducted a survey of employers. Information from this latter survey is not used in this analysis.

11. There is also some information on pensions associated with previous jobs (other than the last job), but we judged these data to be too incomplete to use at this time.

12. About 9 percent of the DB plans were also missing the expected age of retirement. We use the modal response of age sixty-two in these cases.

REFERENCES

Attanasio, Orazio, James Banks, Costas Meghir, and Guglielmo Weber. 1995. "Humps and Bumps in Lifetime Consumption." ERSC working paper no. W95/14.

Board of Trustees of the Federal Old-Age and Survivors Insurance and Disability Insurance Trust Funds. 1995. Annual Report. U.S. Government Printing Office, Washington DC.

Browning, Martin, and Annamaria Lusardi. 1996. "Household Saving: Micro Theories and Macro Facts." *Journal of Economic Literature* 34:1797–1855.

Davies, James B. 1982. "The Relative Impact of Inheritance and Other Factors on Economic Inequality." *Quarterly Journal of Economics* 97:472–98.

Friedman, Milton. 1953. "Choice, Chance, and the Personal Distribution of Income." *Journal of Political Economy* 41:277–90.

Juster, F. Thomas, and James P. Smith. 1994. "Improving the Quality of Economic Data: Lessons from the HRS." July. Mimeograph.

Juster, F. Thomas, and Richard Suzman. 1995. "An Overview of the Health and Retirement Study." *Journal of Human Resources* 30:S7–56.

Kessler, Denis, and Andre Masson. 1988. *Modelling the Accumulation and Distribution of Wealth.* Oxford: Oxford University Press.

Mitchell, Olivia, Jan Olson, and Thomas Steinmeier. 1996. "Construction of the Earnings and Benefits File (EBF) for Use with the Health and Retirement Survey." NBER working paper no. 5707. August.

Samwick, Andrew A. 1996. "Discount Rate Heterogeneity and Social Security Reform." Paper presented at 9th Annual Inter-American Seminar on Economics, Buenos Aires, November.

Shefrin, Hersh M., and Richard H. Thaler. 1988. "The Behavioral Life-Cycle Hypothesis." *Economic Inquiry* 26:609–43.

Shoven, John B., and David A. Wise. 1998. "The Taxation of Pensions: A Shelter Can Become a Trap." NBER working paper no. 5815. In D. Wise, ed., *Frontiers in the Economics of Aging.* Chicago: University of Chicago Press.

Smith, James D. 1980. *Modeling the Distribution and Intergenerational Transmission of Wealth.* Chicago: University of Chicago Press.

Smith, James P. 1995a. "Racial and Ethnic Differences in Wealth in the Health and Retirement Study." *Journal of Human Resources* 30:S158–83.

———. 1995b. "Unequal Wealth and Incentive to Save." *Rand documented briefing.*

Venti, Steven F., and David A. Wise. 1990. "Have IRAs Increased U.S. Saving? Evidence from Consumer Expenditure Surveys." *Quarterly Journal of Economics* 105:661–89.

Wolff, Edward N. 1987. *International Comparisons of the Distribution of Household Wealth.* Oxford: Oxford University Press.

Inheritances and Bequests

James P. Smith

Important strides have been made in recent years in our understanding of the process of wealth accumulation (see Hurd 1990 for an excellent summary). Encouraged by improved data, theoretical models have focused on more fundamental hypotheses about why people save (Bernheim 1987; Deaton 1992). A good deal of the recent literature has attempted to test alternative theoretical models of asset accumulation, of which the life-cycle and bequest motives are the most prominent. While this literature has been growing very rapidly, many central questions remain unanswered. This essay will deal with one of them — the role of inheritances and bequests.

Data restrictions have severely limited our ability to provide informative tests about the role of bequests in shaping the existing extent of wealth inequality in the population as well as the relative importance of bequests as a motive for household savings. The transaction involved — an inheritance left after death — is an inherently difficult one to monitor and frequently escapes detection in traditional household surveys. Since the prospective donor has died, often following a long illness or an extended stay in a nursing home, many have long since attrited from the sample. Even if they were not attritors, the inheritance transaction may occur more than a year after the death of the last surviving spouse. Household surveys typically do not include any postdeath interviews with relatives.

Because of these difficulties, most empirical research on inheritances has relied instead principally on estate records (David and Menchik 1985). While valuable, estate data provide only a limited picture. Many inheritances are below the estate tax thresholds and so do not appear in official estate records.[1] High estate taxation also gives incentives to transfer financial resources to heirs in other ways. The possibility of fraud in reporting through estate records also can not be dismissed. Finally, estate data can only describe realizations for those who are already deceased and are inherently less informative about the role of bequests for younger cohorts.

This essay uses data on planned bequests and actual inheritances received from the recently fielded Health and Retirement Study (HRS) and Asset and Health Dynamics of the Oldest Old (AHEAD). Combined these two surveys span the mature and older ages in the life cycle that are most relevant for bequest behavior. The availability of this data offers another important option to help us understand why so many households have little intention of bequeathing any financial inheritance while so many other U.S. households leave so much.

Motives for Bequests

Outside the life-cycle approach, the savings motive that has received the most attention in the economics literature involves bequests (Abel 1983; Bernheim, Shleifer, and Summers 1985). The importance of bequests relative to life-cycle factors in accounting for aggregate household savings has been a source of considerable controversy. For example, Kotlikoff and Summers (1981) claim that 50–80 percent of personal wealth in the United States is bequeathed while Modigliani (1988) places that number around 20 percent. A number of possible motives for intergenerational bequests have received emphases in theoretical models, including altruistic caring for children, other relatives, or the community at large; strategic or gift exchange; and accidental or unintended bequests associated with the inherent uncertainty of life spans.

Altruistic bequests have received the most prominent attention in the work of Becker and his associates (see Becker 1981). The driving motive for financial transfers in the altruistic model is that parents care for their heirs (children, grandchildren, etc.). A central component of the Beckerian approach is that bequests may take the form of both human capital investments and/or financial transfers. With declining rates of return to human capital investments, families will initially specialize in these investments until their rate of return equals the interest rate. Only then does the family transfer financial resources through either inter-vivos transfers or bequests. The implication is that financial bequests will only begin at higher income levels (Becker 1981). This argument suggests that significant asset accumulation for the purpose of leaving bequests may only be operative at high income levels.

With strategic bequests (Bernheim, Shleifer, and Summers 1985; Cox 1987), transfers between the generations represent contingent payments that will be made, conditioned on the observed behavior of the other generation. For example, parents may use the prospect of future bequests to induce their children to provide assistance to them when they are old. This assistance can include companionship, visits from grandchildren, co-residence in a home, or financial support and time care for their parents if they become ill or infirm. If such services are not rendered, there is an implicit threat to reduce or even eliminate the future bequest.

The final bequest motive centers on uncertainty associated with the date of death (Yaari 1965). Individuals who are luckier than they had planned may be in the awkward situation of having completely depleted their assets with nothing left to live on. When the date of death is uncertain, people may accumulate more assets to protect against this contingency. Even without any explicit bequest motive, in this uncertain world, individuals who die early may have positive asset levels. We may label these remaining assets at death "bequests" although they may be better understood as precautionary savings.

Measurement — Sources of Data

This research relies on two surveys fielded by the Institute of Survey Research at the University of Michigan: the Health and Retirement Survey (HRS) and the Assets and Health Dynamics of the Oldest Old (AHEAD). These data sets have measures of either planned bequests or actual received inheritances. HRS is a national sample of 7,600 households (12,654 individuals) with at least one person in the household fifty-one to sixty-one years old. At baseline, an in-home face-to-face interview was conducted in fall 1992 and winter 1993. Given its focus on the pre-retirement years, the principal objective of HRS is to monitor economic transitions in work, income, and wealth, as well as changes in many dimensions of health status. The first follow-up of HRS respondents was fielded approximately two years after the baseline. The first two HRS waves are used in this research.

The companion survey — AHEAD — includes 6,052 households (8,204 individuals) with at least one person aged seventy and over in 1994. All sampled households with age-eligible respondents under age eighty were obtained from the HRS area probability screen. To guard against underrepresentation of the extremely disabled in a household screen, AHEAD added a supplemental sample of respondents aged eighty and above from the HCFA Medicare enrollment file in the same PSUs as the area probability screen. A baseline AHEAD interview was conducted using computer-assisted telephone techniques for those respondents aged seventy to seventy-nine while in-person interviews were used for respondents aged eighty and over. Given its older age span, AHEAD's objectives shift toward a key concern in its age group: the relationship between changes in physical and cognitive health in old age and dissavings and asset decline. In both HRS and AHEAD, blacks, Hispanics, and residents of Florida were oversampled at a rate of two to one. Baseline response rates were 82 percent in HRS and 81 percent in AHEAD. Only the baseline AHEAD survey was available for this research.

In addition to their information on bequests and inheritances, an important advantage of both surveys is that they all contain high-quality wealth modules (Smith 1995, 1997). In both HRS and AHEAD, a very comprehensive and detailed set of questions was asked to measure household wealth. In addition to housing equity, assets were separated into the following eleven categories: other real estate; vehicles; business equity; IRA or Keogh; stocks or mutual funds; checking, savings, or money market funds; CDs, government savings bonds or treasury bills; other bonds; other assets; and other debt.

Measurement — Measurement of Bequests and Inheritances

Clues about the relative importance of a bequest motive can be obtained either by looking backward at the value of inheritances received by the current generation or by looking forward at this generation's planned amount of bequests. Both HRS and AHEAD include subjective probability measures of planned bequests. For example, HRS respondents were asked during the baseline interview what importance they place on leaving an inheritance to their heirs. The possible responses ranged from very important to not important at all. A quiet different set of questions was used in AHEAD to uncover expectations about future financial inheritances. Each AHEAD respondent was asked a sequence of three questions, all of which relied on subjective probabilities. The first question involved ranking on a scale of 0 to 100 the probability that the respondent or spouse would leave a financial inheritance. With this scale, 0 indicates that there was no chance of any bequest while 100 implied that it was absolutely certain that they would leave an inheritance. The two follow-up questions used an identical scale for the probability that the inheritance would exceed $10,000 or $100,000 in value.[2] Each spouse was asked these questions independently so that within family comparisons are possible.

The second round of HRS switched to the AHEAD question format. The principal difference is that the initial HRS question probed the probability of leaving a bequest of at least $10,000 so that there exists no HRS counterpart to the AHEAD question on the probability of leaving any inheritance at all.[3] Using the same type of probability scale, HRS wave 2 also asked respondents the chances that they would receive an inheritance within the next ten years with a follow-up question on how large they anticipated that inheritance would be.

In household surveys, questions are asked and answers given, but the precise meaning of either is not always clear. Regarding bequests, respondents in both surveys were asked whether they and their spouse or partner would leave an inheritance above a certain threshold. While the survey intent and this wording would imply that assets left to one spouse after the death of the other spouse should not count as part of the inheritance, we can not be certain that all respondents understood this. Respondents were also told to include property and other valuable items as well as money so that the transfer of housing and other tangible assets would seem to be part of any inheritance. Respondents were not asked only to count transfers that were part of their estates. The frequency of "yes" responses implies that they probably understood this intent.

Even with these caveats, it is still not transparent how respondents interpret these probabilities scales. One interpretation is that these subjective probabilities measure preference intentions of what respondents want to bequeath. Another view is that these probabilities index respondents' expectations of what will actually occur. This may seem a subtle difference, but it gets to the heart of theoretical controversies about the very existence of a bequest motive. For example, respondents may know that their precautionary accumulations due to uncertain life may, in an expected value sense, result in positive assets at the time of their death that their heirs would receive. An expectations interpretation would view these answers as summaries of what respondents think will happen — a summary of the interactions of preferences, income, incentives, and other constraints. In this essay, while the term *intentions* is used to describe these scales, I am agnostic about which interpretation is appropriate.

In addition to these questions on planned bequests, HRS also contains information on the actual value of pass inheritances received. As part of the baseline interview, HRS respondents were asked whether they or their spouse had received inheritances or trusts, or other transfers totaling $10,000 or more from relatives, or $10,000 or more as a beneficiary of a life insurance settlement. They were also asked to report the date on which these inheritances or transfers were received. To value all transfers in the same units, all values were first placed into 1992 dollars. In addition, a 3 percent real rate of return was assumed so that all dollar values could be expressed in an equivalent 1992 unit. There were no questions in AHEAD about the value of inheritances received.

Tables 1 and 2 list the distribution of responses to the subjective probability of leaving a financial inheritance arrayed by gender, ethnicity, and race. Table 1 provides these probabilities for leaving any bequest at all (AHEAD only) while table 2 displays the subjective probabilities for the $10,000 and $100,000 thresholds. Large fractions of respondents in both surveys state that either there is no chance they will leave any inheritance or that, at best, the amount of any inheritance is likely to be small.[4] For example, about one-third of all AHEAD respondents claim that there is no chance of a bequest larger than $10,000, and almost half of them state that the odds of bequeathing at least that amount are at best 50–50. These odds are considerably larger in the HRS sample, where roughly only one in every six respondents reports no chance of a bequest greater than $10,000 and two-thirds of HRS respondents put the odds at greater than 50–50.

Not surprisingly, subjective probabilities decline significantly when we raise the bequest threshold to $100,000. The fraction of respondents who are absolutely certain that they will not leave an inheritance worth that amount is two-thirds in AHEAD and more than 40 percent in HRS. In contrast in both surveys, only one in five respondents is certain of bequeathing at least $100,000.

These large numbers of respondents who express little intention of leaving inheritances, especially of reasonably large amounts, is consistent with the common view that financial bequests are not particularly relevant for many U.S. households, whether these households are viewed as donors or as recipients. However, these numbers should not make us ignore the significant fraction of respondents who fully intend to leave financial bequests, often of a considerable amount. The fraction of

TABLE 1.   Probability of Leaving Any Inheritance (percentage distribution in AHEAD)

Probability	All	Male	Female	White	Black	Hispanic
0	27	19	31	23	52	62
1–49	12	10	13	12	13	4
50	14	12	15	14	9	7
51–99	14	17	13	15	9	6
100	33	42	28	36	18	21

middle-aged households (fifty-one to sixty-one years old in HRS) who say that they will bequeath a significant amount is not trivial. For example, only one in every six HRS respondents reports no chance of a bequest greater than $10,000, and about three-quarters assess the odds at 50–50 or better that they will leave at least $10,000.

Similarly, when the bequest threshold is raised to $100,000, one in five HRS respondents is certain of bequeathing at least $100,000, and 43 percent of them give at least even odds for that event. As demonstrated subsequently, these HRS numbers on planned bequests are high relative to what these households have received in financial inheritances from their parents but also relative to what older cohorts (AHEAD) say they intend to leave to their heirs. For example, when the same questions

TABLE 2.   Probability of Leaving an Inheritance of at Least $10,000 or $100,000

Probability	All	Male	Female	White	Black	Hispanic
			> $10,000			
A. AHEAD						
0	34	24	40	29	66	71
1–49	6	6	7	6	7	2
50	8	6	8	8	6	3
51–99	11	12	10	12	5	5
100	41	52	35	45	17	20
B. HRS						
0	16	13	19	13	35	40
1–49	7	7	8	7	9	8
50	10	9	11	10	11	10
51–99	20	20	20	21	14	12
100	46	52	42	49	31	30
			> $100,000			
A. AHEAD						
0	65	54	72	62	90	88
1–49	5	6	4	5	2	2
50	6	8	5	7	3	3
51–99	6	8	5	7	1	2
100	17	23	13	19	4	5
B. HRS						
0	43	37	48	39	66	67
1–49	15	16	14	15	13	10
50	10	10	9	10	6	6
51–99	13	14	12	14	6	7
100	20	23	17	22	9	11

were given to the AHEAD cohort (respondents at least seventy years old), only one in four said that the odds were at least even that an inheritance of at least $100,000 would be left. Such comparisons suggest that there may be important secular trends with the likelihood of receiving or giving financial inheritances rising across generations.

While the behavioral motives that underlie these bequest intentions certainly cannot be read from these responses, these data suggest that bequest motives may exist for a sizable proportion of the U.S. population. Moreover, the population who express bequest intentions are the same people who have been engaged in significant amounts of wealth accumulation.

Tables 1 and 2 also document sharp gender, race, and ethnic differences in the subjective probabilities of leaving bequests. In either survey, men report much higher probabilities of leaving financial inheritances than women do. To illustrate first with the HRS sample (households largely in their fifties), 52 percent of men compared to only 42 percent of women are certain that they will leave an inheritance that exceeds $10,000. The size of this gender disparity may actually grow with age since 35 percent of women compared to 52 percent of men in the AHEAD sample report certain prospects of bequests greater than $10,000.

There are many possible reasons for this gender difference in bequest intentions. First, there may be gender differences in reporting. To cite one example, some respondents may have misunderstood the question and counted as part of inheritances money left to last surviving spouse. Second, preferences for bequests may differ between the sexes. While most of the existing literature argues either for gender neutrality or that women favor their children more than men do (Thomas 1994), inheritances may be the exception to the rule. In many species, there is evidence of a strong male concern with preserving their genetic heritage.

Third, any attempt to isolate parental preferences must first provide adequate control for the quite different amounts of economic resources men and women sometimes possess. One reason for these disparate resources lies in the greater frequency of divorce and separation among women. The lower income and wealth associated with divorce and separation may impinge on a woman's ability to leave much when she dies. A better sample in which to discuss gender differences in bequest preferences involves only married couples, a subject to which we return subsequently.

Race and ethnic differences in bequest intentions are also large. Only three in every ten AHEAD white respondents gave a zero probability that they will leave an inheritance over $10,000 compared to more than two-thirds of the two minority households in that sample. Similarly, roughly nine in ten older minority households are absolutely certain that their bequest will not exceed $100,000, while one in five older white households are just as certain that it will be above that amount. These racial and ethnic differences in intended bequests are equally large in the HRS sample. A question that we will address later in our multivariate analysis is the extent to which such racial or ethnic differences simply reflect the much lower levels of household wealth and income of minority households.

Bequest Expectations of Married Households

An unusual aspect of these subjective probability questions on bequests is that the same questions were asked of both spouses in married families. In addition to any gender differences in how these questions are interpreted or how accurately they are answered, spouses may not agree about how many resources and in what form they should bequeath to their heirs. To provide some insight into this question, table 3 displays the joint distribution of responses in married families.[5]

While there exists considerable overlap in spouses' answers, the overlap is far from perfect. Because respondent answers are concentrated at the endpoints of these scales, the extent of gender similarity is adequately summarized by the fraction of cases in which husbands and wives both gave the same endpoint 0 or 100 response. For example, 46 percent of AHEAD spouses gave the same extreme endpoint response to the $10,000 compared to 34 percent of husbands and wives in HRS households. Similarly, 54 percent of AHEAD and 33 percent of HRS households gave the identical 0 or 100 response when the bequest threshold was raised to $100,000. This narrower gender difference in AHEAD could reflect either a convergence in spousal preferences with age or a reduction in uncertainty about what will happen as the time for bequest realizations grows nearer.

Although in most cases the discrepancy between spouses is not large, this is not always the case. When the husband states that he is certain that the family will leave an inheritance of $100,000, one in six of HRS wives and one in five of AHEAD wives state that there is a zero probability of such an event. These large discrepancies between spouses in their answers suggest the possibility of considerable measurement error in responses. Such measurement error is understandable if respondents have not as yet focused much on these matters. Some respondents may be unfamiliar or uncomfortable with the notion of probability scales, even to the point of confusing or switching the meaning of the endpoints. However, unless there exists a systematic gender bias in reporting, measurement error would not explain gender differences.

Even in married families, men still express a higher intention of leaving inheritances than women do. To clarify this point, table 4 reduces responses to a simple "yes" or "no." This reduction is accom-

TABLE 3. Percentage of Married Men and Women Who Expect to Leave an Inheritance

Men	Women					
	0	1–49	50	51–99	100	All
			> $10,000			
A. AHEAD						
0	13	1	2	2	3	21
1–49	2	1	1	1	1	6
50	1	1	2	1	1	7
51–99	1	1	2	4	5	14
100	4	3	3	9	33	53
All	22	8	9	17	44	
B. HRS						
0	5	1	1	1	2	11
1–49	2	1	1	1	2	6
50	1	1	1	2	3	9
51–99	2	2	3	6	8	21
100	3	3	5	11	29	53
All	13	8	11	22	45	
			> $100,000			
A. AHEAD						
0	42	2	2	2	2	49
1–49	4	1	1	1	0	7
50	3	1	2	2	2	9
51–99	4	1	1	2	3	11
100	5	1	2	4	12	24
All	57	7	8	10	18	
B. HRS						
0	24	4	2	2	2	35
1–49	7	4	2	2	1	16
50	3	2	1	2	2	10
51–99	3	2	2	4	4	15
100	4	3	3	5	9	24
All	41	15	10	14	19	

plished by assigning a yes to anyone with a probability higher than .5 and splitting the 50–50 responses between the yes's and no's.

In both surveys and among married families as well as among all respondents, men are more likely than women to report that the family will leave a financial inheritance above either threshold amount. For example, 39 percent of AHEAD husbands reply "yes" to leaving a financial inheritance in excess of $100,000 compared to about 32 percent of their wives. The magnitude of the gender discrepancy is smaller among married families (especially in AHEAD), suggesting that economic resources are one reason why these gender differences emerge. But the fact that a gender difference remains in married families indicates that differing marital statuses (and the quite different wealth accompanying them) are not sufficient to account for gender differences in bequests intentions.

Correlates of Bequest Preferences: Socioeconomic Status

What factors account for the enormous variation in expected bequests in these samples? A natural place to start is that the less well to do simply have less income or wealth to devote to bequests. We know that households save at quite different rates and that the poor save at much lower rates than the affluent. A partial explanation for higher savings rates among the wealthy may be that they are the only households engaged in significant asset accumulation to leave to their heirs. To depict the relation between economic status and intended bequests, tables 5 and 6 plot mean and median subjective bequest probabilities by deciles of household wealth and income. To complete this portrait, table 7 lists the fraction of individuals who assign a zero probability to a bequest event.

TABLE 4. Percentage Responding "Yes" to Bequest Questions

	Married Families		All Respondents	
	Men	Women	Men	Women
A. AHEAD				
$10,000	70	68	67	49
$100,000	39	32	35	20
B. HRS				
$10,000	77	72	76	67
$100,000	44	39	42	33

Bequest probabilities rise rapidly across either the income or wealth distribution. For example, the median household in the highest income or wealth decile in either survey is virtually certain that it will leave an inheritance of more than $100,000. In contrast, the median household in the lowest decile is just as certain that it will leave no inheritance at all.

These sharp bequest–socioeconomic status (SES) gradients are not surprising. First, within decile levels of income and especially wealth increase sharply in the upper third of these distributions, a reflection of the extreme positive skew to these distributions. Second, theoretical reasoning, as mentioned previously, indicates that intergenerational bequests take the form of human capital investments as well as financial transfers. With declining rates of return to human capital investments, families initially specialize in these investments in their children so that financial bequests will only appear at higher income levels (Becker 1981).

While there is a quite systematic positive relation of expected be-

TABLE 5.   Mean Expectations of Leaving an Inheritance by Economic Deciles

Deciles: Highest to Lowest	Any Inheritance		> $10,000		> $100,000	
	Income	Wealth	Income	Wealth	Income	Wealth
A. AHEAD						
10th	83	85	88	90	67	75
9th	73	77	79	83	49	56
8th	67	72	71	77	35	44
7th	62	65	67	71	29	34
6th	55	63	57	65	19	18
5th	51	53	52	56	18	10
4th	45	43	42	40	13	7
3rd	39	34	37	30	7	5
2nd	26	18	20	13	4	2
1st	18	8	14	4	3	1
B. HRS						
10th	NA	NA	90	92	74	78
9th	NA	NA	85	87	59	66
8th	NA	NA	81	85	49	57
7th	NA	NA	79	81	45	49
6th	NA	NA	74	78	37	41
5th	NA	NA	72	72	33	30
4th	NA	NA	64	67	27	22
3rd	NA	NA	60	56	24	14
2nd	NA	NA	49	46	16	11
1st	NA	NA	37	25	12	7

quests across all dimensions of SES, there also exists considerable heterogeneity in these intentions, even among households with similar
amounts of economic resources. For example, while most households in
the top wealth decile state that they will leave large bequests, among
those in the top wealth decile, one in twenty AHEAD households is
absolutely certain that it will not leave an inheritance that exceeds only
$10,000. Similarly, among those in the median wealth decile, 41 percent
of HRS households state that there is no chance at all of bequeathing
$100,000 while 11 percent of those households in the same decile say
that it is certain that they will do so. Some of this heterogeneity is due to
measurement error in these subjective probabilities. But some of this
variation is no doubt real and parallels the extreme variation in savings
behavior in the population. While economic resources are likely to be an
important reason why households differ in their bequest behaviors, variation among similarly situated households in intended bequests may be
large.

TABLE 6.   Median Expectations of Leaving an Inheritance by Economic Deciles

Deciles: Highest to Lowest	Any Inheritance		> $10,000		> $100,000	
	Income	Wealth	Income	Wealth	Income	Wealth
A. AHEAD						
10th	100	100	100	100	97	100
9th	90	95	100	100	50	50
8th	80	90	100	100	0	0
7th	75	75	90	100	0	0
6th	50	75	75	90	0	0
5th	50	50	50	50	0	0
4th	50	40	20	20	0	0
3rd	20	15	0	0	0	0
2nd	0	0	0	0	0	0
1st	0	0	0	0	0	0
B. HRS						
10th	NA	NA	100	100	93	100
9th	NA	NA	100	100	75	80
8th	NA	NA	100	100	50	60
7th	NA	NA	100	100	50	50
6th	NA	NA	90	98	20	30
5th	NA	NA	90	90	10	10
4th	NA	NA	80	80	0	0
3rd	NA	NA	75	60	0	0
2nd	NA	NA	50	50	0	0
1st	NA	NA	5	0	0	0

Correlates of Bequest Preferences: Health and Bequests

One factor that has received little emphasis in economic modeling of bequests involves the health of respondents. Table 8, which arrays mean and median subjective bequest probabilities by the self-reported current health of respondents, documents that differences in planned bequests by health status can be enormous. For example, more than half of the AHEAD respondents in poor health report that they are absolutely certain that they will not leave an inheritance larger than $10,000. At the same time, more than half of households in excellent health in the same survey are absolutely certain that they will leave such an inheritance. An almost identical pattern describes the bequest-health relation among the younger HRS respondents.

Health may be associated with bequests for many reasons. First, a nontrivial portion of current wealth (from which the future bequest emanates) may be a consequence of current and past health conditions of

TABLE 7. Fraction of Respondents with Zero Subjective Probabilities

Deciles: Highest to Lowest	Any Inheritance		> $10,000		> $100,000	
	Income	Wealth	Income	Wealth	Income	Wealth
A. AHEAD						
10th	5	4	5	5	18	12
9th	8	6	10	8	33	23
8th	11	7	14	8	44	33
7th	11	10	16	13	47	44
6th	17	13	24	17	57	55
5th	21	17	26	22	55	64
4th	26	22	32	32	59	66
3rd	30	32	38	42	66	70
2nd	41	48	47	58	61	72
1st	47	57	54	61	65	66
B. HRS						
10th	NA	NA	2	1	8	7
9th	NA	NA	4	4	17	13
8th	NA	NA	6	4	23	18
7th	NA	NA	7	4	29	25
6th	NA	NA	9	7	37	32
5th	NA	NA	10	10	41	41
4th	NA	NA	16	14	50	53
3rd	NA	NA	20	22	55	63
2nd	NA	NA	32	30	64	69
1st	NA	NA	45	55	74	77

household members (Smith and Kington 1997). Poor health could deplete wealth through several mechanisms. Individuals in poorer health are less able to work, and if they do work, they typically will work fewer hours. This work effect directly reduces income and savings and eventually the ability to bequeath.

Even among people with the same current household wealth, health status may be associated with the prospects and amount of future bequests. Especially within the age range in the HRS sample, poorer health may still reduce current and future period labor supply, earnings, and savings. Controlling for current wealth, this adjustment through labor supply and earnings is less relevant for respondents in the AHEAD sample. In either sample, households with a person in poor health face

TABLE 8. Expectations of Leaving an Inheritance by Health Status

	Any Inheritance	At Least $10,000	At Least $100,000
A. Means			
AHEAD			
Excellent	65	69	39
Very good	63	65	34
Good	54	54	26
Fair	46	47	17
Poor	36	35	13
HRS			
Excellent	NA	80	39
Very good	NA	75	34
Good	NA	66	26
Fair	NA	52	17
Poor	NA	40	13
B. Medians			
AHEAD			
Excellent	90	100	2
Very good	75	95	0
Good	50	70	0
Fair	50	50	0
Poor	5	0	0
HRS			
Excellent	NA	100	50
Very good	NA	99	30
Good	NA	80	10
Fair	NA	50	0
Poor	NA	10	0

higher current and future medical expenses that may deplete their ability to save. Counteracting this effect, current poor health may lower life expectancy, which would tend to leave larger resources available for heirs. Health may also affect the marginal utility of consumption. If the marginal utility of consumption increases with health, then individuals will want to consume more in periods when they are healthier (Lillard and Weiss 1997).

Inheritances Received

Since they link generations, inheritances received and desired bequests represent a continuum and may exhibit similar patterns. In addition to questions about future bequests, HRS also contains information on the actual value of passed inheritances received. HRS respondents were asked in the baseline interview whether they or their spouse had received inheritances, trusts, or other transfers totaling $10,000 or more from relatives or $10,000 or more as a beneficiary of a life insurance settlement. They were also asked the date on which these inheritances or transfers were received.[6]

Table 9 lists HRS prevalence rates of these inheritances alongside the mean and median value among recipients. When households are viewed in their role as recipients, inheritances have not yet been of much consequence for most HRS households. The typical HRS household reports no financial inheritances in any form, although some have received a great deal. Only 30 percent of households in their fifties received any financial inheritance with a mean transfer of $44,000 across all households and almost $150,000 among recipients. Only 3 (1) percent of all HRS households were given inheritances worth more than $292,000 ($625,000). While almost one in three white households reports a financial inheritance, only 10 percent of minority households have received any inheritances. The amounts of these inheritances are quite unevenly

TABLE 9. Value of Inheritances Received

	Percentage Receiving	Recipient	
		Mean	Median
White	34	148,578	58,839
Black	11	85,598	42,478
Hispanic	10	105,707	43,917
All	30	144,517	57,451

distributed. Among recipients, the mean inheritance is close to $150,000, three times its median level.

These low levels of inheritances imply that the large amount of wealth inequality among HRS households is primarily not a consequence of financial wealth being transmitted across generations with the poor unable to give and the well to do insuring that their heirs remain at the top through financial inheritances. To indicate this more concretely, table 10 shows the extent of wealth inequality if we subtract out that part of current wealth that flowed from past financial inheritances.

While the two columns in table 10 are certainly not identical, our perception of the extent of wealth inequality is largely the same when the direct effects of financial inheritances are removed. If wealth dispersion is not due to financial inheritances, then all we have left are persistent interpersonal differences in rates of return and people saving at different rates from their incomes.

The information available on intended bequests and inheritances actually received can be examined together. Using once again for simplicity of exposition the same simple separation of responses into yes or no used in table 4, table 11 compares HRS and AHEAD respondents. Given the roughly twenty-five-year difference in ages in the two samples, the AHEAD respondents can be thought of as representing the parents

TABLE 10. Effect of Inheritances on Household Wealth

	HRS Household Wealth	HRS Household Wealth Inheritances
95	843,598	780,641
90	504,278	469,378
70	193,152	179,143
50	97,506	89,739
30	39,563	33,919
20	16,352	10,969
10	923	923

Source: Smith 1995.

TABLE 11. Secular Trends in Bequest Intentions and Receipts

	Yes to Expected Bequest		Received Inheritance
	$10,000	$100,000	
AHEAD	56	26	NA
HRS	71	38	30

of the HRS respondents. With this generation lag, the expectations of bequests have risen about 50 percent. This will certainly understate the secular growth in bequests as the AHEAD sample represents only the survivors from their generations. Since mortality is strongly correlated with wealth, average bequest intentions in AHEAD overstate the prevalence of bequests for those over age seventy. This bias also appears when we compare bequest intentions in AHEAD with the actual receipts in HRS, which are only 30 percent. While some of this difference reflects understandable discrepancies between givers and receivers, the AHEAD prevalence rates are too high (because of mortality selection). The HRS prevalence rates on receipts are also too low since the process is not over and many of these HRS respondents will receive inheritances in the future. Respondents were asked in wave 2 whether they had received any inheritances between the waves and whether they anticipated that they would receive an inheritance over the next ten years. If these responses are added to baseline inheritances already received 42 percent of HRS respondents will eventually receive inheritances.

Multivariate Models of Bequests

In this section, data descriptive models of respondents' subjective probabilities of leaving bequests are summarized. Using both HRS and AHEAD, the two subjective probability scales estimated are the probability of leaving a bequest in excess of $10,000 and $100,000. Because these subjective scales are bounded by 0 and 100 with many observations at the endpoints, the models were estimated by a two-limit Tobit model. The empirical models include a number of generic variables that correspond to the preceding theoretical discussion: birth cohort, the number of heirs, health status, level of economic resources, medical costs, and retirement income replacement rates. Table 12 presents our estimates for the probability of leaving an inheritance greater than $10,000 while table 13 lists estimates obtained when the inheritance threshold was raised to $100,000.

All models include a set of categorical variables indexing birth cohort of respondents. As with any cross-sectional survey, stratifying sample respondents based on their cohort (age) lends itself to both life-cycle and across-cohort interpretations. On the one hand, bequests should be generally higher among younger cohorts who will have higher levels of lifetime economic resources.[7] The pure aging or life-cycle effect is more difficult to predict a priori. First, there is a question of the impact of mortality selection. Especially in AHEAD, as age increases, the survey samples only the more relatively robust, healthy, and wealthy survivors of the original birth cohort. In fact, one reason for their later than normal demise is that these respondents may be more forward looking in many aspects of their lives. Consequently, the sample of survivors that appears in AHEAD may be more likely to have an operative bequest motive, imparting a positive age gradient to these subjective probabilities. The impact of this mortality selection bias is probably less severe among those in the HRS sample age range.

A more subtle question is what happens to the likelihood of a bequest as a person ages. As respondents become older and closer to the point at which such decisions must be finalized, they may think about bequests more seriously, and their plans may become less vague. The direct implication of this lower uncertainty is that the fraction of endpoint responses (e.g., respondents certain one way or the other) may increase with age. Older respondents with less time left may have less need for precautionary savings due to uncertain life. Consequently, a larger fraction of their remaining wealth may be slotted for bequests.

The birth cohort dummies in these models indicate an asymmetric relation of age to the subjective probabilities of leaving inheritances. In the HRS age range, intentions to leave inheritances are somewhat stronger among more recent cohorts (younger sample members). In contrast, there exists a strong positive age gradient in the AHEAD sample with older individuals reporting higher probabilities of leaving inheritances. Since bequest intentions are much higher in HRS than in AHEAD,[8] the evidence of a secular drift toward more inheritances is powerful. The estimated pattern of cohort dummies within the HRS sample is also evidence of rising prevalence rates for leaving bequests over time. In contrast, the cohort gradient estimated in AHEAD may be strongly influenced by mortality selection as the older sampled survivors are those with a stronger bequest motive compared to the original members of their birth cohort. In addition, a lower need for precautionary savings at very old ages implies that a larger fraction of wealth may be bequeathed.

The presence of children has been used in prior research to decipher the importance of a bequest motive (Hurd 1990). This argument begins with the premise that a bequest motive should be stronger for those with children compared to childless households. Using the original Retirement History Survey (RHS), Hurd (1987) provided such a test by comparing nonhousing wealth changes of retired individuals and couples with and without children. Hurd argues that if households with children have a stronger bequest motive, their wealth profiles should be flatter (e.g., they will dissave less) than households without children. Indeed, if

TABLE 12. Probability of Leaving Inheritance of at least $10,000 (two limit Tobits)

Variables	HRS Coefficient	t	AHEAD Coefficient	t
Birth Cohort				
Group 1[a]	5.62	2.78	−18.28	4.56
Group 2	6.00	2.56	−17.04	4.26
Group 3			−5.91	4.20
Number of Children				
1	13.43	2.68	.38	0.09
2	5.19	1.23	−1.71	0.47
3	—	—	−4.16	1.09
4	1.63	0.38	−12.25	2.36
5 or more	—	—	−12.12	2.93
Education				
12–15	15.59	6.86	7.59	3.00
16 or more	23.82	7.53	15.81	4.03
Professional or Ph.D.			0.12	0.12
Spouse 12–15	3.21	1.30	0.43	0.12
Spouse 16 or more	3.13	1.40	6.65	1.29
Spouse professional or Ph.D.			26.16	1.69
Health				
Excellent	19.26	4.51	1.05	0.22
Very good	18.58	4.55	5.86	1.38
Good	14.97	3.75	−0.47	0.12
Fair	5.25	1.24	3.11	0.76
Poor				
Spouse's Health				
Excellent	0.34	0.08	8.39	1.40
Very good	−4.53	1.09	−0.19	0.04
Good	−4.53	0.99	−0.40	0.08
Fair	8.37	1.89	4.56	0.91
Poor				
Economic Resources				
Income				
1st tercile	.00144	7.80	.00475	7.33
2nd tercile	.00062	5.36	.00158	5.23
3rd tercile	.00004	0.11	.00007	1.66
Wealth				
1st tercile	.00040	9.15	.00160	18.17
2nd tercile	.00036	15.60	.00027	8.75
3rd tercile	.00002	6.64	.00002	3.92
Expect to live 75	1.067	3.35	.1870	5.35

TABLE 12. (*cont.*)

Variables	HRS		AHEAD	
	Coefficient	*t*	Coefficient	*t*
Demographic Variables				
Black	−10.83	3.73	−8.72	2.17
Hispanic	−11.53	3.00	−8.31	1.36
Female	−15.24	8.43	−18.24	7.62
Divorced	11.43	2.40	17.51	2.79
Separated	4.14	0.56	—	—
Widowed	8.29	1.55	26.54	5.72
Never married	−3.80	0.55	10.83	1.41
Partner	−13.19	2.07	11.32	0.92
Nursing home costs			−.0017	2.09
Own medical costs	−.00022	0.96	.0018	2.91
Probability of nursing home			−.0335	0.68
Medical costs use up savings	−.2578	6.75		
Total medical costs	−.00005	1.55		
Length of Horizon				
1 year	1.24	0.36		
1–5 years	2.37	0.91		
5–10 years	4.41	1.64		
> 10 years	6.95	1.92		
Pension replacement rate	7.77	4.60		
Social Security replacement rate	1.27	2.61		
Constant	−28.88	4.40	−72.44	7.46

[a]Birth cohort groups are (1) 1938–, (2) 1935–37 in HRS; and (1) 1919–23, (2) 1914–18, and (3) 1909–23 in AHEAD. In both surveys, the left out group is the oldest cohort.

the stronger assumption is made that childless couples have no bequest motive, Hurd's comparison provides a test of whether there exists an operative bequest motive at all. Based on a series of tests using the RHS, Hurd could not find any statistically significant difference in wealth profiles of households stratified by whether or not they had children.

Our models provide similar contrasts using the subjective probability scales in HRS and AHEAD. The results obtained are quite different in the two samples. For respondents in the HRS age range, the presence of children is associated with a greater expressed intent to bequeath an inheritance above either threshold. However, this intent weakens as the number of children born increases. In contrast, bequest motives in the AHEAD sample appear similar between households with a few children or none at all, but large family sizes lower the expectation of leaving an inheritance in the AHEAD sample.

TABLE 13. Probability of Leaving Inheritance of at Least $100,000

Variables	HRS Coefficient	t	AHEAD Coefficient	t
Birth Cohort				
Group 1[a]	10.08	4.79	−33.09	3.79
Group 2	8.49	3.50	−25.79	2.94
Group 3			−7.12	0.78
Number of Children				
1	15.90	3.03	0.97	.01
2	10.29	2.31	4.32	.60
3	—	—	−1.34	.59
4	1.63	0.38	−7.67	0.88
5 or more	—	—	−19.23	2.15
Education				
12–15	15.17	6.04	16.86	3.10
16 or more	29.15	8.00	41.22	5.64
Spouse 12–15	4.90	1.85	−3.76	0.54
Spouse 16 or more	9.99	2.88	3.26	0.36
Health				
Excellent	18.59	3.75	3.58	0.34
Very good	15.79	3.28	6.79	0.71
Good	11.64	2.45	4.11	0.44
Fair	1.00	0.19	−.16	0.02
Spouse's Health				
Excellent	−2.81	0.56	3.35	0.30
Very good	−3.19	0.71	−14.95	1.48
Good	−3.91	0.86	−7.15	0.73
Fair	1.07	0.23	−20.05	1.93
Economic Resources				
Income				
1st tercile	.00091	4.18	.00747	4.27
2nd tercile	.00106	8.80	.00483	7.14
3rd tercile	.00005	1.75	.00009	2.27
Wealth				
1st tercile	.00015	2.57	.00116	4.56
2nd tercile	.00065	26.63	.00135	19.03
3rd tercile	.00004	12.08	.00006	4.56
Expect to live 75	1.068	3.14	.4814	6.65
Demographic Variables				
Black	−7.47	2.25	−23.54	2.19
Hispanic	1.66	0.38	1.78	0.12
Female	−17.94	9.67	−24.09	7.04
Divorced	12.40	2.32	8.18	0.57
Separated	10.26	1.19	—	—

TABLE 13. (*cont.*)

Variables	HRS		AHEAD	
	Coefficient	*t*	Coefficient	*t*
Demographic Variables (*cont.*)				
Widowed	8.99	1.48	25.32	2.60
Never married	13.48	1.79	23.33	1.47
Partner	−12.33	1.41	−26.14	1.06
Nursing home costs			−.0021	1.99
Own Medical Costs	−.00008	0.29	.0029	2.91
Probability of nursing home			.3180	3.07
Medical costs use up savings	−.6534	7.43		
Total medical costs	−.00004	1.17		
Length of Horizon				
1 year	−7.82	2.09		
1–5 years	0.45	0.16		
5–10 years	0.20	0.07		
> 10 years	5.69	1.54		
Pension replacement rate	2.39	1.70		
Social Security replacement rate	−0.91	0.88		
Constant	−111.26	13.09	−287.16	11.15

[a]Birth cohort groups are (1) 1938–, (2) 1935–37 in HRS; and (1) 1919–23, (2) 1914–18, and (3) 1909–23 in AHEAD. In both surveys, the left out group is the oldest cohort.

One question that has motivated the inclusion of children in bequests models is whether comparisons between childless couples and those with children can be used to deduce whether there is an operative bequest motive. The absence of quantitatively strong effects of children in models such as those summarized in tables 12 and 13 has led some researchers to conclude that there is not. Table 14 takes a closer look at this issue by listing mean subjective probabilities of leaving bequests by whether children exist within selected wealth deciles. Similar to the results obtained from the multivariate models, there are no large difference between those with and without children. However, what is striking about table 14 is not the absence of this difference but the strong intent to leave bequests among childless households. It would appear that childless households can not be assumed to have little bequest motive. Instead, they may simply leave their bequests to others: charities; nieces, nephews, or other relatives; and institutions and causes that they favor. This result turns the original question on its head by asking why childless individuals plan on leaving so many bequests.

Still, it seems puzzling, even allowing that childless households have bequest motives, that this motive appears as strong as the bequest intention in households with children. Some resolution of this puzzle may flow from recognizing that financial transfers through inheritances are only part of the total intergenerational transfer. In particular, human capital transfers such as the education of children can be substantial. For many families, human capital is by far the dominant form of transfer to their children. Since childless couples have little margin for such human capital transfers, our result that childless households and households with children plan similar amounts of financial transfers is consistent with much larger total intergenerational transfers among households with children. The negative effect of very large numbers of children especially in the AHEAD sample may indicate that the total amount of human capital transfers in these large families leaves little room remaining for financial transfers.

There exists a strong gradient of these planned bequests with all alternative SES measures. In all samples, college graduates plan to leave more than high school graduates, who in turn have bequests intentions that exceed those of individuals who did not graduate from high school. Similarly, the intent to bequeath typically rises with either household income or wealth, albeit in a highly nonlinear fashion. The income and wealth estimates in these tables are obtained from linear splines with nodes at terciles of income and wealth. Paralleling the patterns described in the descriptive cross-tabulations earlier, estimated income and wealth coefficients decay quickly as we move up the SES scale. For example, the estimated slopes of planned bequests are thirty times smaller in the upper third of the income distribution compared to the lower third.

In addition to variables measuring current income and wealth, two additional SES variables are included in the HRS model. These variables measure the fraction of current household income that will eventu-

TABLE 14.   Mean Expectations of Leaving Inheritance by Wealth Decile

Wealth Decile	$10,000		$100,000	
	No Children	Children	No Children	Children
1	18	27	3	7
3	55	56	15	14
5	69	72	23	30
7	77	81	40	50
9	88	87	61	67

ally be replaced with two types of annuities — pensions and social security.[9] Presumably, the larger the fraction of current income that will be replaced by annuities, the less the household has to use its assets to finance retirement consumption. Consequently, high replacement rates should be positively associated with intended bequests.

The empirical estimates in tables 12 and 13 support this interpretation. At the low $10,000 threshold, both pension and social security income substitute in favor of higher intended inheritances. Given the progressivity of social security benefit structure, social security annuities are unimportant when the threshold is raised to $100,000. Even at this relatively high inheritance threshold, a higher level of pensions annuities relative to current income still encourages bequests.

Even after controlling for the other covariates in these models, there remain quantitatively large and statistically significant demographic differences in planned bequests. In particular, black respondents are much less likely to plan on a bequest of any amount even after accounting for their current level of economic resources.

A persistent result from all models is that women are far less likely than men to report that they anticipate leaving inheritances. This finding is particularly intriguing since it also exists when the model is estimated only over married spouse present households. Since a couple typically jointly leaves bequests, at first blush, one would think that this relationship should be symmetric.

There are many reasons for this anomaly, many of which rely on the fact that the husband's death typically precedes his wife's. When answering this question, men may be including the wife's recipiency of assets at the time of the husband's death as a bequest even though the intent of the question was clearly otherwise. Second, men may have a lower estimate (relative to their wives) of the yearly consumption flow and health costs expenditures that their wives may incur in the years after their death. Given that men typically die first, assets at the time of the husband's death will eventually be divided between the remaining lifetime consumption of the wife and the amount of assets left for a legacy. While assets have been jointly accumulated by husbands and wives, men may see the financial worth of the family as more of a direct consequence of their past earnings. More so than their spouses, they may believe that their principal link to their heirs is a financial one.

Finally, men are known to be more knowledgeable about household assets. Their inferior knowledge may lead women to systematically understate household wealth, especially if its true size has not been fully revealed by their husbands. Whatever the reasons for this gender discrepancy, the question remains, which partner is a more accurate predictor of what the actual level of inheritances will eventually be?

In simple one-way comparisons, current health status was strongly correlated with bequests intentions in both surveys. When the complete set of covariates is included in these models, however, current health remains a significant correlate of intended bequests only in the HRS sample. Among individuals in their fifties, those in excellent health plan on significantly higher bequests to their heirs than do those respondents whose current health is not as good. However, this strong relationship actually disappears by the time respondents are over age seventy. This sharp difference between the two samples may indicate that the health through earnings mechanism may be a central pathway underlying this relationship. In the age span covered by the HRS sample (e.g., respondents in their fifties), poorer health reduces future labor supply and earnings, lowering the resources available for inheritances. This causal pathway is much less relevant in the AHEAD age range.

The models in tables 12 and 13 experimented with a number of health cost variables obtaining quite mixed results. Current out-of-pocket medical costs have no systematic effect on intended bequests. The principal health cost variable that has a statistically significant effect on intended bequests is the subjective probability scale of whether medical expenses will use up all of one's family's saving during the next five years. These estimates imply that an increase in this subjective probability reduces planned bequests.

A persistent finding in all models is that a higher subjective probability of living to a future age actually increases intended bequests. Almost any standard life-cycle model would suggest the opposite. For any given amount of wealth, greater life expectancies imply longer periods over which assets will have to be used (and depleted) to order to sustain consumption. This longer period of depletion would then imply fewer remaining assets to bequeath. One possible explanation for the anomaly concerns the way respondents answer subjective probability questions. Those respondents who are optimists by nature may give high probabilities both to questions on life expectancy and on the probability of leaving bequests.

Conclusion

This essay examined intentions to leave bequests to heirs as well as the past receipt of financial inheritances from parents. The bequest intentions were derived from new subjective probability scales used in the

HRS and AHEAD surveys. While many people do not intend to bequeath, a significant and growing fraction of Americans appear to be accumulating assets in part to leave to their heirs.

Among other things, these bequests appear to be closely related to the health of respondents. Our results may indicate that health shocks and bequests may be close substitutes. Individuals may plan on leaving nontrivial sums to their heirs. However, if they experience episodes of poor health with high out-of-pocket expenses that often accompany those episodes, they use dollars that would have gone to their heirs instead of significantly lowering their own consumption.

NOTES

This essay was prepared for a conference in honor of Tom Juster held in Ann Arbor, Michigan, in December 1996. This research was supported by grants from the National Institute of Aging and the NICHD. Excellent programming assistance was supplied by Iva Maclennan and David Rumpel. Charles Brown and Michael Hurd provided many useful comments.

1. For example, Mulligan (1995) reports that only 5–10 percent of those who died past age forty-five file estate tax returns. The current threshold at which estate taxes start is $600,000 for an individual and can be as high as $1,200,000 for a married couple.

2. Respondents were not asked the second question on whether the amount would exceed $10,000 if they had previously said that the probability of leaving any inheritance was zero. Similarly, they were not asked the third question about the amount exceeding $100,000 if they either said that there was a zero chance of leaving any inheritance or a less than 31 percent chance of leaving more than $10,000.

3. Respondents who reported that there was a zero probability of leaving an inheritance of $10,000 or more were not asked the follow-up question on leaving an inheritance totaling $100,000 or more.

4. Apparently, a common characteristic of subjective probability questions is that responses tend to bunch at the 0, 50, and 100 values. This bunching is not unique to questions about inheritances. See Hurd and McGarry 1995.

5. Because the question on whether one will leave any inheritance was not asked in HRS, to conserve space the remaining tables in the essay are restricted to the two threshold questions about $10,000 or $100,000.

6. To value all transfers in the same units, within each category, all values were first put into 1992 dollars. In addition, a 3 percent real rate of return was assumed so that all values could be expressed in an equivalent 1992 unit.

7. While wealth is included in these models, the across-cohort argument in the text still applies. To illustrate with a concrete example, in tables 11 and 12,

we are comparing a fifty year old and a sixty year old with the same wealth. Given rising wealth with age over this age span, the fifty year old will have more wealth in ten years than the sixty year old has now.

8. The strong mortality bias in the AHEAD sample suggests that raw differences in intentions actually understate the extent of cohort drift toward more bequests among younger cohorts.

9. See Smith 1995 for a derivation.

REFERENCES

Abel, Andrew B. 1983. Bequests and Social Security with uncertain lifetimes. *American Economic Review* 75:777–91.

Becker, Gary S. 1981. *Treatise on the Family.* Cambridge, MA: Harvard University Press.

Bernheim, B. Douglas. 1987. The economic effects of social security: Toward a reconciliation of theory and measurement. *Journal of Public Economics* 33 (3): 273–304.

Bernheim, B. Douglas, Andrei Shleifer, and Lawrence H. Summers. 1985. The strategic bequest motive. *Journal of Political Economy* 93 (6): 1045–76.

Cox, Donald. 1987. Motives for private income transfers. *Journal of Political Economy* 95:508–46.

David, Martin, and Paul L. Menchik. 1985. The effect of Social Security on lifetime wealth accumulation and bequests. *Economica* 52:421–34.

Deaton, Angus. 1992. *Understanding Consumption.* Oxford, UK: Clarendon Press.

Hurd, Michael D. 1989. Mortality risk and bequests. *Econometrica* 57 (4): 779–813.

———. 1990. Research on the elderly: Economic status, retirement, and consumption and saving. *Journal of Economic Literature* 28:565–637.

Hurd, Michael D., and Kathleen McGarry. 1995. Evaluation of the subjective probabilities of survival in the health and retirement study. *Journal of Human Resources* 30 (supplement): S268–92.

Kotlikoff, Laurence J., and Lawrence H. Summers. 1981. The role of intergenerational transfer in aggregate capital accumulation. *Journal of Political Economy* 89 (4): 706–32.

Lillard, Lee, and Yoram Weiss. 1997. Uncertain health and survival: Effect on end-of-life consumption. *Journal of Business and Economic Statistics* 15, no. 2: 254–68.

Modigliani, Franco. 1988. Life cycle, individual thrift, and the wealth of nations. *American Economic Review* 76 (3): 297–313.

Mulligan, Casey B. 1995. Economic and biological approaches to inheritance: Some evidence. Working paper.

Smith, James P. 1995. Racial and ethnic differences in wealth. *Journal of Human Resources* 30:S158–83.

————. 1997. Wealth inequality among older Americans. *Journal of Gerontology* 52B (May): 74–81.

Smith, James P., and Raynard Kington. 1997. Demographic and economic correlates of health in old age. *Demography* (February): 159–70.

Thomas, Duncan. 1994. Like father, like son, or like mother, like daughter: Parental education and child health. *Journal of Human Resources* 29 (4): 950–89.

Yaari, Menahem E. 1965. Uncertain lifetime, life insurance, and the theory of the consumer. *Review of Economic Studies* 32:137–50.

Pension and Social Security Wealth in the Health and Retirement Study

Alan L. Gustman, Olivia S. Mitchell,
Andrew A. Samwick, and Thomas L. Steinmeier

The purpose of this essay is to evaluate the importance of pension and social security wealth in influencing the economic security of a cohort of people on the edge of retirement. The data set we analyze is the Health and Retirement Study (HRS), a nationally representative data set that carefully measures income and wealth for respondents who were ages fifty-one to sixty-one in 1992.[1] A contribution of this study is that we use matched employer-provided pension data to estimate the contribution of pensions to wealth and to income within the HRS sample. Estimates of social security wealth are also included, but they are based on self-reported earnings histories.

The analysis shows the overwhelming importance of pensions and social security in the wealth and income of the HRS population. After correcting for some imperfections in the data, the wealth equivalents of pensions and social security together amount to almost half of the wealth held by all households. Moreover, together pensions and social security account for well over 60 percent of total net wealth for households who are in the 45th to 55th percentile of net wealth holders. In addition, pension and social security accrual are found to account for about 9 percent of income, where income is not only measured conventionally to include earnings and returns to a variety of assets but also includes accrual of pension value and social security value. The study also includes the value of employer-provided health insurance in income and retiree health insurance in wealth. Thus our measure of income includes important elements of total compensation.

In our data, total net wealth exceeds ten times earnings. This finding suggests that households may be better prepared for retirement than some studies have suggested. For a single male, this implies that wealth accumulation to around age fifty-six may generate enough income in retirement to replace at least two-thirds of earnings, and for a couple, their wealth could be sufficient to replace at least half of earnings and probably more.[2]

For the HRS population, about half of the surveyed age-eligible population had a pension, and two-thirds of households are covered by a pension from a current or past job.[3] Pension wealth measured from employer-provided plan descriptions accounts for over a fifth of all household wealth and almost a fifth of the wealth of the median 10 percent of households.[4] As a share of total net wealth, pensions are just slightly less important than social security.

Pension wealth also proves to be quite unevenly distributed, accounting for 7 percent of wealth for those in the bottom quarter of wealth holders, 18 percent of wealth for the median 10 percent of households ordered by their wealth holding, and 31 percent of wealth for those in the 75th to 95th percentile of households arrayed by wealth. There are major differences in retirement wealth between households with and without pensions. Households with a pension average $573,090 in total net wealth, while those without a pension average $337,233.

As wide as these wealth differences are, they are narrower than the differences in income between those with and without pensions. If the differences in income are taken as a proxy for differences in lifetime wealth, these findings are in contrast to the findings in some other studies that nonpension, non-social-security wealth is positively correlated with pension coverage. They are consistent with the possibility that pension wealth is substituted for other forms of wealth.

Pension accrual, social security benefit accrual, and health insurance account for about 13 percent of income. Pension accrual rates are especially volatile for the Health and Retirement Study population. For workers covered by defined benefit plans, in the year before reaching early retirement age, pension accrual may be as important as earnings in total compensation.

The share of social security in total net wealth is only slightly greater than the share of pensions.[5] However, the effect of social security on the distribution of wealth is equalizing, while pension wealth is an increasing share of wealth as wealth rises. Moving up the wealth distribution, the share of total net wealth due to pensions increases as the share of total net wealth due to social security falls. Together, pensions and social security account for half or more of wealth for households in all but the top decile of the wealth distribution.

This study justifies all of the effort by Tom Juster and his colleagues to collect pension data in the Survey of Consumer Finances and pension and social security data in the Health and Retirement Study.[6] Our findings suggest that those who ignore pensions and social security when studying the income and wealth of the population do so at their peril.[7]

This essay relies for its estimates of pension wealth on employer-provided pension plan descriptions of defined benefit (DB) plans and defined contribution (DC) plans provided by the HRS.[8] Eventually, more accurate estimates of pension values will be obtained by combining the information from the employer-provided plan descriptions with information obtained from the respondents.[9] Until then, these first order estimates of pension values and other components of wealth provide a good indication of the size of assets and income from pensions, social security, and other components of income and wealth.[10]

The next section discusses preparation of the data. Estimates of the role of pension and social security wealth in the distribution of wealth, and of pension and social security accrual in the distribution of income, are reported for the HRS sample in the "Pensions and Other Sources of Income and Wealth" section. The following section analyzes incentives for retirement, again using employer-provided pension plan descriptions. The last section concludes the essay.

The Data

This section explores issues in the construction of the components of income and wealth for the respondents in the HRS.

Pensions

HRS respondents who reported that they had a pension in their current job were asked the name and address of their employer. The survey staff of the Institute for Social Research (ISR) then contacted these employers to try to obtain pension plan Summary Plan Descriptions (SPDs) (which are publicly available documents).[11] In cases where that did not work, a backup plan was used whereby the records at the Department of Labor were searched for the Summary Plan Descriptions. Of the 5,713 individuals in the HRS who indicated they were covered by a pension, this strategy resulted in plan descriptions being gathered for 3,834 individuals, or about 67 percent of those who indicated that they were covered. A program to evaluate these pensions under various sets of assumptions has been developed at the Institute for Social Research (ISR) and is being adapted for use on personal computers. Because the program is not complete, this essay uses a program for evaluating pensions developed by Gustman and Steinmeier (1989, 1998).

In valuing the defined benefit plans, we have cleaned isolated errors in the coded Summary Plan Descriptions.[12] We also have departed from some of the assumptions made by the coders and, in particular, have assumed in a number of cases that dollar amounts reported in the surveys will increase as wages grow. Other problems are not so obvious.[13] Some have to do with segments of the benefit formulas that cover different employment periods but then fall silent about benefits for employment into the future, when in fact they probably meant to apply the most recent formula to the future years. With regard to other problems, the answer may not be in the SPD. In some cases the error produces a plan that clearly has properties that are not feasible; for example, when a very sharp decline in plan value on becoming eligible for early retirement seems to be due to an obvious coding error or when the solution looks reasonably obvious but cannot be confirmed. In such cases, we have adopted a correction in the formula.

For defined benefit plans, the employer-provided plan descriptions make it possible to calculate benefit amounts relatively accurately. The asset value of the pension is simply the discounted value of these benefits to early retirement age, prorated on the basis of work to date. So if a person is fifty-seven, will qualify for early retirement at sixty-two, and has been with the firm for fifteen years, three-quarters of the pension wealth that will eventually be accumulated will have been accumulated based on work to date.[14] We prorate pension wealth to put it on equal footing with the other wealth reported, which represents savings to date. Otherwise to put other assets in the same time frame as pension wealth, if we used full pension wealth as of the date of retirement, we would have to project savings to that same date.[15]

For defined contribution plans, we also use the employer-provided pension formula to estimate the value of the pension. The total attributed to the defined contribution plan is the sum of employer contributions plus mandatory contributions made by the individual. For plans with mandatory contributions, the amounts of these contributions are used. When there are voluntary contributions, as in Samwick and Skinner 1998, the amounts in the defined contribution plans assume that individuals contribute up to a maximum of 5 percent whether or not there is matching. That is on top of any mandatory contribution. The firm does whatever the plan prescribes for a voluntary contribution of 5 percent on the part of the respondent. If the plan has a maximum contribution of less than 5 percent, the individual is assumed to contribute only the maximum amount. For the rare plans where the minimum contribution is above 5 percent, the individual is assumed not to contribute. Similar assumptions are adopted for 401(k), profit sharing, and other defined contribution plans.

In the case of old plans, that is, plans from previous jobs, we count an individual as covered by a pension where the individual indicates that he or she was included in the pension, but we exclude those who indicate they received a cash settlement when they left or lost their benefits. We have not counted any old plans where the individual is also covered by a pension on the current job. The older the plan the less likely that hot-decking from the SPD collected in 1992 will provide an accurate indication of the plan value. For this reason our estimates understate the value of pensions held on previous jobs.

The appendix indicates the match rates for employer-provided pensions by firm size and respondent reported plan type. When a pension match is not available for an individual who indicates pension coverage, we impute a plan to the individual. Imputations use a match of individuals based on occupation, industry, full-time/part-time status, government vs. private employment, and earnings level. Thus either a defined benefit or a defined contribution plan, or both, may be attributed to an individual without a matched pension, depending on which donor is chosen from a hot decked plan. In the case of old plans, we impute a pension plan from the list of current plans on the basis of the characteristics mentioned previously.

As will be seen subsequently in the "Incentives for Retirement" section, this approach to imputation is somewhat biased, but the bias is likely to be less than 4 percentage points of the pension values we estimate. The sample of pensions obtained from employers contains a higher fraction of DB plans than the fraction of DB plans reported by respondents. We have not reweighted the data to correct for the disproportionate representation of defined benefit plans.[16]

The analysis to follow also makes a number of descriptive calculations focusing on the role of pensions. We compare wealth for those with and without pensions and compute asset values, by family status, race, education, and union and veteran status.

In valuing the pension asset, there is a consideration that was first made prominent by Ippolito (1985). Should a defined benefit pension be valued as though the worker were going to leave the job today (the legal value), or should it be valued as the prorated share based on work to date of the value the pension would have if the worker were to stay until the date he or she expects to retire (the projected value)? The difference in these two values can be quite large. In previous work on the subject, we have calculated that for an average pension-covered individual, the difference can equal a year's worth of wages (Gustman and Steinmeier

1989, 66). Further, the question of whether to choose the legal or the projected value does not appear to have a determinate answer; rather, the answer depends on the purpose of the valuation. Subsequently we present distributions of wealth and income primarily using the projected value of the pension, but we also compare findings as to projected values with values obtained using the legal liability definition.

In addition to reporting computed values of pension wealth, it is also of interest to report pension accrual, the difference between the pension wealth computed at the beginning and end of the year, allowing for mortality in the intervening year. In this essay we equate pension accrual with pension income.

Assumptions Made in Calculating Pension Wealth

In computing pension wealth for those who are currently covered by a pension, we benchmark the benefit based on the worker's current annual earnings in 1992. We assume that wages in the future for each of these covered individuals increase with the overall growth of wages, but given the respondent's age, we do not add any premium for increasing tenure.[17] Job tenure is reported in the HRS.

For purposes of simulation we use a 4 percent cost of living increase, 5 percent nominal wage growth, and 6.3 percent nominal interest rate, the intermediate assumptions adopted by the Social Security Administration (SSA) (Board of Trustees 1995). Thus real wage growth is 1 percent, and the real interest rate is 2.3 percent, which also is the return assumed on assets invested in DC plans. The life table used is a projected life table from the Social Security actuaries used to analyze the funding status of social security under the intermediate funding assumptions (see Mitchell, Olson, and Steinmeier 1996).

Social Security

For the present study, we were not able to use the matched descriptions of social security covered earnings history and benefits that HRS has obtained from the Social Security Administration. This is because at the time we conducted our analysis, the Memorandum of Understanding currently in force betwen the HRS and the Social Security Administration prohibited using the social security earnings and benefit data together with the detailed pension plan descriptions. In particular, researchers were not allowed to calculate the present value of HRS respondents' pensions using the employer record and in the same computer file calculate the present value of the social security benefit based on the earnings record obtained from SSA and attribute that to the HRS respondent. This restriction was relaxed subsequently, but here we have chosen to use the employer-provided pension plan descriptions and to estimate social security wealth from the self-reported HRS respondent's earnings history. Also at the time we wrote this essay we did not have access to the detailed battery of questions included in wave 3 of the HRS that asks about covered earnings history. Therefore we used only the earnings reports from HRS respondents in wave 1 on their current job (section F), last job if not currently employed (section G), and previous job (section H). We also consider any other past jobs that were reported by the respondent because they offered a pension.

To estimate a respondent's covered earnings history, we assume that all males in the HRS worked in jobs covered by social security from the time of leaving school until the time that the first job reported to the HRS began. For single women, we assume that they also worked in jobs covered by social security since leaving school. For married women, however, we assume they were covered only for the length of the period they report working on their current job, last job, and any previous job reported. The anchor for projecting the wage is the latest wage reported in each job to the HRS.[18]

Previous analysis of the social security earnings records of HRS respondents shows that married men averaged a total of 125 covered quarters through 1991, married women averaged 72 covered quarters, nonmarried men averaged 115 covered quarters, and nonmarried women averaged 85 covered quarters (Mitchell, Olson, and Steinmeier 1996, table 1). Even though the procedure of matching only the years for which work is explicitly reported for married women will understate their covered work history, we do not expect this procedure to result in too large an error in the value of social security in married households. The reason is, in accordance with rules affecting dual beneficiaries, the wife is assumed in our algorithm to be eligible for half the benefit her husband is entitled to. Moreover, in most households, when the husband dies, the widow receives the benefit her husband was entitled to; even if she worked, the benefit she receives based on her husband's record is larger than that based on her own work history. In the case of unmarried women, we knew we would be overstating the value of social security benefits, and we expected also to overstate them for men, since men do suffer some interruption in their work history. In most cases this is likely to be mitigated when the average indexed monthly wage is calculated and only the high thirty-five years of indexed earnings are counted. As will be seen subsequently, the values of social security wealth calculated using respondents' reports of partial reported earnings histories and the assumption that men and single women worked fully from time of leaving school to beginning the earliest reported job on the survey overstate by about 13 percent the values obtained by Mitchell, Olson, and Steinmeier (1996) using Social Security Administration records.

The potential social security benefit amount is calculated using the rules in place after 1977, as applicable to the relevant cohort. Once the benefit amounts are calculated, the value of the asset stream is obtained by discounting the benefit amounts in different years, allowing for the intervening mortality. This is not quite as simple as it at first appears, since for a family we must calculate whether the spouses are better off taking benefits on their own accounts or as spouses, and survivor benefits must also be included in the asset values. Consistent with the social security rules, the spouse is credited with the highest benefit to which she is entitled.

When we calculate the accrual rate of social security, in contrast with the method used for pensions, we used a legal liability concept. Social security accrual is calculated by differencing social security wealth accumulated through the beginning vs. the end of the year, on the assumption that there would be no further covered work in the future. That is, the same method used in Mitchell, Olson, and Steinmeier 1996 is used here. By conforming with their methodology we can measure the error in our findings from having to use the constructed earnings histories rather than the SSA record of covered employment. That measurement error is discussed in the following.

The accrual rate we report is in the present value of social security benefits. We do not take account of social security taxes.

Health Insurance

The value of health insurance is a difficult concept to measure and so has frequently not been included in discussions of retiree income and wealth. Because the costs of health insurance have increased so much in recent years, and therefore the value of the insurance has risen so much, it is useful to investigate how the value of health insurance affects measures of the distributions of income and wealth.

With regard to income, it is clear that it is not the cost of the insurance that should be counted but rather the value of the employer's share of the cost. The employee's share of the cost is part of the employee's wage, and hence to count the entire cost of the insurance would be double counting the employee's share. For the purposes of this study, we build on work that the census has already done in the area of imputing the employers' share of health insurance costs. Beginning 1992, the census has included on the March Current Population Survey (CPS) a variable measuring the employers' share of health insurance costs. This variable is based on the National Medical Care Expenditure Survey (NMCES).[19]

To estimate the amount of the employers' contributions to health insurance for individuals in the HRS, we match individuals in the 1992 CPS with individuals with health insurance in the HRS on the basis of the variables described in step 2 of note 19. Contributions are reduced by about 70 percent to 30 percent (actually to 777/2,606) after the individual becomes eligible for Medicare (GAO 1989).

The employer's contribution to current health insurance should certainly be included as income, but should it be added to household assets? The answer is that unless a calculation of wealth is to include potential wealth from human capital, which our estimates of wealth do not, the contribution to current health insurance does not have any asset value, any more than the current wage has asset value. What does have asset value is the promise of the employer to contribute to the cost of health insurance after the individual retires (retiree health insurance). The calculation of the asset value of retiree health insurance is more complicated than the calculation of the income value of the employer's contribution to current health insurance, but the two calculations share many of the same features.

When a retiree reaches sixty-five, Medicare becomes the first payer for retirees. This means that employer contributions to health insurance go down, since they no longer have to cover what Medicare picks up. The GAO (1989) reports that employer contributions to retiree health insurance are only 30 percent as large for retirees over sixty-five years old as they are for retirees under sixty-five. The cost estimates for payments after sixty-five adjust for the reduction in benefit payments as employers pay only for medigap insurance.[20]

Having calculated the employer contributions to retiree health insurance, it is a relatively simple matter to take the present discounted value of the future contributions and arrive at an asset value for the commitment of the firm to maintain its contributions to the health insurance plan. For those employees who have not completed the age and/or service requirements for retiree health insurance but who will be eligible if they continue working, a similar ambiguity arises as for the pension plans. On a legal basis, the current value of the retiree health insurance asset is zero because retiree health insurance is not vested prior to retirement, and in many cases, not even after retirement. On a projected basis, the value is the value of the asset, prorated according to the percentage of the age and/or service requirement attained. In this latter case, there should also be an income amount imputed to be the increase in the value of the prospective retiree health insurance asset from working this year.

The income measure for employer-provided health insurance discussed subsequently includes an estimate of the increase in the present value of the retiree health benefit plus the current employer contribution toward health insurance in the current year. The wealth equivalent includes only the share of the present value of retiree health benefits accrued on the basis of work to date.

Financial Assets and Housing

Yet another advantage of using the HRS in this study is its high-quality information on financial assets. A typical survey question on assets is of the form, "If you sold all of your stocks and mutual funds and paid off anything you owed on them, how much would you have?" If appears that many respondents, when confronted with such a question, interpret the question as requiring a precise answer. Hence, they reply, "I don't know." For these "don't know" responses (and for the refusals as well), the HRS employed an "unfolding" technique. If the respondent answered that he or she didn't know the amount of assets, there was a follow-up question, "Would it amount to $25,000 or more?" If the respondent answered yes to this question, he or she received a second follow-up question, "Would it be $100,000?" If the answer to the first question was no, the second question was, "Would it be $5,000?" In principle, this unfolding could go on indefinitely, but as a practical matter no more than two unfolding questions were asked for any particular asset category, mostly to keep the interviews from becoming too long and to keep from annoying the respondents too much.[21]

The differences of the imputations (random assignments drawn from the valid data cases that fall into the same bracket) from those that would been made in the absence of the bracket data can only be described as enormous. Relative to valid cases, refusal households have triple the mean amount of business and farm equity, triple the amount of real estate equity, about fifty percent larger IRS or Keogh accounts, and more than three times the amount of stock. The use of these unfolding techniques on the HRS gives a much clearer picture of the components of net worth, and the comparable importance of pensions and health insurance, than could be obtained from other surveys.

Smith (1996) questions the fluctuations in asset amounts between waves of the survey. Hurd and McFadden (1996) have raised questions about the sensitivity of these estimates to the anchor — that is, the initial value presented to the respondent in a question asking if a certain type of asset holding exceeded the specified amount. Investigation of brackets has suggested to the designers of the HRS that the bracket amounts used in HRS 1 were not optimal; bracket amounts were subsequently changed for later waves of the survey. Despite all of these problems, for this investigation of the importance of pensions and social security in wealth and income of HRS respondents, our findings use only the data from wave 1 of the HRS and make no adjustment for the anchoring problem.

Earnings

Earnings in 1991 of HRS respondents are explored in a set of more or less standard questions. Since these questions do not differ significantly from similar questions in other surveys, we simply note that earnings are the primary component of most HRS respondents' income in 1991. Hence the variation in earnings is the principal source of the variation in incomes.

Measuring Observations for Households

Several of the income measures and most of the wealth measures in the HRS were collected at the household level rather than for individuals. Because of this, the analysis of wealth and income patterns in the HRS must be cast in a household framework. For couples, the interviewer asked which member of the couple was most knowledgeable about finances, and that individual was designated as the primary respondent. Usually that person's partner was designated as the secondary respondent. The primary respondent answered the sections of the HRS questionnaire having to do with housing, income, assets, and insurance. For 284 households, interviews were only obtained with the primary respondent. The primary respondent did give some information about the partner, such as the age, gender, race, and income. This made it possible to "hotdeck" the missing spouse from other cases in the survey by finding another respondent who was a member of a couple and who had the same age, gender, race, approximately the same individual income, and approximately the same family income. For 95 households in the HRS, interviews were obtained only with the secondary respondent. These households must be dropped from the analysis because none of the financial sections of the questionnaire were asked, leaving 7,607 households in the analysis.

Household income measures also include labor earnings, income from assets, government transfer income, and so forth. Asset measures include housing wealth, business assets, financial assets, and retirement assets (IRAs and Keoghs). All of these are included in the subsequent calculations.

In tabulations to follow we present total household income and wealth calculated separately for single households and couple households. Single households are further broken down into males and females. In most cases we also present findings arrayed by household income and wealth percentiles (5, 10, 25, 50, 75, 90, and 95 percent). Statistics reported using weighted data include the weighted percentage of nonzero amounts, the weighted average of the nonzero amounts, the overall weighted average and the percentile breaks for such variables as total assets, housing wealth, business assets, financial assets, retirement assets and the value of retiree health insurance (both total household and by male/female), and analogous quantities for the income quantities.

Pensions and Other Sources of Income and Wealth

Income by Type

Total annual income among households in wave 1 of the HRS is reported in table 1 (all figures are in 1991 dollars). While we will continue to call the reported figures income, they are closer to compensation

TABLE 1. Household Income by Source: HRS 1 (in 1991 dollars)

Source of Income	Mean for Sample		Value for Median 10 Percent of Households	
	Value ($)	Percentage of Total Income	Value ($)	Percentage of Total Income
Total	48,203	100	36,006	99
Earnings	35,313	73	28,027	78
Pension accrual	2,767	6	1,062	3
Social security accrual	1,517	3	1,356	4
Health insurance	1,775	4	1,655	5
Transfers	941	2	958	3
Asset income	5,304	11	2,516	7
Other	586	1	432	1
Unweighted number of observations	7,607			

Source: Authors' calculations using HRS Wave 1. Pension accrual is based on SPD data and is calculated using the projected method from employer-provided plan descriptions for DB plans and contributions for DC plans. Social security values are based on the self-reported earnings histories and the authors' imputations. Median 10 percent of households are those with total incomes in the 45th to 55th percentiles. See the text for explanations. All data are weighted by HRS sample weights.

since they include accruals from pensions and from social security, as well as the value of health insurance provided by the employer. Column 2 reports the mean values of income by type for each household. We have chosen to include all households. The reader should be aware that these figures mix together retired households and those that continue to work. Column 3 indicates the fraction of income accounted for by the indicated category. Column 4 presents the value of income by type for the households having the median 10 percent of total income, that is, for households falling between the 45th and 55th percentiles in terms of total income.[22] Column 5 indicates the fraction of total income accounted for by these categories for those falling into the middle 10 percent of households.

Line 1 of table 1 indicates that on average, all HRS households received $48,203 in income in 1992. Income for the median 10 percent of households was $36,006. The difference reflects the well-known skewness of the income distribution, where those in the upper part of the distribution receive a disproportionate share.

Earnings
Line 2 in table 1 reports the most important source of income, earnings.[23] On average, earnings total $35,313 per year in HRS households, accounting for 73 percent of total household income. For the median 10 percent of HRS households, earnings were an even more important source of income, accounting for 78 percent of total income. It should be recalled that only about a fifth of HRS wave 1 households are retired (Gustman, Mitchell, and Steinmeier 1995a).

Columns 2 and 3 in table 2 report the fraction of families receiving

TABLE 2.   Household Income by Source and Value among Recipients and All Households: HRS 1 (in 1991 dollars)

Source of Income	Percentage with Income from Indicated Source	Average Value of Income among Recipients ($)	Average Value of Income among All Households ($)
Earnings	84	42,063	35,313
Pension accrual	50	5,569	2,767
Social security accrual	57	2,665	1,517
Health insurance contribution	51	3,464	1,775
Transfers	20	4,650	941
Asset income	47	11,262	5,304

Source: See table 1. All data are weighted by HRS sample weights.

income by type and the average value of income by type for those receiving the indicated source of income. For purposes of comparison, the last column again reports the average amount of income by type across all households.

From table 2 it can be seen that 84 percent of households received earnings, averaging $42,063 per household receiving earnings.

Pension Contributions
For those with a defined contribution (DC) plan, the pension contribution is the amount the employer deposits in the plan. For those with a defined benefit (DB) pension, the pension contribution is the accrual rate from working one more year, where pension accrual is calculated on a projected liability basis.[24] The figures on pension contribution in tables 1 and 2 represent only the increment in the real present value of the pension from additional work. In order to avoid double counting of income and wealth from the same source, pension income is not in our calculation of income for those whose pensions are in pay status. The pension income from interest on tax free balances and the income equivalent arising from the fact that the lump sum promised under a pension is coming closer in time, as well as any pension incomes from plans that are in pay status, also are not included in the pension contribution category. In this sense, the pension contribution reported here understates what pension income would be if it were reported using the same criteria as some other categories of asset income. Similarly, we do not report the rental value of housing realized by those who live in their own homes as income, and we also do not report unrealized capital gains on stocks or other holdings.

As seen in line 3 of table 1, on average the pension contribution is $2,767 per household. This amounts to 6 percent of household income and to 8 percent of average household earnings. For the median 10 percent of households, the pension contribution amounts to $1,062 but accounts for 3 percent of total household income. As seen in table 2, of the 50 percent of households with income from pension accrual, the average accrual per household is $5,569.

Social Security
The average HRS household accrues social security benefits at a rate of $1,517 per year, accounting for 3 percent of income. Accrual is measured as the difference in wealth from working an additional year and assumes that in all future years outside the calculation there are zero recorded earnings.[25] For the median 10 percent of households, social security benefit accrual accounts for $1,356 per year, or about 4 percent

of household income. According to table 2, 57 percent of households continue to accrue credits under social security, averaging $2,665 per household that is still accruing benefits.

Health Insurance Contributions by Employers
The average value of the health insurance contribution by employers among HRS employees is $1,775 per household, or 4 percent of average household income. This benefit is received by 51 percent of households, averaging $3,464 per household that receives the benefit. Health insurance contributions average $1,655 for the median 10 percent of households arrayed by income, which amounts to 5 percent of household income.

Pensions, Social Security, and Health Insurance
Altogether pension accrual, social security benefit accrual, and health insurance contributions account for 13 percent of average income. For the median 10 percent of households, pensions, social security, and health insurance together account for 12 percent of household income.

Income from Transfers
Income from transfers[26] amounts to 2 percent of average HRS household income, or $941 per household. For the median 10 percent of households, the figure is $958, which accounts for 3 percent of the income of the median 10 percent of families. Altogether, 20 percent of HRS households receive transfer income, averaging $4,650 per recipient household.

Asset Income
For the HRS households, 47 percent have asset income,[27] with households with asset income averaging $11,262 per year and asset income to all households accounting for 11 percent of household income, or $5,304 per household. The figure is half that for the median 10 percent of income recipients among households. The median households receive $2,516 per household in asset income, amounting to 7 percent of their household income.

Other Income
Other sources[28] amount to 1 percent of income, $586 per household.

Total Net Wealth by Type

Table 3 reports on the level of total net wealth, that is, total assets net of liabilities, by type owned by households in 1992.[29] The first column reports the source of wealth. Column 2 indicates average wealth by category, while column 3 presents the fraction of wealth represented by wealth in each category. Columns 4 and 5 present the same figures for households falling within the median 10 percent of all households.

On average, row 1 of table 3 indicates that all HRS households own $499,187 in net wealth in 1992. Wealth for the median 10 percent of households is $339,725. About 99 percent of HRS households reported some wealth value.

Total Wealth vs. Total Income

One way to assess the reported magnitudes of wealth is to compare average wealth with average earnings, or with average income net of pensions, social security, and health insurance. Average wealth in the HRS totals fourteen times annual earnings and twelve times income net of pension accrual, social security benefit accrual, and health insurance. Using the life tables and interest rate returns underlying our wealth estimates, at age sixty-two a single male can replace two-thirds of income with wealth of ten times income. A couple can replace half of income if the same expenditure is maintained even after one spouse dies and a

TABLE 3.   Household Wealth Net of Liabilities by Source: HRS 1 (in 1992 dollars)

Source of Wealth	Mean for Sample		Value for Median 10 Percent of Households	
	Value ($)	Percentage of Total	Value ($)	Percentage of Total
Total	499,187	100	339,725	100
Pension value	116,012	23	60,102	18
Social security value	133,662	27	144,801	43
House value	78,826	16	67,716	20
Business assets	78,951	16	14,511	4
Financial assets	42,140	8	19,274	6
Retirement assets	19,613	4	10,948	3
Retiree health insurance	7,600	2	7,771	2
Other	22,383	4	14,602	4
Unweighted number of observations	7,607			

Source: Authors' calculations using HRS Wave 1. Net wealth is defined as net worth, assets less liabilities. Pension value is based on SPD data and is calculated using the projected method from employer-provided plan descriptions for DB plans and contributions for DC plans. Social security values are based on the self-reported earnings histories and the authors' imputations. See the text for explanations. Median 10 percent of households are those with net wealth in the 45th to 55th percentiles. All data are weighted by HRS sample weights.

larger fraction if consumption of a surviving spouse is reduced below the consumption of the couple. And HRS respondents average age fifty-six, and will accrue pension benefits over years until retirement. Thus wealth accumulated by the respondents to the HRS appears to be substantial.

Pension Wealth

The importance of pension wealth to HRS respondents is very clear. As seen in row 2 of table 3, on average pension wealth is $116,012 per household, which accounts for 23 percent of all wealth among households, including households with no pension. For the median household, pensions average $60,102, which accounts for 18 percent of total net wealth. This suggests that pensions are distributed more unevenly than total net wealth. Table 4 indicates that among all households, 64 percent have some pension wealth, worth $181,926 to those with pension wealth.

Wealth Value of Social Security

Only slightly more important than pensions in this survey is social security. As would be expected, 96 percent of all households are expected to receive social security benefits (see table 4).[30] The present value of social security wealth for all households averages $133,662. Thus social security wealth on average totals 27 percent of household wealth, only slightly more than pensions. With such a large fraction of households covered by social security, table 4 shows that average social security wealth is not much higher for covered HRS households at $138,878 than for all households.

To provide an indication of how close our calculations come to estimating social security wealth using the covered earnings histories, we

TABLE 4.   Household Wealth Net of Liabilities by Source and Value among Recipients and All Households: HRS 1 (in 1992 dollars)

Source of Wealth	Percentage with Wealth from Indicated Source	Average Value of Wealth among Recipients ($)	Average Value of Wealth among All Households ($)
Pension value	64	181,926	116,012
Social security value	96	138,878	133,662
House value	80	98,456	78,826
Business assets	32	250,198	78,951
Financial assets	88	47,709	42,140
Retirement assets	42	46,716	19,613
Retiree health insurance	32	23,841	7,600

Source: See table 3. All data are weighted by HRS sample weights.

need to skip ahead into the next set of tables, which include findings for couples and singles. For couples we estimate average social security wealth of $162,610. For married men, as of 1992 Mitchell, Olson, and Steinmeier (1996, table 3), using social security earnings histories, estimated couple's benefits of $148,198 when focusing on men and $161,780 when focusing on women. (The HRS men are married to younger women, some of whom are out of the sample range, while the women are married to older men, some of whom are out of the sample age range, which accounts for the higher social security wealth figure when focusing on women.) Therefore compared to the $155,000 average of their estimates, our present estimates are only slightly high (by about 5 percent). For single men, we estimate social security wealth in 1992 of $75,164. Using the HRS earnings records, Mitchell, Olson, and Steinmeier (1996) estimate social security wealth of $67,777. Thus for single men we are high by about 11 percent. For single women, our estimate of social security wealth is high by about 38 percent since we estimate social security wealth of $69,703, while they estimate social security wealth of $50,678. Because single women accumulated 85 total quarters on average, and we assume they worked full time since leaving school, or 140 quarters, it is not surprising that here we overstate their social security wealth. All told then, our estimates of social security wealth overstate the figures from Mitchell, Olson, and Steinmeier by about 13 percent.

House Value
Average house value[31] for HRS households is $78,826 per household, accounting for 16 percent of total assets. House value for the median 10 percent of households is $67,716, accounting for 20 percent of total net wealth for this group. For the 80 percent of households who own a home, the average value of housing assets is $98,456.

Business Assets
Business assets[32] account for the same fraction of average wealth as housing assets, 16 percent. Overall, business assets amount to $78,951 per household. Average business assets for the median 10 percent of households arrayed by wealth amount to $14,511, which when compared to mean assets suggests that the distribution of business assets is highly unequal. With 32 percent of all households reporting they own business assets, the average value for those with business assets is $250,198.

Financial Assets
The average level of financial assets[33] is $42,140 over all households, accounting for 8 percent of assets held by households. With 88 percent

of households reporting having some financial assets, average holdings by those with financial assets are $47,709. The median 10 percent of households has $19,274 in assets, accounting for 6 percent of total assets held by the median 10 percent of wealth holders.

Retirement Assets

Overall, 42 percent of households report having some retirement assets.[34] On average retirement assets amount to $19,613 over all households and account for 4 percent of total assets. Among households with retirement assets, these assets are worth $46,716 per household. For the median 10 percent of all wealth holders, retirement assets average $10,948 and account for 3 percent of household wealth.

Asset Value of Retiree Health Insurance

The average asset value expected due to employer-provided retiree health insurance amounts to 2 percent of household assets, or $7,600 per household. Only 32 percent of HRS households have assets from retiree health insurance, amounting to $23,841 per household with such benefits. For the median 10 percent of wealth holders, retiree health benefits average $7,771, which is also 2 percent of household assets.[35]

Other Assets

Another 4 percent of total assets falls in the other category[36] and amounts to $22,383 on average for the sample.

Pensions and the Distributions of Incomes and Wealth by Type among Couples and Singles

The distribution of total income among HRS couples and singles in 1992 is reported in table 5. On average, all couples, including those with no income, received $58,895 in income in 1992. Columns 3 and 4 report income components for male and female members of couple households for those components that can be decomposed in that way. Assets and social security benefits are attributed to the full household. Columns 5 and 6 report the analogous results for single males and females.

Singles have lower incomes than couples on a per capita basis.[37] Average income for all singles is $25,225, which is 43 percent of average income for couples. Income for the median 10 percent of singles is $17,855, which is 38 percent of the income for the median 10 percent of couples of $47,492, so that more income is concentrated in the upper tail for singles. For single males, average income is $34,094, while for single females it is $21,064.

Pension contributions accrue to 37 percent of single males, which is below the 41 percent of male partners with pension contributions. The average pension contribution for male singles of $1,876, which includes those with a zero contribution, is below the pension contribution of $2,076 for men in couples. Female singles' average pension contribution is $1,571, with 36 percent of female singles reporting pension contributions. Both figures are in excess of those for female partners in couples, where 31 percent report pension contributions, amounting to $1,202 when averaged across all couples. Pension contributions for male singles average 8 percent (1,876/24,738) of total earnings, while the figure for female singles is 10 percent (1,571/15,072) of total earnings. For couples, the pension contribution for the male partner averaged 7 percent (2,076/31,118) of the men's earnings, while the pension contribution of the female partner averaged 10 percent (1,202/12,177) of the women's earnings. Thus holding marital status constant, differences in pension contributions between men and women are lower than the differences in their earnings.

The distribution of total assets among singles and couples in 1992 is reported in table 6. On average, all couples, including those with no assets, own $610,749 in assets in 1992. Asset value for the median 10 percent of asset holders who are couples is $440,285. Assets held by all singles average $259,424, or 42 percent of the assets held by couples. Thus on a per capita basis, singles hold fewer assets than couples. Single males hold significantly more assets than single females, $359,122 for single males versus $212,641 for single females.

TABLE 5. Household Income by Source, Marital Status, and Sex: HRS 1 (in 1991 dollars)

	Couples			Singles	
Source of Income	Household ($)	Male ($)	Female ($)	Male ($)	Female ($)
Total	58,895			34,094	21,064
Earnings	43,296	31,118	12,177	24,738	15,072
Pension accrual	3,278	2,076	1,202	1,876	1,571
Social security accrual	1,873			818	721
Health insurance	2,248	1,618	630	874	702
Transfers	1,107	945	162	4,812	518
Asset income	6,508			727	1,734
Other	585			249	746
Unweighted number of observations	5,234			741	1,632

Source: See table 1. All data are weighted by HRS sample weights.

On average pension wealth is $141,278 for all HRS couples, including those with no pension wealth, with 72.5 percent of couples reporting assets in the form of a pension. This amounts to 23 percent (141,278/ 610,749) of all assets for couples. The median amount of pension wealth accrued to date from current work by the median 10 percent of wealth holders among all couples is $96,567.

Among all HRS couples, 62 percent report pension assets from a male partner, averaging $113,078 including zero values, and 36 percent of couples report pension assets due to a female partner, averaging $28,199 among all couples. Thus 80 percent of pension assets held by couples are due to the male earner.[38]

Among all singles, 45 percent have pension wealth. This is a much smaller ratio than the 73 percent figure found for couples. Among all singles, including zeros, pension values average $61,713. Thus HRS singles average 44 percent of the pension wealth owned by couples. The ratio of pension wealth to total net wealth held by singles of 24 percent is similar to the 23 percent ratio of pension wealth to total wealth held by couples.

Among all HRS single males, 52 percent report pension wealth, well below the 62 percent figure reported for male partners in couples. For single males, including those with no pension assets, pension assets average $111,570, below but close to the average value for male partners in couples of $113,078. Among female singles, 42 percent report having pen-

TABLE 6.   Household Net Wealth by Source, Marital Status, and Sex: HRS 1 (in 1992 dollars)

	Couples			Singles	
Source of Wealth	Household ($)	Male ($)	Female ($)	Male ($)	Female ($)
Total	610,749			359,122	212,641
Pension value	141,278	113,078	28,199	111,570	38,318
Social security value	162,610			75,164	69,703
House value	94,818			42,592	45,332
Business assets	101,603			55,614	18,374
Financial assets	50,324			35,025	19,638
Retirement assets	24,592			10,736	8,057
Retiree health insurance value	9,574	7,349	2,225	4,353	2,889
Other	25,950			24,068	48,648
Unweighted number of observations	5,234			741	1,632

Source: See table 3. All data are weighted by HRS sample weights.

sion assets, which is above the 36 percent figure reported for the pension assets due to a female partner in couples. For single women, pension assets average $38,318, compared to $28,199 for the female partners with pensions in couples.

Income and Assets by Pension Status, Race, Education, Union Status, and Veteran's Status

Table 7 reports income and wealth by subgroups in the population that are of special interest. In the first two rows of the table it can be seen that income and wealth differ substantially between households in which a member is covered by a pension and households with no pension. Incomes are more than twice as high on average in pension households. When households with pensions are identified and are ordered by income and average income is computed for the median 10

TABLE 7. Household Income and Net Wealth by Pension Status, Race, Education, Union Status, and Veteran Status: HRS 1

Category	Unweighted Number of Observations	Average Income ($)	Income for Median 10 Percent ($)	Average Wealth ($)	Wealth for Median 10 Percent ($)
Pension Status					
With pension	5,085	57,441	46,368	573,090	421,864
No pension	2,522	27,960	14,709	337,233	149,277
Education					
Less than high school	1,680	18,554	12,118	219,567	131,577
High school graduate	2,519	35,913	30,071	410,395	315,141
Some college	1,653	50,680	44,846	500,480	377,534
College graduate	1,757	84,062	67,459	821,044	587,014
Race					
White and other	5,467	52,650	40,690	553,180	383,542
Black	1,424	28,904	19,100	259,550	163,096
Hispanic	716	26,653	16,362	245,239	153,430
Union Status					
Union member	2,388	49,037	43,268	524,186	418,374
Not union member	5,219	47,800	31,895	487,918	298,531
Veteran Status					
Veteran	2,103	67,189	56,069	690,041	529,653
Not veteran	5,505	40,452	28,071	421,268	268,740

Source: See tables 1 and 3. Income is in 1991 dollars, wealth in 1992 dollars. All data are weighted by HRS sample weights.

percent of households, and the same is done for households without pensions, the income differences are more than three to one in favor of households with pensions. Average wealth is 70 percent higher in households with pensions than in nonpension households. When households with and without pensions are ordered according to wealth, the average assets for the median 10 percent of households with pensions is 2.8 times the average assets for the median 10 percent of households without pensions.

It is instructive to compare both income and wealth differences between households with and without pensions. Because medians reorder households when rankings are based on income as opposed to wealth, we prefer to look at means. The ratio of mean income in households with pensions to those without is 2.05 to 1. The ratio of total mean wealth is 1.7 to 1. In a simple life-cycle model with no precautionary, bequest, or other motive for savings, if individuals treated pension wealth the same as other wealth, there would be perfect substitution between pension wealth and other wealth, and the wealth ratios would be the same as the income ratios.[39] In a model in which pensions added to total wealth accumulation, that is, in which there was not a perfect offset, then the ratio of total wealth between those with and without pensions would be higher than the ratio of incomes. The fact that wealth ratios between those with and without pensions are lower than income ratios suggests that substitution between pension wealth and other wealth may be substantial. Multivariate analysis reported in Gustman and Steinmeier (forthcoming), however, suggests that pensions cause very little displacement of wealth, so that the overall effect of pensions is to increase total wealth, probably by considerably more than half the value of the pension.[40]

The next comparison made in table 7 is by schooling. The schooling level for the household is defined as the highest level achieved by either spouse. The ratios of income and wealth between the highest and lowest education categories are at least 3.7 to one.

Following that is a comparison by race. Whites and others have twice the household income of Hispanics, and almost twice the household income of blacks. Average wealth for whites and other households is twice as high as it is for black and Hispanic households. When the median 10 percent of households are identified within each group and compared, the differences in wealth are more than two to one in favor of whites and others.

Next we consider whether either partner in a household is a union member.[41] Average incomes are very close between union and nonunion households, but when households with median income are identified within each group, the average income for the median group is one third higher for union households, reflecting the more equal distribution of incomes among union households. Union households have about 8 percent more wealth than nonunion households on average, but the differences in wealth between the medians are much wider, with the median of union household wealth being over a third higher than the median for nonunion households. Notice that 31 percent of the households in the HRS have a union member. This high number is the result of two things. The union measure identifies households in which either partner is a member of a union and so should be higher than the average rate of unionization in the population. In addition, the 1931–41 birth cohort is more likely to be unionized than are younger cohorts. In 1992, union membership among the employed is 25 percent for men and 19 percent for women in the HRS (Gustman, Mitchell, and Steinmeier 1995b).

The final set of results presents something of a puzzle. For the HRS cohort we find that both the income and wealth of households with a veteran are higher than the income and wealth for households without a veteran. The HRS cohort, born from 1931 to 1941, largely was too young for the Korean War and too old for Vietnam. Their experience may be different from those who were of draft age during the Vietnam era, where veterans exhibited lower incomes than nonveterans. Nevertheless, it is noteworthy that we find such a large income difference in favor of households with veterans in them.

Table 8 focuses on pensions. It reports the fraction of income and wealth due to pensions for these different population groups.

Among households with pensions, the pension accounts for 7 percent of average income and 29 percent of average wealth. The comparable numbers are lower for median households at 4 percent and 25 percent respectively.

Pensions grow in importance as a source of income and as a source of wealth with the level of schooling. On average for college graduates the share of pensions in income and wealth is two-thirds bigger than the share of pensions in income and wealth for those with less than a high school education. For median families within these schooling categories, the share of total income represented by pensions is five times as large for families with a college education as for those with less than high school, while the comparable difference in share of wealth represented by pensions among median households is more than three to one.

For blacks the share of average wealth represented by pensions is higher than for whites and others.[42] Although the share of incomes represented by pensions is similar between Hispanics and whites and others, the share of average wealth represented by pensions is considerably lower for Hispanics, and the difference is even wider between the median families for each group. Looking at the figures for households with median wealth, the share of wealth represented by pensions is 4 percent for Hispanics, 19 percent for white and other households, and 15 percent for the median black households.

The share of average incomes represented by pension accrual is similar for veterans and nonveterans. The share of wealth in the form of pensions is clearly higher for veterans than for nonveterans.

Pensions, Social Security, and Health Insurance in the
Distribution of Income and Wealth in the Health and
Retirement Study

The Distribution of Income

Table 9 reports the distribution of income in the HRS. Percentiles are reported in column 1, where households are ordered on the basis of total income. Column 2 indicates the average value of income in each percen-

TABLE 8. Proportion of Household Income and Net Wealth Due to Pensions, by Pension Status, Race, Education, Union Status, and Veteran Status: HRS 1

Category	Average Income (%)	Income for Median 10 Percent (%)	Average Wealth (%)	Wealth for Median 10 Percent (%)
Pension Status				
With pension	7	4	29	25
No pension	0	0	0	0
Education				
Less than high school	4	1	16	7
High school graduate	5	4	22	17
Some college	5	4	23	18
College graduate	7	5	26	26
Race				
White and other	6	3	23	19
Black	6	3	28	15
Hispanic	6	2	16	4
Union Status				
Union member	6	2	31	28
Not union member	5	3	20	14
Veteran Status				
Veteran	6	4	28	28
Not veteran	6	4	20	16

Source: See tables 1 and 3. All data are weighted by HRS sample weights.

tile category. In column 3 we report average earnings to facilitate analysis for those in the bottom 5 percent of the income distribution who have negative incomes. Column 4 reports the lower bracket limit for the percentile category. As is widely known, there is considerable skewness in the distribution of income in the United States, and this is clearly seen in the data in table 9. The gini coefficient for the distribution of income among households is .5026.[43] Also reflecting the skewness of the distribution of income among households, the average income for the median 10 percent of households is $36,006, which is about three-fourths of the average income of all households. Negative incomes for the bottom 5 percent of households reflect negative accrual on some assets, including business losses, pensions, and social security. Thus those in the very bottom of the income distribution may have higher assets than one might at first expect.[44]

Pensions and the Income Distribution

Table 10 focuses on the distribution of pension accruals within the distribution of household income. Again the first column of the table indicates the percentile category in the income distribution. The fraction of households with a pension is reported in column 2. In column 3 the data report on average pension accrual for those with a pension, while in column 4 the data report the average pension accrual for all households in the percentile category. In column 5 the data indicate average pension

TABLE 9.   Distribution of Household Incomes and Earnings in the HRS Population: HRS 1 (in 1991 dollars)

Income Percentile	Average Value of Incomes in Percentile Category ($)	Average Value of Earnings in Percentile Category ($)	Lower Bracket Income Limit for Percentile Category ($)
95–100	219,869	145,126	128,027
90–95	110,570	80,303	98,880
75–90	78,471	59,515	63,770
50–75	49,062	38,297	35,656
25–50	25,069	19,014	15,000
10–25	8,677	4,963	3,020
5–10	1,504	421	398
0–5	−113	344	
All	48,203	35,313	
45–55	36,006	28,027	

Source: See table 1. All income categories are those included in table 1. All data are weighted by HRS sample weights.

accrual as a percentage of average income. Over 70 percent of those in the top half of the income distribution have a pension. Pension accruals range from $19,594 for the average household in the top 5 percent of the income distribution down to −$540 for those in the bottom 5 percent of the income distribution.[45]

The last column of table 10 shows that except for the lowest 5 percent of income recipients, pension accrual increases as a share of income, rising to 9 percent of income for the top 5 percent of income recipients. For those in the bottom 5 percent of the income distribution some families have both negative income and negative pension accrual, producing a large positive ratio of pension accrual to income.

Social Security and the Income Distribution
The structure of table 11 is similar to that of table 10, but it reports on the importance of social security accrual as a fraction of total income. Column 2 shows the proportion of households with social security. Those with no social security coverage include those who have worked for state and local governments, who have been employed in other uncovered work, or who have not had a sufficient work history to qualify for social security benefits. As noted previously, social security accrual is calculated on a legal liability basis, comparing what would be received if the respondent worked until 1992 vs. 1991 and then left paid employ-

TABLE 10.   Pension Accruals in the Distribution of Household Incomes: HRS 1

Income Percentile	Percentage with Pension	Average Accrual Value of Pension for Those with Nonzero Pensions in Percentile Category ($)	Average Accrual Value of Pension for All Households in Percentile Category ($)	Percentage of Income Accounted for by Pension Accrual
95–100	75	26,159	19,594	9
90–95	76	11,448	8,724	8
75–90	78	6,212	4,819	6
50–75	69	2,882	1,996	4
25–50	47	1,346	627	3
10–25	9	−48	−4	−0
5–10	2	−749	−14	−1
0–5	1	−46,975	−540	478
All	50	5,569	2,767	6
45–55	60	1,766	1,062	3

Source: See table 1. All data are weighted by HRS sample weights.

ment. Because social security benefits are calculated on the basis of the high thirty-five years of earnings, in both calculations, zeros are added in for average indexed monthly earnings after ceasing to work. The negative social security accruals for a small number of cases in the bottom 5 percent of the income distribution probably represent households where one member is outside the age range of the HRS, most likely couples with an older husband. That alone is not sufficient to land the household in the bottom 5 percent of income recipients. Some negative asset or pension accrual is also probably involved.

Employer-Provided Health Benefits and the Income Distribution

Table 12 reports similar results for the value of employer-provided health benefits. (Medicare is not counted here.) Among the three-quarters of the households with highest incomes, the majority has employer-provided health benefits. As seen in the last column, the share of income accounted for by employer-provided benefits declines as income rises from the fifth percentile of income households on up. Employer-provided health benefits are worth only about 4 percent of income on average, but for those from the 5th to the 20th percentile, they are worth about 12 percent of income. By the time we hit the top 10 percent of the

TABLE 11. Social Security Accruals in the Distribution of Household Incomes: HRS 1

Income Percentile	Percentage with Social Security	Average Accrual Value of Social Security for Those with Nonzero Social Security in Percentile Category ($)	Average Accrual Value of Social Security for All Households in Percentile Category ($)	Percentage of Income Accounted for by Social Security Accrual
95–100	68	5,932	4,052	2
90–95	72	4,882	3,515	3
75–90	70	4,119	2,886	4
50–75	72	2,613	1,886	4
25–50	65	1,278	824	3
10–25	32	640	206	2
5–10	7	−662	−45	−3
0–5	1	−920	−12	11
All	57	2,665	1,517	3
45–55	77	1,774	1,356	4

Source: See table 1. All data are weighted by HRS sample weights.

income distribution, employer-provided benefits are worth only 2 percent of income.

The Distribution of Wealth

The distribution of net wealth in the HRS is reported in table 13. The median wealth of households is $339,751, which closely corresponds to

TABLE 12. The Value of Employer-Provided Current and Retiree Health Insurance in the Distribution of Household Incomes: HRS 1

Income Percentile	Percentage with Employer-Provided Current and Retiree Health Insurance	Average Value of Health Insurance for Those with Nonzero Health Insurance in Percentile Category ($)	Average Value of Health Insurance for All Households in Percentile Category ($)	Percentage of Income Accounted for by Health Insurance
95–100	66	4,949	3,249	1
90–95	74	4,708	3,480	3
75–90	70	4,306	3,008	4
50–75	63	3,371	2,115	4
25–50	51	2,423	1,223	5
10–25	32	2,906	935	11
5–10	12	1,876	223	15
0–5	1	2,363	19	−17
All	51	3,464	1,775	4
45–55	58	2,849	1,655	5

Source: See table 1. All data are weighted by HRS sample weights.

TABLE 13. Distribution of Household Net Wealth in the HRS Population: HRS 1 (in 1992 dollars)

Wealth Percentile	Average Value of Wealth in Percentile Category ($)	Lower Bracket Limit for Percentile Category ($)
95–100	2,543,780	1,397,823
90–95	1,162,428	987,875
75–90	762,738	608,118
50–75	457,376	339,751
25–50	252,119	169,678
10–25	122,965	77,396
5–10	61,322	45,650
0–5	9,248	0
All	499,187	
45–55	339,725	

Source: See table 3. Net wealth is defined as net worth, assets less liabilities. All assets are those included in table 3. All data are weighted by HRS sample weights.

the average value of assets for the middle 10 percent of households of $339,725. Households in the upper 5 percent average more than seven times the wealth of the median household. The bottom 5 percent of households has less than $10,000 in wealth, or less than 3 percent of the wealth of the median wealth holder.[46]

Pensions and the Wealth Distribution

Table 14 reports on the importance of pension wealth within the overall distribution of wealth. In all brackets from the 25th percentile upward, at least 65 percent of households have pension wealth. From the 50th to 95th percentile, over 80 percent of households have pension wealth. For those in the 25th to 50th percentile, pension wealth for the two-thirds of households with a pension averages $55,557. For those in the third quarter of the wealth distribution, for the 83 percent of households with a pension, the pension is worth $133,346. While only 4 percent of those in the bottom 5 percent of the wealth distribution have pensions, and those with a pension have a plan worth $27,855, for the 65 percent of households in the top 5 percent of the wealth distribution who have a pension, their pensions are worth $732,861 on average.

The last column of table 14 shows that, except for the extreme upper and lower 5 percent of wealth holders, the share of pension wealth in total net assets rises as total net assets rise. For those in the 75th to

TABLE 14. Pension Wealth Values in the Distribution of Household Net Wealth: HRS 1 (in 1992 dollars)

Wealth Percentile	Percentage with Pension	Average Value of Pension for Those with Nonzero Pensions in Percentile Category ($)	Average Value of Pension for All Households in Percentile Category ($)	Percent of Wealth Accounted for by Pension
95–100	65	732,861	475,267	19
90–95	82	442,948	363,966	31
75–90	86	278,805	239,727	31
50–75	83	133,346	109,967	24
25–50	67	55,557	36,987	15
10–25	37	22,103	8,100	7
5–10	11	10,775	1,171	2
0–5	4	27,855	1,205	13
All	64	181,926	116,012	23
45–55	76	79,280	60,102	18

Source: See table 3. Wealth is defined as net worth, assets less liabilities. All assets are those included in table 3. All data are weighted by HRS sample weights.

95th percentiles, pensions account for almost a third of total net assets. For those in the 5th to 10th percentiles, pensions account for only 2 percent of total net assets. In between, pensions increase steadily as a share of total net wealth, accounting for 18 percent of total assets for the median 10 percent of all households. However, pensions account for 13 percent of assets for those in the bottom 5 percent of the wealth distribution, where a number of families have negative wealth, and pensions account for 19 percent of the total net wealth of those in the top 5 percent of wealth holders.

Social Security and the Asset Distribution

Table 15 reports on the importance of social security wealth to those in different percentiles of the wealth distribution. As noted previously, social security wealth accounts for 27 percent of average wealth and 43 percent of wealth for the median 10 percent of wealth holders. Reflecting the progressive benefit formula, social security wealth accounts for a declining portion of wealth as average wealth increases, falling from over 100 percent of net wealth for the bottom 5 percent of households (counting those with negative wealth) and falling smoothly as one proceeds up the wealth distribution to 7 percent of wealth for the top 5 percent of the distribution.

TABLE 15.   Social Security in the Distribution of Household Net Wealth: HRS 1 (in 1992 dollars)

Wealth Percentile	Percentage with Social Security	Average Value of Social Security for Those with Nonzero Social Security in Percentile Category ($)	Average Value of Social Security for All Households in Percentile Category ($)	Percentage of Assets Accounted for by Social Security
95–100	99	185,825	184,399	7
90–95	100	188,506	187,709	16
75–90	100	179,766	178,888	23
50–75	100	158,119	157,649	34
25–50	99	129,542	127,967	51
10–25	99	90,309	89,090	72
5–10	92	56,755	52,380	85
0–5	47	35,384	16,567	179
All	93	138,878	133,622	27
45–55	99	145,620	144,801	43

Source: See table 3. Net wealth is defined as net worth, assets less liabilities. All assets are those included in table 3. All data are weighted by HRS sample weights.

Retiree Health Benefits from Employers and the
Asset Distribution
Table 16 reports similar results for the wealth value of retiree health benefits provided by private employers. Over a third of the median 10 percent of the population is entitled to retiree health benefits worth about 2.3 percent of their total net wealth. Fewer than 10 percent of the bottom quarter of the wealth distribution are entitled to retiree health benefits from their employers. For those in the top 5 percent of the wealth distribution, employer-provided retiree health insurance, altogether worth $10,587, accounts for less than half a percent of their total net wealth. Thus for most of the distribution, the share of wealth accounted for by retiree health benefits is low, peaking roughly in the middle of the distribution.

Summarizing the Distribution of Pension Wealth, Social
Security Wealth, and Wealth from Employer-Provided
Retiree Health Insurance
If one wishes to understand the distribution of pension wealth, social security wealth, and the wealth equivalent of retiree health benefits in the context of the current distribution of wealth, the preceding tables

TABLE 16.   Retiree Health Insurance in the Distribution of Household Net Wealth: HRS 1 (in 1992 dollars)

Wealth Percentile	Percentage with Retiree Health Insurance	Average Value of Retiree Health Insurance for Those with Nonzero Retiree Health Insurance in Percentile Category ($)	Average Value of Retiree Health Insurance for All Households in Percentile Category ($)	Percentage of Assets Accounted for by Retiree Health Insurance
95–100	35	30,628	10,587	0.4
90–95	53	29,905	16,190	1.4
75–90	54	27,403	14,768	1.9
50–75	45	23,273	10,525	2.3
25–50	25	18,316	4,498	1.8
10–25	13	13,762	1,748	1.4
5–10	3	12,677	282	0.5
0–5	1	21,953	266	2.9
All	32	23,684	7,600	1.5
45–55	37	21,082	7,808	2.3

Source: See table 3. Net wealth is defined as net worth, assets less liabilities. All assets are those included in table 3. All data are weighted by HRS sample weights.

provide the required information. While the share of total net wealth represented by pensions increases with the place of the individual in the wealth distribution, the share of wealth represented by social security declines. Together, pensions and social security account for more than half of total net wealth for all but those in the top 10 percent of the wealth distribution.

Figures 1 and 2 picture the variation in the shares of pension wealth, social security wealth, wealth from retiree health insurance benefits, and all other wealth among those in different segments of the wealth distribution. The two middle bars in each figure represent the wealth distribution of the middle fifty percent of the population. The two bars at each end of the distributions cover the highest and lowest 5 percent segments of the population, that is, the top and bottom deciles. In figure 1, the relationships are shown in dollar amounts, emphasizing the major differences in total net wealth from the bottom to the top of the wealth distribution. Because the shares of wealth for the lower end of the distribution are obscured when the same dollar scale is used for those at both ends of the wealth distribution, figure 2 presents the percentage distribution of wealth for those in different parts of the wealth distribution.[47] These findings make it very clear that the share of pensions grows with increasing wealth as the share of social security wealth declines with increasing wealth. The exception is the top 5 percent of the wealth distribution.

Table 17 collects results on the total shares of income and wealth due to pensions, social security, and health insurance. These three sources contribute 13 percent of income on average, while on average they account for 52 percent of wealth. When households are arrayed by income, 11 percent of income for the median 10 percent of households consists of pension and social security accrual and health insurance. When households are arrayed by wealth, 63 percent of the wealth of the median 10 percent of households is comprised of pensions, social security, and retiree health benefits. The share of wealth due to pensions, social security, and retiree health insurance is 68 percent for those in the 25th to 50th percentile; 60 percent for those in the 50th to 75th percentile; and 48 percent for those in the 90th to 95th percentile.

One might also wish to summarize the distributions of wealth, pensions, social security, and the wealth equivalent of retiree health insurance independently of the other elements constituting wealth. The inequality of the distributions of each of these elements of wealth may be summarized by the appropriate gini coefficient. The gini coefficient for the distribution of all wealth among households is .5001.[48] Pension wealth is less equally distributed with a gini coefficient of .7067. Social

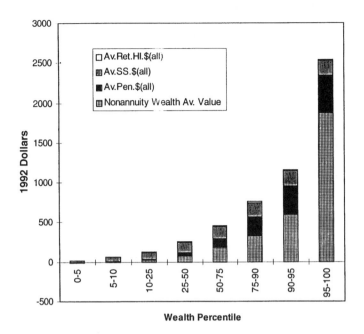

Fig. 1. Household wealth by type, by wealth percentile (in 1992 dollars)

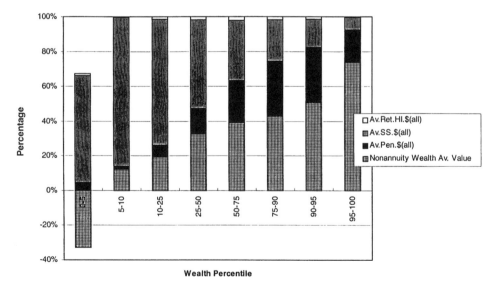

Fig. 2. Percentage distribution of household wealth by type, by wealth percentile

security wealth, in contrast, is more equally distributed and has a gini of .2630. For retiree health insurance, the gini coefficient is .7788, indicating an even less equal distribution than pensions.

Legal vs. Projected Method of Evaluating Pensions

Throughout the discussion so far, we have assumed that pensions are measured by the projected liability method. That is, the estimates assume that the individual will remain with the firm until qualifying for early retirement benefits and that the proper way to measure the liability at the current time is to prorate the ultimate tenure at the firm, crediting the individual with a fraction of the liability that will be realized at retirement that is equal to the ratio of tenure to date divided by tenure accrued at retirement.

Table 18 presents estimates of pension wealth values that assume that the reporting period is the last period of employment at the firm and compares them to the pension wealth estimates based on the projected liability method. The effect is to reduce the value of benefits under defined benefit plans since if employment is terminated, these benefits are calculated for those with defined benefit plans using the current wage and service accrued to date, rather than the projected wage and tenure at retirement, adjusted by the proportion of ultimate tenure accrued to date.[49] Defined contribution benefits have been calculated throughout on a legal liability basis.

TABLE 17. Household Income and Net Wealth from Pensions, Social Security, and Health Insurance by Place in the Distribution: HRS 1

Income or Wealth Percentile	Percentage of Income from Pension Accrual, Social Security Accrual, and Health Insurance	Percentage of Wealth from Pensions, Social Security, and Retiree Health Insurance
95–100	12	26
90–95	14	48
75–90	14	56
50–75	12	60
25–50	11	68
10–25	13	80
5–10	11	88
0–5	472	195
All	13	52
45–55	11	63

Source: See table 3. All data are weighted by HRS sample weights.

From table 18 it can be seen that the mean pension wealth measures based on the legal or projected methods differ by only about 6 percent. There are two reasons for this. First, some people have passed the early retirement age, in which case the rates of pension accrual under the legal and projected methods come together. Second, even though there are sharp spikes at the moment of attaining eligibility for early retirement, the pension wealth values calculated with the two different methods approach each other as the individual approaches the early retirement age.

The mean pension accrual computed on a legal liability basis, $3,579, is 29 percent larger than the mean pension accrual computed on a projected liability basis, $2,767. The pension accrual rates computed for the median 10 percent of households arrayed by income are very close.

With regard to pension wealth, as expected higher values are obtained on a projected liability basis. The means are $116,012 when pension wealth is calculated on a projected liability basis and $109,144 on a legal liability basis. For the median 10 percent of households, the figures are $60,102 and $53,051 on a projected and legal liability basis respectively.

Incentives for Retirement

Tables 19 to 22 report the pension values by age and the characteristics of pensions that affect the incentive to retire. These data are restricted to age eligibles for whom an employer-provided plan description was available and who began their job before age 50.

TABLE 18. Pension Values for HRS Households Based on Projected vs. Legal Liability Methods: HRS 1 (in 1992 dollars)

Method of Calculating Pension	Pension Accrual		Pension Wealth	
	Mean among All Households ($)	Within Households with Median 10 Percent of Income ($)	Mean among All Households ($)	Within Households with Median 10 Percent of Income ($)
Projected liability basis	2,767	1,062	116,012	60,102
Legal liability basis	3,579	944	109,144	53,051

Source: See tables 1 and 3. All data are weighted by HRS sample weights.

Table 19 reports the distribution of plan early and normal retirement ages for defined benefit plans that were matched with the HRS sample. Average early retirement age is 54.4, and average normal retirement age is 61. The modal and median early retirement age is 55, but given their ages of entry, over a quarter of the sample with DB plans could retire before age 55. Only 6 percent have an early retirement age above 60. Forty percent face a normal retirement age of 65, with 14 percent having normal retirement at age 62, over 20 percent having normal retirement at age 60, and over a fifth having a normal retirement age below 60.

Table 20 reports pension value by age, pension value in 1992, and

TABLE 19. Distribution of Early and Normal Retirement Ages of Defined Benefit Plans: HRS 1

Age	Percentage with Early Retirement Age	Percentage with Normal Retirement Age
<50	8.9	1.5
50	11.4	3.2
51	1.9	0.2
52	1.7	1
53	1.6	0.6
54	2	0.8
55	45.8	8.4
56	2.6	1.3
57	2.9	1.4
58	2.3	2.4
59	2.5	1.9
60	10	20.6
61	0.8	1.2
62	4.3	13.7
63	0.1	0.4
64	0.3	0.5
65	0.7	40.6
66	0	0
67	0	0
68	0	0
69	0	0
70	0	0
>70	0	0.1
Average	54.4	61

Source: Authors' calculations using HRS wave 1. Retirement age calculations are based on SPD data as applied to information provided by HRS respondents on work and earnings history. All data are weighted by HRS sample weights.

TABLE 20. Pension Wealth Values by Age (in thousands of 1992 dollars): HRS 1

	Age					1992	ER Age	NR Age
	50	55	60	65	70			
			Defined Benefit					
Mean	99	158	198	209	205	154	159	204
Standard deviation	143	188	209	208	204	188	186	210
First quartile	15	41	70	86	86	39	46	78
Second quartile	51	96	150	165	163	94	105	155
Third quartile	122	214	258	265	261	206	210	261
Number of observations	1,615	1,615	1,615	1,615	1,615	1,615	1,615	1,615
			Defined Contribution					
Mean	52	72	90	107	123	72		
Standard deviation	55	64	74	83	93	64		
First quartile	8	20	29	37	45	18		
Second quartile	29	44	56	69	83	44		
Third quartile	74	100	120	141	159	100		
Number of observations	347	347	347	347	347	347		

Source: Authors' calculations using HRS Wave 1. Pension value calculations are based on SPD data as applied to information provided by HRS respondents on work and earnings history, using the projected liability method. All data are weighted by HRS sample weights.

Note: ER Age = the time of qualification for early retirement benefits. NR Age = the time of qualification for normal retirement benefits.

TABLE 21. Annual Pension Accruals for Defined Benefit plans by age (in thousands of 1992 dollars): HRS 1

	Age				
	50	55	60	62	65
Mean	10.2	7.5	2	−3.7	− 6.2
Standard deviation	31	12.4	10.5	7.9	9.8
First quartile	2.1	1.6	−1.8	−5.6	−8.7
Second quartile	5.5	4.6	1.5	−2.2	−4.4
Third quartile	10.3	9.2	4.6	−0.1	−1.6
Number of observations	1,615	1,615	1,615	1,615	1,615

Source: Authors' calculations using HRS Wave 1. Pension accrual calculations use the projected method for DB plans and are based on SPD data as applied to information provided by HRS respondents on work and earnings history. All data are weighted by HRS sample weights. Reported number of observations is unweighted.

TABLE 22.   Annual Pension Accruals for Defined Benefit Plans by Relation to Early and Normal Retirement Age (in thousands of 1992 dollars): HRS 1

		Plans with Early Retirement			Plans without ER	
	Pre-retirement	ER Age	ER Age–NR Age	NR Age	NR Age	After NR Age
Pension Accrual ($000)						
Mean	8.5	42.7	5.6	5.1	48.5	−1
Standard deviation	8.3	74.4	6.3	40	93.9	4.9
First quartile	3.3	4.5	2.1	−0.9	7.6	−3
Second quartile	6.1	13.8	4.7	2.7	19.8	−0.6
Third quartile	10.6	51.4	8.2	7.3	46.1	1
Number of observations	1,615	1,274	1,274	1,274	341	1,615
Pension/Wage Accrual (%)						
Mean	21.9	102.3	16.5	18.4	117.8	−2.5
Standard deviation	17.7	176.2	9.7	149.6	177.5	17
First quartile	11.3	18	9	−3.1	33.8	−9.4
Second quartile	19.2	40.5	17.3	13	54.4	−2.1
Third quartile	29.4	135.1	24.4	26	164.4	4.6
Number of observations	1,615	1,274	1,274	1,274	341	1,615

Source: Authors' calculations using HRS Wave 1. Pension accrual calculations use the projected method for DB plans and the legal liability method for DC plans and are based on SPD data as applied to information provided by HRS respondents on work and earnings history. All data are weighted by HRS sample weights.

Note: Preretirement Years = the third through first year before qualifying for early retirement benefits, if available, or the three years before normal retirement age if there is no early retirement. ER Age = the year during which the individual qualifies for early retirement benefits. ER Age–NR Age = the years between early and the year before qualifying for normal retirement. NR Age = the year just before qualifying for normal retirement benefits. After NR Age = the three years immediately following qualification for normal retirement benefits.

pension value at the early retirement age and normal retirement age for those respondents with a matched plan. The pension values reported in table 20 are the full values of the pension at the indicated ages or dates. That is, in contrast to the earlier tables, pension values are not prorated on the basis of work to date as a fraction of time from date of hire until retirement. Means, standard deviations, and values separating quartiles are reported. At the early retirement age, the average pension value is $159,000 for defined benefit plans. At the normal retirement age, the average respondent with a DB plan has a pension worth $204,000.[50] These values are higher than the wealth equivalents of pensions reported for the whole population since they pertain only to covered individuals.

For those with defined contribution plans, the plans are valued on the basis of amounts accrued to the indicated age or date. The mean value of the DC plans in 1992 is significantly below the comparable values for DB plans. One reason for the difference is that the cumulative earnings paid to date to those covered by DC plans are about 20 percent lower than are the cumulative earnings paid to those covered by DB plans.

As noted earlier, the sample of plans is not representative of the distribution of all plans. The table in the appendix shows the distribution of plan matches by respondent reports of plan coverage and plan type. Both weighted and unweighted results are reported. It is clear from these data that the fraction of employer plan descriptions that were matched was much higher for employees of large firms and also was much higher for those who were covered by a defined benefit rather than a defined contribution plan. At the extremes, looking at the raw counts, a person reporting a defined benefit or combination plan and working in a firm with over five hundred employees had a 77 percent chance of a pension match. A person with a DC plan only in a similarly sized firm had a 66 percent chance of a pension match. A person with a DB or combination plan in a firm with twenty-four to ninty-nine employees had a 52 percent chance of having the employer plan matched, while the figure for a person with a DC plan only in the same sized firm was 32 percent.

It is possible to make a crude calculation of the upper limit of the effect of oversampling DB plans on the value of pension wealth estimated previously. In the self-reported information on plan types, when asked what type of pension they had, of those who reported, 68 percent (weighted) of HRS respondents indicated they were covered by some type of DB plan, with the rest covered exclusively by a 401(k) or other DC plan. For this group, at age sixty-five, on average DB plans are worth 15.5 percent of the cumulative earnings. On average, at age sixty-five DC plans are worth 9.2 percent of the cumulative earnings. But 76 percent (weighted) of respondents with a matched pension are treated as being covered by a DB plan. If respondents are reporting the correct mix of plan types, so that the proper mix includes 68 percent DB and mixed plans and 32 percent DC only plans, and we have used a mix of 76 percent DB and mixed plans and 24 percent DC only plans, then if earnings were the same, and if we randomly assigned employer plans to respondents, we would overstate the value of average pensions in retirement by about 3.7 percent: $(.76 \times .155 + .24 \times .092)/(.68 \times .155 + .32 \times .092)$. Since pensions were assigned to respondents without an employer-provided plan on a number of characteristics so as to reduce this bias, 3.7 percent is an upper limit estimate.

Tables 21 and 22 indicate pension accrual for those with DB and mixed (i.e., both DB and DC) plans covering HRS age-eligible respondents who began their job before age fifty and for whom the employer provided a matched plan. Table 21 reports on the increments in the projected present value of the pension by age. The accrual rates decline with age after age fifty as a larger fraction reaches the early retirement age.[51] Notice also that the change in the accrual rate with age depends on both the requirements of plans and the age and tenure of workers covered by those plans in the HRS sample.[52]

Table 22 reports on increments in present values of pensions by relation to early and normal retirement age. The figures in table 21 will smooth spikes in DB plan accrual profiles since those covered by different plans will face different retirement ages. By focusing on the years just before and just after attaining eligibility for early and normal retirement, table 22 highlights the spikes in the accrual profiles. Column 2 in table 22 reports on the increment when the covered individual is in the third through first year before qualifying for early retirement benefits, if available, or for three years before normal retirement age if there is no early retirement (Preretirement). The next three columns refer to those plans that will provide early retirement benefits. Column 3 refers to the increment in the pension in the year during which the individual qualifies for early retirement benefits (ER Age), column 4 to the increment between early and the year before qualifying for normal retirement age (ER Age–NR Age), column 5 to the benefit increment in the year just before qualifying for normal retirement benefits (NR Age) for those whose plans offer early retirement benefits, column 6 to the increment in the year before qualifying for normal retirement for those whose plans do not allow for early retirement, and Column 7 refers to the increment in benefits in the three years immediately following qualification for normal retirement benefits. Thus results are separated between the four-fifths of respondents who will be eligible for their plan's early retirement benefits and the one-fifth of respondents who will not be eligible for early retirement benefits.

The bottom of table 22 reports the size of the annual pension accrual relative to annual earnings. The figures are the means of the ratios. These results are also pictured in figure 3 for those in plans where they are eligible for early retirement benefits. The numbers reported in table 22 for pension accrual before early retirement ages are about a third higher than the comparable values calculated using the 1983 Survey of Consumer Finances (SCF) (Gustman and Steinmeier 1989). In the year before early retirement, the HRS pension accrual rate is worth about one year's earnings on average. The same is true at normal retirement age for those who will not be eligible for early retirement benefits. One

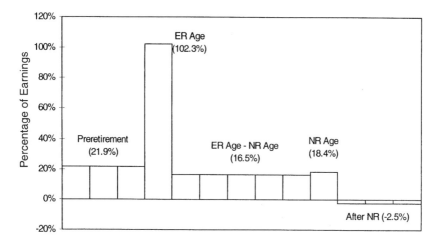

Fig. 3. Pension/earnings accruals for early and normal retirement ages

noteworthy difference between the pensions sampled in the HRS and those in the 1983 SCF is that the increment in pension value after normal retirement age is significantly higher in absolute terms (less negative) in the HRS data than in the SCF data—that is, in the HRS data there is less negative accrual after normal retirement age. This presumably reflects the changes in law regarding age discrimination, which now require that after the normal retirement age the pension be credited on something approaching an actuarially fair basis. In the period the SCF sample was taken, firms were free to halt pension accruals for those remaining employed beyond the normal retirement age.

Conclusion

This essay has confirmed the overwhelming importance in the Health and Retirement Study of including the wealth equivalent of pensions and social security when analyzing wealth. In the HRS data, the sum of pension and social security wealth is about as important as the total of all other sources of wealth taken together, including housing.

Our findings are comparable to others in terms of the importance of pension and social security wealth, as is shown in table 23.[53] Two groups of studies are summarized. Studies in the top panel compute pensions and social security as a share of total income for selected groups in the population that are sixty-five or older.[54] The set in the bottom panel

TABLE 23. Pensions and Social Security as a Percentage of Total Income or Wealth in Various Studies

Study	Population	Year and Interest Rate	Sources of Income or Wealth Other than Pensions and Social Security	Pensions as a Percentage of Income or Wealth	Social Security as a Percentage of Income or Wealth
		Mean Income of Selected Groups Age 65 or Older			
Gustman and Juster (1996, table 2.2)	AHEAD, ages 70–74	1992	Earnings, asset income, transfers, other income	26	41
Grad (1994, table 7.2)	CPS ages 65 and older	1992	Earnings, asset income, public assistance, other	19	40
Grad (1994, table 7.1)	CPS ages 65–69	1992	Earnings, asset income, public assistance, other	19	31
		Mean Wealth			
Present analysis	HRS firm reported pension data ages 51–61	1992, $i = .063$	Business, financial, and retirement assets, house value, retiree health insurance	23	27
Smith (1995a, table 13)	HRS respondent reported pension	1992, $i = .0675$	Business, financial, and retirement assets, house value	22	26
Poterba, Venti, and Wise (1994, table 1)	SIPP, ages 65–69	1991, $i = .06$	Financial assets, home equity, other property. Other assets include 401(k) balances.	20	32

computes the share of wealth represented by pensions and social security, where pension and social security wealth is computed by the authors of the studies on the basis of self-reported incomes of those over sixty-five. Our estimates of the share of wealth due to pensions based on employer-provided pension data are a few percentage points above the shares of pensions in incomes of those sixty-five to sixty-nine in the study by Grad (1994) or the share of pensions in wealth given by Poterba, Venti, and Wise (1994), who used data from the Survey of Income and Program Participation (SIPP). They are close to the estimates of the share of pensions in wealth by Smith (1995a), who used respondent reported data on pensions from the HRS.[55] The estimates of pension wealth for those in their seventies from Gustman and Juster (1996) are somewhat higher than our estimates for the HRS cohort. Our estimates of social security as a share of total net wealth are in line with those from Smith for the HRS but fall below the estimates in the other studies. The older the cohorts included in the studies, the more important is social security as a share of income or wealth.

It is comforting to note that the overall levels of wealth computed from firm reported HRS pension data and the self-reported data in Smith are close to one another. It suggests that researchers may obtain reasonable estimates of pension wealth from self-reported pension data. Nevertheless, it is still likely that self-reports on pension accruals will prove to be inadequate for analysis of retirement behavior and possibly also for analyzing savings behavior. This is because analysis of behavior at the microlevel requires detailed and precise information on the location of spikes in the accrual profile. Self-reports tend to be much less precise as to the location and size of spikes, but the extent to which this is true in the HRS data should be the subject of future research.

While pensions and social security represent half of total net wealth on average, our findings also suggest that for households in the middle of the wealth distribution, the share of wealth represented by pensions and social security is even larger. For all but the highest decile of the wealth distribution, pension and social security wealth together account for more than half of wealth. The share of pensions in net wealth rises with place in the wealth distribution as the share of wealth in social security falls, so that even for those in the 90th to 95th percentile, pension and social security wealth together account for 47 percent of wealth.

Our findings on pension wealth by age and by plan type, and pension accrual rates for the respondents with matched pension plan descriptions from their employers, are consistent with earlier findings based on employer-provided data from the 1983 Survey of Consumer Finances. Absolute benefits are higher in the HRS, a survey ten years more recent than the 1983 SCF, but the accrual profiles still look very similar up until normal retirement age.

Our numbers also indicate the importance of pension accrual, social security benefit accrual, and health insurance benefits in the incomes of those approaching retirement. It is important to include these major elements of compensation when discussing the level and distribution of income.

The results reported in this essay involve three assumptions that may cause us to overstate the importance of pensions and social security in overall wealth. First, we have had to use the self-reported earnings histories in computing social security wealth. Comparing the figures we have calculated with those calculated by Mitchell, Olson, and Steinmeier (1996) using covered earnings histories obtained from the Social Security Administration, we estimate that this approach overstates social security wealth by about 13 percent. Second, we have estimated pension wealth without fully correcting the pool of employer-provided pension plans for overrepresentation of defined benefit plans. The estimated effect may be to overstate pension wealth by as much as 4 percent. Third we have used only the employer-provided plan descriptions in computing wealth from defined contribution plans. Although we have the contribution rate for those cases where contributions are mandatory, in the case of voluntary contributions we have used the average figure from the SCF of a 5 percent contribution rate in those plans where contributions are voluntary. We then have assumed that firms match as called for by the plan.

Even after making allowances for some overstatement of social security and pension wealth in these first pass estimates, it remains the case that pension and social security wealth are overwhelmingly important in determining the level and distribution of wealth of HRS respondents. Anyone who studies wealth or savings in the HRS and ignores pensions and social security does so at the peril of misstating the underlying behavior of HRS households.

These findings also raise questions about whether current generations of workers are badly underprepared for retirement, as some claim. We have not calculated income replacement rates in retirement for those in the HRS cohort. However, the wealth numbers generated here appear to be sizable once social security and pensions have been taken into account. On average HRS respondents are fifty-six years old, with average wealth that is more than ten times annual earnings. Even after allowing for the fact that a fifth of the HRS wave 1 participants have already retired, their accumulated assets are substantial enough to replace two-thirds of income for single men and half or more of incomes for couples, depending on how consumption is curtailed after one spouse dies. To be sure, we recognize that heterogeneity in savings patterns is important and that many people enter retirement with inadequate assets. And of course, many people are heavily dependent on social security, which in the long run will not be financially sustainable at current benefit levels.[56] But on the whole, the population entering retirement may not be in such bad shape as some have led us to believe. Clearly an important next step is to systematically study replacement rates with pension and social security wealth equivalents included.

There are other steps that naturally follow this analysis. One is to integrate the information obtained from employer-provided pension plan descriptions with self-reported pension data. Because of the incomplete availability of employer-provided pension plan descriptions, we had to do a significant amount of imputation. Pension values obtained from respondents will provide useful information to supplement the firm reported data. Moreover, the information obtained from the self-reported data could be used to significantly improve the imputation of pensions. This is not a simple task because self-reported pension data are often reported with error, some of which is systematic. At best, an individual's knowledge of his or her anticipated pension is incomplete. Thus it is not obvious how one should resolve certain conflicts between the employer's and respondent's reports.[57] In addition, because respondents are asked to report pension value at retirement age, it is important to adjust the dollar amounts for those in the sample who are using future rather than current dollars.[58] At this stage, none of the programs for computing pension values from employer-provided Summary Plan Descriptions separates the defined contribution component in plans that are both DB and DC, so merging respondent reports of DC amounts with employer reported pension plans is not currently possible and can only be accomplished after a significant amount of reprogramming. Life tables and prorating of benefits for those who have not yet retired need to be standardized; life tables that take account of the relation between wealth and mortality should be used, and other assumptions underlying calculations should also be standardized. Nevertheless, combining the information provided by respondents with plan descriptions obtained from employers will probably improve estimates of pension wealth, pension income, and incentives from pensions. It will be especially important to obtain the closest estimates possible of the pension accrual profile when conducting retirement studies. If the spikes in the pension accrual profile are not correctly placed, it is likely that any estimates of respondent preferences governing retirement decisions will be poorly estimated.

Those who wish to improve on pension estimates presented here will also have to concern themselves with the imputation methodology and the issue of selection bias. Refining the imputation of pension values for those with missing data requires understanding what determines the likelihood that employees with different plans will have a matched employer-provided plan description. It is clear from the frequencies reported in the table in the appendix that the probability of matching an employer plan description is much higher in larger firms and for defined benefit plans. A similar analysis will be required to understand the patterns of missing data in the self-reported plan descriptions and to correct both sets of data in light of systematic patterns of missing data.

Another source of improvement in these estimates will come when researchers use both the employer-provided pension plan descriptions and the social security earnings records in the same study, under a carefully controlled set of restricted access conditions. Not only will estimates of social security benefits be improved, but the information on earnings history will also be useful in computing pension wealth.

For all of these reasons, the estimates presented here provide only a preliminary picture of the role of pensions and social security in income and wealth determination. Nevertheless, these findings demonstrate that one must take full account of pensions and social security when examining the distribution of income and wealth. This is a lesson that was taught to us by Tom Juster, who has led the way in designing surveys that take full account of pensions and social security in the distribution of income and wealth.

APPENDIX

Pension Matching Rates by Firm Size, Weighted and Unweighted Results

	Firm Size					
	<24	24–99	100–499	500+	Unknown	All
	Unweighted Counts					
No Pension	2,238	431	353	672	113	3,807
Pension						
SR[a] DB or combo						
Unmatched plan	79	97	147	503	8	834
Matched plan	39	107	303	1,683	21	2,153
SR DC only						
Unmatched plan	144	139	133	238	13	667
Matched plan	36	65	131	464	7	703
SR Unknown						
Unmatched plan	15	23	35	95	4	172
Matched plan	2	4	14	34	0	54
All Plans						
Unmatched plan	238	259	315	836	25	1,673
Matched plan	77	176	448	2,181	28	2,910

	Firm Size					
	<24	24–99	100–499	500+	Unknown	All
	Weighted Counts (00 omitted)					
No Pension	43,698,128	8,569,556	6,027,238	10,892,398	1,754,368	70,941,768
Pension						
SR DB or combo						
Unmatched plan	1,782,030	2,084,695	2,785,766	10,214,940	153,721	17,021,168
Matched plan	875,047	2,286,421	6,636,897	33,882,888	443,132	44,124,408
SR DC only						
Unmatched plan	3,168,715	3,216,292	2,942,495	4,730,529	287,710	14,345,736
Matched plan	804,111	1,275,550	2,771,571	9,065,339	128,041	14,044,617
SR Unknown						
Unmatched plan	300,495	468,208	546,089	1,851,844	83,464	3,250,099
Matched plan	39,536	38,233	248,553	406,774	0	733,096
All Plans						
Unmatched plan	5,251,240	5,769,193	6,274,349	16,797,324	524,896	34,617,004
Matched plan	1,718,694	3,600,205	9,657,022	43,354,988	571,173	58,902,092

Source: Authors' calculations using HRS Wave 1.

[a]SR = self-reported.

NOTES

This essay is a revised version of a paper presented at the Retirement Conference in Honor of F. Thomas Juster, December 13 and 14, 1996. Gustman and Steinmeier are grateful for support under Contract No. J-9-P-5-0097 from the U.S. Department of Labor, Pension and Welfare Benefits Administration, and from the National Institute on Aging. Mitchell acknowledges support from the Aging Research Center and the Pension Research Council at the University of Pennsylvania. We are grateful for comments from Charlie Brown, Lee Lillard, Anna Lusardi, David McCarthy, and conference participants. Charlie Brown and Mel Stephens were very helpful in resolving questions about coded pension plan descriptions. Opinions expressed are those of the authors and not of the sponsoring agencies.

   1. The HRS is a panel study of a nationally representative population base with a least one spouse who was born from 1931 to 1941. The first wave of the survey, fielded in 1992, includes 12,652 individuals. We identify 7,607 households with usable records for the present study.

   2. Of course, this will depend on mortality experience as well as investment earnings.

   3. In the HRS sample of households where the financially knowledgeable member responded to the survey, we count 6,170 individuals as having been covered by either a current or past pension that was not cashed out or lost upon

leaving. In 1992 four-fifths of those who were covered by a pension or by social security from their own work had not yet retired. These and other descriptive numbers are reported in Gustman, Mitchell, and Steinmeier 1995a, 1995b. The numbers (raw counts) of households by marital status and probability of pension coverage in our sample are as follows: single males = 741; .519; single females = 1,631; .418; married males = 5,234; .618; married females = 5,234; .357).

4. In an innovative study using employer-provided pension plan descriptions from the Survey of Consumer Finances, McDermed, Clark, and Allen (1989) found higher shares of pension wealth in total wealth than we do here. However, their estimates of total wealth do not include social security wealth.

5. Another major innovation in the HRS is the inclusion of earnings histories and benefit payments obtained for each respondent from the Social Security Administration. This study does not use the social security earnings histories. The agreement with the Social Security Administration at the time the essay was written did not permit the social security data collected for HRS participants to be used together with employer-provided pension plan descriptions. Accordingly, we had to estimate social security wealth from self-reported but incomplete earnings histories provided by respondents. We will describe the construction of our estimate of social security wealth subsequently in the text. For estimates of social security wealth in the HRS based on matched earnings records from the Social Security Administration, see Mitchell, Olson, and Steinmeier 1996. In the aggregate, our estimates of social security wealth using self-reported earnings histories are seen later in the text to be about 13 percent higher than the estimates obtained by Mitchell, Olson, and Steinmeier. This means that our estimates of social security wealth overstate their share of total net wealth by about 3 percentage points.

6. Richard Curtin collected firm provided pension plan descriptions for the Survey of Consumer Finances and surpervised their coding and analysis. Robert Peticolas collected the pension information for the HRS and supervised its coding. Tom Juster directed both surveys.

7. Until pension plan descriptions from employers were included in surveys of income and wealth, students of savings and wealth determination and distribution found it extremely difficult to calculate reliable estimates of pension wealth and pension income, especially in surveys that included many people who remained at work. Many studies of savings and wealth determination did not include pensions and social security. See, for example, Diamond and Hausman 1984; Avery and Kennickell 1991; U.S. Congressional Budget Office 1993; Bernheim and Scholtz 1993; Kennickell and Starr-McCluer 1996. Some studies of income and wealth include pensions by focusing on the retired population. See, for example, Grad 1994; and Poterba, Venti, and Wise 1994. As will be seen in the concluding section of this essay, our findings as to the importance of pensions and social security in total net wealth and income for the HRS population, which includes many who have not yet retired, are consistent with the findings in these studies for recent generations of retirees.

Some surveys, including those based on the Health and Retirement Study, obtain information about pensions by asking the respondents about their plans. These data are quite informative, including detailed descriptions from the covered individual or from the spouse. Frequently, however, the plan descriptions are incomplete. They are most valuable when used in concert with information from employer-provided pension plan descriptions. Thus it is of interest to compare our findings with those from studies based on respondent-provided pension plan descriptions, such as in Smith 1995a. We make such a comparison in the concluding section. Pension data obtained from the respondents to the Health and Retirement Study have also been analyzed by McGarry and Davenport (1996).

8. A defined benefit pension plan determines the yearly benefit a worker will receive on retiring by using a formula that depends on the employee's earnings, years of service, and retirement age. A very simple DB plan might pay benefits equal to 1 percent of final salary times the number of years worked at the company. In contrast, a defined contribution pension plan establishes an account that is held in each covered worker's name, and benefits accrue according to a contribution formula that determines how much is deposited in the account in each year (plus investment earnings or losses). At retirement, benefit payments depend on the cumulated value of contribution amounts, as well as investment income from the accumulated funds. Under a DB plan, pension payments do not depend on pension fund returns, since when investment returns are lower than expected, the employer is ultimately responsible for covering the shortfall (along with a government insurance fund, if the firm goes bankrupt). There are many varieties of defined contribution plans including 401(k) plans, profit sharing, stock ownership, and money purchase plans, where payment may be in a lump sum or may take the form of an annuity (Turner and Beller 1992). Workers can, and often do, have both DB and DC plans. For descriptive statistics on these plans, see Gustman, Mitchell, and Steinmeier 1995a and 1995b.

9. Estimates of the value of financial and other assets reported here have been reported previously (e.g., Smith 1995a, 1995b; Moon and Juster 1995; Gustman and Juster 1996) and are based on the innovative methodology applied in the HRS, which results in a substantial improvement in the quality of the information on these assets.

10. The amounts reported in defined contribution plans are estimated from the earnings history and from the plan description. For defined contribution plans with required contributions, we use the mandated rate as the rate of contribution. When a DC plan has a voluntary component, we use a 5 percent contribution rate, which is the average rate found by Samwick and Skinner (1998) in data from the Survey of Consumer Finances.

11. The HRS is one of three surveys to have collected pension plan descriptions from employers. The others are the Survey of Consumer Finances (SCF) and the National Longitudinal Survey of Mature Women (NLS-MW). Neither the SCF nor the NLS-MW incorporates the bracketing technique for reporting of assets used in the HRS to obtain substantially improved estimates of the value of financial and other assets.

12. A number of errors and anomalies have been identified, and the plan

descriptions have been altered from those originally coded in order to correct the errors. Many of the errors result in pension accrual profiles that are discontinuous in unreasonable ways, have negative slopes, and in other ways appear to be unreasonable. In some cases the source of the error is obvious; for example, a decimal is moved. For some cases the error is obvious, but the cure is not. A plan description might prescribe a benefit for a worker employed in 1989, a higher benefit for a worker employed in 1990, and a still higher benefit for a worker employed in 1991. But the description may fall silent for work in 1988, the last year the respondent worked.

13. A number of plans were identified as having ten-year vesting although private pension law requires shorter vesting for all but multiemployer plans. (The Small Business Job Protection Act enacted on August 20, 1996, was the first legislation to require faster than ten-year cliff vesting for multiemployer plans, and it has a three-year phase-in.) In some cases the plans are public plans. But some of the plan descriptions are quite old and go back to a period when the vesting could exceed ten years.

14. More specifically, the retirement age used in prorating the projected value of DB plans is taken to be the lowest of the ages specified in any DB component to the retirement plan. The projected value is based on service and earnings projected to the early retirement age, that is, the age the respondent will be eligible for early retirement benefits. The prorated share of the projected value of the pension takes the fraction of the projected value equal to the fraction of years from date of hire to early retirement date that have been worked as of 1992. For anyone in the sample who is still working beyond the early retirement age, the pension value is increased accordingly. Variation in the value of DB plans with different ages of retirement is explored in the "Incentives for Retirement" section of this essay.

15. Because we provide pension wealth on the basis of work to date, our findings as to pension wealth accrued to date are not very sensitive to the date we take for retirement. We prorate pension wealth from the early retirement date. But if we had prorated pension wealth from a later date, like normal retirement age or the retirement age expected by the individual, then while total pension wealth rises with additional work until normal retirement age, the fraction of pension wealth earned to date falls since a smaller fraction of the number of years that will ultimately be worked has been worked to date.

16. One strategy we will employ in the future is to compare HRS respondents' reports of plan type with firm reports of plan type for those where respondent- and employer-provided pension descriptions are available. Knowing the difference one could then use the individual reports of plan type to impute type of plan for those without a matched employer plan.

17. For an analysis of wage growth among older workers, see Gustman and Steinmeier 1985.

18. The earnings function used to project earnings in earlier years assumes only economy-wide wage growth but ignores wage growth due to tenure and experience. As a result, we are overstating earnings at younger ages.

19. The construction of this variable is described in the publication *Measuring the Effect of Benefits and Taxes on Income and Poverty: 1979 to 1991* (U.S. Bureau of the Census 1993, B-3).

1. An enhanced NMCES data file was prepared by adding two variables not on the original file (total annual earnings and usual hours per week) by statistically matching NMCES and CPS using the appropriate demographic and economic variables available from both sources. The match made it possible to assign earnings and full-time/part-time variables to the NMCES file.
2. The enhanced NMCES file was used to estimate a model that related employer contributions to a set of explanatory variables that were also available on the CPS file. These variables included type of plan (family or individual), proportion of cost paid for by employer (part or all), earnings, type of worker (full-time or part-time), industry, occupation, sector (private or government), region, residence, age, race, marital status, and education.
3. The model was run on the March CPS file to obtain estimates of the amount of employer contributions for each worker whose employer paid all or part of the cost of his or her health plan. The model was run as deflating 1991 earnings to 1977 dollars. The estimates produced by this model were then inflated to 1991 estimates by multiplying the 1977 level estimates by the 1977 to 1991 change in employer contributions per covered worker.
4. For those persons who worked for the federal government in 1991, the amount of employer contribution was calculated using administrative data. Separate calculations were made for postal and nonpostal employees.

20. Gustman and Steinmeier (1994) include the wealth equivalent of employer-provided health insurance in the opportunity set affecting the worker's retirement decision.

21. The unfolding techniques have been examined in Juster and Smith 1994. Their conclusions are as follows.

1. Most respondents who cannot or will not provide an estimate of the value of a net worth component are willing to respond to the bracket question.
2. The proportion of people willing to respond to the bracket questions is much higher for respondents who reply, "Don't know," to the original question about the amount (about 90 percent) than for respondents who refused to answer the question (about 50 percent).
3. Respondents who either report that they don't know or refuse to answer a question about the value of a net worth component are very different from respondents who provide valid responses to the amount question,

and the differences cannot be accounted for by differences in some measurable characteristic of the respondent.

22. The concept of the median 10 percent of families arrayed by wealth or income is a bit awkward to deal with. However, it is not appropriate to focus only on the median family because we are interested in the distribution of wealth or income for the median group and the family with median income or wealth may not have a representative distribution among various categories of wealth or income.

23. Earnings include wages, salaries, bonuses, overtime, tips, income from professional trade and practice, income from second jobs, and income from the military reserve.

24. For pensions at various ages, the accrual is the difference between the currently available pension and the pension available one year hence, less the accumulated interest. This represents the accrual from this year's work.

25. To remind the reader, we do not take the payroll tax into account in this calculation.

26. Transfers include unemployment insurance, workers' compensation, veterans' benefits, Supplemental Security Income (SSI), and welfare.

27. Asset income includes business income, rent, dividends, interest, and income from trust funds and royalties. We have checked the totals obtained here against results obtained by Gustman and Juster (1996) and by Venti and Wise (this volume). The totals and individual items are consistent.

28. Other income includes alimony, child support, regular support from friends and relatives, and other income sources.

29. Notice that in reporting wealth we have not included the capitalized value of future earnings. This leads to an understatement of full expected wealth on the part of the household.

30. Note once again that these figures for social security wealth are based on past earnings history reported by the respondent rather than on reported covered earnings from the Social Security Administration. In the case of men and single women, we assumed that they worked continuously since leaving school. According to the social security records for the sample provided by Mitchell, Olson, and Steinmeier (1996, table 1), however, even from age thirty forward, men averaged 10 to 12 percent of years with zero reported social security earnings and additional but unspecified years with earnings that may on average be overstated by our procedure of projecting wages backward from the earliest job reported in the HRS. In addition, as noted earlier, we have estimated earnings at younger ages assuming that earnings increase each year by the rate of economy-wide wage growth in earnings, but we have not included increases in wages with tenure and experience. The effect is that we overstate earnings at younger ages.

31. House value includes ranch, farm, home on partly owned ranch, mobile home site, mobile home, mobile home and site, house/apartment, first mortgage, second mortgage, third mortgage, home equity line of credit, second home, mortgage on second home, and net value of motor home.

32. Business assets include real estate and business assets.

33. Financial assets include stocks and mutual funds, checking and savings accounts, CDs, government savings bonds or treasury bills, and other bonds or bond funds and are net of debts.

34. Retirement assets include Keoghs and IRAs.

35. Note that the wealth measure of the health insurance variable is based only on the present value of retiree health insurance. The income measure of health insurance also includes the value of employer-provided health insurance covered as part of ongoing compensation for continuing work.

36. Other assets include vehicles and other assets.

37. See Smith 1995b for a very informative discussion of the income and wealth of singles and couples.

38. It would be of interest to further decompose gender differences in pension wealth into differences in plan coverage, plan type, plan generosity, wage and employment history, planned retirement date, and life expectancy. Such a decomposition is beyond the scope of the present essay.

39. We do not mean to suggest that the simple life-cycle model is the appropriate model to use in predicting how wealth will vary with higher incomes; these simple comparisons are only very roughly suggestive. Many other complications should be taken into account before making judgments on the basis of a comparison between income and wealth differences for those with and without pensions. Among the considerations not taken into account in the simple comparisons are the following. For a number of reasons, those with and without pensions may retire at different times. On the one hand, pension incentives may encourage earlier retirement. On the other hand, other things the same, those with pensions may have a stronger taste for work than those without pensions, and that taste difference may be correlated with date of retirement. Transitory incomes may affect the comparisons. There may be systematic unmeasured differences in the jobs held by those with and without pensions. Income growth may differ between those with and without pensions. For all of these reasons, a measure of full earnings, based on a concept of lifetime earnings adjusted for realizations of various outcomes that are uncertain ex ante, should be used in these comparisons, instead of measures of current income. Moreover, social security is nondiscretionary, so that total wealth may be higher than many low-income families would prefer if they were free to dissave and to consume. Also, housing wealth may not be transformed willingly into other forms of consumption. Clearly, the question of how total wealth varies with income and pension coverage deserves a much closer examination, in the context of a more realistic model that includes careful measurement of pension and social security wealth, than we can produce by simply comparing income and wealth for those with and without pensions. For a related discussion and a list of additional issues, see Gale 1998.

40. Those with lower incomes, which we are taking here as a crude index of lifetime income, are entitled to higher replacement rates from social security. Again, in a simple life-cycle model, the social security benefits would substitute

for other savings. The fact that those with pensions have lower replacement rates from social security would suggest that they should save more in other forms.

41. Union jobs are not identified in section H, previous job. They are identified in section F, current job, and section G, last job for those with no current job. That means we may be missing some union members who were on long-term union jobs but retired from them a number of years ago.

42. Remember that the absolute value of total net wealth for blacks is half that for whites and others.

43. Because some respondents have negative incomes, use of gini coefficients is not entirely appropriate here. Comparisons between means and medians and consideration of the amounts found in the brackets at different percentiles of the distribution provide the clearest indication of the skewness of the distribution.

44. There also are other seeming anomalies. For example, transfers are high for those with high incomes. There are twenty observations with income greater than $100,000 and transfers greater than $8,000. Almost all have veterans' benefits in the $20,000 to $40,000 range.

45. The large negative numbers for the 1.1 percent with a pension, out of the bottom 5 percent of the income distribution (i.e., 6 hundredths of a percent of the sample fall in this category), reflect two things. First, the income percentile and the wage used in computing the pension are calculated from different measures that may diverge and in rare circumstances may substantially diverge. In calculating incomes, earnings in 1991–92 are used. To fall in the bottom 5 percent of the income distribution, those earnings must be low. But pensions are computed based on the reported wage, which for the 1992 survey year may be high. The wage must be high if it is associated with a pension of high enough value to accrue a negative $46,975 on average. The negative accrual in the pension in turn must reflect the effect of the individual having passed at least the early retirement age and in the case of the $46,975 figure, probably the normal retirement age. That is, the individual is losing one year of a highly valued pension from continuing at work, is listed as receiving earnings that are very low despite the high wage, and is not accruing future pension value at nearly a high enough rate to make up for the forgone pension. These negative pension accrual figures may also reflect the collection of an older plan than the one actually in operation in 1992. Older plans may not credit work after having reached retirement age to the extent that the courts and law now require such work to be credited. As seen subsequently in table 21, the accrual rate for the sample DB plans averages −2.5 percent after the individual qualifies for normal retirement and for the bottom quartile averages −9.4 percent. In plans in place in 1983 collected by the Survey of Consumer Finances, the bottom quartile averaged an accrual rate of −17 percent after normal retirement age (Gustman and Steinmeier 1989, table 11).

46. A number of the households falling within the bottom 5 or 10 percent of wealth holders have high assets in particular categories. For example there are seven observations with less than $7,000 in total wealth but more than $25,000 in business assets. All of then have negative total assets. Four of them listed large

negative financial assets (debts) that have more than offset the business assets. Three of them had large negative housing assets, which were either mortgages or home equity lines of credit that substantially exceeded the value of the house. The worst case by far was an observation that listed business assets of $2,625,000 and a third mortgage of $3,500,000.

47. On average, those in the bottom 5 percent of the wealth distribution have negative nonannuity wealth, which accounts for a portion of the first bar in figure 2 falling below the 0 percent axis.

48. When the gini coefficient is calculated for all wealth, but negative wealth values are excluded, it falls to 0.4976.

49. For further discussions of the legal and projected liability methods, and for comparisons of pension values under each method in the 1983 Survey of Consumer Finances, see Gustman and Steinmeier 1989. See also McGill et al. 1996.

50. Pension values associated with DB plans include the value of any plan that has a defined benefit component. Thus the amounts shown include the sum of defined benefit plus defined contribution components for those whose plans include elements from each plan type.

51. For pensions at various ages, the accrual is the difference between the currently available pension and the pension available one year hence. This represents the accrual from this year's work. In table 22, where accrual is reported by relation to early and normal retirement age, the accrual is the difference in the pension value in the indicated period, for instance, the year before early retirement age.

52. Conceptually, it is also possible to calculate plan accrual rates for a person with a standardized earnings history, so as to isolate the effects of plan provisions, but we do not do that in table 21 or table 22. (See Gustman and Steinmeier 1989, for related calculations.)

53. There are many differences among the studies, so the comparisons are very crude. For example, the various wealth estimates make different assumptions about life expectancy and cost of living adjustments. Moreover, we prorate pension and social security wealth based on the fraction of total work accomplished to date, while Smith (1995a) reports total wealth at retirement. Although the assumptions about interest rates are not far apart, these and other assumptions should be standardized to obtain a clearer understanding of the wealth differences obtained.

54. For the first set of studies in table 23, we are comparing shares of incomes for the older populations examined with shares of wealth in our computations. This comparison implicitly assumes that the income from assets at the various points in the retirement period examined in these studies will be roughly proportionate to the shares of wealth in studies that focus on asset equivalents over the full retirement period. But incomes from pensions and social security change over time within the retirement period. See, for example, Gustman and Steinmeier 1993, which finds substantial variation in pension incomes after retirement for a sample from the PSID panel.

55. McGarry and Davenport (1996) estimate pension wealth from self-reported HRS data, but they do not estimate social security wealth. Their mean estimate of pension wealth of $88,000 for all households is well below the mean of $116,000 estimated in this study. Over households with nonzero pension wealth they report average wealth of $152,000 compared to $182,000 in the present study. There also is a major difference in other wealth beside pensions and social security. They report $180,000 in nonpension, non-social-security wealth, while we report an average of $250,000 per household. Accordingly, while our estimates indicate that pension wealth is 46 percent of other (non-pension, non-social-security) wealth, McGarry and Davenport find that pension wealth based on self-reported data is 49 percent of other wealth on average. Because these calculations are based on many different assumptions, they are only roughly comparable.

56. On the prospects for social security, see Technical Panel 1995. There also is the question of how to treat housing wealth: Will housing wealth become more of a retirement asset as reverse mortgages become more popular?

57. Consider some of the following issues: (1) If a worker reports a DB plan and the employer reports a DC plan only, or vice versa, what should the researcher do? Suppose the worker has reported a DC balance, but the firm has submitted an SPD for a DB plan only. (2) If a worker reports a DB and a DC plan, but the firm submits an SPD for a DB plan only, what does one do with the DC plan? Hotdeck it or ignore it? (3) If the worker says DB and the firm says both DB and DC, does one assume the worker is not participating in the DC or that the worker has failed to report it but is participating? (4) If a worker claims to have both DB and DC plans, but the firm files no plans, should the DB and DC plans be hotdecked separately, or is it better to hotdeck from joint DB and DC plans? Some of the answers to these questions are contained in the detailed descriptions from the SPDs, which are not always apparent from the coded plan descriptions. For example, some plans are essentially DB but guarantee a very low minimum return on the contribution of the employee, a return that is so low that it will never be realized. Nevertheless, these plans have been coded as both DB and DC.

58. Respondents are asked about the wage just before retirement to allow adjustment in responses between present and future dollars.

REFERENCES

Avery, Robert B., and Arthur B. Kennickell. 1991. "Household Saving and Portfolio Change: Evidence from the 1983–89 SCF Panel." Board of Governors. Mimeo.
Bernheim, B. Douglas, and J. Karl Scholtz. 1993. "Private Saving and Public Policy." In J. Poterba, ed., *Tax Policy and the Economy,* 7:73–110. Cambridge: MIT Press.
Board of Trustees, Federal Old Age and Survivors, Insurance and Disability

Trust Funds. 1995. Annual Report. Washington, DC: U.S. Government Printing Office.

Diamond, Peter A., and Jerry Hausman. 1984. "Individual Retirement and Saving Behavior." *Journal of Public Economics* 23:81–114.

Gale, William G. 1998. "The Effects of Pensions on Wealth: A Re-evaluation of Theory and Evidence." *Journal of Political Economy* 106:706–23.

Grad, Susan. 1994. *Income of the Population 55 or Older, 1992.* Washington, DC: U.S. Department of Health and Human Services, Social Security Administration.

Gustman, Alan L., and F. Thomas Juster. 1996. "Income and Wealth of Older American Households: Modeling Issues for Public Policy Analysis." In Eric Hanushek and Nancy L. Maritato, eds., *Assessing Knowledge of Retirement Behavior,* 11–60. Washington, DC: National Academy Press.

Gustman, Alan L., Olivia S. Mitchell, and Thomas L. Steinmeier. 1995a. "Older Union and Nonunion Workers and Their Jobs in the Health and Retirement Survey." *Proceedings, Industrial Relations Research Association.*

———. 1995b. "Retirement Research Using the Health and Retirement Survey." *Journal of Human Resources* 30 (supplement): S57–83.

Gustman, Alan. L., and Thomas L. Steinmeier. 1985. "The Effects of Partial Retirement on Wage Profiles of Older Workers." *Industrial Relations* 24, no. 2:257–65.

———. 1989. "An Analysis of Pension Benefit Formulas, Pension Wealth and Incentives from Pensions." In Ronald Ehrenberg, ed., *Research in Labor Economics,* 10:33–106. Greenwich, CT: JAI Press.

———. 1993. "Cost-of-Living Adjustments in Pensions." In Olivia S. Mitchell, ed., *As the Workforce Ages: Costs, Benefits and Policy Challenges,* 147–80. Ithaca, NY: ILR Press.

———. 1994. "Employer-Provided Health Insurance and Retirement Behavior." *Industrial and Labor Relations Review* 47, no. 3.

———. 1998. "Changing Pensions In Cross-Section and Panel Data: Analysis With Employer Provided Pension Plan Descriptions." *Proceedings: National Tax Association.*

———. Forthcoming. "Effects of Pensions on Savings: Analysis with Data from the Health and Retirement Study." *Carnegie-Rochester Conference on Public Policy.*

Hurd, Michael, and Daniel McFadden. 1996. "The Effects of Anchoring on the Distribution of Consumption and Saving." Paper presented at the NBER Summer Institute Session on Aging.

Ippolito, Richard. 1985. "The Labor Contract and True Economic Pension Liabilities." *American Economic Review* 75, no. 5: 1031–43.

Juster, F. Thomas, and James P. Smith. 1994. "Improving the Quality of Economic Data: Lessons from the HRS." Ann Arbor, MI. Mimeo.

Kennickell, Arthur B., and Martha Starr-McCluer. 1996. "Household Saving and Portfolio Change: Evidence from the 1983–89 SCF Panel." Board of Governors. Mimeo.

McDermed, Ann A., Robert L. Clark, and Steven G. Allen. 1989. "Pension Wealth, Age-Wealth Profiles, and the Distribution of Net Worth." In Robert E. Lipsey and Helen S. Tice, eds., *The Measurement of Saving, Investment and Wealth,* 689–731. Chicago: University of Chicago Press for NBER.

McGarry, Kathleen, and Andrew Davenport. 1996. "Pensions and the Distribution of Wealth: Differences by Race and Sex." Paper presented at the Center for Pension and Retirement Research Conference, Miami University, Oxford, Ohio, May 31–June 1.

McGill, Dan M., Kyle N. Brown, John J. Haley, and Sylvester J. Schieber. 1996. *Fundamentals of Private Pensions.* 7th ed. Philadelphia: University of Pennsylvania Press, for the Pension Research Council, the Wharton School of the University of Pennsylvania.

Mitchell, Olivia, S., Jan Olson, and Thomas L. Steinmeier. 1996. "Construction of the Earnings and Benefits File (EBF) for Use with the Health and Retirement Survey." NBER working paper no. 5707.

Moon, Marilyn, and F. Thomas Juster. 1995. "Economic Status Measures in the Health and Retirement Study." *Journal of Human Resources* 30 (supplement): S138–57.

Poterba, James M., Steven F. Venti, and David A. Wise. 1994. "Targeted Retirement Saving and the Net Worth of Elderly Americans." *American Economic Review* 84, no. 2: 180–85.

Samwick, Andrew A., and Jonathan Skinner. 1998. "How Will Defined Contribution Pension Plans Affect Retirement Income?" NBER working paper no. 6645, Hanover, NH.

Smith, James P. 1995a. "Racial and Ethnic Differences in Wealth Using the HRS." *Journal of Human Resources* 30 (supplement): S158–83.

———. 1995b. "Marriage, Assets and Savings." Rand working paper no. 95–08.

———. 1996. "Wealth Accumulation between the Waves." Rand Corporation. Photocopy.

Technical Panel on Trends and Issues in Retirement Saving. 1995. Final Report, U.S. Department of Health and Human Services. 1994–95 Advisory Council on Social Security, ⟨http://www.ssa.gov⟩.

Turner, John A., and Daniel J. Beller. 1992. *Trends in Pensions, 1992.* Washington, DC: U.S. Government Printing Office.

U.S. Bureau of the Census. 1992. *Measuring the Effect of Benefits and Taxes on Income and Poverty: 1979 to 1991.*

U.S. Congressional Budget Office. 1993. *Baby Boomers in Retirement: An Early Perspective.*

U.S. General Accounting Office (GAO). 1989. *Employee Benefits, Companies' Retiree Health Liabilities Large, Advance Funding Costly.* June.

The Size Distribution of Wealth in the United States: A Comparison among Recent Household Surveys

Edward N. Wolff

Over the past fifteen years or so there has been a near explosion in the number of surveys of household wealth holdings. After a twenty-year drought, during which little information was collected on household wealth between the 1962 Survey of Financial Characteristics of Consumers (SFCC) and the 1983 Survey of Consumer Finances (with the slight exception of the 1979 Income Survey and Development Program), the problem in this area today is an embarrassment of riches. There are at least a dozen surveys that cover one or more years in the period from 1983 to 1995 and are conducted on a regular basis that contain questions on household assets and liabilities. These include the Federal Reserve Board's Survey of Consumer Finances (SCF) for years 1983, 1986 (a partial resample of the households included in the 1983 survey), 1989, 1992, and 1995; the U.S. Bureau of the Census's Survey of Income and Program Participation (SIPP) for 1984, 1988, 1991, and 1993; and the Institute for Social Research's Panel Survey of Income Dynamics (PSID) for 1984, 1989, and 1994. Yet, this wealth of wealth data — insofar as it has been analyzed — has often produced contradictory and inconsistent estimates of the distribution of household wealth.

In contrast, there are now official estimates of the size distribution of household income. The U.S. Census Bureau conducts an annual survey in March, called the Current Population Survey, which provides detailed information on individual and household earnings and income. On the basis of these data, the U.S. Census Bureau constructs its estimates of both family and household income inequality. Moreover, the Current Population Surveys have been conducted in the United States for almost half a century. As a result, there exists a consistent time series on household income distribution for the United States that covers this entire period. There is, in addition, considerable consistency in household income estimates that are obtained from other survey sources, such as the decennial Census of Population, SIPP, and the Consumer Expenditure Survey.

Unfortunately, there do not exist comparable data on the size distribution of household wealth for the United States or, for that matter, for any other country in the world. There are no official household surveys conducted on an annual basis for this purpose. As a result, researchers in this field have had to make estimates of household wealth inequality from a variety of sources, which are often inconsistent and, indeed, contradictory. Compounding this problem is the fact that household wealth is much more heavily concentrated in the upper percentiles of the distribution than income. Thus, unless surveys or data sources are especially designed to cover the top wealth groups in a country, it is quite easy to produce biased estimates of the size distribution of wealth. The net result is that time-series estimates of household wealth distribution have been less reliable than those of income.

In this essay, I present comparisons of wealth estimates derived from the SCF, SIPP, and PSID. Three time periods are highlighted: (1) the 1983 SCF, the 1984 SIPP, and the 1984 PSID; (2) the 1989 SCF, the 1988 SIPP, and the 1989 PSID; and (3) the 1992 SCF, the 1991 and 1993 SIPP files, and the 1994 PSID. In many ways, my work here updates the seminal and very comprehensive study (seventy-six pages worth) of Curtin, Juster, and Morgan (1989), which investigated differences in wealth estimates drawn from the 1983 SCF, the 1984 SIPP, and the 1984 PSID. Their main conclusion is as follows: "Measured against the standards set by previous household wealth surveys, all three of these data sets stand up quite well. They do not differ substantially among themselves when it comes to measuring total wealth and the distribution of wealth in the great bulk of the U.S. population" (544).

I do not intend to try to replicate the extensive analyses of these data conducted by Curtin, Juster, and Morgan but will, instead, focus on a few issues. Moreover, where relevant, I will try to assess whether the comparative performances of these surveys have changed much since the early 1980s.

The next section of this essay, "Methodological Issues and Data Sources," briefly reviews some of the methodological issues involved in the estimation of household wealth from household surveys. The "Time Trends in the Size Distribution of Wealth" section presents a comparison of time-series trends on the overall distribution of household wealth over the period 1983–94 from the three sources. The "Comparison of Ownership Rates and Means by Asset Type" section delves more deeply into the relative performances of the three surveys in the three periods. Concluding remarks are made in the last section of the essay.

Methodological Issues and Data Sources

An extensive treatment is provided by Curtin, Juster, and Morgan (1989) of the methodological issues involved in assessing the quality of wealth data from household surveys. Here, I will highlight two major issues: (1) the sample design and (2) asset and liability coverage (questionnaire design).

Sample Design

Because household wealth is extremely skewed, the upper tail of the distribution is often considerably underrepresented in representative samples. All three data sources — the SCF, SIPP, and PSID — use a representative sample as their basic survey instrument. The PSID also includes a special low-income supplement, originally drawn from the 1966–67 Survey of Economic Opportunity. Of the three, only the SCF includes a high-income supplement. This is drawn from the Internal Revenue Service's Statistics of Income data file. For the 1983 SCF, for example, an income cutoff of $100,000 of adjusted gross income is used as the criterion for inclusion in the supplemental sample. Individuals were then randomly selected for the sample within predesignated income strata.

The advantage of the high-income supplement is that it provides a much "richer" sample of high income and therefore potentially very wealthy families. The disadvantage is that weights must be constructed to meld the high-income supplement with the core representative sample. The construction of the weights is further complicated by differential response rates among families in the high-income supplement and the cross-section sample. According to Curtin, Juster, and Morgan, only 9 percent of the families chosen for the high-income supplement in 1983 agreed to be interviewed. However, of this group, the response rate was 95 percent, compared to 71 percent for the families in the cross-section sample. Two major studies conducted by the Federal Reserve Board — Kennickell and Woodburn 1992 for the 1989 SCF and Kennickell, McManus, and Woodburn 1996 for the 1992 SCF — discuss the problems associated with developing these weights and propose alternative sets of weights as solutions.

The PSID also has sampling problems because it is a panel survey.

The original 1968 sample had 2,930 families in the basic cross-section survey and 1,872 in the low-income supplement. The PSID has followed the individuals in the original sample over time. However, because of severe attrition in the original sample over time (by 1993, over half of the individuals in the 1968 sample had dropped out of the survey), new weights must be continually constructed for the families that remain in each new annual survey. The SIPP is a partial panel, with each base sample of households resurveyed every six months and remaining in the sample for two and a half years (five waves). As a result, attrition problems for the SIPP are not nearly as severe as those for the PSID.[1]

Asset and Liability Coverage

Another critical difference among the three samples is the degree of detail with regard to asset and liability information. The SCF is designed primarily as a wealth survey, whereas SIPP and the PSID are primarily income surveys, so that the SCF asks for and provides the user with much more detailed information on wealth holdings than the other two. In fact, the SCF has many hundreds of questions on assets and liabilities — for example, balances on each checking account, savings account, credit card, consumer loan, and so on, are listed separately. In contrast, the PSID includes only eleven categories in its questionnaire: (1) liquid assets, (2) stocks, (3) bonds, (4) primary residence, (5) other real estate, (6) vehicles, (7) businesses, (8) pension entitlements, (9) mortgage debt, (10) vehicle debt, and (11) other household debt. The SIPP includes twenty-one asset categories and twelve liabilities categories in its wealth supplement.

It is likely that the more detailed the questions asked, the better the coverage of household wealth. However, it is also the case that item nonresponse is much higher in the SCF than the other two samples. The Federal Reserve Board imputes information for missing items in the SCF, as does the Census Bureau for missing information in the SIPP.

Time Trends in the Size Distribution of Wealth

In this study, I use marketable wealth (or net worth), which is defined as the current value of all marketable or fungible assets less the current value of debts. Net worth is thus the difference in value between total assets and total liabilities or debt. Total assets are defined as the sum of the following: (1) the gross value of owner-occupied housing; (2) other real estate owned by the household; (3) the gross value of vehicles; (4)

cash and demand deposits; (5) time and savings deposits, certificates of deposit, and money market accounts; (6) government bonds, corporate bonds, foreign bonds, and other financial securities; (7) the cash surrender value of life insurance plans; (8) the cash surrender value of pension plans, including IRAs and Keogh plans; (9) corporate stock, including mutual funds; (10) net equity in unincorporated businesses; and (11) equity in trust funds. Total liabilities are the sum of the following: (1) mortgage debt; (2) consumer debt, including auto loans; and (3) other debt.

Time Trends in Medians and Means

I begin with summary statistics on median and mean net worth from the three surveys over the period 1983 to 1994. There are surprising differences among the three with regard to time trends and levels (see table 1). According to the SIPP data, median net worth fell by about 4 percent in real terms between 1984 and 1988 and by another 14 percent from 1988 to 1993. Over the entire period, the annual rate of growth of real median household net worth was −2.1 percent. In contrast, the PSID data show almost no change in real median household wealth between 1984 and 1989 and then a 7 percent increase from 1989 to 1994. Over the entire ten years, real median net worth grew by 0.8 percent per year.

For the SCF, I show two sets of estimates. The first (panel C) are based on the original data in the SCF files. The only change I have made is to use a somewhat different set of weights for the 1992 SCF data based on my analysis of some anomalies in the size distribution of income in the survey that arise from the weights provided by the Federal Reserve Board (see Wolff 1996 for details). According to these estimates, real median net worth increased by 6 percent between 1983 and 1989 and then fell by 8 percent from 1989 to 1992. Over the full nine years, real median wealth fell by 0.3 percent per year. If I use the original weights in the 1992 SCF, then there is almost no change in real median wealth between 1983 and 1992. Moreover, if I limit the 1983 SCF sample to the base cross-section sample only (1983-CS), median net worth is almost identical to the full-sample estimate.[2]

The second set of SCF estimates (panel D of table 1) is based on my adjustments to the original asset and liability values in the surveys. This takes the form of the alignment of asset and liability totals from the survey data to the corresponding national balance sheet totals. In most cases, this entails a proportional adjustment of underreported values of balance sheet items in the survey data (for details, see Wolff 1987, 1994, and 1996).[3] The time trends in median net worth are similar to those

TABLE 1. Summary Statistics on Median and Mean Net Worth, from the SIPP, PSID, and SCF, 1983–94 (in 1993 dollars)

Source and Year	Median Net Worth	Mean Net Worth	Number of Households (in thousands)
A. SIPP[a]			
1984	45,432	109,500	86,790
1988	43,670	112,396	91,554
1991	40,846	107,885	94,692
1993	37,587	99,772	96,468
Growth rate, 1984–93			
(percentage per year)	−2.11	−1.03	1.17
B. PSID[b]			
1984	42,333	133,262	
1989	42,882	145,650	
1994	45,836	143,010	
Growth rate, 1984–94			
(percentage per year)	0.80	0.71	
C. SCF: Original Entries[c]			
1983	51,780	185,668	
1989	55,125	211,462	
1992–adjusted weights	50,600	216,952	
Growth rate, 1983–92			
(percentage per year)	−0.26	1.73	
Addendum			
1983-CS	51,872	150,299	
1992–original weights	51,582	191,942	
D. SCF: My Adjustments[d]			
1983	55,287	195,624	83,893
1989	59,129	225,332	93,010
1992–adjusted weights	52,419	218,849	95,463
Growth rate, 1983–92			
(percentage per year)	−0.59	1.25	1.44

[a]*Source:* 1984 — U.S. Bureau of the Census 1986, tables 1 and 3; 1988 — U.S. Bureau of the Census 1990, tables 1 and 3; 1991 — "Asset Ownership of Households: 1993," P70–47, on the Internet, tables 4a and 5a; and 1993 — "Asset Ownership of Households: 1993," P70–47, on the Internet, tables 4 and 5.

[b]*Source:* Hurst, Luoh, and Stafford 1998, 277.

[c]*Source:* Own computations from the 1983, 1989, and 1992 SCF. Net worth includes vehicles. The 1992 figures are based on my adjusted weights. See Wolff 1996 for details. 1983-CS refers to the cross-sectional sample only (i.e., the full sample excluding the high-income supplement).

[d]*Source:* Own computations from the 1983, 1989, and 1992 SCF. Net worth includes vehicles. Asset and liability entries are fully aligned to national balance sheet totals. The 1992 figures are based on my adjusted weights. See Wolff 1987, 1994 and 1996 for details.

calculated from the original entries. Median net worth increased by 7 percent between 1983 and 1989 and then fell by 11 percent from 1989 to 1992, for an annual growth rate of −0.6 percent over the nine years.

Results on time trends in real mean household net worth also vary among the three samples. The SIPP data show that it rose by 3 percent from 1984 to 1988 and then fell by 11 percent from 1988 to 1993, for an overall annual growth rate of −1.0 percent. The PSID shows mean net worth rising in real terms by 9 percent between 1984 and 1989 and then falling by 2 percent from 1989 to 1994, for an overall annual growth rate of 0.7 percent. The original SCF data (with my adjusted weights for 1992) show mean wealth rising by 14 percent between 1983 and 1989 and then by only 3 percent between 1989 and 1992, for an overall growth of 1.7 percent per year over the whole period. If the original weights are used for the 1992 data, then mean net worth is found to decline by 9 percent over the last three years, for a 1.4 percent annual growth rate over the 1983–92 period. My adjusted data show a 15 percent growth in mean wealth in 1983–89 followed by a 3 percent decline in 1989–92, for an overall annual rate of growth of 1.3 percent over the entire 1983–92 period.

It is quite striking that there is virtually no consistency among the three samples with regard to time trends in either median or mean household net worth. The SIPP data show a very large decline in the median between the mid-1980s and the mid-1990s, the PSID an increase, and the SCF a very small decline. With regard to mean wealth, the SIPP data show a decline over this period whereas the PSID indicates a moderate gain and the SCF a large increase, though both the PSID and the SCF show all the growth occurring during the first subperiod. Part of the difference in results might be attributable to slight differences in the periods covered by the three surveys, but this factor does not seem nearly sufficient to account for the very large differences in time trends.

Time Trends in the Size Distribution of Wealth

Tables 2 and 3 continue to investigate differences in time trends among the three samples by focusing on changes in the size distribution of net worth. Table 2 compares the SIPP and the SCF. The wealth class groupings are based on published data from the SIPP and are fixed over time in nominal values (see the footnotes to the table for references). On the basis of Gini coefficients calculated from the nine wealth intervals, the SIPP data show no change in overall inequality between 1984 and 1988, a rise from 0.69 to 0.71 from 1988 to 1991 and then a subsequent decline

TABLE 2. Trends in the Size Distribution of Household Wealth: Comparison of the SIPP, 1984–93, and the SCF, 1983–92 (in current dollars)

A. SIPP Data[a]

Wealth Class (current dollars)	1984		1988		1991[b]		1993	
	Size Dist., House-holds	Size Dist., Net Worth	Size Dist., House-holds	Size Dist., Net Worth	Size Dist., House-holds	Size Dist., Net Worth	Size Dist., House-holds	Size Dist., Net Worth
Negative or zero	11.0	−0.5	11.1	−0.6	12.6	−1.1	11.5	−0.8
$1 to $4,999	15.3	0.4	15.1	0.3	14.2	0.3	13.7	0.3
$5,000 to $9,999	6.4	0.6	6.2	0.5	6.5	0.5	6.3	0.4
$10,000 to $24,999	12.4	2.6	11.5	2.1	11.2	1.9	10.8	1.8
$25,000 to $49,999	14.5	6.7	13.0	5.2	12.2	4.5	12.2	4.4
$50,000 to $99,999	19.3	17.5	16.7	13.1	15.1	11.0	16.5	11.7
$100,000 to $249,999	15.3	29.6	17.5	30.1	17.6	27.7	18.5	28.6
$250,000 to $499,999	4.0	17.2	6.0	22.2	7.0	24.2	6.9	23.1
$500,000 and over	1.9	25.9	2.8	27.1	3.5	31.1	3.6	30.5
Overall mean net worth	$78,734		$92,017		$107,885		$99,772	
Gini coefficient based on nine intervals	0.691		0.691		0.711		0.693	

B. SCF Data[c]

Wealth class (current dollars)	1983		1989		1992	
	Size Dist., House-holds	Size Dist., Net Worth	Size Dist., House-holds	Size Dist., Net Worth	Size Dist., House-holds	Size Dist., Net Worth
Negative or zero	7.7	−0.1	11.2	−1.2	9.9	−0.3
$1 to $4,999	15.7	0.2	12.3	0.1	11.6	0.1
$5,000 to $9,999	6.1	0.3	4.8	0.2	5.5	0.2
$10,000 to $24,999	12.2	1.5	10.1	0.9	10.5	0.8
$25,000 to $49,999	14.6	4.0	11.2	2.2	12.0	2.1
$50,000 to $99,999	17.7	9.4	15.5	5.9	15.0	5.1
$100,000 to $249,999	16.3	18.7	20.3	16.6	20.7	15.4
$250,000 to $499,999	5.5	14.4	8.2	14.8	7.5	12.2
$500,000 and over	4.2	51.5	6.3	60.6	7.3	64.2
Overall mean net worth	$134,839		$193,365		$212,488	
Gini coefficient based on nine intervals	0.760		0.781		0.770	

[a]*Source:* 1984 — U.S. Bureau of the Census 1986, tables 1 and 3; 1988 — U.S. Bureau of the Census 1990, tables 1 and 3; 1991 — "Asset Ownership of Households: 1993," P70–47, on the Internet, tables 4a and 5a; and 1993 — "Asset Ownership of Households: 1993," P70–47, on the Internet, tables 4 and 5.

[b]1991 size distribution categories are based on 1993 dollars.

[c]*Source:* Own computations from the 1983, 1989, and 1992 SCF. Asset and liability entries are fully aligned to national balance sheet totals. Net worth includes vehicles. See Wolff 1987, 1994, and 1996 for details.

to 0.69 in 1993, about the same level as in 1984 and 1988. The pattern is somewhat different on the basis of my adjusted SCF data. This source shows an increase in the Gini coefficient over the period 1983 to 1989, from 0.76 to 0.78, followed by a decline to 0.77 in 1992. The 1992 level of inequality is greater than the 1983 level.

The SIPP data show the proportion of households in the top three wealth classes ($100,000 and above) rising steadily over time, whereas the SCF data indicate a sharp increase in this proportion between 1983 and 1989 and then little change between 1989 and 1992. Moreover, according to the SIPP data, the share of wealth owned by the top three wealth classes increased between 1984 and 1991 and then remained relatively unchanged in 1993. The SCF data show a similar pattern, with a large jump in this share over the 1983–89 period and virtually no change between 1989 and 1992. On the basis of the SIPP data, the percentage of households with zero or negative net worth rose slightly between 1984 and 1991 (from 11.0 to 12.6) and then declined slightly in 1993 (to 11.5). Calculations from the SCF indicate a very sharp increase in the proportion of these households between 1983 and 1989 (from 7.7 to 11.2 percent) followed by a decline to 9.9 percent.

Table 3 shows comparisons of the size distribution of wealth by quintile and upper percentiles between the PSID and the SCF. The overall Gini coefficients, calculated from the seven intervals shown in

TABLE 3.   Shares of Total Household Wealth Held by Quintiles: Comparison of the PSID, 1984–94, and the SCF, 1983–92 (in percentages, except for the Gini coefficients)

Quintile or Percentile	PSID[a]			SCF[b]		
	1984	1989	1994	1983	1989	1992
Bottom quintile	−0.4	−0.6	−0.9	0.0	−1.2	−0.2
Second quintile	1.6	1.5	1.7	1.7	1.4	1.4
Middle quintile	6.4	6.0	6.6	5.7	5.4	4.9
Fourth quintile	15.5	15.8	16.5	13.0	12.8	11.9
Top quintile	76.8	77.4	76.1	79.6	81.6	82.0
Top 10 percent	61.9	61.1	59.1	66.5	68.7	69.9
Top 5 percent	49.5	47.0	44.5	54.5	57.2	58.2
Gini coefficient based on seven intervals	0.739	0.742	0.732	0.757	0.787	0.780

[a]*Source:* Hurst, Luoh, and Stafford 1998, table 2. Calculations include net equity in the principal residence.

[b]*Source:* Own computations from the 1983, 1989, and 1992 SCF. Asset and liability entries are fully aligned to national balance sheet totals. Net worth includes vehicles. See Wolff 1987, 1994, and 1996 for details.

the table, reveal somewhat different trends. The PSID data show a very small increase in overall wealth inequality between 1984 and 1989, from 0.739 to 0.742, followed by a moderate decline in 1994, to a value of 0.732. The SCF calculations show a sharp rise in inequality from 1983 to 1989 (0.757 to 0.787), followed by a modest decline in 1992 (to 0.780). However, while the PSID data indicate that wealth inequality was lower in 1994 than in 1984, the SCF shows a higher level of inequality in 1992 compared to 1983.

The time trends by percentile group are even more dissimilar between the two samples. According to the PSID data, the share of wealth owned by the top 5 percent of households declined continuously between 1984 and 1994, from 50 to 44 percent, while the share of the top 10 percent remained constant between 1984 and 1989, at 62 percent, and then fell in 1994, to 59 percent. In contrast, from the SCF, the share of both the top 5 and the top 10 percent rose between 1983 and 1989 (from 55 to 57 percent and from 67 to 69 percent, respectively) and then increased again in 1992 (to 59 and 70 percent, respectively). Moreover, the PSID data show that the share of wealth held by each of the middle three quintiles rose between 1984 and 1994 and that of the top quintile declined, while the SCF results indicate that the shares of the middle three quintiles declined between 1983 and 1992 and the share of the top quintile increased.

In sum, all three surveys show some kind of increase in wealth inequality between the mid-1980s and the late 1980s or early 1990s (though the increase is much more extreme for the SCF than SIPP and larger for SIPP than the PSID), followed by a decline in the mid-1990s. However, the SIPP data show about the same level of inequality in the mid-1990s as in the mid-1980s, the SCF shows higher inequality in the 1990s, and the PSID shows a lower level of inequality in the later period. Moreover, the SCF shows a much larger increase of wealth shares in the top wealth classes than SIPP between the mid-1980s and the mid-1990s, and according to the SCF the shares of the top 5, 10, and 20 percent increased over this period while the PSID data show declines.

Year-by-Year Comparisons of the Size Distribution of Wealth

In the next three tables, tables 4 to 6, I confront the estimates of the size distribution of wealth derived from each of the three sources in each period. As will become apparent, estimates derived from the three surveys differ substantially with regard to mean net worth and the degree of wealth concentration.

Table 4 compares estimates for 1983–84. The SIPP data report a much higher percentage of families with negative or zero net worth in 1984 and a much smaller percentage of families with net worth in the top wealth class compared to the 1983 SCF. Indeed, the share of households in the top group is more than double in the SCF compared to the SIPP and almost 80 percent higher in the SCF when it is restricted to the base cross-section sample alone (SCF-CS). Median wealth computed from the 1983 SCF is somewhat higher than the SIPP estimate (a difference of 9 to 17 percent, depending on the SCF version). However, mean wealth is considerably higher in the SCF than in the SIPP data — 63 percent higher on the basis of the original entries in the SCF (SCF-O),

TABLE 4.   Comparisons of the Size Distribution of Household Wealth, Mid-1980s: SIPP-1984, SCF-1983, and PSID-1984

Wealth Class (current dollars)	SIPP[a]	SCF-O[b]	SCF-A[c]	SCF-CS[d]	CJM Estimates[e]		
					SIPP	PSID	SCF
Percentage of Households by Wealth Class							
Negative or zero	11.0	7.7	7.7	7.6	10.9	10.3	8.0
$1 to $4,999	15.3	16.7	15.7	16.6	15.1	13.0	17.0
$5,000 to $9,999	6.4	6.2	6.1	6.3	6.4	7.1	6.1
$10,000 to $24,999	12.4	12.4	12.2	12.4	12.3	11.5	12.3
$25,000 to $49,999	14.5	15.4	14.6	15.4	14.6	14.7	15.3
$50,000 to $99,999	19.3	17.5	17.7	17.8	19.8	17.7	17.8
$100,000 to $249,999	15.3	15.2	16.3	15.1	16.1	17.8	14.6
$250,000 to $499,999	4.0	5.1	5.5	5.3	3.5	5.7	5.0
$500,000 and over	1.9	3.9	4.2	3.4	1.3	2.2	3.8
Total	100.0	100.0	100.0	100.0			
Addendum							
Median net worth (in thousands)	32.7	35.7	38.1	35.8		30.4	
Mean net worth (in thousands)	78.7	128.0	134.8	103.6		95.8	
Mean of highest wealth class (in hundred thousands)	1.07	1.71	1.66	1.22		1.31	
Gini coefficient based on nine intervals	0.691	0.767	0.760	0.724		0.700	

[a]*Source:* U.S. Bureau of the Census 1986.

[b]*Source:* Own computations from the 1983 SCF. These calculations are based on the original, unadjusted asset and liability figures in the SCF. Net worth includes vehicles.

[c]*Source:* Own computations from the 1983 SCF. Asset and liability entries are fully aligned to national balance sheet totals. Net worth includes vehicles.

[d]*Source:* Own computations from the 1983 SCF. 1983-CS refers to the cross-sectional sample only (i.e., the full sample excluding the high-income supplement). These calculations are based on the original, unadjusted asset and liability figures in the SCF. Net worth includes vehicles.

[e]*Source:* Curtin, Juster, and Morgan (CJM) 1989, 487, 492. Mean and median net worth for the PSID are from Hurst, Luoh, and Stafford 1996. The Gini coefficient is based on my own calculations.

71 percent on the basis of my adjusted asset and liability figures in the SCF (SCF-A), and 32 percent higher in the cross-section component of the SCF (SCF-CS).

The mean value of the open-ended wealth interval is also considerably higher in the full SCF samples (1.7 million) compared to the SIPP (1.1 million) and somewhat higher in SCF-CS (1.2 million). The corresponding estimates of overall inequality, based on a Gini coefficient

TABLE 5.   Comparisons of the Size Distribution of Household Wealth, Late 1980s and Early 1990s: SIPP-1988 and SCF-1989 and SIPP-1992 and SCF-1992

Wealth Class (current dollars)	1988–89			1992			
	SIPP[a]	SCF-O[b]	SCF-A[c]	SIPP[d]	SCF-O[e]	SCF-A[f]	SCF-OW[g]
Percentage of Households by Wealth Class							
Negative or Zero	11.1	11.4	11.2	12.1	10.2	9.9	10.3
$1 to $4,999	15.1	12.5	12.3	14.0	11.7	11.6	11.7
$5,000 to $9,999	6.2	5.0	4.8	6.4	5.5	5.5	5.5
$10,000 to $24,999	11.5	10.2	10.1	11.0	10.8	10.5	10.8
$25,000 to $49,999	13.0	11.6	11.2	12.2	12.1	12.0	12.1
$50,000 to $99,999	16.7	16.0	15.5	15.8	15.4	15.0	15.5
$100,000 to $249,999	17.5	19.8	20.3	18.1	20.1	20.7	20.2
$250,000 to $499,999	6.0	7.6	8.2	7.0	7.3	7.5	7.3
$500,000 and over	2.8	5.9	6.3	3.6	6.9	7.3	6.6
Total	100.0	100.0	100.0	100.0	100.0	100.0	100.0
Addendum							
Median net worth (in thousands)	35.8	47.3	50.7	38.0	49.1	50.9	48.5
Mean net worth (in thousands)	92.0	181.5	193.4	103.8	210.7	212.5	184.8
Mean of highest wealth class (in hundred thousands)	0.89	1.81	1.85	0.90	1.95	1.88	1.67
Gini coefficient based on nine intervals	0.691	0.785	0.781	0.702	0.777	0.770	0.759

[a]*Source:* U.S. Bureau of the Census 1990.

[b]*Source:* Own computations from the 1989 SCF. These calculations are based on the original, unadjusted asset and liability figures in the SCF. Net worth includes vehicles.

[c]*Source:* Own computations from the 1989 SCF. Asset and liability entries are fully aligned to national balance sheet totals. Net worth includes vehicles.

[d]Average of figures from the 1991 and 1993 SIPP. *Source:* Internet.

[e]*Source:* Own computations from the 1992 SCF. These calculations are based on the original, unadjusted asset and liability figures in the SCF but use my adjusted weights. Net worth includes vehicles.

[f]*Source:* Own computations from the 1992 SCF. Asset and liability entries are fully aligned to national balance sheet totals and use my adjusted weights. Net worth includes vehicles.

[g]*Source:* Own computations from the 1992 SCF. These calculations are based on the original, unadjusted asset and liability figures in the SCF and use the original weights. Net worth includes vehicles.

TABLE 6. Comparisons of the Size Distribution of Household Wealth by Quintile, 1983–94: The PSID and the SCF

Quintile or Percentile	1983 or 1984 (in 1983 dollars)				1989		
	PSID[a]	SCF-O[b]	SCF-A[c]	SCF-CS[d]	PSID[a]	SCF-O[e]	SCF-A[f]
Mean Values by Group							
Bottom quintile	(2.2)	0.1	0.0	0.1	(3.8)	(11.5)	(11.3)
Second quintile	8.1	10.0	11.1	10.2	9.6	12.2	13.1
Middle quintile	31.8	36.0	38.6	36.1	38.3	47.4	51.9
Fourth quintile	76.4	81.0	87.6	80.4	101.7	116.8	124.1
Top quintile	379.2	512.7	536.9	391.3	497.9	740.5	789.0
Top 10 percent	611.1	864.9	896.5	625.5	787.0	1,247.0	1,327.4
Top 5 percent	976.2	1,433.8	1,468.4	966.8	1,210.1	2,083.9	2,210.5
Median wealth (in thousands)	30.4	35.7	38.1	35.8	36.8	47.3	50.7
Mean wealth (in thousands)	95.8	128.0	134.8	103.6	125.0	181.5	193.4
Gini coefficient based on seven intervals	0.739	0.763	0.757	0.720	0.742	0.788	0.787

	1994 or 1992 (in 1992 dollars)			
	PSID[a]	SCF-O[g]	SCF-A[h]	SCF-OW[i]
Bottom quintile	(6.0)	(2.1)	(2.0)	(2.1)
Second quintile	11.7	13.9	14.7	13.7
Middle quintile	46.0	50.4	52.3	49.9
Fourth quintile	114.9	122.8	126.9	121.0
Top quintile	530.6	868.2	870.7	741.5
Top 10 percent	823.6	1,488.8	1,484.9	1,242.7
Top 5 percent	1,240.1	2,497.8	2,474.6	2,028.3
Median wealth (in thousands)	44.5	49.1	50.9	48.5
Mean wealth (in thousands)	138.9	210.6	212.5	184.8
Gini coefficient based on seven intervals	0.732	0.785	0.780	0.766

[a]*Source:* Hurst, Luoh, and Stafford 1998, p. 277. Calculations include net equity in the principal residence.

[b]*Source:* Own computations from the 1983 SCF. These calculations are based on the original, unadjusted asset and liability figures in the SCF. Net worth includes vehicles.

[c]*Source:* Own computations from the 1983 SCF. Asset and liability entries are fully aligned to national balance sheet totals. Net worth includes vehicles.

[d]*Source:* Own computations from the 1983 SCF. 1983-CS refers to the cross-sectional sample only (i.e., the full sample excluding the high-income supplement). These calculations are based on the original, unadjusted asset and liability figures in the SCF. Net worth includes vehicles.

[e]*Source:* Own computations from the 1989 SCF. These calculations are based on the original, unadjusted asset and liability figures in the SCF. Net worth includes vehicles.

[f]*Source:* Own computations from the 1989 SCF. Asset and liability entries are fully aligned to national balance sheet totals. Net worth includes vehicles.

[g]*Source:* Own computations from the 1992 SCF. These calculations are based on the original, unadjusted asset and liability figures in the SCF but use my adjusted weights. Net worth includes vehicles.

[h]*Source:* Own computations from the 1992 SCF. Asset and liability entries are fully aligned to national balance sheet totals and use my adjusted weights. Net worth includes vehicles.

[i]*Source:* Own computations from the 1992 SCF. These calculations are based on the original, unadjusted asset and liability figures in the SCF and use the original weights. Net worth includes vehicles.

computed from the nine wealth intervals, are, not surprisingly, higher in the two full SCF samples (0.76 and 0.77) than in SIPP (0.69) and also somewhat higher in SCF-CS (0.72). It seems apparent that both the addition of a high-income supplement to the sampling frame in the SCF and the more detailed asset and liability questions in the SCF than in the SIPP contribute to the higher estimates of mean net worth and overall inequality.

The last three columns of table 4 show the corresponding estimates made by Curtin, Juster, and Morgan (1989). Fortunately, they line up very closely with my own estimates for the SIPP and the SCF data. Estimates made by Curtin, Juster, and Morgan from the 1984 PSID are also shown. Though median wealth computed in the PSID is somewhat lower than the corresponding SIPP figure, estimates of mean wealth, the mean value of the open-ended wealth class, and overall inequality are higher in the PSID than the SIPP data and line up rather closely with my own estimates derived from the SCF-CS sample.

Table 5 shows a similar set of comparisons between SIPP and the SCF for 1988–89 and 1992. As will be apparent, the deviation between the SCF and the SIPP data has grown over time. The percentage of households in the top wealth class is again more than double in the 1989 SCF on the basis of both the original asset and liability information (SCF-O) and my adjusted values (SCF-A) than in the 1988 SIPP. Mean wealth estimated from both the 1989 SCF-O and the SCF-A samples is now double that of the corresponding estimate from the 1989 SIPP data. Even median wealth is considerably higher in the SCF sample than the SIPP (32 percent greater on the basis of SCF-O and 42 percent greater on the basis of SCF-A). The mean wealth of the highest wealth class derived from the SCF is now double that reported in the SIPP data. Moreover, the difference in Gini coefficients calculated from the SCF and SIPP data has grown from about 0.075 in 1983–84 to 0.09 in 1989.

Results for 1992 are very similar to those for 1989. The various estimates of median net worth derived from the 1992 SCF are about 30 percent greater than the median reported in the 1992 SIPP, mean wealth is about double, and the mean value of the open-ended wealth class also about double. The Gini coefficient estimated from the SCF data ranges from 0.76 to 0.78, compared to a value of 0.70 computed from the SIPP data.

Table 6 compares the size distribution of wealth derived from the SCF and the PSID data files by quintile. The mean values of net worth by quintile derived from the 1984 PSID and the 1983 SCF match up very closely for the bottom four quintiles. However, for the top quintile, the top 10 percent, and the top 5 percent, the mean values computed from the two full-sample SCF files (SCF-O and SCF-A) are 40–50 percent higher than the corresponding values from the PSID. In contrast, mean values by quintile match up almost exactly between the PSID data and the 1983 SCF-CS sample (the cross-section data only). The Gini coefficient calculated from these seven intervals is about 0.02 higher in the 1983 SCF-O and SCF-A samples than the PSID but actually 0.02 points higher in the PSID than the SCF-CS sample.

Differences between the two data sources are more marked in the 1989 data. Mean values of net worth are again close for the bottom four quintiles but in this case differ by 49–58 percent for the top quintile, by 58–69 percent for the top 10 percent, and by 72–83 percent for the top 5 percent. Mean net worth is 45 percent greater in the 1989 SCF-O file than the 1989 PSID and 55 percent greater in the SCF-A file, and the difference in Gini coefficients between the SCF and the PSID has now grown to 0.045 points.

The 1992–94 match between the PSID and the SCF is even worse than the 1989 comparison. Mean values for the bottom four quintiles are again close, but the mean value of the top quintile is about 64 percent higher in the SCF data on the basis of my adjusted weights than the PSID file, about 80 percent higher for the top 10 percent, and about 99 percent higher for the top 5 percent (the mean values are somewhat closer between the PSID data and the 1992 SCF-OW — the SCF data using the original weights). Median wealth is somewhat lower in the PSID data, but mean wealth is 52 percent greater in the SCF data (on the basis of my adjusted weights). The difference in Gini coefficients calculated from the PSID and the SCF datasets has now grown slightly to 0.048 points.

Comparison of Ownership Rates and Means by Asset Type

In order to obtain more information on the source of the deviation in results between the SCF and the other two datasets, I next investigate differences among the three sources by asset type. Table 7 shows the first set of comparisons — between the PSID and the SCF data. The percentage of households reporting ownership of the various assets listed in table 7 generally lines up closely between the PSID and SCF data. The exceptions are liquid assets, for which the SCF figures are about 8–10 percentage points higher, and stock ownership, for which the PSID figures are higher. However, the latter may be due to definitional differences between the two data sources (in particular, to the fact that the

TABLE 7. Comparison of Percentage Holding and Mean Holdings by Asset and Liability Type, 1983–94: PSID and SCF[a]

Asset or Liability	1984[b] PSID	1983[b] SCF	Ratio SCF/ PSID	1989[c] PSID	1989[c] SCF	Ratio SCF/ PSID	1994[d] PSID	1992[d] SCF	Ratio SCF/ PSID
A. Percentage of Households Owning Item									
Principal residence	60.1	63.4		60.9	62.8		63.5	64.1	
Vehicles	83.2	84.4		83.1	83.7		85.4	86.3	
Liquid assets[e]	80.8	88.1		81.2	86.1		77.8	87.8	
Liquid assets[f]		88.3			86.8			88.8	
Other real estate	20.1	18.9		19.6	19.1		17.7	19.6	
Unincorporated business	12.2	14.2		13.4	11.1		13.2	12.1	
Stocks and mutual funds[g]	24.8	20.7		27.9	19.8		34.5	22.3	
Other assets[h]	23.4	45.6		26.3	59.6		24.5	52.8	
Nonmortgage debt	46.3	63.6		50.2	64.5		50.6	64.7	
B. Mean Value, Holders Only (in thousands)									
Net worth	95.8	134.8	1.4	125.0	193.4	1.5	138.9	212.5	1.5
Principal residence (net equity)	46.1	56.2	1.2	67.3	74.8	1.1	65.5	75.8	1.2
Vehicles[i]	6.4	5.8	0.9	9.4	9.7	1.0	11.8	10.1	0.9
Liquid assets[e]	14.5	25.9	1.8	21.9	40.7	1.9	23.4	31.2	1.3
Liquid assets[f]		28.4	2.0		47.6	2.2		51.3	2.2
Other real estate (net equity)	65.6	112.1	1.7	118.3	119.5	1.0	127.4	139.4	1.1
Unincorporated business (net equity)	130.2	198.7	1.5	171.8	335.9	2.0	155.8	352.4	2.3
Stocks and mutual funds[g]	27.5	65.4	2.4	46.5	75.9	1.6	77.6	88.2	1.1
Other assets[h]	67.5	33.8	0.5	22.4	46.8	2.1	36.3	56.7	1.6
Nonmortgage debt	3.8	14.3	3.8	5.8	9.5	1.6	11.3	9.6	0.9

[a]*Source* for PSID: Hurst, Luoh, and Stafford 1998, p. 270. *Source* for SCF: Own computations from the 1983, 1989, and 1992 SCF. Net worth includes vehicles. Asset and liability entries are fully aligned to national balance sheet totals. The 1992 figures are based on my adjusted weights.

[b]In 1983 dollars.

[c]In 1989 dollars.

[d]In 1992 dollars.

[e]For the PSID, this category includes checking accounts, savings accounts, money market funds, CDs, U.S. savings bonds, U.S. treasury bills, and IRAs. For the SCF, this category includes checking accounts, savings accounts, money market funds, CDs, and U.S. savings bonds.

[f]For the SCF, this category includes checking accounts, savings accounts, money market funds, CDs, U.S. savings bonds, and IRAs, Keogh plans, 401(k) plans, and other pension accounts.

[g]For the PSID, this includes stocks held in IRAs and Keogh plans; for the SCF, this excludes stocks held in IRAs.

[h]For the PSID, this includes trusts and estates, bond funds, life insurance policies, and special collections. For the SCF, this includes trusts and estates, bond funds, life insurance cash surrender value, and special collections, as well as mortgages held from the sale of real estate, the amount due from sale of a business, and other financial investments.

[i]Net value in PSID; gross value in SCF.

PSID categorizes stocks held in IRAs and other pension funds in the stocks and mutual funds category). The SCF also reports a larger percentage of households holding "other assets" than the PSID, though here, too, definitional differences and also the greater coverage of a wide assortment of assets in the SCF questionnaires may be largely responsible. The SCF figures also show a higher percentage of households holding nonmortgage debt in each of the three years than the PSID, a result that may also be attributable to the more extensive coverage of household liabilities in the SCF questionnaire than in the PSID.

A comparison of mean values of assets for asset owners only is shown in panel B of table 7. As noted previously, average net worth calculated from the SCF data is higher than the corresponding PSID figure — about 40 percent higher in 1983–84 and 1992–94 and 50 percent higher in 1989 and 1992/4. However, mean values line up very closely between the two surveys for own home and vehicles. Average holdings of liquid assets are found to be higher in the SCF data — the exact difference depends on the treatment of pension assets in the PSID. The ratio in net equity in other real estate between the SCF and the PSID is 1.7 in 1983–84 but about 1.0 in the other two years. Mean net equity in unincorporated business is 50 percent higher in the SCF data in 1983–84 and double that of the PSID in the two later years.

The ratio of corporate stock holdings declines from 2.4 in 1983–84 to 1.6 in 1989 and then to almost unity in 1992–94. This trend for 1989 to 1992–94 is particularly surprising. The SCF data, for example, show that the average value of corporate stock among stock owners increased by 16 percent in nominal terms between 1989 and 1992, while the Standard and Poors 500 index increased by 29 percent — an apparent fluke in the SCF data. On the other hand, the PSID data show that average stock holdings among holders actually doubled between 1989 and 1994, while the Standard and Poors 500 index went up by 43 percent — also a questionable result. Both results deserve a closer look.

Table 8 shows similar comparisons between the SIPP and SCF data. The patterns are similar. The SCF and SIPP data are quite close with regard to the percentage of households owning for own homes, motor vehicles, and liquid assets held at financial institutions. Figures for ownership rates of nonhome real estate (shown as rental property and other real estate equity in the SIPP), own business or profession, and stocks and mutual funds are also remarkably similar. The SCF data show almost the same rate of ownership of other interest-earning assets (corporate bonds and the like) in 1983–84 but much higher rates for 1988–89 and 1992. Interestingly, the SIPP data indicate that almost twice as many households held IRAs or other pension accounts in 1984 than in the

TABLE 8. Comparison of Percentage Holding and Mean Holdings by Asset and Liability Type, 1983–92: SIPP and SCF[a]

Asset or Liability	1984[b] SIPP	1983[b] SCF	Ratio SCF/ SIPP	1988[c] SIPP	1989[c] SCF	Ratio SCF/ SIPP	1992[d] SIPP	1992[d] SCF	Ratio SCF/ SIPP
A. Percentage of Households Owning Item									
Own home	64.3	63.4		63.6	62.8		64.5	64.1	
Motor vehicles	85.8	84.4		86.3	83.7		86.1	86.3	
All interest-bearing assets	72.4	79.2		73.5	73.4		72.7	70.4	
Interest-earning assets at financial institutions[e]	71.8	78.8		72.9	71.0		72.2	68.9	
Other interest-earning assets[f]	8.5	7.7		9.4	16.6		8.8	14.2	
Checking accounts[g]	53.9	78.6		48.3	80.8		46.0	83.6	
U.S. savings bonds	15.0	20.4		17.5	23.8		18.3	22.3	
IRA or Keogh accounts[h]	19.5	10.9		24.2	23.2		23.0	38.2	
Nonhome real estate	—	18.9		—	19.1		—	19.6	
Rental property equity	9.8	—		9.0	—		8.7	—	
Other real estate equity	10.0	—		10.5	—		10.0	—	
Own business or profession	12.9	14.2		12.5	11.1		11.3	12.1	
Stocks and mutual funds	20.0	20.7		21.8	19.8		20.8	22.3	
Other assets[i]	3.5	14.2		3.3	27.2		2.7	20.7	
Mortgages held from sale of property	2.9			2.3					
B. Mean Value, Holders Only (in thousands)									
Net worth	75.5	134.8	1.8	96.5	193.4	2.0	100.8	212.5	2.1
Own home (net equity)	48.5	56.2	1.2	65.2	74.8	1.1	67.5	75.8	1.1
Motor vehicles[j]	5.3	5.8	1.1	6.5	9.7	1.5	7.5	10.1	1.3
All interest-bearing assets	15.4	35.9	2.3	19.1	53.7	2.8	18.5	52.2	2.8
Interest-earning assets at financial institutions[e]	15.2	27.7	1.8	18.7	46.1	2.5	18.0	35.9	2.0
Other interest-earning assets[f]	27.8	81.6	2.9	42.8	40.5	0.9	51.7	84.3	1.6
Checking accounts[g]	0.9	5.0	5.6	1.1	6.6	6.0	1.1	7.1	6.3
U.S. savings bonds	2.4	2.1	0.9	3.1	3.0	1.0	3.9	5.0	1.3
IRA or Keogh accounts	8.5	20.1	2.4	16.8	27.3	1.6	26.0	45.9	1.8
Nonhome real estate	—	112.1		—	119.5		—	139.4	
Rental property equity	69.1	—		84.2	—		76.1	—	
Other real estate equity	33.0	—		39.3	—		50.5	—	
Own business or profession (net equity)	60.5	198.7	3.3	67.6	335.9	5.0	61.3	352.4	5.7
Stocks and mutual funds	25.8	65.4	2.5	28.7	75.9	2.6	37.3	88.2	2.4
Other assets[k]	53.5	41.7	0.8	43.3	64.0	1.5	56.3	65.1	1.2

[a]*Source* for SIPP: 1984—U.S. Bureau of the Census 1986; 1989—U.S. Bureau of the Census 1990; 1992—average of figures from the 1991 and 1993 SIPP (source: Internet). *Source* for SCF: Own computations from the 1983, 1989, and 1992 SCF. Net worth includes vehicles. Asset and liability entries are fully aligned to national balance sheet totals. The 1992 figures are based on my adjusted weights.

[b]In 1983 dollars.

[c]In 1989 dollars.

[d]In 1992 dollars.

corresponding SCF data, about the same ownership rate in 1988–89, and a much lower ownership rate in 1992 than the SCF.

Overall net worth reported in the SCF data was about twice as great as that recorded in the SIPP data (see panel B). The two sources, however, are very close for mean values of own homes, vehicles, and U.S. savings bonds. The major differences appear to occur for interest-bearing assets (both time and savings accounts and bonds and other securities), IRA and Keogh accounts, nonhome real estate, and, especially, the net equity in unincorporated businesses and stocks and mutual funds, where the SCF asset values are double or more than double the corresponding SIPP values.

Table 9 shows comparative values of mean net worth derived from the SIPP and SCF data for selected demographic groups. The pattern is quite striking. The SIPP figures are closer to the corresponding SCF figures the poorer the group. This pattern is clearest when wealth figures are compared by family income quintiles. The SIPP and SCF mean values are almost identical for the bottom two income quintiles. For the third and fourth, the SCF averages are about 30 percent greater than the SIPP data indicate, and for the top income quintile, the estimated mean wealth in the 1992 SCF data is 3.4 times as great as in the SIPP data.

The same relationships hold by education group, where the SIPP and SCF mean net worth values are almost identical for households with less than twelve years of schooling, the SCF values are 30–40 percent greater for high school graduates, 60–90 percent greater for those with

---

Notes to Table 8. (*cont.*)

   eFor SIPP, this includes passbook savings accounts, money market deposit accounts, certificates of deposit, and interest-earning checking accounts. For the SCF, this includes all savings accounts and time deposits, money market funds, certificates of deposit, and the cash surrender value of life insurance.

   fFor SIPP, this includes money market funds, U.S. government securities, municipal and corporate bonds, and other interest-earning assets. For the SCF, this includes U.S. government securities, municipal and corporate bonds, and other interest-earning securities.

   gFor SIPP, this includes only non-interest-bearing checking accounts; for SCF, this includes all checking accounts.

   hFor the SCF, this also includes 401(k) plans and other individual pension accounts.

   iFor SIPP, this includes amount due from sale of a business, unit trusts, other financial investments, and, in 1992, mortgages held from sale of real estate. For the SCF, this includes the amount due from sale of a business, trusts and estates, special collections, mortgages held from the sale of real estate, and other financial investments.

   jNet value in SIPP; gross value in SCF.

   kFor SIPP, this includes amount due from sale of a business, unit trusts, other financial investments, and, mortgages held from sale of real estate in all three years. For the SCF, this includes the amount due from sale of a business, trusts and estates, special collections, mortgages held from the sale of real estate, and other financial investments.

TABLE 9. Comparison of Mean Net Worth by Demographic Characteristics: 1983–92: SIPP and SCF[a] (in thousands of dollars)

Demographic Characteristic	1984[b] SIPP	1983[b] SCF	Ratio SCF/ SIPP	1992[c] SIPP	1992[c] SCF	Ratio SCF/ SIPP
All households	75.5	134.8	1.8	100.8	212.5	2.1
Race and Hispanic Origin of Householder						
White	82.8	157.0	1.9	110.4	254.5	2.3
Black	19.4	31.8	1.6	28.1	50.2	1.8
Hispanic origin[d]	34.5	28.0	0.8	40.2	59.3	1.5
Age of Householder						
Less than 35 years	21.8	31.3	1.4	27.0	47.4	1.8
35 to 44 years	66.6	97.6	1.5	77.2	153.9	2.0
45 to 54 years	110.5	204.8	1.9	125.9	299.1	2.4
55 to 64 years	125.1	222.5	1.8	164.3	381.3	2.3
65 years and over	100.5	211.8	2.1	157.3	298.4	1.9
65 to 69 years	120.2	310.6	2.6	172.6	354.7	2.1
70 to 75 years	99.2	187.0	1.9	164.3	309.8	1.9
75 years and over	86.5	138.4	1.6	142.2	250.6	1.8
Education of Householder						
Less than 12 years	49.5	54.8	1.1	60.6	69.1	1.1
High school: 4 years	66.8	89.4	1.3	82.7	119.9	1.4
College: 1 to 3 years	75.8	124.3	1.6	93.8	178.1	1.9
4 or more years	125.8	319.5	2.5	173.3	433.5	2.5
Type of Household by Age of Householder						
Married-couple households	97.7	180.5	1.8	131.1	303.5	2.3
Less than 35 years	38.8	37.9	1.0	37.7	67.1	1.8
35 to 54 years	110.6	178.1	1.6	122.2	292.9	2.4
55 to 64 years	150.4	297.3	2.0	203.4	497.5	2.4
65 years and over	149.9	315.6	2.1	218.1	473.1	2.2
Male householder	46.9	192.4	4.1	69.4	126.8	1.8
Less than 35 years	18.2	51.5	2.8	21.9	35.5	1.6
35 to 54 years	51.7	217.8	4.2	73.9	125.9	1.7
55 to 64 years	82.2	283.6	3.5	120.4	326.8	2.7
65 years and over	86.3	540.7	6.3	131.9	233.6	1.8
Female householder	43.1	96.0	2.2	60.7	90.7	1.5
Less than 35 years	8.7	42.1	4.9	12.2	20.4	1.7
35 to 54 years	39.4	106.5	2.7	43.6	66.7	1.5
55 to 64 years	64.6	115.1	1.8	91.6	137.6	1.5
65 years and over	65.0	130.1	2.0	103.0	139.3	1.4
Labor Force Activity of Householders under 65 Years						
Total	68.9	116.5	1.7	85.2	188.4	2.2
With labor force activity	68.3	119.3	1.7	85.5	197.6	2.3
With job entire period	72.9	130.5	1.8	89.5	209.1	2.3
With job part of period	33.7	105.1	3.1	48.2	259.7	5.4
No job during period, spent time looking or on layoff	22.5	29.0	1.3	34.7	53.5	1.5
No labor force activity	72.8	94.8	1.3	83.3	128.2	1.5

TABLE 9. (*cont.*)

Demographic Characteristic	1984[b] SIPP	1983[b] SCF	Ratio SCF/ SIPP	1992[c] SIPP	1992[c] SCF	Ratio SCF/ SIPP
Monthly Household Income[e]						
Less than $900	28.4	30.2	1.1			
$900–1,999	50.5	58.4	1.2			
$2,000–3,999	76.8	109.1	1.4			
$4,000 and over	232.0	663.5	2.9			
Lowest quintile				35.7	32.6	0.9
Second quintile				61.5	65.4	1.1
Third quintile				79.8	106.8	1.3
Fourth quintile				103.4	133.8	1.3
Highest quintile				223.9	765.9	3.4
Tenure						
Owner	109.5	197.7	1.8	146.1	306.8	2.1
Renter	14.2	25.8	1.8	18.5	44.4	2.4

[a]*Source* for SIPP: 1984 — U.S. Bureau of the Census 1986; 1992 — average of figures from the 1991 and 1993 SIPP (source: Internet). *Source* for SCF: Own computations from the 1983 and 1992 SCF. Net worth includes vehicles. Asset and liability entries are fully aligned to national balance sheet totals. The 1992 figures are based on my adjusted weights.

[b]In 1983 dollars.

[c]In 1992 dollars.

[d]In SIPP, persons of Hispanic origin may be of any race. In the SCF, the white and black classifications exclude Hispanics.

[e]In the SCF, annual income is converted into a monthly equivalent.

one to three years of college, and 2.5 times as great for college graduates than in the corresponding SIPP data. Likewise, the deviation between the SCF and SIPP mean net worth figures increases with the age of the household almost monotonically until the peak wealth age group (sixty-five to sixty-nine years in 1983 and fifty-five to sixty-four years in 1992) and then declines.

Concluding Remarks

If we use the SCF as the benchmark for estimates of the size distribution of household wealth, the main finding is that both SIPP and the PSID did a better job in matching up with the SCF estimates in the mid-1980s than in the late 1980s or the early to mid-1990s. Both SIPP and the PSID were more successful in capturing the relatively big wealth holders in 1984 than in 1988 or in 1992–94.

A second major finding is that both the difference in sampling frame between the SCF and the other two data sources — in particular, the addition of a high-income supplement in the SCF — and the more detailed questionnaire used in the SCF than in the other two contributed to the higher estimates of mean wealth and overall wealth inequality. This is apparent from the 1983–84 comparisons, where the SCF-CS estimates lie almost exactly in between the SIPP estimates and the figures derived from the full SCF sample. However, the 1984 PSID estimates line up more closely with the 1983 SCF-CS than do the calculations from the 1984 SIPP.

As a consequence, time trends derived from the three sources are radically dissimilar. The SIPP data show both median and mean net worth in real terms declining continuously between 1984 and 1993; the PSID indicates that median wealth remained almost constant between 1984 and 1989 and then increased in 1994, while mean wealth increased in the 1980s but declined in the 1990s; and the SCF data (both the original data and my adjusted data) show both median and mean wealth rising from 1983 to 1989 and then falling in 1992.

The inequality patterns also differ. On the basis of the SIPP data, inequality, as measured by the Gini coefficient, was the same in 1988 as in 1984, rose in 1991, and then fell in 1993 to the same level as in 1984. According to the PSID, wealth inequality rose slightly between 1984 and 1989 and then fell in 1994 to a level below that in 1984. On the basis of the SCF data (my adjusted version), inequality increased between 1983 and 1989 and then declined in 1992, though its level was higher than in 1983. It is quite striking that each of these three data sources gives a very different story of wealth changes between the mid-1980s and mid-1990s.

The comparisons made in the last three tables in this essay provide some indications for why the SIPP and PSID wealth data seem to have steadily deteriorated since the early 1980s (relative to the SCF). The SIPP and the PSID data do a very good job in capturing the major forms of wealth held by the middle class — particularly, own home, vehicles, savings bonds, some forms of liquid assets, and pension accounts (such as IRAs). The shortfall occurs for investment-type assets, such as unincorporated business equity, stocks and mutual funds, corporate bonds and other securities, and nonhome real estate, and these are held mainly by the rich. Moreover, a comparison of the SIPP and SCF data by demographic group reveals that the SIPP data do a reasonable job of capturing the wealth of the bottom four income quintiles but grossly underestimate the wealth of the top quintile. Moreover, the relative shortfalls of the SIPP and the PSID both by asset type and, in the case of

SIPP, by demographic group have not altered very much over time. Rather, the worsening performance of these two datasets over time appears due to the fact that almost all the growth of wealth between the mid-1980s and mid-1990s has accrued to the rich and has taken the form of investment-type assets held by the rich.[4]

There are two provisos to these overall conclusions. First, the years do not match up exactly between the SCF data and the SIPP and PSID results. Thus, part of the difference in results may be due to changes in the size distribution of wealth between years (in particular, between 1983 and 1984, between 1988 and 1989, and between 1992 and 1994). However, on the basis of past analysis, it seems unlikely that the size distribution of wealth can change sharply enough over such short periods to account for the total or even a significant part of the difference in results on both the overall inequality of wealth and median and mean net worth between data sources.

Second, it is possible that the definition of household wealth may differ somewhat among the three data sources. According to the list of assets and liabilities included with the three sources, there do not appear to be any glaring differences. However, it still may be the case that certain assets, such as trust funds; IRAs, Keoghs, 401(k), and other defined contribution pensions plans; loans from the family to the family business and vice versa; and the valuation of antiques, art, and other collectibles may be handled differently in the three datasets.

On a policy note, if the SCF data can be taken as a reliable benchmark, then I would urge both the U.S. Bureau of the Census and the Survey Research Center to analyze more carefully their sampling frame and the accuracy of their responses in order to understand why the quality of their wealth data appears to have deteriorated over time. With regard to the latter, this may take the form of direct interviews with a subsample of respondents in conjunction with detailed record checking on the part of the interviewer.

NOTES

1. For the 1988 panel, for example, sample loss was 18.5 percent at the end of the fifth wave (see U.S. Bureau of the Census 1990, 29).

2. The 1983 SCF provides a variable to differentiate between observations in the cross-section and high-income supplements. Unfortunately, it is not possible to isolate the two samples in the later 1989 and 1992 SCF.

3. It should be noted that in table 1, as in the rest of the essay, my definition

of net worth includes the value of vehicles. As a consequence, the results from the SCF data here differ from those reported in my previous three articles, which exclude vehicles in the definition of net worth.

4. I thank Tom Juster for this point.

REFERENCES

Curtin, Richard T., F. Thomas Juster, and James N. Morgan. 1989. "Survey Estimates of Wealth: An Assessment of Quality." In R. Lipsey and H. Tice, eds., *The Measurement of Saving, Investment, and Wealth,* Studies of Income and Wealth, 52:473–548. Chicago: University of Chicago Press.

Hurst, Erik, Ming Ching Luoh, and Frank P. Stafford. 1998. "Wealth Dynamics of American Families, 1984–1994." *Brookings Papers on Economic Activity,* no. 1: 267–357.

Kennickell, Arthur B., Douglas A. McManus, and R. Louise Woodburn. 1996. "Weighting Design for the 1992 Survey of Consumer Finances." Mimeo, Federal Reserve Board, March.

Kennickell, Arthur B., and R. Louise Woodburn. 1992. "Estimation of Household Net Worth Using Model-Based and Design-Based Weights: Evidence from the 1989 Survey of Consumer Finances." Mimeo, Federal Reserve Board, April.

U.S. Bureau of the Census. 1986. Current Population Reports, Series P-70, No. 7, *Household Wealth and Asset Ownership, 1984.* Washington, DC: U.S. Government Printing Office.

———. 1990. Current Population Reports, Series P-70, No. 22, *Household Wealth and Asset Ownership, 1988.* Washington, DC: U.S. Government Printing Office.

Wolff, Edward N. 1987. "Estimates of Household Wealth Inequality in the United States, 1962–83." *Review of Income and Wealth* 33 (September): 231–56.

———. 1994. "Trends in Household Wealth in the United States, 1962–1983 and 1983–1989." *Review of Income and Wealth* 40, no. 2 (June): 143–74.

———. 1996. "Trends in Household Wealth, 1983–1992." Report submitted to the Department of Labor, July.

Health, Work, and Economic Well-Being of Older Workers, Aged Fifty-One to Sixty-One: A Cross-National Comparison Using the U.S. HRS and the Netherlands CERRA Data Sets

Richard V. Burkhauser, Debra Dwyer,
Maarten Lindeboom, Jules Theeuwes,
and Isolde Woittiez

Work in the marketplace is the principal source of income in modern industrial societies, and ameliorating the risks associated with exit from the labor force due either to health problems or "old age" is a fundamental goal of modern social welfare systems. Yet the mix of private and public insurance against such risks varies greatly across countries, and the resulting structure of retirement institutions and the signals they send with respect to how and when to leave the labor market are more likely to explain the dramatic differences in work at older ages than underlying health conditions in those countries.

No two countries better demonstrate the importance of institutional signals on retirement than the United States and the Netherlands. In this essay we make use of the first waves of two extraordinary new data sets—the U.S. Health and Retirement Study (HRS) and the Netherlands CERRA Retirement Panel Study—that began in the early 1990s to look at the health, work, and economic well-being of men and women transitioning into retirement. We find that in the United States work still dominates the income of men aged 51 to 61, while a large share of Dutch men this age have already transitioned out of the labor force. Based on this first run through the data, we suggest that differences between U.S. and Dutch institutions, rather than differences in the underlying health conditions of men in this age group in the two countries, are more likely to explain this phenomenon. In the next section we describe the data. In the third section we contrast the U.S. and Dutch retirement systems. In the fourth section we report our findings on the health, work, and economic well-being of our two age cohorts, and the concluding section summarizes our results.

Data

The U.S. Health and Retirement Study (HRS) has been described in previous essays in this volume and in Juster and Suzman (1995). The CERRA data are less well known. This Dutch retirement panel study is produced by the Center for Economic Research on Retirement and Aging (CERRA) at the University of Leiden.

The CERRA retirement panel is a representative sample of the older working-age population of the Netherlands. The first wave of the CERRA panel was conducted in October 1993 and consists of a primary sample of 3,581 households with a head aged 53 to 63 and a secondary sample of 1,145 households with a head aged 43 to 52. Both household head and spouse (if present) are interviewed. The total number of respondents in the primary sample is 4,726, with 2,013 respondents in the secondary sample. The second wave of CERRA was conducted in October 1995, and the total number of respondents reinterviewed was 3,461.

In structure and content the CERRA panel resembles the HRS. The first wave of the panel consists of a household section covering personal demographic characteristics, nationality, family composition, and education; a labor market section covering job characteristics, earnings, benefit levels, job search behavior, and early retirement; a health section covering personal health characteristics, health care, and use of health care facilities, as well as a housing section covering housing characteristics and mobility; and a financial section covering wealth and debt.

A survey of respondent employers was also conducted in 1994. It provides general information on the organization (firm size, financial performance, etc.), as well as information concerning retirement opportunities within the organization and the organization's attitude toward older workers. Of the 2,200 different employers of respondents in CERRA, 752 completed the employer survey.

Internal evaluations of item nonresponse and representativeness of the first wave of data show them to be of high quality. In general, item nonresponse was not a problem. Nonresponse was, however, relatively high for the income questions, with a nonresponse rate of up to 30 percent for some income sources. CERRA data were compared to data from the Netherlands Central Bureau of Statistics. These data were comparable based on age, sex, labor status, and education.[1]

The first public use wave of CERRA data is available from the Steinmetz Archives in Amsterdam. An English language version of the first wave household questionnaire is available to the research community.[2] This data set can be used to answer questions regarding the health and work experience of the cohort of workers who transitioned into retirement in the 1990s in the Netherlands. But it is also valuable for cross-national comparisons with the HRS. Since both data sets are similar in design, they allow retirement outcomes in the United States to be compared with those in the Netherlands, a country with substantially different labor market institutions.

Retirement Systems in the United States and the Netherlands

Long-Term Trends in Male Labor Force Participation Rates

The roots of most social welfare programs in the United States can be traced to New Deal legislation of the 1930s, when the current Old-Age, Survivors, and Disability Insurance system was established. Hence, it is instructive to trace the labor force participation rates of older workers in the United States from those times.

Table 1 provides the labor force participation rates of men in the United States from 1940 to 1996. If the "normal" retirement age of men in a society is defined as the age at which only one-half of them remain in the labor force, then normal retirement occurred at about age 70 in 1940 and remained so over the next decade. It was not until the 1950s, as an increasing share of workers became eligible for social security retirement benefits at age 65, that the normal retirement age began to drop. By 1960 normal retirement had fallen to age 66, and by 1970 it was age 65. However, over the next fifteen years it continued to fall, so that by 1985 it was approximately age 62. Hence, between 1960 (the year just prior to the establishment of early Social Security benefits for men in 1961) and 1985, the labor force participation of men aged 62 fell from 79.8 to 50.9 percent. While the labor force participation rates of men between ages 55 and 62 have also fallen substantially since 1960, particularly between 1970 and 1985, these declines were not as precipitous as the fall in labor force participation rates of men aged 62 through 65. The downward trend in labor force participation rates for men aged 62 and over in the United States ended in the mid-1980s. Over the last decade — 1985 to 1996 — while the labor force participation rates of men aged 55

TABLE 1.   Male Labor Force Participation Rates by Age in the United States, 1940 to 1996

Year	Age						
	55	60	61	62	63	64	65
1940[a]	93.8	85.5	83.6	80.0	80.4	77.0	70.0
1950[a]	90.6	84.7	82.3	81.2	79.8	76.8	71.7
1960[a]	92.8	85.9	81.6	79.8	77.8	71.5	56.8
1970	91.8	83.9	80.1	73.8	69.4	64.4	49.9
1975	87.6	76.9	73.5	64.4	58.3	54.2	39.4
1980	84.9	74.0	69.6	56.8	52.3	48.8	35.2
1985	83.7	71.0	66.5	50.9	44.7	42.2	30.5
1990	85.3	70.5	67.0	52.5	45.5	40.9	31.9
1995	81.1	68.9	62.0	51.3	43.2	40.3	33.5
1996	81.9	67.5	64.8	51.5	45.3	40.6	33.4

Year	Age					
	66	67	68	69	70	72
1940[a]	68.1	60.3	58.5	56.3	48.6	—
1950[a]	67.1	59.4	57.7	54.5	49.8	39.3
1960[a]	49.0	42.7	42.0	39.0	37.2	28.0
1970	44.7	39.4	37.7	34.0	30.1	24.8
1975	34.2	30.5	23.7	25.8	23.7	22.6
1980	30.4	27.9	24.1	23.0	21.3	17.0
1985	26.5	23.7	20.5	19.5	15.9	14.9
1990	27.2	27.0	23.4	19.0	17.1	16.4
1995	30.2	25.8	22.4	21.9	20.6	16.0
1996	31.7	26.5	22.7	22.2	21.3	16.3

Source: Labor force participation figures from 1970 to 1996 are based on unpublished data from the Current Population Survey (CPS).

[a]Based on adjusted U.S. Bureau of the Census labor force participation data. The adjustment is based on the ratio of CPS figures and census figures in 1970.

through 61 continued to fall, for the most part, the labor force participation of men at most ages over 61 exceeded their mid-1980s troughs.[3]

The social welfare system in the Netherlands is one of the most generous and comprehensive in Europe. While its roots also extend back to pre–World War II years, the great expansion in its programs occurred in the 1960s and 1970s. Table 2 contains historical information on male labor force participation rates in the Netherlands. While the age categories in table 2 are not as disaggregated as in table 1, table 2 does provide a comparable long-term view.

In 1920 one-half of men aged 65 and over were in the labor force in the Netherlands. By the end of World War II only about one-third of men this age were in the labor force. By 1960 one in five was participating, but by 1980 labor force participation rates for men aged 65 and older had fallen to less than one in twenty. While the labor force participation rates of men aged 50 to 64 were relatively constant between 1920 and 1960 they have fallen substantially since the 1960s. While 91.1 percent of men this age were in the labor force in 1960, by 1980 only 70.3 percent were in the labor force and only 59.4 percent by 1985. Over the last decade the drop in labor force participation continued but at a much slower rate, so by 1993 the labor force participation rate for men aged 50 to 64 was 56.2 percent. In contrast, there has been only a modest decline in the labor force participation rate of younger men — aged 40 to 49 — since 1920, and all of that occurred in the 1960s and 1970s. Hence, the decline in the male labor force participation rates in the Netherlands has been steeper and deeper than in the United States both for those over age 65 and for those in their late 50s and early 60s. Furthermore, the decline in labor force participation rates of older men in the Netherlands appears to have slowed considerably over the last decade, while the United States has actually seen slight increases in the work effort of men aged 62 and over.

TABLE 2. Male Labor Force Participation Rates by Age in the Netherlands, 1920 to 1993

	Age		
Year	40 to 49	50 to 64	65 and Older
1920	97.5	91.4	50.0
1930	97.2	88.5	42.6
1947	97.7	89.5	35.5
1960	98.3	91.1	19.9
1980	92.0	70.3	4.7
1981	91.5	67.4	3.8
1983	90.8	63.6	3.8
1985	90.8	59.4	3.3
1987	91.2	57.6	5.2
1988	90.5	57.7	4.8
1989	90.7	56.7	4.6
1990	90.8	56.6	4.5
1991	91.1	55.9	4.0
1992	91.8	56.5	3.9
1993	91.8	56.2	3.8

Source: From "Vijfennegentig jaren statistiek in tijdreeksen" 1899–1994, Central Bureau of Statistics, Gravenhage, Sdu Uitgevers.

Retirement Program Goals and Structures

Citizens of modern industrial democracies like the United States and the Netherlands turn to government to reduce the risk of economically threatening events. Perhaps the most basic economic risks in these countries are associated with a transition out of the labor force at older ages. The results in both countries have been a mixture of government-regulated private insurance and pension programs as well as specific government-run social insurance and welfare programs. In the United States, the Old-Age, Survivors, and Disability Insurance (OASDI) system provides earnings-based retirement benefits to workers and their families beginning as early as age 62. These social security benefits are nearly universal. The spouses of workers are eligible to receive a benefit, as are survivors aged 60 and over. A surviving parent and his or her dependent children are eligible to receive benefits at any age. In addition, the majority of workers who receive OASDI are also eligible to receive employer-based retirement beneifts.[4] The earliest age of eligibility for employer pension benefits varies but is typically earlier than age 62, and many plans offer benefits as early as age 55.

For those aged 65 and over with very low income from other sources, Supplemental Security Income (SSI), a means-tested benefit program, provides a federally guaranteed income. In 1994, the benefit was $669 per month for a couple and $446 per month for an individual with no other sources of income. This amount is supplemented in some states. Persons on this program are also eligible for in-kind transfers—food stamps, health insurance, and so on.

Social Security Disability Insurance (SSDI) benefits are available to workers at any age, if they have worked a sufficient number of years in the system, who are unable to perform "any substantial gainful activity" in the economy. Beneficiaries are also entitled to Medicare. Supplemental Security Income (SSI) is also available at any age for those who meet the disability test for SSDI but do not quality for SSDI benefits because of an insufficient work history or whose SSDI benefits are below the guaranteed social minimum. The United States has no permanent unemployment insurance program and no universal income maintenance program, so the primary sources of government-provided non-work-based income available to persons younger than age 62 who do not care for children are the SSDI and SSI programs.[5]

Social welfare programs in the Netherlands are among the most generous and comprehensive in Europe, far more so than those in the United States. Flat-rate social insurance programs and means-tested welfare programs safeguard the subsistence levels of all Dutch residents. Old age insurance programs provide a minimum level of income to those aged 65 and over, and government-mandated employer pensions supplement these basic programs and allow for early retirement. Disability insurance provides income for those of working age who have a health impairment. Survivors' insurance provides benefits to a deceased worker's surviving spouse and dependent children. Long-term unemployment insurance provides benefits to those who lose their jobs. Long-term welfare programs provide protection to all those with insufficient income and those whose unemployment coverage runs out. In addition to income maintenance, medical and child care expenses are also covered by insurance-based programs. As a result of this comprehensive social welfare system, the Netherlands has a much more elaborate set of financial avenues out of the labor market for its population, many of which begin well before the official retirement age of 65, than does the United States.

Since 1957 all residents of the Netherlands have been entitled to flat-rate social security benefits at age 65.[6] The monthly benefit amount, like the universally guaranteed income program for younger persons, is tied to the government-mandated minimum wage — 2,162.20 guilders per month in 1994. (This is approximately $1,130 per month using a 2 guilders = $1 exchange rate.) Prior to 1993, a couple with a head aged 65 received a social security benefit equal to 100 percent of the after-tax value of the minimum wage — 1,771.54 guilders per month in 1994.[7]

Almost all workers can supplement these basic social security benefits with mandated employer pension benefits. Meuwissen (1993) estimates that 80 percent of households with a head aged 65 or over received some form of supplementary occupational pension in 1989. Kapteyn and de Vos (1997) report that almost all occupational pensions are defined benefit plans (usually basing benefits on some share of final year's earnings) and that, together with social security benefits, they replace between 60 and 69 percent of the median retiree's pretax earnings.

In addition to mandated benefits, most pension plans in the Netherlands offer early retirement options that begin well before age 65. Typically, they offer an employee a benefit equal to 70 to 80 percent of his or her previous year's earnings, which will be paid up to age 65 when normal retirement benefits begin. Because such "early retirement bonuses" are provided with no loss of normal retirement benefits, they offer significant actuarial incentives to retire at the earliest possible age. (See Kapteyn and de Vos 1997 for descriptions of these incentives and evidence of their effects.)

In addition to the generous and widespread early retirement options of its occupational pensions system, the Netherlands has an extremely generous and easily accessible disability system. The modern disability system in the Netherlands can be traced to the Disability Insurance Act of 1967.[8] Following this legislation, program participation increased at an average annual rate of 9 percent in the 1970s and 2 percent in the 1980s. Although attempts were made beginning in the 1970s to stem the tide of beneficiaries and to slow program growth, especially by means of the reforms of 1987, it was not until the reforms of 1993 that program growth finally was stopped. (See Aarts, Burkhauser, and De Jong 1996 for a detailed history of these reforms.)

The first level of protection against income loss in the Dutch disability system is the sickness benefit. Until 1985, sickness benefits replaced 80 percent of gross wage earnings. Since 1985, this program replaces 70 percent of earnings, but most employees (90 percent) and all civil servants have collective bargaining agreements with their employers to supplement the program payment to fully replace all net-of-tax earnings. Sickness benefits can be paid for a maximum of one year. Employees who are still receiving these benefits after that time are evaluated to estimate residual earning capacity. If they have a chronic condition that reduces their capacity to perform work commensurate with their job training and work history, they are eligible for disability benefits.[9] Those who are judged partially disabled are eligible for partial benefits; the minimum level of impairment for eligibility is 15 percent.

The most controversial aspect of the disability system in the Netherlands has been how the determination of eligibility for total benefits is made. Before 1987, disability adjudicators were instructed to take into account, in their judgment of earning capacity, the difficulties a person with a partial disability might experience in finding commensurate employment. This was called the "labor market consideration." In practice, this regulation resulted in all unemployed persons with disabilities, even those with partial disabilities as low as 15 percent, being awarded full disability benefits. The 1987 reforms attempted to disentangle the disabilities and unemployment components in the disability program by eliminating labor market considerations from disability assessments. This rule change, which was anticipated several years before it was officially implemented, together with other reforms, appears to be in part responsible for the slowdown in new beneficiaries on the rolls in the 1980s and 1990s (see Aarts, Burkhauser, and De Jong 1996).

Disability benefits are paid out of two funds. Basic disability benefits come from the National Disability Pension Act of 1976 and provide a flat benefit to all disabled residents aged 18 to 64. The maximum national disability benefit equals 70 percent of the gross minimum wage. Benefits from the second fund, mandated private and public sector employees' disability insurance, are earning related and supplement the national benefit amount. Hence, most totally disabled workers — those who are judged to have lost 81 to 100 percent of their earning capacity — have joint benefits that replace 70 percent of after-tax wages. Employee-based social insurance benefits were capped at 4,367 guilders per month in 1994. In addition to these statutory benefits, over one-half of all employers provide supplemental benefits up to 90 to 100 percent of after-tax earnings during the first year of entitlement to these mandated disability benefits.

Table 3 shows the relative importance of disability transfer programs between 1970 and 1994 in the United States and the Netherlands. As was shown in tables 1 and 2, over this entire period, labor force participation rates were lower in the Netherlands at older ages — especially past age 60. In addition, the use of disability transfers was greater, so the ratio of disability transfer recipients per thousand employed workers was dramatically higher in the Netherlands then in the United States, especially at older ages. However, program growth slowed in the 1980s compared to the 1970s, and the number of recipients per worker declined in the Netherlands between 1990 and 1994. These dramatic differences in within-country and between-country disability transfer recipient rates appear to be more closely correlated to differences in the program histories of the two countries than to underlying health differences.

The unemployment program in the Netherlands is also considerably more generous and longer lasting than unemployment benefits in the United States. The first six months of unemployment in the Netherlands

TABLE 3. Disability Transfer Recipients per Thousand Employed Workers by Age in the United States and the Netherlands

Population	1970	1975	1980	1985	1990	1994
Aged 15 to 64						
United States	27	42	41	41	43	62
The Netherlands	55	84	138	142	152	151
Aged 15 to 44						
United States	11	17	16	20	23	38
The Netherlands	17	32	57	58	62	66
Aged 45 to 59						
United States	33	68	83	71	72	96
The Netherlands	113	179	294	305	339	289
Aged 60 to 64						
United States	154	265	285	254	250	294
The Netherlands	299	437	1,033	1,283	1,987	1,911

Source: Aarts, Burkhauser, and De Jong 1996. Reprinted by permission.

are covered by the standard unemployment insurance programs. Prior to 1985, these programs covered 80 percent of before-tax earnings; this has been reduced to 70 percent since 1985. In 1994 the maximum benefit was 200 guilders per day. Prior to the 1987 reforms, two years of long-term unemployment benefits were available at 70 percent of before-tax wages. Since the 1987 reforms, maximum benefit duration depends on age, with a maximum of five years provided for those aged 59 and older. The long-term unemployment program effectively permits workers who become unemployed at age 59 to continue to receive unemployment insurance until they become eligible for normal retirement benefits at age 65.

Generous retirement, disability, and unemployment benefits available in the Netherlands provide easy avenues for early withdrawal from the workforce. Therefore, it is not surprising that labor force participation rates have rapidly fallen for Dutch workers in their 50s.

Health, Work, and Economic Well-Being in the United States and the Netherlands

Tables 1 and 2 show that the labor force participation rates of older men have dropped dramatically in the United States and the Netherlands since World War II. The labor force participation rates of male workers aged 62 and over leveled off in the mid-1980s in the United States, at a rate well above the concurrent Dutch rates, and appear to have increased modestly since then. Dutch male labor force participation rates plummeted to virtually zero past age 65 by the 1980s and have shown no sign of recovery. While the labor force participation rates of Dutch men aged 50 to 64 are well below those of similar men in the United States, they appear to have stabilized in the 1990s.

Labor Force Participation and Income Source

In table 4 we take advantage of data from HRS and CERRA to look at the work efforts of men aged 51 to 61 in the early 1990s in much greater detail than has previously been possible. In the first column of each country component in table 4 we show the percentage of men who are currently working by age. Work patterns for those aged 51 through 53 appear to be quite similar in the two countries. But for all ages between 54 and 61, work is less prevalent in the Netherlands—at age 54 fewer than three in four men work; by age 58 fewer than one in two work; by age 60 only one in five works. In the United States, while work declines past age 54, the fall is much less precipitous—from 85 to 66 percent by age 61. As we saw in table 1, it is not until age 62 that work dramatically drops in the United States.

Table 4 also provides information on the sources of income for those not currently working. Not surprisingly, given the relative generosity of and access to disability benefits in the Netherlands, disability

TABLE 4.   Prevalence of Work and Transfer Benefits for Men by Age in the Netherlands and the United States

		Not Working		
Age	Working[a]	Disability Transfers[b]	Employer Pension[c]	Other[d]
		United States		
51	82.6	4.1	0.9	12.4
52	84.9	3.0	2.4	9.9
53	82.8	3.5	0.5	13.2
54	84.6	2.9	2.7	9.8
55	78.5	4.5	1.8	15.3
56	76.9	5.0	6.3	11.8
57	80.3	4.6	7.0	8.0
58	71.5	7.5	9.2	12.0
59	68.9	6.5	9.3	15.3
60	67.9	6.1	12.6	13.3
61	65.9	5.6	16.0	12.5
		The Netherlands		
51	83.3	13.7	0.0	3.0
52	87.5	8.1	1.9	2.5
53	81.9	14.1	1.7	2.3
54	74.6	17.2	1.9	6.2
55	72.2	16.7	3.5	7.5
56	59.0	23.9	10.2	6.8
57	58.7	17.4	15.6	8.3
58	49.0	25.0	19.0	7.0
59	44.1	23.2	27.5	5.2
60	20.9	33.3	42.3	3.5
61	16.8	26.9	50.5	5.8

Source: Data from the Netherlands are weighted values of the 1993 Wave 1 CERRA Retirement Panel Study. Data from the United States are weighted values of the 1992 Wave 1 Gamma Release of the Health and Retirement Study.

[a]Those who are working at the time of the interview — 1993 in the Netherlands and 1992 in the United States.

[b]Those who are not working and are receiving disability transfers at the time of the interview.

[c]Those who are not working or receiving disability transfers but who are receiving private pension benefits at the time of interview.

[d]Those who are not working and receiving neither disability transfers nor private pension benefits at the time of interview.

transfers play a much more important role in the provision of income to men in this age cohort in the Netherlands than in the United States. Those who report they are not working and are receiving disability transfers range from about 3 to 8 percent in this age range in the United States but from 8 to 33 percent in the Netherlands. Consistent with the numbers reported in table 3, at ages 60 and 61 more Dutch men are receiving disability transfer benefits than working.

In the next column we look at men who are not working and are receiving employer pensions.[10] Employer pensions play a more important role than disability transfers in the United States past age 60. Employer pensions recipt follows a similar pattern in the Netherlands, but the prevalence of employer pension income is much higher than in the United States past age 55. Again, this is not surprising since employer pensions are mandated in the Netherlands and form a major part of their integrated social security retirement system. By age 59 more than one man in four in the Netherlands is receiving benefits from an employer pension, and this rises to one in two by age 61.

In the final column we look at nonworking men who receive neither disability nor employer pensions. Once again a profound difference appears between the two countries. While the vast majority of men aged 51 to 61 in the United States work, of those who do not, a large share neither receive disability transfers nor employer pension benefits. In fact, for those men aged 51 through 55 who do not work, the majority receive no such transfers. Furthermore, even after age 55, when disability and employer pensions are more common, a large share of nonworking men this age still do not receive them — even at age 61 at least one in three nonworkers is receiving neither disability nor employer pension benefits. In contrast, the vast majority of nonworking Dutch men at every age in table 4 receive either disability transfers or employer pension income. Hence, even though the Dutch social welfare system provides long-term unemployment benefits and a guaranteed minimum income, at this age these programs are not highly utilized because most nonworkers are already receiving even more generous disability transfers or early employer pension benefits. In the United States, where eligibility for disability transfers is far more restricted and early retirement benefits are less widespread, nonworkers are much more likely to have neither of these sources of income to rely upon.

Work and Health

While the link between work and health is well established, the dramatic differences in the work patterns of men in the two countries captured in table 4 cannot be primarily related to the underlying health of men in the two age cohorts.[11] As can be seen in table 5, based on several measures of health there appears to be little difference in health characteristics of these cohorts. Both surveys ask a battery of questions on the health status of respondents. Column 2 reports the number of activities of daily living (ADL) or instrumental activities of daily living (IADL) reported

TABLE 5. Health Status Measures for Workers Aged 51 to 61 in the Netherlands and the United States

	Sample Size	ADL/IADL[a]	Outpatient Visits[b]	Nights in Hospital[c]	Work Limitations (%)[d]
		United States			
All	4,552	0.44	4.3	1.09	20.4
Working[e]	3,425	0.39	2.8	0.55	10.1
Not working	1,127	0.43	7.0	3.51	54.7
Disabled[f]	236	0.46	11.0	6.68	93.6
Pensioner[g]	236	0.35	5.4	2.49	36.6
Other[h]	613	0.46	6.1	2.73	48.1
		The Netherlands			
All	2,183	0.34	4.4	0.89	36.6
Working[e]	1,261	0.20	3.5	0.49	20.5
Not working	922	0.53	5.7	1.45	58.4
Disabled[f]	444	0.87	8.3	2.11	94.8
Pensioner[g]	359	0.20	3.2	0.64	21.9
Other[h]	119	0.24	3.8	1.41	33.1

Source: Data from the Netherlands are weighted values of the 1993 Wave 1 CERRA Retirement Panel Study. Data from the United States are weighted values of the 1992 Wave 1 Gamma Release of the Health and Retirement Study.

[a]This index counts the number of activities of daily living (ADL) or instrumental ADLs that are problematic, accounting for the hierarchical nature of these symptoms. The value increases with poorer functional status. Note that 3,598 of the 4,552 male respondents have no problems with ADL/IADLs in the United States and 1,572 out of 2,183 have no problem in the Netherlands. Data are for 1992 in the United States and 1993 in the Netherlands.

[b]Outpatient visits in 1991 in the United States and in 1992 in the Netherlands.

[c]Nights spent in a hospital in 1991 in the United States and in 1992 in the Netherlands.

[d]In the United States, this variable equals 1 if the respondent reports having a health condition that limits the amount or kind of paid work he can do and 0 otherwise. In the Netherlands this variable equals 1 if the respondent reports a health problem that limits doing one's job and 0 otherwise. Data are for 1992 in the United States and 1993 in the Netherlands.

[e]Those who are working at time of interview.

[f]Those who are not working and are receiving disability transfers at time of interview.

[g]Those who are not working or receiving disability transfers but who are receiving private pension benefits at the time of interview.

[h]Those who are not working and are receiving neither disability transfers nor private pension benefits at the time of interview.

as problematic in the cohorts aged 51 to 61 in the Netherlands and the United States. While work is far more prevalent in the United States than in the Netherlands within this age cohort, the mean value of ADL/IADL problems, 0.44, is actually slightly higher in the United States than the 0.34 mean reported in the Netherlands. In both countries workers have on average fewer ADL/IADL problems than those who are not working. Note, however, that the difference is much larger in the Netherlands (0.20 versus 0.53) than in the United States (0.39 versus 0.43). In both countries, those receiving disability transfers report a higher prevalence of ADL/IADL problems than those receiving employer pensions.

Patterns of outpatient visits and nights spent in the hospital between the two countries are similar, although they suggest that men this age in the United States spend more time in the hospital than do men in the Netherlands.[12]

When the health measure is the report of a health condition that limits the amount or kind of paid work performed, the patterns found for the other health measures remain the same within each country — workers have a smaller prevalence of work-limiting conditions than non-workers, and those nonworkers who receive disability transfers have larger prevalence rates than other nonworkers. The major difference between these countries is that the overall level of work limitation reported in the Netherlands is nearly twice as high in this age group as that reported in the United States (36.6 percent versus 20.4 percent).[13]

Sources of Income

If the differences in the work activity of men aged 51 to 61 in the two countries cannot be traced to underlying health conditions, what other possible explanations are there? A look at the retirement systems in the two countries and the incentives they provide for job exit offers one such explanation. As was discussed previously, easier entry into disability programs, availability of private pensions at younger ages, and more generous and longer lasting unemployment benefits all suggest that the Netherlands offers greater incentives to leave the labor force at older "working" ages — 51 to 61 — than is the case in the United States. The greater use of these programs as income sources is verified in table 6.

Table 6 provides information on household income from the two data sets to show the sources of income for the households in which the men in our samples live. Table 6 reinforces the view from table 4 that work is a far more important source of income for men aged 50 to 60 in the United States than it is in the Netherlands.[14] Overall, 86.0 percent of men in the United States reported income from own work in the previous calendar year (1991) while only 57.8 percent of men report income from own work in the previous year (1993) in the Netherlands.[15] The mean share of own work in total household income in the U.S. sample is 56.2 percent compared with 48.6 percent in the Netherlands sample. Work of other household members accounts for 25.5 percent of total household income in the United States but only 7.1 percent of household

TABLE 6. Total Amount and Sources of Household Income for Men Aged 50 to 60 in the United States and the Netherlands (total household income in U.S. dollars and Dutch guilders)

	United States		
Source	Percentage with Positive Income	Mean (dollars)	Mean Share of Total Income[b] (%)
Own work	86.0	$35,419	56.2
Work of other household members	69.2	14,756	25.5
Disability transfers	10.8	820	3.6
Employer pension transfers	16.9	2,362	5.6
Other government transfers	11.8	433	2.6
Private assets	49.6	4,758	5.9
Others	2.6	153	0.5
Total household income	100.0	$58,701[a]	

	The Netherlands		
Source	Percentage with Positive Income	Mean (guilders)	Mean Share of Total Income[b] (%)
Own work	57.8	ƒ44,496	48.6
Work of other household members	24.7	7,053	7.1
Disability transfers	23.8	7,380	17.3
Employer pension transfers	19.9	10,947	14.9
Other government transfers	18.5	3,536	6.1
Private assets	18.5	1,409	1.4
Others	18.6	3,612	4.6
Total household income	100.0	ƒ78,433[a]	

Source: U.S. data are weighted values from the 1992 Wave 1 Gamma Release of the Health and Retirement Study based on yearly income values for 1991. The Netherlands data are weighted values from the 1993 Wave 1 CERRA Retirement Panel Study based on 1993 income year information. HRS sample includes 4,506 age-eligible men who report income information. CERRA sample includes 2,183 age-eligible men who report income information.

[a]Median household size–adjusted income is $30,600 in 1991 for the United States and ƒ41,152 in 1993 for the Netherlands. The exchange rate in 1991 was approximately ƒ2 = $1.

[b]Mean of the sum of each source's share of total household income across all households.

income in the Netherlands. In contrast, no other source of income in the United States accounts for more than a 6 percent share of household income. Disability and employee pension income shares are quite low (3.6 and 5.6 respectively) in the United States but account for 17.3 percent and 14.9 percent shares of household income in the Netherlands. Table 6 makes clear that men's own work and that of other household members are the dominant sources of income for the households of U.S. men aged 50 to 60, while income from work is far less important for similar households in the Netherlands.

One explanation for the dramatic differences in work and transfer receipt patterns in this age cohort is that the relative reward for exiting the labor market versus continuing to work at these ages is larger in the Netherlands than in the United States. In table 7 we provide information on the relative economic well-being of workers and nonworkers by disaggregating our age cohorts by principal source of household income. In the United States there are enormous differences across main source of income categories. The mean income of households in which either own work or the work of others dominates is far larger than the mean income in households where employer pensions, disability transfers, and other government transfers dominate. Those households where private assets dominate look more like work-dominated households than transfer-dominated households.

In contrast, the gap in mean income between work- and transfer-dominated households is much narrower in the Netherlands. The higher safety net provided by the Dutch disability transfer system is evident in the narrow gap between mean income in households dominated by disability transfers and both work- and employer pension–dominated households. Contrast the very large gap in mean income in the United States between disability transfer–dominated households and work- and employer pension–dominated households with the much smaller gap among these three groups in the Netherlands. Furthermore, the very low mean income of government transfer–dominated households in the United States demonstrates the extremely modest safety net that exists for those with little or no disability transfers or employer pension benefits who are not working at this age. In contrast, in the Netherlands men in this cohort in other government transfer–dominated households have income that is even somewhat greater than that of disability-dominated households. This is primarily due to workers receiving short-term unemployment benefits. When their unemployment benefits run out, long-term unemployment benefits begin that are in most instances lower than disability transfers.

TABLE 7. Total Amount and Sources of Household Income for U.S. and Dutch Men Aged 50 to 60 in 1991 across Primary Income Source Categories (total household income in 1991 U.S. dollars and Dutch guilders)

	Primary Sources of Personal Income					
Sources	Own Labor Earnings[a]	Other Labor Earnings[b]	Disability Transfers[c]	Employer Pension Transfers[d]	Private Assets[e]	Other Government Transfers[f]
United States						
Own work	72	26	3	14	33	6
Work of other household members	17	60	11	11	13	17
Disability transfers	0	2	43	2	3	3
Employer pension transfers	2	4	7	64	5	8
Private assets	8	6	6	6	45	4
Other government transfers	0	1	22	1	1	61
Others	0	0	8	1	0	0
Total mean household income (= 100%)	$64,953	$54,455	$14,922	$33,178	$49,677	$10,322
The Netherlands[g]						
Own work	84		0	0		0
Work of other household members	8		6	5		8
Disability transfers	2		80	0		0
Employer pension transfers	0		2	84		6
Private assets	1		2	2		3
Other government transfers	2		4	4		68
Others	3		6	5		15
Total mean household income (= 100%)	ƒ92,841		ƒ44,998	ƒ75,840		ƒ51,146

Source: U.S. data are weighted values from the 1992 Wave 1 Gamma Release of the Health and Retirement Study based on yearly income values for 1991. The Netherlands data are weighted values from the 1993 Wave 1 CERRA Retirement Panel Study based on 1993 income year information. HRS sample includes 4,506 age-eligible men who report income information. CERRA sample includes 2,183 age-eligible men who report income information.

[a]Those men living in the household whose largest share of income came from their own labor earnings: $n =$ 3,031 US, 1,261 NL.

[b]Those men living in the household whose largest share of income came from other household members' labor earnings: $n = 977$ US.

[c]Those men living in the household whose largest share of income came from their own disability transfers: $n = 225$ US, 444 NL.

[d]Those men living in the household whose largest share of income came from their own employer pension transfers: $n = 180$ US, 359 NL.

[e]Those men living in the household whose largest share of income came from private assets: $n = 56$ US.

[f]Those men living in the household whose largest share of income came from other transfers: $n = 37$ US, 119 NL.

[g]There are not enough observations in the columns "Other Labor Earnings" and "Private Assets" in CERRA for a reliable comparison. Persons in these categories were put into the next most dominant source category.

Measuring Income Inequality

Table 8 looks more closely at the relative economic well-being of the households of men aged 50 to 60 in the two countries. Because men live in households of different size, it is necessary to adjust for the number of people in the household before making comparisons of their relative economic well-being. There is a great deal of variation in the choice of equivalence scale used in such measures.[16] Here we use a scale commonly used in cross-national comparisons. This "international experts" scale divides household income by the number of household members to the 0.5 power. Hence, for example, a family of four would be assumed to require exactly twice as much income ($20,000) as a single person ($10,000) to have each of its household members at the same level of economic well-being ($10,000 = ($20,000/4$^{.5}$)). It is also assumed that income is equally shared within the household.[17]

As can be seen in table 8, the differences across primary income source categories narrow relative to table 7. This is caused both by the use of median rather than mean income, which reduces the importance of outliers, and by the adjustments for household size. Nonetheless, the across-group income pattern found in table 7 remains. In the United States, households dominated by income from work or personal assets are substantially better off than households whose primary source of income comes from transfers. Households in which employer pensions dominate are better off than households where disability transfers are the primary source of income; both of these household types are much better off than households in which government transfers dominate.

In the Netherlands the differences are much less pronounced. The median income of households dominated by own labor earnings is only 15 percent higher than that of households dominated by employer pensions. While both these types of households are substantially better off than households dominated by either disability benefits or other government transfers, the differences are much smaller than in the United States, especially for those receiving other government transfers.

We infer from tables 7 and 8 that the differences in work patterns in the two countries are much more likely to be related to differences in the relative rewards for job exit than to differences in underlying health. The Dutch effort to ameliorate income losses following labor market exits associated with poor health, job loss, or "old age" through their generous and comprehensive social welfare system has yielded prevalence rates of retirement and disability benefits recipients among men aged 51 to 61 that are substantially higher than those in the United States. The consequences of this policy on income distribution have also

TABLE 8. Measures of Household Size–Adjusted Income Inequality for U.S. and Dutch Men Aged 50 to 60 in 1991 within and across Primary Income Source Categories[a] (total household size–adjusted income in U.S. dollars and Dutch guilders)

Household Size–Adjusted Income Deciles		Distribution of Men within Total Income Distribution Deciles[c]					
	All Men (n = 4,506)	Own Labor Earnings (n = 3,031)	Other Labor Earnings (n = 977)	Disability Transfers (n = 225)	Employer Pension (n = 180)	Private Assets (n = 56)	Other Government Transfers (n = 37)
Median income (in dollars)[b]	$30,600	$34,043	$28,475	$8,289	$18,599	$24,575	$3,396
90/10[b]	7.01	5.61	5.50	7.54	5.02	6.90	20.47
Gini[b]	0.43	0.41	0.37	0.44	0.37	0.40	0.56
Theil[b]	0.30	0.27	0.21	0.32	0.23	0.28	0.57
Share of overall inequality[c]	100.00	62.00	14.40	4.60	3.10	1.20	1.20
Weighted share of population	100.00	68.50	21.00	4.30	4.10	1.30	0.70
Ratio of overall inequality to weighted share of population	—	0.90	0.70	1.07	0.77	0.94	1.90
			The Netherlands				
	(n = 2,183)	(n = 1,261)		(n = 444)	(n = 359)		(n = 119)
Median income (in guilders)[b]	ƒ41,152	ƒ50,086		ƒ25,529	ƒ42,930		ƒ26,496
90/10[b]	4.70	3.86		3.23	3.60		4.29
Gini[b]	0.34	0.31		0.28	0.30		0.35
Theil[b]	0.12	0.17		0.15	0.15		0.24
Share of overall inequality[c]	100.00	56.10		9.60	13.90		4.70
Weighted share of population	100.00	54.90		21.30	18.00		5.70
Ratio of overall inequality to weighted share of population	—	1.02		0.45	0.77		0.82

Source: U.S. data are weighted values from the 1992 Wave 1 Gamma Release of the Health and Retirement Study based on yearly income values for 1991. The Netherlands data are weighted values from the 1993 Wave 1 CERRA Retirement Panel Study based on 1993 income year information. HRS sample includes 4,506 age-eligible men who report income information. CERRA sample includes 2,183 age-eligible men who report income information. There are not enough observations in the columns "Other Labor Earnings" and "Private Assets" in the CERRA survey to warrant a reliable comparison. Persons in these categories were put in the next most dominant category.

Note: An equivalence scale of 0.5 is used for calculating household size–adjusted income, which is then arrayed from lowest to highest.

[a]See table 7 for definitions of each primary personal income category source.

[b]Within primary household size-adjusted income source category.

[c]Between-group inequality equals 13.5 percent in the United States and 15.7 percent in the Netherlands.

been substantial. As table 8 shows, the Netherlands has a far more economically egalitarian society than does the United States. Table 8 uses three standard measures of income inequality — the 90/10 ratio and the Gini and Theil (I_1) coefficients. (See the appendix for a discussion of these three inequality measures.) Regardless of measure, inequality is found to be far greater in the United States than in the Netherlands both within and across the subcategories of men aged 50 to 60.

In the United States the male household size–adjusted income at the 90th percentile of the household size–adjusted income distribution is 7.01 times that of the male at the 10th percentile, much higher than the 90/10 value of 4.70 for similarly positioned Dutch men. Income inequality varies greatly within households with different dominant sources of income in these two countries. In the United States, household size–adjusted income is most varied in the Other Government Transfers, Disability Transfers, and Private Assets groups. Those in the Own or Other Labor Earnings groups have less within-income category inequality and those with Employer Pensions the last inequality in the United States. Inequality is also highest within the group with Other Government Transfers — this is mostly due to differences between long- and short-term unemployment benefits — but the difference between this group and the other three groups is relatively small. What is particularly remarkable for the Netherlands compared to the United States is the relatively low within-group income inequality of Disability Transfers beneficiaries. Their inequality is on the same level as the Own Labor Earnings and Employer Pensions groups, while in the United States inequality within the Disability Transfers group is quite large relative to all groups except Other Government Transfers.

Our Theil (I_1) inequality measure is additively decomposable, which permits overall inequality to be portioned into differences between subgroups and within subgroups (see Shorrocks 1980). Thus, we can show how much of overall inequality is due to inequality between primary income groups and how much is due to inequality within income groups. In the United States 13.5 percent of overall inequality is explained by inequality between groups while in the Netherlands 15.7 percent is explained in this manner. In the United States the primary source of overall inequality comes from within the Own Labor Earnings group — 62.0 percent. This is true primarily because it is the largest population group. A more important finding is that the ratio of overall inequality to the weighted share of population in the United States is greatest within the Disability Transfers and Other Government Transfer groups, suggesting, as do the individual within-group inequality measures, the greatest variation in outcomes in this group. In the Netherlands all nonworking groups have much lower inequality ratios than does the working group.

Measuring Income Mobility

Two waves of the HRS data were available to us. The 1993 wave of CERRA is drawn from another survey that contains questions about income levels in 1991. This makes it possible to measure changes in income over a two-year period in both data sets.[18] Because household composition may change, we choose as our unit of analysis the individual and trace his economic well-being over a two-year period. Table 9 shows that the median change in household size–adjusted income was positive for men in both countries over the two-year period.[19] More importantly it shows that not only is the single-period inequality shown in table 8 greater in the United States than in the Netherlands, but income movements over the two-year period were far greater. In the Netherlands only about one in four men experienced income changes of more than 20 percent over that period, while in the United States three in five men experienced such large changes. Furthermore, in the Netherlands, large gainers outnumber large losers by more than 2.4 to 1, while in the United States this ratio is only 1.2 to 1.

TABLE 9. Changes in Household Size–Adjusted Income between 1991 and 1993 for U.S. and Dutch Men Aged 50 to 60 in 1991

	Household Size–Adjusted Income	
Year	United States (in dollars)	The Netherlands (in guilders)
Median change in income (1993–91)	$1,000	ƒ2,380
Size of Change		
Decrease of 20 percent or more	27.7	7.80
Decrease or increase of less than 20 percent	39.4	73.22
Increase of 20 percent or more	32.9	18.99

Source: U.S. data are weighted values from the 1992 Wave 1 Gamma Release of the Health and Retirement Study together with income values from the 1994 Wave 2 Beta Release of the Health and Retirement Study. The Netherlands data are weighted values from the 1991 AVO and from the 1993 Wave 1 CERRA Retirement Panel Study.

Note: U.S. sample size is 3,465. The decline in sample size compared to previous tables is due to missing values for income in the 1994 Wave 2 Alpha release of the Health and Retirement Survey. Sample size in the Netherlands is 1,796 who are both in the 1991 Dutch Social and Cultural Planning Bureau AVO sample and in Wave 1 of the CERRA Household Survey.

TABLE 10. Transitions across Household Size–Adjusted Income Quintiles, for U.S. Men Aged 50 to 60 in 1991, by Primary Income Source Categories (total household size–adjusted income in U.S. dollars)

1991 Income Quintiles	1993 Household Size–Adjusted Income Quintiles					1991 Median
	Lowest	Next Lowest	Middle	Next Highest	Highest	
All Men						
Lowest	62.7	24.9	5.6	4.0	2.7	$11,489
Next lowest	19.3	40.4	26.2	10.2	3.8	24,028
Middle	9.9	18.2	38.4	23.5	10.1	33,333
Next highest	4.5	10.1	21.7	44.1	19.6	44,990
Highest	3.7	6.6	8.5	17.9	63.3	70,213
1993 median	$9,787	$22,989	$33,959	$46,848	$79,787	
Own Labor Earnings						
Lowest	54.6	32.1	7.2	2.7	3.5	13,040
Next lowest	17.2	39.2	29.8	9.3	4.4	24,143
Middle	9.4	18.1	39.6	23.1	9.7	33,213
Next highest	4.5	9.4	21.3	45.1	19.6	44,681
Highest	3.3	5.6	8.1	16.1	66.8	71,731
1993 median	$10,490	$23,000	$34,000	$47,341	$80,179	
Other Labor Earnings						
Lowest	55.5	28.0	6.0	7.8	2.8	12,057
Next lowest	23.8	40.9	17.9	14.6	2.8	23,584
Middle	9.9	21.1	34.2	22.4	12.5	33,237
Next highest	1.8	12.2	24.3	42.5	19.2	46,099
Highest	4.8	10.1	8.5	26.0	50.7	69,431
1993 median	$10,828	$23,399	$33,665	$46,069	$75,372	
Disability Transfers						
Lowest	92.2	4.5	0.0	3.4	0.0	7,338
Next lowest	20.0	60.0	16.0	4.0	0.0	23,169
Middle	52.6	0.0	5.3	42.1	0.0	31,773
Next highest	0.0	0.0	0.0	100.0	0.0	53,901
Highest	0.0	0.0	0.0	0.0	0.0	—
1993 median	$7,320	$21,302	$29,401	$47,270	—	
Employer Pensions						
Lowest	67.0	23.6	4.7	2.8	1.9	12,057
Next lowest	26.5	46.9	20.4	4.1	2.0	23,050
Middle	10.5	5.3	42.1	34.2	7.9	34,752
Next highest	6.3	12.5	31.3	31.3	18.8	44,777
Highest	0.0	10.5	21.1	26.3	42.1	65,390
1993 median	$11,952	$21,844	$34,057	$47,343	$86,648	

TABLE 10. *(cont.)*

1991 Income Quintiles	1993 Household Size–Adjusted Income Quintiles					1991 Median
	Lowest	Next Lowest	Middle	Next Highest	Highest	
Private Assets						
Lowest	51.2	0.0	19.5	14.6	14.6	$10,250
Next lowest	27.6	27.6	27.6	13.8	3.4	14,721
Middle	0.0	20.0	60.0	20.0	0.0	23,794
Next highest	27.6	17.2	0.0	27.6	27.6	48,562
Highest	25.0	25.0	25.0	0.0	25.0	76,454
1993 median	$9,068	$21,816	$33,004	$44,691	$89,362	
Other Government Transfers						
Lowest	100.0	0.0	0.0	0.0	0.0	2,950
Next lowest	0.0	100.0	0.0	0.0	0.0	20,390
Middle	0.0	0.0	0.0	0.0	0.0	—
Next highest	0.0	0.0	0.0	0.0	0.0	—
Highest	0.0	0.0	0.0	0.0	0.0	—
1993 median	$7,236	$24,000	—	—	—	—

Source: U.S. data are weighted values from the 1992 Wave 1 Gamma Release of the Health and Retirement Study together with income values from the 1994 Wave 2 Beta Release of the Health and Retirement Study.

Note: Total sample size 3,465.

In tables 10 and 11, we look more closely at mobility in the two countries. We do so by comparing the initial position of each man in the household size–adjusted income distribution in 1991 with his relative position in 1993. We do this for the overall sample and within primary income subcategories.

In table 10 we compare movement across household size–adjusted income quintiles in the United States — 62.7 percent of the men in the lowest quintiles in 1991 remained there in 1993. The immobility rate of men in the highest quintiles in 1991 was 63.3 percent. Immobility in the middle three quintiles was smaller, with about two workers in five remaining in each of these quintiles over the two years. While sample sizes are small in some of the primary income categories, it appears that immobility does not vary greatly among the Own Labor Earnings, Other Labor Earnings, and Employer Pensions categories. Less mobility appears to occur in the Disability Transfers category and more in the Private Assets category.

In the Netherlands mobility rates are on average lower than in the United States. About three men in four in the highest and lowest income categories remained in these quintiles, and from 56 to 67 percent of men remained in middle quintiles over the two-year period. Immobility in the

TABLE 11. Transitions across Household Size–Adjusted Income Quintiles for Dutch Men Aged 50 to 60 in 1991, by Primary Income Source Categories (total household size–adjusted income in Dutch guilders)

1991 Income Quintiles	1993 Household Size–Adjusted Income Quintiles					1991 Median
	Lowest	Next Lowest	Middle	Next Highest	Highest	
All Men						
Lowest	74.5	18.2	4.4	2.2	0.8	ƒ11,860
Next lowest	13.8	55.7	21.1	6.0	3.5	16,047
Middle	5.1	15.6	55.5	16.8	7.0	19,651
Next highest	0.9	3.4	13.4	67.1	15.1	24,419
Highest	1.1	3.4	4.3	14.3	76.8	34,186
1993 median	ƒ12,209	ƒ17,677	ƒ21,565	ƒ27,151	ƒ37,209	
Own Labor Earnings						
Lowest	65.3	22.1	7.1	3.5	2.0	15,000
Next lowest	20.9	46.7	23.1	6.7	2.7	18,081
Middle	6.8	25.4	50.0	9.8	8.0	22,326
Next highest	2.0	6.8	14.8	63.5	12.9	26,512
Highest	1.8	2.9	3.5	17.1	75.0	34,884
1993 median	ƒ16,163	ƒ20,291	ƒ24,302	ƒ29,477	ƒ40,698	
Disability Transfers						
Lowest	65.4	23.1	3.8	1.3	6.4	9,767
Next lowest	9.6	63.5	26.9	0.0	0.0	11,860
Middle	5.7	5.7	64.3	24.3	0.0	13,116
Next highest	1.8	5.5	14.6	65.4	12.7	14,860
Highest	7.9	4.8	3.2	4.8	79.4	20,930
1993 median	ƒ9,767	ƒ11,860	ƒ12,907	ƒ14,651	ƒ20,930	
Employer Pensions						
Lowest	75.6	13.3	2.2	4.5	4.4	14,930
Next lowest	20.0	70.0	2.5	2.5	5.0	18,140
Middle	4.1	12.3	75.5	4.1	4.1	20,930
Next highest	0.0	2.6	2.6	81.6	13.2	25,116
Highest	0.0	0.0	7.1	16.7	76.2	31,395
1993 median	ƒ15,174	ƒ18,837	ƒ22,326	ƒ26,165	ƒ34,186	
Other Transfers						
Lowest	66.6	20.0	0.0	6.7	6.7	8,372
Next lowest	14.3	35.6	21.4	28.8	0.0	10,988
Middle	17.6	35.3	41.2	5.9	0.0	12,209
Next highest	0.0	5.3	21.0	58.0	15.8	17,384
Highest	0.0	11.0	0.0	0.0	89.0	27,907
1993 median	ƒ8,498	ƒ10,772	ƒ12,209	ƒ15,479	ƒ26,163	

Source: The Netherlands data are weighted values from the 1991 AVO and from the 1993 Wave 1 CERRA Retirement Panel Study.

Note: Total sample size is 1,796.

Netherlands is greater in the Other Transfers category, but even in the Own Labor Earnings category immobility ranges from about one in two to three in four.

Not only is there greater income equality in the cohort of Dutch men aged 51 to 61, but there is greater stability in the distribution over the two years of our analysis than is the case in the United States. Differences in Dutch and U.S. social policy are undoubtedly responsible for both the greater relative level of income equality and the lower level of work in this age cohort in the Netherlands.

Conclusion

We show that the labor force participation rates of men have dropped dramatically for older male workers in the United States and the Netherlands since World War II. The labor force participation rates of male workers over age 62 leveled off in the mid-1980s in the United States, at a rate well above the Dutch rates of that era, and they appear to have increased modestly since then. Dutch male labor force participation rates plummeted to virtually zero past age 65 by the 1980s and have shown no sign of recovery. While in the United States work still dominates the income of men aged 51 to 61, a large share of men this age have already transitioned out of the labor force in the Netherlands.

When we compare information on the source of income for those not currently working we find that disability transfers and employer-based early retirement benefits play a much more important role in the provision of income to men in the cohort aged 51 to 61 in the Netherlands than in the United States. While the vast majority of men aged 51 to 61 in the United States work, of those who do not, a large share receive neither disability transfers nor employer pension benefits. In contrast, the vast majority of nonworking Dutch men in the same age group receive either disability transfers or employer pension income. Income from work both by men and by other members of their households is the dominant source of income for U.S. men aged 51 to 61, while income from work is far less important for similar men in the Netherlands.

Based on our data from the HRS, we find enormous differences across main source of income categories in the United States. The mean household income of households in which either own work or the work of others dominates is by far larger than the mean income in households where employer pensions, disability transfers, or other government transfers dominate. In contrast, using our data from CERRA, we find the gap in mean income between work- and transfer-dominated households is much narrower in the Netherlands. The bigger safety net provided by the

Dutch disability transfer system is evident in the narrow gap between mean income in households dominated by disability transfers and both work- and employer pension–dominated households.

We infer that the differences in work patterns between the two countries are much more likely to be related to differences in the relative rewards for job exit than to differences in underlying health. This is not to say that health does not play a role in early withdrawal from the labor market in both countries. Within both countries those not at work are more likely to have difficulty with ADL/IADL activities than are workers. However, the differences in health between the two countries cannot explain the enormous differences in labor force attachment we observe. The Dutch effort to ameliorate income losses following labor market exits associated with poor health, job loss, or "old age" through a generous social welfare system has resulted in prevalence rates of retirement and disability transfer recipients among men aged 51 to 61 that are substantially higher than those in the United States.

The consequences of this policy on income distribution have also been substantial. The Netherlands has a far more economically egalitarian society than does the United States. Not only is there greater income equality in the cohort of Dutch older "working-age" men, but there is greater stability in their income mobility over the two years of our analysis than is the case in the United States.

Different social policy goals in the two countries are undoubtedly responsible for both the greater level of income equality and the lower level of work we observe. Our comparisons of the Netherlands and the United States reveal the classic trade-off between equality and productivity that lies at the heart of all social choices that people of different countries must make through their representative governments. The voting population in the Netherlands clearly has shown a much greater willingness to accept reduced employment to obtain greater equality and stability of income than is the case in the United States. Whether the Dutch will be able to continue to afford their social welfare system as their population ages and as international competition and European unification intensify over the next decade remains to be seen.

APPENDIX

Work Status Variables

While the HRS and CERRA data provide similar information, there are some differences. The HRS is a representative sample of men and women aged 51 to

61 in 1992. The first wave of CERRA data contains a primary sample of Dutch household heads (a head of household is defined as the household member with the highest individual income) aged 53 to 63 and a secondary sample of household heads aged 43 to 52 in 1993. We reweighted the two Dutch samples using population proportions so that the weighted CERRA sample we use is comparable to the HRS sample. The reweighted CERRA sample used in this essay is representative of Dutch men aged 51 to 61 in 1993.

In the HRS data we categorize respondents into work status groups in two ways. Tables 4 and 5 look at current work status by current age and health status. In these two tables we use respondent self-reports of work status that reflect their situation at the time of the interview. The remainder of the tables focus on annual income by previous year work status. In the HRS data we use previous year work status because our annual income measures reflect behavior in the year prior to the interview. Current work status reports may not accurately explain past income in this case. To resolve this issue in the HRS we designate work status in tables 6 through 10 based on the greatest source of income for that year—annual income in 1991. These categorizations are described in more detail in the following.

Self-Reports (tables 4 and 5):   The "Working" category in the HRS includes those who report themselves as currently working at the time of the 1992 interview. The "Not Working" category is divided into three mutually exclusive subcategories of respondents who do not report themselves as working in 1992. Those receiving income from SSDI, SSI, or the Workers' Compensation program are categorized as "Disabled." Those not receiving any disability transfers but who are receiving income from private pension are categorized as "Pensioners." Those neither receiving disability transfers nor private pension benefits are categorized as "Other."

The "Working" category in the CERRA includes those who report themselves as currently working at the time of the 1993 interview. The "Not Working" category is divided into three mutually exclusive subcategories of respondents who do not report themselves as working in 1993. Those receiving income from disability programs (WAO, AAW, IAOW, and IAOZ) are categorized as "Disabled." Those not receiving any disability transfers but who are receiving income from early retirement schemes (VUT) and normal retirement pension income are categorized as "Pensioners." Those neither receiving disability transfers nor early retirement benefits nor normal retirement private pension benefits are categorized as "Other." In the Netherlands, a large component of the "Other" category receives unemployment benefits.

Income Derived (tables 6 through 10):   As discussed previously, work status categories in the HRS are derived from sources of 1991 annual household income. The "Working" category consists of those men whose primary source of household income in 1991 was from their 1991 labor earnings. The "Other Labor Earnings" category consists of respondents whose main source of household income comes from the labor earnings of other household members. Those whose primary source of household income was from SSDI, SSI, and Workers' Compensation are referred to as "Disabled." Private pensions are the primary source of household income for "Pensioners." The "Private Assets" category is for those men whose primary source of household income is interest, dividends, rent, and so on. The final category, "Other Government Transfers," consists of those whose primary income sources are government transfers not related to disability or private assets. Note that because those income sources are from the previous year, the age category in these tables is men aged 50 to 60.

In the CERRA data, yearly income is primarily derived from previous monthly income values so work status correlates almost perfectly with greatest source of income. Hence, for the Dutch case we continue to use the current work status variables discussed previously.

Health Variables

Both surveys offer a variety of health measures from which to choose. We were restricted to choose among measures that were comparable across the two surveys. The ADL/IADL index is a detailed eleven scale hierarchical index based on work done by Katz et al. (1963). The index increases as health worsens and takes into account the severity of symptoms. ADLs included in the index are transferring, bathing, dressing, and feeding. The IADLs used are proxies for shopping and transportation, since these are not available in the HRS. We used variables measuring the ability to lift ten pounds (e.g., a bag of groceries) and walking several blocks.[20] In the CERRA data the ADL/IADL index is based on questions regarding the ability to lift and push or pull objects.

Other objective measures of health include the number of outpatient office visits in 1991 (in 1992 for the Netherlands) and the number of nights spent in a hospital in 1991 (in 1992 for the Netherlands).

For the HRS, the self-report of work limitations takes a value of 1 if the respondent reports a health condition that limits the amount or kind of paid work he can do and 0 otherwise. For CERRA, the self-report of work limitations takes a value of 1 if the respondent reports a health problem that limits doing one's job and 0 otherwise.

Household Income

Household income is adjusted by the number of people in the sharing unit in tables 8 through 11. The HRS sharing unit includes all members of the dwelling unit who are married or partners plus all other blood relatives. We call the sharing unit the household. Household income is measured as annual 1991 household size–adjusted gross income in the HRS. It is adjusted using an equivalence scale of 0.5. It includes all sources of household income. Information on respondents' own earnings comes from a question about their labor income in the previous year. Data for labor earnings of other household members come from similar questions about spouse and about other household members. Employer pension transfers measures household income from private pensions in 1991. Disability transfers consist of SSDI, SSI, and Workers' Compensation transfers to anyone in the household. Private assets consist of household income from rent, interest, and dividends. Other government transfers are any income from government transfers not related to disability. In the mobility tables we use similar data created by John Phillips as part of Phillips 1997. He calculated annual 1993 household size–adjusted gross income based on the Wave 2 Beta Release of the HRS information.

The income questions in CERRA are for either the previous month or year. The survey was fielded in October 1993 so data are primarily for 1993. Monthly expenses were adjusted to make them yearly. A further complication is that respondents were asked to provide an after-tax measure of income rather than a before-tax measure. To make these values consistent with the before-tax values provided in the HRS data, we calculated gross (before-tax) yearly income from the information on net monthly or yearly income using a tax program that allowed us to go from net after-tax income to gross before-tax income using standard tax deductions and tax rates. In CERRA, respondent's own earnings come from a question about their net labor income in the previous month or year. Labor earnings of other family members come from similar questions about the spouse or other family members. Employer pension transfers measure respondent's income from an early retirement (VUT) or normal retirement pension plan. Disability transfers consist of WAO, AAW, IAOW, or IAOZ transfers to anyone in the household. Private assets consist of household income from rent, interest, and dividends. Other government transfers include any income from government transfers not related to disability and will in most cases be unemployment benefits (WW) or social welfare benefits (Bijstand).

While CERRA is a panel study, wave 2 CERRA data for 1995 were not available at the time we wrote this essay. Happily the 1993 CERRA data were in part drawn from the 1991 Dutch Social and Cultural Planning Bureau AVO sample (Aanvullend voorzieningen onderzoek). Hence, for the subsample of the 1993 CERRA drawn from the 1991 AVO sample, we have information on their net income for 1991. Since we do not have information on the income of other household members, we computed all other household income using information from the 1993 CERRA. We then derived gross before-tax income from our tax program.

Income Inequality Measures

We use three conventional relative measures of income inequality. The 90/10 ratio is one relative measure of income inequality. It is the ratio of income at the 90th percentile to that of the 10th percentile. This shows the magnitude of the difference between those at the top of the distribution and those at the bottom. This is done overall and within groups as well. We also use the Gini coefficient, which measures relative income inequality by comparing differences in individual incomes to the mean. Finally, we use a Theil coefficient (I_0), which sums the log ratio of mean income to individual income, adjusted for sample size to evaluate deviations from the mean. This measure has the advantage of being additively decomposable into within- and between-group categories of inequality.

Theil $I_1(Y)$ and Theil $I_0(Y)$

$$\text{Theil } I_1(Y) = \frac{1}{n} \sum_i \frac{y_i}{\mu} \log \frac{y_i}{\mu}$$

and

$$\text{Theil } I_0(Y) = \frac{1}{n} \sum_i \log \frac{\mu}{y_i'}$$

where n equals the number of individuals, y_i equals the income of individuals I, and μ is mean income.

Gini Coefficient

$$\text{GINI} = \left[\frac{1}{2n^2\mu} \right] \sum_{i=1}^{n} \sum_{j=1}^{i} |y_i - y_j|,$$

in which y is individual income, n is the number of individuals, and μ is mean income.

90/10 Percentile Point Measure

$$90/10 \text{ ratio} = \frac{y_{90\text{th percentile}}}{y_{10\text{th percentile}}},$$

where Y is equivalent household income assigned to all members of the household.

NOTES

This study was funded by the National Institute on Aging, Program Project No. 1-PO1-AG09743–01, "The Well-Being of the Elderly in a Comparative Context," and by the Dutch NESTOR Program on Aging and the Leiden University Speerpunten Program. Burkhauser was at Syracuse University, Dwyer was a National Institute on Aging postdoctoral fellow at Syracuse University and Lindeboom and Theeuwes were at the University of Leiden while the bulk of this essay was written.

1. For a more complete discussion of the CERRA data quality, see Fokkema 1996 and Struijs 1994.

2. Those interested in receiving the English language questionnaire as well as further information on the data and how to obtain them should write to Prof. J. J. M. Theeuwes, SEO, University of Amsterdam, Roetersstraat 11, 1018 WB Amsterdam, the Netherlands; e-mail: j.theeuwes@seo.fee.uva.nl.

3. Burkhauser and Quinn (1997), using Current Population Survey data, show the labor force participation rates of men aged 60 to 64 and aged 65 to 70 from 1964 through 1996 and use a linear time trend based on the 1964 to 1985 data to project labor force participation rates from 1986 through 1996. They find actual rates since 1985 have been substantially above projected rates.

4. Burkhauser, Couch, and Phillips (1996), using the first two waves of the HRS, find that 59 percent of workers who turned age 62 between 1992 and 1994 were eligible to receive an employer pension and 65 percent of men who took early social security benefits at age 62 were also eligible for employer benefits.

5. Workers' Compensation, a state-based program, is also an important source of income for persons who have a work limitation that can be traced to their job. The vast majority of Workers' Compensation benefits are temporary full or permanent partial payments. For a fuller discussion of the United States disability system, see Burkhauser and Haveman 1982 and Berkowitz and Burkhauser 1996. For persons who care for children, Aid to Families with Dependent Children (AFDC) and other child-based programs that include health care are available. But since 1996 they are time limited.

6. While this program was officially introduced in 1957, it was based on provisional laws that date back to the immediate post–world War II years.

7. The system was slightly modified in 1994. While a married couple, both age 65, continues to receive 100 percent of the after-tax minimum wage, total benefits are reduced if the spouse is under age 65 and working.

8. See Emanuel 1979 for a discussion of disability programs prior to 1967.

9. In the reforms of 1993 and 1994 the concept of commensurate work was broadened to include all generally accepted jobs that are compatible with one's residual capacity.

10. Because some people who receive disability transfers may also receive employer pension income, the number of people who are not working and receiving employer pensions in this table is understated. It is also important to note that this number does not capture all those receiving employer pensions, since some men who are currently working may also be receiving such benefits. The same can be said of our disability transfer count. These measures are arbitrary but convenient means of segmenting the population without double counting.

11. There is strong evidence in the economics literature that poor health negatively impacts on work at older ages within both the United States and the Netherlands. (For recent evidence using the HRS and CERRA, see Dwyer and Mitchell forthcoming and Kerkhofs and Lindeboom 1995.) But the dramatic difference in work at older ages cannot be primarily caused by underlying health conditions in the two countries.

12. The HRS asks respondents to predict their probability of surviving until ages 75 and 85. When we average self-reported probabilities for each of the population categories in table 5, normalizing the rates between 0 and 1 (see Hurd and McGarry 1995), we find a pattern similar to those we described for the other measures of health—workers predict higher probabilities of survival than nonworkers, and among nonworkers, those receiving disability benefits predict the lowest probabilities. (These values are available from the authors upon request.)

13. For a further discussion of the health characteristics of Dutch men using these data, see Kerkhofs and Lindeboom 1995. For a further discussion of the health characteristics of U.S. men using these data, see Dwyer and Mitchell forthcoming.

14. In the previous tables, we have used information from HRS and CERRA on current work status and income sources to categorize persons in our sample. In the remaining tables, we use HRS information for the previous year to categorize people and estimate income from various sources. See the appendix for details.

15. As discussed in more detail in the appendix, the HRS reports income in the previous calendar year while in CERRA income is based on either the previous month or previous year from the time of the survey—October 1993.

16. See Burkhauser, Smeeding, and Merz 1996 for a discussion of this topic and examples of how the choice of scale can influence the outcome.

17. This scale, called the "international experts scale" by Burkhauser, Smeeding, and Merz (1996), has often been used in international comparisons of economic well-being. Recently cross-national studies sponsored by OECD (Atkinson, Rainwater, and Smeeding 1995) and by the Statistical Office of the European Commission (Hagenaars, de Vos, and Zaidi 1998) have used this scale. (See Coulter, Cowell, and Jenkins 1992 for a fuller discussion of the use of parametric equivalence.)

18. For more details on the 1991 Dutch data set, see the appendix.

19. Since we require two years of information, sample sizes fall for both the United States and the Netherlands relative to previous tables.

20. Alternative indices were considered and tested following Katz et al. 1963.

REFERENCES

Aarts, Leo J. M., Richard V. Burkhauser, and Philip P. De Jong, eds. 1996. *Curing the Dutch Disease: An International Perspective on Disability Policy Reform.* Aldershot, UK: Avebury.

Atkinson, Anthony, Lee Rainwater, and Timothy M. Smeeding. 1995. *Income Distribution in OECD Countries: Evidence from the Luxembourg Income Study.* Paris: OECD.

Berkowitz, Edward D., and Richard V. Burkhauser. 1996. "A United States Perspective on Disability Programs." In Leo J. M. Aarts, Richard V.

Burkhauser, and Philip P. De Jong, eds., *Curing the Dutch Disease: An International Perspective on Disability Policy Reform*, 71–92. UK: Avebury.

Burkhauser, Richard V., Kenneth A. Couch, and John W. Phillips. 1996. "Who Takes Early Social Security Benefits: The Economic and Health Characteristics of Early Beneficiaries." *Gerontologist* 36, no. 6 (December): 789–99.

Burkhauser, Richard V., and Robert H. Haveman. 1982. *Disability and Work: The Economics of American Policy.* Baltimore, MD: Johns Hopkins University Press.

Burkhauser, Richard V., and Joseph F. Quinn. 1997. "Pro-Work Policy Proposals for Older Americans in the 21st Century." Center for Policy Research policy brief no. 9, the Maxwell School. Syracuse, NY: Syracuse University.

Burkhauser, Richard V., Timothy M. Smeeding, and Joachim Merz. 1995. "Relative Inequality and Poverty in Germany and the United States Using Alternative Equivalency Scales." *Review of Income and Wealth* 42, no. 4 (December): 381–400.

Coulter, Fran, Frank A. Cowell, and Stephen P. Jenkins. 1992. "Equivalent Scale Relativities and the Extent of Inequality and Poverty." *Economic Journal* 102 (September): 1067–82.

Dwyer, Debra, and Olivia S. Mitchell. Forthcoming. "Health Problems as Determinants of Retirement: Are Self-Rated Measures Endogenous?" *Journal of Health Economics.*

Emanuel, Han. 1979. "Achtergronden van het arbeidsongeschiktheidsvershijnsel in Nederland." In J. J. Klant, W. Driehuis, H. J. Bierens, A. J. Butter, eds., *Samenleving en Onderzoek.* Leiden: Stenfert Kroese.

Fokkema, Tineke. 1996. "Residential Moving Behavior of the Elderly: An Explanatory Analysis for the Netherlands." Ph.D. diss., Free University of Amsterdam.

Hagenaars, Aldi J., Klaas de Vos, and M. Zaidi. 1998. "Patterns of Poverty in Europe." In Stephen P. Jenkins, Ari Kapteyn, and Bernard van Praag, eds., *The Distribution of Welfare and Household Production,* 25–49. Cambridge: Cambridge University Press.

Hurd, Michael M., and Kathleen McGarry. 1995. "Evaluation of the Subjective Probabilities of Survival in the Health and Retirement Study." *Journal of Human Resources* 30 (Supplement): S268–92.

Juster, F. Thomas, and Richard M. Suzman. 1995. "An Overview of the Health and Retirement Survey." *Journal of Human Resources* 30 (supplement): S7–56.

Kapteyn, Arie, and Klaas de Vos. 1997. "Social Security and Retirement in the Netherlands." Paper written for the NBER project on International Social Security Comparisons. Mimeo, University of Tilburg.

Katz, Sidney, Amasa B. Ford, Roland W. Moskowitz, Beverly A. Jackson, Marjorie W. Jaffe, and M. A. Cleveland. 1963. "Studies of Illness in the Aged: The Index of ADL: The Standardized Measure of Biological and Psychosocial Function." *Journal of the American Medical Association* 185: 914–19.

Kerkhofs, Marcel, and Maarten Lindeboom. 1995. "Subjective Health Measures and State Dependent Reporting Errors." *Health Economics* 4, no. 3: 221–35.

Meuwissen, P. J. J. 1993. "AOW-ontuanges en aanvullend (pensionen) inkomen." *Statistisch Magazine,* 11–13.

Phillips, John W. 1997. "Essays on the Accumulation and Transfers of Wealth at Older Ages." Ph.D. diss., Syracuse University.

Shorrocks, Anthony. 1980. "The Class of Additively Decomposible Inequality Measures." *Econometrica* 48:613–25.

Struijs, Martin. 1994. "Analyse van Nonresponse: Het imputeren van ontbrekende inkomens in de CERRA enquête." CERRA technical note.

Labor Market Transitions in the HRS: Effects of the Subjective Probability of Retirement and of Pension Eligibility

Michael D. Hurd

In models of intertemporal decision making under uncertainty, the probability distributions of future stochastic events enter the decision problem. Faced with the requirement of supplying such distributions for empirical work, researchers have typically either simplified the problem by assuming rational expectations in the context of a model or they have substituted population probabilities. Both are excessively restrictive: rational expectations because there is no reason for people to have the expectations that are consistent with the model; population probabilities because in many contexts people have private information that causes them to form individualized probabilities and they act on those probabilities. An alternative to assuming rational expectations or using population probabilities is to base estimation on subjective probabilities, the probabilities the individual holds about the stochastic events. If a subject will reveal the probabilities on which he or she bases behavior, they can be used in intertemporal models to account for heterogeneity.

The Health and Retirement Study (HRS), a biennial panel, had at baseline and in subsequent waves a number of questions that were meant to elicit subjective probabilities. Subjects were queried about the chances of a number of personal events such as survival, retirement, and job loss and about the chances of a number of macro events such as inflation and recession. The most heavily studied of these questions is about survival. Subjects, most of whom were aged 51 through 61 at baseline, were asked about their self-assessed chances of surviving to 75 and to 85. In cross section, the average survival probability is close to a comparable average from life tables, and the survival probabilities covary in an appropriate way with known risk factors (Hurd and McGarry 1995a). For example, smokers give lower survival probabilities than former smokers, who, in turn, give lower probabilities than lifetime nonsmokers. Based on this kind of covariation, one can fairly confidently state that the subjective survival probabilities will have predictive power for actual mortality.

Between waves 1 and 2 of the HRS about 1.7 percent of the age-eligible subjects died, and, indeed, they had stated subjective survival probabilities at wave 1 that were about one-third lower than the survival probabilities of those who survived between the waves (Hurd and McGarry 1995b). Further, even after controlling for a number of known risk factors, the subjective survival probability has predictive power for actual mortality. Despite the close agreement with the life table, however, it is not known whether the subjective survival probability is appropriately scaled in the sense that the variation across risk groups is the same as the variation in actual mortality outcomes. This is because the target age is 75, so it will be many years before an age-eligible cohort (which is population representative) reaches that age. Until that time an assessment of scaling will of necessity partly depend on a mortality model that can specify mortality rates of subjects in their 50s as a function of their survival probability to age 75. Should the mortality predictions not accord with the actual mortality experience between the waves, it may be that the subjective survival probabilities are not properly scaled; alternatively it could be that the mortality model is not correct.

The subjective questions about retirement concerned the probability that workers would be working full time after age 62 and age 65. While it is very much more difficult to find a basis for a comparison with the population probability, a somewhat informal calculation shows the average stated probability to be rather close to a population probability (Hurd and McGarry 1993). Just as with the subjective survival probabilities, the subjective probabilities of working vary with known risk factors for retirement such as eligibility for defined benefit (DB) pensions. For example, the average probability of working full time after age 62 among full-time workers lacking a DB pension was 0.53. The average among workers who were eligible for full benefits before the age of 62 was 0.30, and among workers not eligible until age 65 it was 0.67. Thus the subjective probability of continued work varies in a manner very similar to the variation in actual continuation of work such as in Kotlikoff and Wise 1989: early eligibility leads to reduced participation whereas late eligibility leads to increased participation relative to workers lacking a DB pension. Therefore, the subjective probability of continued work should be predictive at least qualitatively of actual rates of labor force participation.

While these kinds of cross-section analyses are informative, we would like to find if the subjective probability predicts actual labor market behavior in panel and if it can help predict behavior at the individual level. The goal of this essay is to describe labor force transitions between waves 1 and 2 of HRS, with the particular objective of assessing whether the wave 1 subjective probabilities of working have predictive power for actual retirement. This will be done by comparing retirement outcomes of an appropriate group with their stated subjective work probabilities. An assessment of scaling will be done by comparing the variation by observable characteristics in actual retirement with the variation in the subjective probability of working. Their quantitative importance will be assessed by comparing their effects with the effects of DB pensions, which are known to have substantial effects on retirement.

The plan of the essay is first to describe the labor market transitions between waves 1 and 2 of the HRS to establish the broad patterns of retirement and other transitions. These transitions will be related to the availability of DB pension benefits and to the subjective probabilities. Because of the expected influence of DB plans on retirement it will be of interest to find if the subjective probabilities have independent predictive power for labor market transitions.

Data

The data come from waves 1 and 2 of the HRS. At baseline in 1992, the HRS was a nationally representative sample of 12,652 individuals born in the years 1931–41 and their spouses.[1] The age-eligible respondents were approximately 51–61 years old at wave 1.

Data were collected about employment, including pensions and their structures (as self-reported by workers), income and assets, health, cognition, and family relationships. Because expectations are important determinants in decisions of an intertemporal nature such as retirement, the HRS developed several innovative questions about the respondents' assessment of the probabilities of future events, in particular the subjective probabilities of survival and of working past the age of 62 and the age of 65. The survival question was as follows: "On a scale of 0 to 10 where 0 means *absolutely no chance* and 10 equals *absolutely certain* what do you think are the chances you will live to be 75 or more?" Those who were working at baseline were asked, "Thinking about work generally and not just your present job, what do you think are the chances that you will be working full time after you reach age 62? . . . after 65?" Ages 62 and 65 are the target ages, and I will call the responses to the questions about them $P62$ and $P65$, the probabilities of working full time after ages 62 and 65. A major goal of this essay is to compare actual labor market status in wave 2 of the HRS with the stated values of $P62$ in wave 1.

Labor Force Status at Wave 1 and Transitions to Wave 2

Because the subjective probability question refers to full-time work, I will define labor market categories that are consistent with a categorization as to full time or part time. Therefore, I assign to each person in the baseline survey one of four labor market categories defined by labor market status at the wave 1 interview: working full time (thirty-five hours per week or more), working part time, unemployed, or not in the labor force. A similar categorization is made of those interviewed at wave 2.

In wave 1 of the HRS labor force participation was measured to be somewhat higher than in the Current Population Survey (CPS). For example among men 55–59 years old, the HRS participation rate was 82 percent, yet in the CPS it was 78 percent (1993 average). It is not clear what could cause the difference, although a difference in the population actually sampled could be an explanation. The HRS had a baseline response rate of 82 percent, and it may well be that those who refused or could not be located had labor force participation rates that were lower than those who were actually interviewed. For the purposes of this essay with its emphasis on the variation in participation by covariates such as the subjective work probabilities and DB pension eligibility, the difference is not important.

As in other data, in the HRS the rate of labor force participation by men gradually declines after about age 55, reaching about 70 percent at age 61. Men in their early 50s typically work full time: about 82 percent of the population at age 51. This percentage gradually declines with age as men retire, reaching 58 percent by age 61. Among men part-time work is not very important, being always less than 10 percent of the population, although there is a modest tendency for an increase in the later 50s.

Among women participation is considerably lower: about 70 percent until age 56 when it declines to about 60 percent. It is about 50 percent at age 61. Thus, the participation rate of women is about 20 percentage points lower than men holding age constant. Furthermore, the division between full time and part time is rather different: about 20 percent of women work part time, approximately independent of age, so that the fall in the participation rate of women is due to leaving full-time work, not part-time work. By age 61 just 31 percent of women work full time, so that the rate of full-time work among men is about twice the rate among women.

While the cross-section participation rates by age show considerably different employment patterns among men than among women, they combine two different effects: the fraction of the population entering age 51 in the different labor market states and transitions from one state to another, conditional on being in a particular labor market status at wave 1. The effects can be separated by studying the transitions from one labor market status to another between the waves.

The transition probability from state *i* at wave 1 to state *j* at wave 2 is calculated as the fraction of those in state *i* at wave 1 that were in state *j* in wave 2. Figures 1–4 have selected transition probabilities. The classification is by age in wave 2 rather than by age in wave 1 to make possible a more valid comparison between the subjective probability and the actual probability. For example, were the classification to be by age at wave 1, some 60 year olds would not have attained age 62 by wave 2 because the time between interviews was not exactly two years: thus, the comparison between labor market status in wave 2 and the baseline subjective probability would only be valid for some. Eligibility for Social Security at age 62 is an important determinant of retirement, providing a further reason for categorizing by age at wave 2.

Figure 1 shows the transitions of men from full-time work in wave 1 to the four labor market categories in wave 2. For example, among men who were age 53 at their wave 2 interview and who were working full-time at wave 1, 91 percent were working full time at wave 2, 4 percent were not in the labor force, 3 percent were working part time, and 2 percent were unemployed. The figure is notable for the high rates of transition from full time to full time until about age 59 (wave 2). Most of this, of course, would simply be a continuation of work on the same job as in wave 1. At greater ages, the transition probability to full-time work declines, particularly at age 63, when it is just 53 percent. Thus, among those men of approximate age 61 in wave 1 and who were working full time, just 53 percent were working full time at wave 2.

The decline in the transition to full-time work was mainly accompanied by an increase in the transition to not in the labor force, especially at age 63. This is notable because 62 is the youngest age at which a worker can claim Social Security benefits. Among the 63 year olds (who were approximately 61 in wave 1) 31 percent had left the labor force completely by wave 2.

Full-time male workers have very low rates of transition into part-time work, although the number increases slowly, reaching about 7

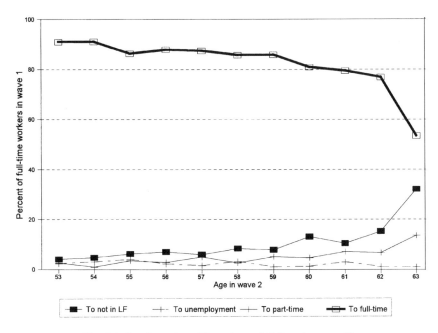

Fig. 1. Labor force transitions (men full time in wave 1)

percent by age 62. Of course, some workers may have spent some time in the years between the waves in part-time work, but generally these results are consistent with findings from the 1969–79 Retirement History Survey. In that panel survey the dominant mode of transition to retirement among men was from full time to not in the labor force with rather little time spent in part-time work (Rust 1990). This happens despite the stated preference by workers to retire gradually, and it is undoubtedly related to the limited availability of well-paying part-time jobs. Typically a change from full-time to part-time employment at older ages is associated with a wage reduction of 35–50 percent (Hurd 1996). A further explanation is the earnings test under Social Security, which although approximately actuarially fair apparently is not perceived by workers to be fair.

Transitions from full time to unemployment are very low, from 2 to 4 percent, and at ages 62 and 63 they are about 1 percent.[2] The decline is surely due to the availability of Social Security benefits beginning at age 62: men prefer to retire and take Social Security benefits at that age rather than continue in unemployment.

Figure 2 shows transitions by men from not in the labor force in wave 1 to the four labor market categories in wave 2. About 90 percent

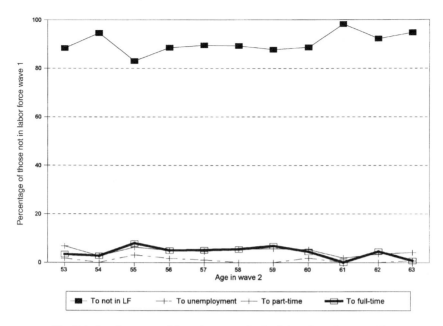

Fig. 2. Labor force transitions (men not in the labor force in wave 1)

remain out of the labor force, and this percentage increases at the ages 61–63. The rates of transition to part time and to full time are about equal at 5 to 6 percent until age 60 and then decline to a few percentage points. Unemployment and part time are quantitatively not important, so transitions from those states in wave 1 are not shown.

Overall for men, by far the dominant channel to retirement is from full-time work to not in the labor force, and once out of the labor force they tend to remain out.

The transitions of women from full time have the same general pattern as those of men, but the rate from full time to full time is much lower at all ages except 63 (fig. 3). Correspondingly women have higher rates of transition to not in the labor force until about age 57; after that age there is on average very little difference between the sexes. Women also have higher transition rates to part time, and the rate increases with age, so that by age 63 (wave 2) it is about 15 percent. As with men transitions to unemployment from full time are not quantitatively important.

Figure 4 shows very low rates of labor market entry among women, especially at older ages: by age 63 (wave 2) just 4 percent of those not in the labor market at wave 1 were in the labor market at wave 2. Among those that do enter the labor market the important transition is to part

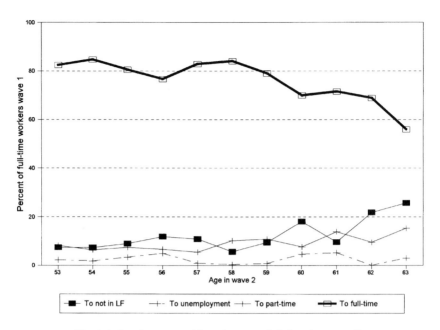

Fig. 3. Labor force transitions (women full time in wave 1)

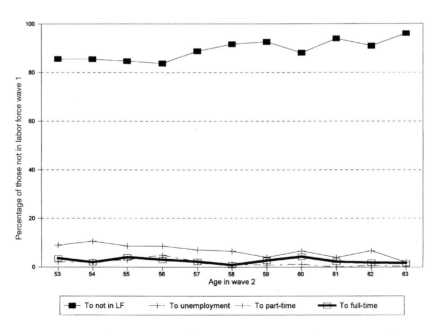

Fig. 4. Labor force transitions (women not in the labor force in wave 1)

time. For example, at age 54, that rate is about 10 percent. It declines with age, reaching very low levels at 63. The rate of transition to full time is considerably smaller.

Among women working part time in wave 1 most continue in part-time employment (about 60 percent), and that transition rate is approximately constant with age (not shown). Notable trends are the increase in transition to not in the labor force and the decline in the transition to full-time.

Overall among women part-time work is much more important than for men both in levels and in transitions. For men, not in the labor force is almost an absorbing state, whereas among women there is considerably more movement into employment, particularly in their early 50s. All transitions both for men and for women show important effects at ages near 62. Full time to part time increases; full time, part time, and not in the labor force to not in the labor force increases, and in many cases the increases are rather sharp. As a consequence the transition from labor force participation to not in the labor force increases substantially after age 62.

Labor Market Transitions and Pensions

Prior research based on firm-level data has shown that the details of a DB pension plan are important. DB plans reduce departures prior to eligibility for benefits, and they accelerate departures after eligibility (Kotlikoff and Wise 1989). Figure 5 shows the rate of transition from in the labor force to not in the labor force (the retirement hazard) among those with DB pensions as a function of whether they are not yet eligible for full pension benefits by wave 2, whether they became eligible between the waves (newly eligible), or whether they were already eligible at wave 1 (previously eligible). For reference the retirement hazards of workers who do not have a DB pension plan are also shown.[3]

Among those 53–56 at wave 2, the retirement hazard is about 9 percent among those that lack a DB pension on their present job. That is, 9 percent of those in the labor force in wave 1 (almost all employed) were not in the labor force in wave 2. If someone had a DB pension but was not yet eligible for full retirement benefits, the hazard was 5 percent. If someone became eligible between wave 1 and wave 2 the retirement hazard approximately doubled, and it tripled if the worker was eligible before wave 1 (previously eligible). Therefore, having a plan but not being eligible reduces labor market transitions. A similar pattern obtains among those 57–60 and 61–63, except that the hazards are

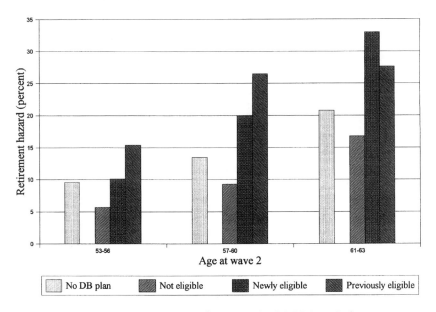

Fig. 5. Retirement rates (eligibility for full DB benefits)

greater. For example, at 61–63 the retirement hazard is just 17 percent among those not eligible while it is 33 percent among those newly eligible. An interesting example of selection comes from comparing the hazards of the newly eligible and previously eligible at age 57–60 with the same groups at ages 61–63. In the first age group the previously eligible had a considerably higher hazard, and those with a weak attachment to the labor force retired. In the second age group, only those with a relatively strong labor force attachment remained, whereas the newly eligible included those with a weak attachment. Thus the overall retirement rate was higher among the newly entitled.

These results confirm in a nationally representative sample prior results that were based on job separation from individual employers (Kotlikoff and Wise 1989). Because the prior samples were not nationally representative and because the workers could not be followed after their separation from a particular employer, the prior results could not be generalized to reflect national retirement rates whereas these results can be.

Overall, DB pensions influence the retirement hazards very strongly. Among those who have a DB plan but are not yet eligible the hazards are substantially reduced compared with those already eligible and also compared with those who have no pension plan. When workers are eligible either for reduced or full benefits the retirement hazards are increased substantially.

Labor Market Transitions and Subjective Probabilities

A valid comparison of $P62$ with actual labor market behavior requires ascertaining the age at which the event "working full time" should be determined for comparison with $P62$. The question about $P62$ is, ". . . [what are] the chances that you will be working full time after you reach age 62?" Based on earlier work (Hurd and McGarry 1993), I believe that the question is somewhat ambiguous and has been interpreted by some respondents to refer to the time when they turn 62 or shortly after that, whereas some respondents interpreted it to be the time when they turn 63.[4] Because the rate of retirement is high when people are 62, the ambiguity could lead to an invalid comparison between $P62$ and the rate of full-time work among 62 year olds.

Figure 6 shows by age at wave 2 the probability of working full time at wave 2 conditional on working full time at wave 1 and the average value of $P62$ over those same individuals. Thus if $P62$ is accurate the lower line gives for most subjects their average rate of full-time work at some future date (after they reach age 62), with the possible exceptions of those aged 62 or 63 at wave 2. Depending on the interpretation of the underlying question, a comparison is valid at one or the other of those ages.

The figure shows an upward trend in $P62$ from age 60 (about age 58 in wave 1). The actual rate of full-time work declines slowly, and because of a sharp decline in the rate of full-time work, the predicted rate from $P62$ and the actual rate are about the same at age 63. That is, those full-time workers who were age 61 in wave 1 accurately predicted their average rate of full-time work at age 63. There is a difference between the two rates at age 62 of about 15 percentage points. This is likely due to a combination of the ambiguity in the subjective probability questions about the actual target age and the fact that some workers would have been just a few months older than age 62 and had not adjusted their work to the availability of Social Security and pensions. Overall I view the averages of the subjective probability to be a remarkably accurate predictor of average full-time work.

Figure 7 shows the retirement rates between waves 1 and 2 by the 11 discrete values of $P62$ for the ages 63, 62, 54, and 53.[5] The top line pertains to full-time workers at wave 1 who were aged 63 in wave 2. Among those with $P62$ of zero in wave 1, about 80 percent had retired

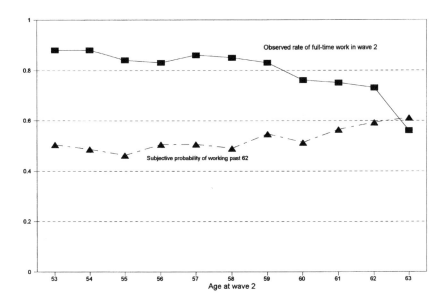

Fig. 6. Probability of full-time work (full-time workers in wave 1)

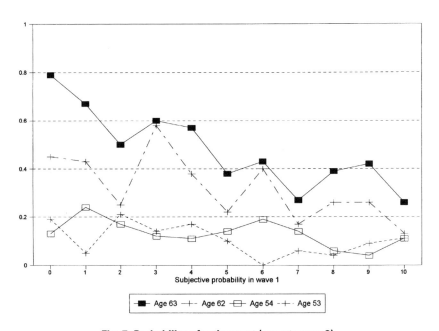

Fig. 7. Probability of retirement (age at wave 2)

by wave 2. Generally the line has a negative slope, so that among those with *P62* of 1.0 the average retirement rate was just 26 percent. The slope of the line is −0.43 (OLS), and *P62* explains 76 percent of the variation in the average retirement probabilities. Thus, among those where a comparison between *P62* and actual retirement is likely to be valid, the subjective probability has considerable explanatory power, although the regression coefficient is less than one. Furthermore, the rates of retirement at the focal points of 0, 5, and 10 are consistent with the overall pattern of retirement, which provides evidence against the view that focal point responses are uninformative.

The variation in the retirement rate among 62 year olds (wave 2) is more random: the slope is considerably less, and the variation around the slope is greater. Nonetheless the subjective probability has considerable explanatory power. For example just 12 percent of those giving *P62* = 1.0 had left full-time work by wave 2. At lower probabilities some subjects may consider that they have not yet reached the target age, and the retirement rate is correspondingly lower. In the lowest age groups (53 and 54) the slopes are smaller still: nonetheless those giving small probabilities of working past 62 are more likely to retire than those giving large values.[6]

The overall impression from figure 7 is that the subjective probability has considerable explanatory power for retirement at older ages, particularly at 63. Of course, it should be expected that it is a weaker predictor of retirement at younger ages because the target age is quite distant. For example, some workers in their early 50s might intend to retire in their late 50s, and so they could be rather certain they will work two more years but not past 62; therefore, they would state that *P62* is zero, yet their observed participation rate in wave 2 would be one.

Although the average of *P62* over the 63 year olds is very close to their average rate of participation, indicating that at least the stated level of *P62* is appropriate, it does not indicate whether *P62* varies across individuals in an appropriate way. One interpretation of figure 7 is that *P62* is observed with error, which is the reason that the slope is less than one. It could also have happened that the variation is not correctly scaled. A method of studying the scaling is to group observations by risk factors for retirement and then to find if the variation in the average of *P62* is the same as the variation in the retirement rate. In the results to follow the averages will be taken over 62 and 63 year olds (wave 2) because some of the 62 year olds may not have reached their own (subjective) target age, yet some of the 63 year olds may have retired shortly after reaching age 62, which they considered to be their target age.

As a way to control for the difference in the average rate of full-time work and the average of the subjective probability caused by question ambiguity, the results will be given in terms of relative rates of continuing in full-time work. For example, the first panel of table 1 shows the continuation rates of women in full-time work relative to men measured both as actual continuation rates and as the average subjective probability of working full time. The table shows that women anticipated about the same continuation rate (subjective) as men but their actual continuation rate was about 5 percent lower. Reference to figures

TABLE 1. Relative Probability of Working Full Time: 62 and 63 Year Olds in Wave 2 Who Were Working Full Time in Wave 1

Characteristic	Actual	Subjective Probability
Male[a]	1.00	1.00
Female	0.95	1.02
No DB plan	0.80	0.95
DB: not eligible for reduced benefit	1.14	1.12
DB: newly eligible for reduced benefit	0.86	0.81
DB: already eligible for reduced benefit	0.83	0.72
DB: not eligible for full benefit[a]	1.00	1.00
DB: newly eligible for full benefit	0.77	0.62
DB: already eligible for full benefit	0.84	0.69
Social Security Quartile		
Lowest	1.35	0.98
Second[a]	1.00	1.00
Third	1.14	0.97
Highest	1.37	1.40
Health Insurance on Job		
No[a]	1.00	1.00
Yes	1.11	1.01
Retiree Health Insurance		
No[a]	1.00	1.00
Yes, not paid for by employer	1.01	0.90
Yes, partly paid	0.81	0.82
Yes, fully paid	0.79	0.74
Subjective Health		
Excellent	1.01	1.07
Very good	1.00	1.01
Good[a]	1.00	1.00
Fair	0.64	0.92
Poor	0.54	0.60

Source: Author's calculations based on HRS Waves 1 and 2.
[a]Normalization.

1 and 3 shows that the difference is due to a higher rate of continuation in full time among 62-year-old men.

The next panel shows the relative continuation rates in full-time work as a function of eligibility for DB pension benefits. The reference group is those with a DB plan but who are not yet eligible for full benefits. The pattern and many of the levels of relative actual continuation in full time are similar to the pattern and levels of subjective continuation in full time. For example, among those not eligible for reduced benefits the actual continuation rate in full time was about 14 percent higher than the continuation rate of those in the reference group. According to the subjective probabilities the continuation rate should have been about 12 percent higher. There is a similar correspondence in the patterns by variation in eligibility for reduced and full benefits. Thus, for example, those who knew in wave 1 that they would become eligible for full benefits between the waves (newly eligible) anticipated an average continuation rate in full-time work of 62 percent of those who would not become eligible. The actual continuation rate was 77 percent.

The magnitude of Social Security benefits should influence retirement. I estimated Social Security benefits from questions in the survey about the benefits respondents anticipate and the age at which they anticipate receiving them. From these questions I adjusted anticipated benefits for the early retirement reduction or the delayed retirement credit as appropriate to approximate the Primary Insurance Amount (PIA). The next panel shows variation by PIA quartile. There is considerable discrepancy between the actual continuation rates and the subjective continuation rates among those in the lowest Social Security income quartile. A possible cause is that until just prior to a date at which a retirement decision has to be made workers in general have rather imprecise information about the level of Social Security benefits they will receive. Those in the lowest quartile could then have been surprised at the low level of benefits, causing them not to retire at the rate they had anticipated. Particularly in the highest quartile the correspondence between actual and anticipated retirement is almost exact.

As far as actual retirement is concerned the second, third, and highest quartiles show approximately increasing continuation in full time. Those in the higher quartiles are likely to have personal and job characteristics that encourage later retirement, and, of course, those are not controlled for in these cross tabulations.

The difference in $P62$ by availability of on-the-job health insurance is negligible. However, in fact health insurance acts to retain workers, increasing the continuation rate in full-time work by about 11 percent.

The availability and structure of retiree health insurance should affect retirement decisions among 63 year olds because they are not yet eligible for Medicare. By law continuing health insurance coverage must be made available if the firm offers health insurance to its employees, but the cost, which need not be paid by the employer, can be rather high. Thus, health insurance that is paid for by the employer can have a different effect on retirement than retiree health insurance that is not paid for by the employer. The next panel shows that the difference affects retirement substantially: the actual continuation rate in full-time employment is 22 percent lower when the employer pays for retiree health insurance than when the employer does not pay. The subjective probabilities reflect quite closely this pattern, and the levels are similar.

It is well known that self-assessed health status is a powerful predictor of retirement. The last panel shows this to be the case when health is fair or poor, but it shows no difference among the three better health categories. *P*62 shows a similar pattern in that worse health is associated with a decline in working past age 62; there is, however, a fairly substantial difference between the subjective probability and the actual probability among those with fair health in wave 1. It is rather remarkable that those in poor health had continuation rates in full time that were about half the continuation rates of those in excellent health whether measured as actual continuation or as subjective continuation.

My overall conclusion from these cross tabulations is that the scaling of *P*62 is reasonably good: in most of the cross tabulations the patterns and magnitude of the variation in *P*62 and actual participation were similar. Even in those where they were not, there was no systematic pattern of failure that would suggest a lack of adequate scaling. For example, were the *P*62 not properly scaled, their variation with some observable characteristic would be consistently either too small or too large compared with the variation in actual participation. The cross tabulations did not show that. Rather they showed that sometimes both *P*62 and participation had no systematic variation with a characteristic, and the difference between the two was not systematic.

Pension Eligibility and the Subjective Probability of Working

As the cross tabulations show, both the details of pension eligibility and the subjective probability of continued work have considerable explanatory power for actual retirement. Furthermore, their effects are not linear in that both interact with age. Table 2 has the estimated coefficients of a linear probability model where the left-hand variable takes

TABLE 2. Effects on Transition from Full-Time Work to Part Time or Not in the Labor Force (full-time workers in wave 1; linear probability model)

Variable	Effect	t-Statistic
Constant	0.25	12.4
Age 53–55		
Subjective probability of working		
0	—	—
0.1–0.4	0.01	0.4
0.5	−0.06	2.1
0.6–0.9	−0.09	3.3
1.0	−0.09	3.3
Has DB plan		
Not yet eligible for benefits	−0.14	6.5
Eligible for reduced benefits		
Previously	0.08	1.6
Newly	0.03	0.5
Eligible for full benefits		
Previously	0.05	0.7
Newly	0.01	0.1
Age 56–59		
Subjective probability of working		
0	0.06	2.1
0.1–0.4	−0.07	2.3
0.5	−0.06	2.0
0.6–0.9	−0.10	3.8
1.0	−0.08	2.9
Has DB plan		
Not yet eligible for benefits	−0.10	4.5
Eligible for reduced benefits		
Previously	−0.03	0.9
Newly	0.02	0.4
Eligible for full benefits		
Previously	0.21	4.6
Newly	0.05	0.8
Age 60–61		
Subjective probability of working		
0	0.21	5.7
0.1–0.4	−0.00	0.1
0.5	0.01	0.2
0.6–0.9	−0.06	1.5
1.0	0.00	0.0
Has DB plan		
Not yet eligible for benefits	−0.16	3.9
Eligible for reduced benefits		
Previously	0.05	1.0
Newly	−0.07	0.8
Eligible for full benefits		
Previously	0.11	1.8
Newly	0.28	3.5

TABLE 2. *(cont.)*

Variable	Effect	*t*-Statistic
Age 62–63		
Subjective probability of working		
0	0.41	9.7
0.1–0.4	0.29	5.7
0.5	0.09	1.9
0.6–0.9	0.10	2.5
1.0	−0.01	0.2
Has DB plan		
Not yet eligible for benefits	−0.19	3.0
Eligible for reduced benefits		
Previously	0.05	0.6
Newly	0.07	1.0
Eligible for full benefits		
Previously	0.03	0.4
Newly	0.07	1.2
All Ages		
Has DB plan		
Eligibility for reduced missing	0.03	0.9
Eligibility for full missing	0.10	2.2
Has DC plan		
Not yet eligible	−0.11	5.2
Previously eligible	0.01	0.3
Newly eligible	0.05	1.1
Eligibility missing	0.02	0.7
Plan type unknown	−0.06	1.2

Source: Author's calculations based on HRS Waves 1 and 2.

the value one if a full-time worker in wave 1 is not working full-time at wave 2 ("retired") and zero otherwise. The explanatory variables are categories of $P62$ interacted with age categories and details of pension eligibility also interacted with age categories. The reference group has $P62 = 0$, age 53–55, and lacks a DB pension. The objective of the estimation is to find if the very large effects of the subjective probabilities remain after controlling for pension details.

The results in table 2 show that $P62$ has substantial effects on retirement and that the interactions with age are important. For example, the effect of a change in $P62$ from zero to one is −0.09 at age interval 53–55; −0.14 at age interval 56–59; −0.21 at age interval 60–61; and −0.42 at age interval 62–63. Furthermore, there are nonlinearities in the probability that vary with age. In the last age interval the retirement varies as $P62$ varies throughout its range; yet, in the other age intervals the main variation in the retirement rates happens as *P*62 varies between zero and any other value. Apparently at younger ages when someone gives a value of zero that person has in mind a definite plan for early retirement, and in some cases that age happens between the waves. Larger values of *P*62 reveal uncertainty or lack of a definite plan.

The DB variables continue qualitatively to have the same kinds of effects as in the cross tabulations, but they are attenuated. For example, if someone has a DB plan at age 60–61 but is not yet eligible, the probability of retirement is reduced by 0.16 compared with someone that does not have a DB plan. If someone was previously eligible for both reduced and full benefits the probability is increased by 0.16. The table also reveals an interesting pattern of the effects of eligibility for reduced and/or full benefits by age compared with not having a DB plan: the effects of being eligible for benefits are largest in the age intervals 56–59 and 60–61. A likely explanation is that at earlier ages, people are still far from the margin of retiring so adding pension availability will not put them over the margin. Furthermore, such early pensions may well not have much value. In the oldest age group (62–63) the base level is already high, probably because of the availability of Social Security, so an additional effect from pensions is relatively small.

The relative magnitudes of DB pensions and the subjective probabilities are shown in table 3. The entries for DB show the variation in the predicted retirement probability from varying pension eligibility from "not yet eligible" to eligible for both reduced and full benefits at baseline. For example among 53–55 year olds in wave 2 being fully eligible would increase the probability of leaving full-time work by 0.27 compared with "not eligible." The entries for the subjective probability show the effect of varying *P*62 from zero to one. It is apparent that eligibility for a DB plan has a strong influence on retirement and that the influence is almost uniform over all age groups.[7] As previously discussed, the

TABLE 3.   Effects on Leaving Full-Time Work: Comparison of DB Pensions with Subjective Probabilities

Age in Wave 2	DB Effects: Fully Eligible at Baseline versus Not Yet Eligible	Subjective Probability Effects: *P*62 = 1.0 versus *P*62 = 0.0
53–55	0.27	−0.09
56–59	0.28	−0.14
60–61	0.32	−0.21
62–62	0.27	−0.42

Source: Table 2.

effect of the subjective probability varies substantially with age, and by the time subjects have reached the target age it is capable of producing larger variations in the retirement probability than DB plans.

The last part of table 2 shows the effects of eligibility for DC plans. Not being eligible for benefits under a DC plan reduces the rate of leaving full-time employment by 0.11. Because under typical DC plans there are no effects on the wealth value of the DC plan either from continuing or not continuing employment, the effect is likely due to a liquidity constraint.

Other Indicators of Retirement Intentions

The HRS has several other indicators of retirement intentions. In particular, respondents were asked if they had thought at all about retirement, and if so, they were asked details about the intended retirement age. Thinking about retirement and intending to retire are likely to be simultaneous acts in many cases. Thus an indicator variable for having thought about retirement should predict actual retirement.

The fraction of workers who have thought about retirement increases with age as would be expected (not shown). Table 4 has the distributions of $P62$ at three ages by whether the respondent has thought about retirement. At age 51 among those who have thought about retirement the distribution of $P62$ is shifted toward zero, which is evidence that thinking about retirement and having intentions about an early

TABLE 4.   Distribution of the Subjective Probability of Working past Age 62

Subjective Probability	Age at Wave 1					
	51		55		61	
	Thought	Not Thought	Thought	Not Thought	Thought	Not Thought
0.0	33.8	15.2	34.1	18.4	27.1	6.5
0.1–0.4	19.6	16.5	12.4	14.5	12.8	7.5
0.5	10.8	18.1	12.0	18.4	13.3	7.5
0.6–0.9	21.2	25.5	20.6	20.6	15.1	24.7
1.0	14.2	24.3	20.6	26.8	31.2	53.8
Total percentage[a]	99.6	99.6	99.7	98.7	99.5	100

Source: Author's calculations from HRS Wave 1.
Note: "Not thought" means respondent has not given much thought to retirement.
[a]Does not total 100 percent because of missing values.

TABLE 5.   Two-Year Rate of Retirement among Full-Time Workers (percentage)

Age in Wave 2	Subjective Probability of Working past Age 62					
	0.0		0.5		1.0	
	Thought	Not Thought	Thought	Not Thought	Thought	Not Thought
53–55	17.5	15.0	13.4	10.6	11.3	9.6
56–59	27.7	20.7	19.8	7.3	13.2	12.9
60–61	43.8	35.4	21.2	22.7	17.0	23.8
62–63	61.8	50.0	34.6	17.9	23.3	14.1

Source: Author's calculations from HRS Waves 1 and 2.
Note: "Not thought" means respondent has not given much thought to retirement.

retirement are part of the same process. At 55, the distribution is similarly shifted except that among those who have thought about retirement a considerably greater number have $P62$ of one. Among those who have not thought about retirement the distributions at 51 and 55 are similar. At age 61 both distributions have shifted considerably toward one, especially among those who have not thought about retirement.

Table 5 has the associated rates of retirement. Among those with $P62 = 0$, those who have thought about retirement always have higher retirement rates. This implies that the reliability of $P62$ as a predictor of retirement can be enhanced by interacting it with, or conditioning it on, other variables. The largest difference is at $P62$ of 0.5, where those who have thought about retirement retired at a rate fairly close to their average of $P62$ whereas those who had not retired at a very much lower rate. An interpretation of this difference is the following. If a response of 0.5 is assumed to be uninformative, then actual retirement probabilities will not be likely to be close to 0.5, and that is what obtains over those who have not thought about retirement. But as the table shows, when the probability is calculated over those who have thought about retirement the probability is much closer to 0.5. Again this indicates that a variable such as whether someone has thought about retirement may be used to judge the reliability of the subjective probability.

Conclusion

The main conclusion is that subjects in the HRS were able to give quantitative information about their retirement intentions, and the information is informative about actual retirement. Although the question itself induced some ambiguity about the target age, the subjective probabilities corresponded in level very closely with actual behavior. The variation with risk factors was similarly close. These results should increase our confidence that subjective probabilities have good scaling properties, not just index properties: subjects apparently understand the nature of the probability question and respond appropriately in levels, not just in a relative way with variation in risk factors. Previous work has found broadly similar results with respect to the subjective survival probabilities, but that work was barred from a direct test of the scaling properties because the subjects had not yet reached the target age.

Even so, using the subjective probabilities of continued work in behavioral models will not be easy. The difficulties can be illustrated by comparing retirement hazards to mortality hazards. Survival is a stochastic process, and individuals have rather low levels of control over the process. There is considerable heterogeneity in risk that persists over long periods. An important and natural model of such a process is a proportional hazards model. Individuals have differing levels of fitness that subject them to differing levels of mortality risk at all ages: someone in his or her 50s with a low probability of survival to age 75 will have a low probability of survival over all shorter time periods. Therefore, the stated subjective survival to age 75 can be used to estimate a proportional hazards model that can be used to predict survival over two waves of HRS.

Retirement is partly stochastic. A worker could become ill or be terminated from employment and retire earlier than expected; a worker could need more money because of unexpected expenses and work longer. However, a few factors such as eligibility for Social Security benefits or pension benefits are very important predictors of retirement, and these factors are likely to be quite well known. This implies that retirement is mostly a controlled process. In the extreme case where it is completely controlled a worker either will or will not work past age 62. If $P62$ is reported to be 1.0 and the worker is less than 60, the worker will be certain to work over the next two years. If $P62$ is zero and the worker is less than 60, retirement over two waves will depend on age and other covariates that affect the two-year retirement rate among workers who will not work past the age of 62. The result is that the actual rate of retirement among workers near the target age will be strongly related to the probability of working past the target age whereas the rate among workers far from the target age will be only weakly related to the subjective probability. This is, of course, what we saw in figure 7.

An implication of this reasoning is that a proportional hazards model based on $P62$ is not a useful model of retirement behavior. A model needs to accommodate greater complexity. In particular at ages considerably less than the target age a large value of *P*62 should map into a high estimated probability of continued work; a small value of *P*62 would signal that *P*62 itself is not a reliable estimate of the probability of continued work. The estimated probability would have to be based on observed population probabilities perhaps with covariates.

NOTES

Prepared for the symposium to honor F. Thomas Juster, December 1996. Financial support from the NIA and from RAND is gratefully acknowledged. Many thanks to Kathleen McGarry for helpful discussions and to Julie Zissimopoulos for excellent research assistance.

1. See Juster and Suzman 1995 for a description of the HRS.
2. Of course some may have spent time in unemployment between the waves, which would not appear in these transitions.
3. The pension is measured only on the present job.
4. Evidence for the ambiguity comes from a comparison of *P*62 with a stated age of retirement.
5. I use the term *retirement*. The actual transition is calculated as the transition from full time in wave 1 to not full time in wave 2 so that it corresponds to *P*62, which queries about full-time work after age 62. As indicated in figures 1 and 3, the great majority of transitions are to retirement.
6. In mortality models, a high survival rate to a distant target age typically implies a correspondingly high survival rate to a near age. Then a proportional hazards model may be approximately accurate for mortality. However, it is not likely to be accurate for retirement. This is because among a rather large part of the workforce, retirement is a controlled process, with little random element. In that situation one person may have a high probability of retiring at, say, 58 compared with another worker, but that does not at all imply that the first worker is more likely to retire at, say, 54. In fact, because of the structure of DB plans the opposite may well be true.
7. Of course, the effect on retirement rates in the working population will vary with age group because the fraction of workers that is eligible for full benefits varies with age.

REFERENCES

Hurd, Michael D. 1996. "The Effect of Labor Market Rigidities on the Labor Force Behavior of Older Workers." In *Advances in the Economics of Aging,* ed. David A. Wise, 11–58. Chicago: University of Chicago Press.
Hurd, Michael D., and Kathleen McGarry. 1993. "The Relationship between

Job Characteristics and Retirement." Paper presented at the HRS Early Results Workshop, Ann Arbor, September, and NBER working paper no. 4558.

———. 1995a. "Evaluation of the Subjective Probabilities of Survival in the HRS." *Journal of Human Resources* 30:S268–92.

———. 1995b. "The Predictive Validity of the Subjective Probabilities of Survival in the Health and Retirement Survey." Paper presented at the HRS2 Early Results workshop, Ann Arbor, October.

Juster, F. Thomas, and Richard Suzman. 1995. "An Overview of the Health and Retirement Study." *Journal of Human Resources* 30:S7–56.

Kotlikoff, Laurence J., and David A. Wise. 1989. "Employee Retirement and a Firm's Pension Plan." In *The Economics of Aging,* ed. David A. Wise, 279–330. Chicago: University of Chicago Press.

Rust, John P. 1990. "Behavior of Male Workers at the End of the Life-Cycle: An Empirical Analysis of States and Controls." In *Issues in the Economics of Aging,* ed. David A. Wise, 317–79. Chicago: University of Chicago Press.

The Impact of Education and Heart Attack on Smoking Cessation among Middle-Aged Adults

Linda A. Wray, A. Regula Herzog,
Robert J. Willis, and Robert B. Wallace

Considerable evidence supports the premise that higher levels of education lead to enhanced health, including protective health behaviors, in both older and younger adults (Adler et al. 1994; Antonovsky 1967; Feinstein 1993; Feldman et al. 1989; Kitagawa and Hauser 1973; Ross and Wu 1995; Syme and Berkman 1976). This essay focuses more closely on how education affects one health behavior known to lead to enhanced health: the cessation of smoking. In particular, we examine the extent to which education influences the decision to quit smoking by middle-aged adults following a heart attack — a potentially life-threatening health event. Thus, we study one step in the process linking education and enhanced health in a highly selective group of middle-aged smokers. Specifically, these smokers may differ from younger smokers in several ways. They may represent a group of longer-term and, thus, more heavily addicted or otherwise committed smokers who have successfully resisted decades of widely available information on the health dangers of cigarette smoking. Their unique characteristics may also contribute to their resisting current public health programs targeted to the smoking community at large or to younger smokers. This study aims to understand the role that higher levels of education may play in changing smoking behavior in the face of a health crisis.

Given the available literature, we hypothesize that middle-aged adults with more formal education will stop smoking more readily than middle-aged adults with less education following the experience of a heart attack. Second, we ask what other factors might underlie and explain such an effect. In exploring these issues, we bring together two voluminous bodies of literature that crosscut such disciplines as sociology, psychology, medicine, economics, and epidemiology: one pertaining to the predictors of smoking cessation and the other to the relationship between education and health. Using longitudinal data, we track changes in individual smoking behavior after a heart attack while controlling for documented correlates of smoking and heart attack plus other factors associated with education, heart attack, and smoking that may also influence whether a person quits.

Previous Research

Previous studies dealing with smoking cessation as well as the links between education and health are wide and varied. Each area is summarized briefly in the following.

Smoking Cessation

The first Surgeon General's Report on Smoking and Health in 1964 as well as all subsequent reports from that office demonstrate that cigarette smoking is the foremost preventable cause of death in the United States and, in particular, of those deaths resulting from cardiovascular diseases and cancers (Centers for Disease Control 1987; U.S. Department of Health and Human Services 1989, 1990). Although the 1990 Surgeon General's Report indicates that the proportion of smokers who stop smoking has increased consistently since 1964 (U.S. Department of Health and Human Services 1990), the reasons why some people quit and others continue to smoke are not entirely clear.

Education clearly plays a role in smoking cessation: the rates of quitting smoking since the 1964 Surgeon General's Report have consistently increased (and increased more rapidly over time) for those with more education. For example, although the overall quit rates have increased from 33 percent in 1965 to 44 percent in 1987, college graduates have quit at significantly higher rates than high-school graduates (U.S. Department of Health and Human Services 1990), suggesting that people with higher educational attainment may have better understood the risks of cigarette smoking and acted on the surgeon general's recommendations.

Several other health as well as demographic, environmental, and psychosocial factors may also influence smoking behavior. Studies have shown that not smoking or quitting smoking is highest among older adults, people who are not married to other smokers, and workers not employed in manufacturing or day labor jobs (O'Loughlin et al. 1997;

U.S. Department of Health and Human Services 1990; Wister 1996; Wray et al. 1996). In contrast, smoking cessation is lowest among people who are depressed (Anda, Williamson, and Escobedo 1990; Glassman, Helzer, and Covey 1990) or heavy alcohol users (Breslau et al. 1996; U.S. Department of Health and Human Services 1994). Smoking cessation may also be lower among individuals with poorer self-assessed health (Nevid, Javier, and Moulton 1996). More heavily addicted smokers — people who smoke more than one pack of cigarettes a day — are also less likely to quit (Marbella, Layde, and Remington 1995). In addition, studies have shown that smoking cessation may differ by gender, some indicating that women are more likely to quit smoking and others that men quit more often (Escobedo and Peddicord 1996; Jarvis 1995; Rogers, Nam, and Hummer 1995; U.S. Department of Health and Human Services 1989; Wenger 1995).

In general, although smokers perceive their health risks for cardiovascular diseases and cancer to be greater than those of nonsmokers, they also underestimate their health risks (Strecher, Kreuter, and Kobrin 1995). Nevertheless, higher proportions of smokers quit smoking once they experience a heart event compared to smokers who did not experience such an event (U.S. Department of Health and Human Services 1989). In addition, the proportion of those quitting following any heart event increases with the severity of the event (Baile et al. 1982). Given the well-established relationship between smoking and heart attack, smoking behavior may also be affected indirectly by modifiable risk factors associated with the experience of heart attacks or other heart-related conditions such as physical inactivity, high blood pressure, and obesity (Brownson et al. 1996; Bucher and Ragland 1995; Wenger 1995; Winkleby et al. 1996) as well as by enduring factors such as gender and race/ethnicity (Brownson et al. 1996; Nevid, Javier, and Moulton 1996; Ransford 1986; Strecher, Kreuter, and Kobrin 1995).

Education and Health

Decades of studies have documented that higher levels of education are linked to a variety of measures of enhanced health, including protective-health behaviors such as weight management, regular exercise, and moderate drinking (Wray et al. 1996). Although the link between education and health is well established across academic disciplines, the meaning of this association is open to debate (see Adler et al. 1994; Ettner 1996; Ross and Wu 1996). Four interpretations of the association are possible: two suggesting direct relationships between education and health (Grossman and Kaestner 1997), a third looking at an indirect relationship due to the existence of other factors that are associated with both education and health (Behrman 1997; Coburn and Pope 1974; Grossman and Kaestner 1997; Matthews et al. 1989; Ross and Wu 1995, 1996), and a fourth examining a conditional relationship that indicates that education and health outcomes are associated only under selected circumstances.

The third and fourth possibilities—which have received far less analytic attention than the other two primarily due to data constraints—serve as the basis for this study's conceptual framework. We begin by examining whether heart attack or education exerts direct effects on smoking cessation among middle-aged smokers as demonstrated in the literature for all smokers or, alternatively, whether they interact in some way to change smoking behavior. That is, perhaps educational attainment moderates the relationship between heart attack and smoking cessation so that the move to quit smoking varies across levels of education. In particular, it may be that higher levels of education produce more of the necessary knowledge, skills, and abilities that help a person to understand the link between cigarette smoking and heart attacks and, in turn, the advisability of quitting smoking following the experience of a heart attack.

We also consider the extent to which selected psychological, social environment, and resources consequences of education may mediate the process of quitting smoking. From a psychological perspective, acquiring higher levels of education in childhood and young adulthood may reinforce or augment cognitive ability in adulthood—particularly in the dimension of knowledge-based intelligence (Perlmutter 1986) or product intelligence (Salthouse 1991, 1996). People who function at a higher cognitive level may be better able to use their educational resources to apply the ever-changing health data to their own lives (Kenkel 1991), thereby decreasing their propensity to smoke and, in turn, their risk for heart attack (Hamilton 1972; Ippolito 1979; Lewit, Coate, and Grossman 1981; Schneider, Klein, and Murphy 1981). Further, some smokers with higher levels of education and, relatedly, higher levels of cognitive ability may have been more positively influenced by evidence that ten to fifteen years of abstaining from smoking returns the all-cause mortality risks of past smokers to those of nonsmokers and—perhaps more saliently—that even one year of abstention significantly reduces the risks of dying from various diseases (Samet 1992; U.S. Department of Health and Human Services 1990).

Another psychological factor that may explain a link among education, heart attack, and smoking cessation is a personality characteristic that predisposes people to invest in the future through "good" health behaviors in the present (Becker, Grossman, and Murphy 1991, 1994;

Becker and Murphy 1988; Farrell and Fuchs 1982; Fuchs 1982; Grossman and Kaestner 1997; Kenkel 1991; Rakowski et al. 1987). People with higher levels of education are more likely than people with lower levels of education to engage in healthful behaviors overall, including never smoking (Matthews et al. 1989; Wagenknecht et al. 1990; Winkleby et al. 1992), and thereby reduce their risk of many diseases (Antonovsky 1967; Diez-Roux et al. 1995; Wray et al. 1996). They may do so because they are more willing to plan or "invest" in the future rather than "consume" in the present. Thus, we speculate that differences in future orientation may explain the education-health association.

Alternatively, a social-environment perspective posits that educational levels may influence a person's choice of where to live or work that may differentially reinforce beneficial health behaviors or discourage harmful health behaviors through "social control" in the form of peer norms or values (Diez-Roux et al. 1995; Rogers, Nam, and Hummer 1995; Ross and Wu 1995; Umberson 1987). As noted earlier, smoking cessation is reported to be highest among people whose spouse or other household members are nonsmokers (O'Loughlin et al. 1997; Wister 1996). Similarly, rates of smoking vary by job categories: workers in professional or higher-status jobs are disproportionately nonsmokers compared to workers in lower-status jobs (Wray et al. 1996). Since less-educated people tend to marry other people with less education and work in jobs that require less education, it is possible that they are faced with disproportionately greater numbers of smokers in their immediate environment. The lower-status jobs may also include more physically demanding and repetitive tasks as well as less autonomy and flexibility, factors that may combine to increase job-related boredom and stress and, potentially, the likelihood of smoking to counter the boredom and stress. Thus, people with lower levels of education may be more likely to start or continue smoking not because of their levels of educational attainment per se but instead because of influences in their social environment which are related to educational level.

A similar logic applies to a resources perspective: higher levels of education may "buy" better health through higher income and wealth that then purchase more health insurance or greater access to high-quality health care (Grossman and Kaestner 1997; Patterson, Kristal, and White 1996; Schultz 1975; Welch 1970). Rather than advanced education linking directly to fewer heart attacks or to the cessation of smoking, it may be that the greater wealth or employer-provided health insurance associated with higher levels of education protect against heart attack or encourage a decision to quit smoking following a heart attack.

Whatever the true meaning of the education-health association, increased years of education are consistently found to be positively associated with many aspects of enhanced health in both younger and middle-aged adults. Whether education contributes directly, indirectly, or conditionally to enhanced health in the form of smoking cessation among a particular group of older smokers is the question that is the focus of this essay.

Method

Data

The lack of conclusive research on the process by which education changes health behaviors is due in part to the paucity of data sets containing appropriate longitudinal data to study this question. Ideally, such a data set would contain individual social, health, and economic characteristics as well as other individual and environmental factors that may influence making certain behaviors and decisions. The Health and Retirement Study (HRS), a large, nationally representative sample of preretirement-age Americans, is uniquely suited for exploring this study's issues for two primary reasons. First, the HRS is rich in information central to our interests, containing considerable sociodemographic, physical and emotional health, health behavior, function, work and retirement, income and assets, and health- and life-insurance data as well as measures on cognitive ability, future orientation, risk aversion, and subjective probabilities. Second, the HRS is a panel study that has collected three waves of data to date,[1] enabling us to explore a range of dynamic processes relating to health and economic decision making among preretirement-age individuals.

Questions and Hypotheses

Based on our review of studies on smoking behavior and the health benefits of education, we expect that education will be an important — and perhaps even predominant — predictor of smoking cessation among middle-aged smokers. In addition, given the documented link between the experience of a heart attack and smoking cessation, we anticipate that education will interact with the experience of a heart attack so that rates of smoking cessation will differ across educational levels. Because education is a proxy for knowledge, skills, and abilities developed over half a lifetime in the case of our HRS cohort, we also test whether selected psychological, social environment, and resources factors perceived as consequences of education might explain any of the effects of education or the interaction of education and heart attack on the decision to quit smoking. We anticipate that these education-related factors may be all the more important in decision making for this particular group of middle-aged smokers. Because they are more likely to be highly addicted to cigarettes after many smoking years, their smoking behavior may also be influenced considerably more by each of the education-related factors to which they have been exposed for longer periods of time compared with their younger counterparts.

In this essay, we ask the following questions about middle-aged adults.

1. Does education affect smoking cessation? Does the experience of a heart attack affect smoking cessation? Do education and the experience of a heart attack interact to affect smoking cessation such that people with more formal education are more likely to quit smoking following a heart attack than are people with less formal education?
2. Is there any evidence for psychological, social-environment, or resources factors explaining an education or an education–heart attack interaction effect on smoking cessation?

Based on our study questions and the extant literature, we test three primary hypotheses relating to smoking cessation among middle-aged adults.

1. Smokers with higher levels of education are more likely to quit smoking than are smokers with lower levels of education.
2. Smokers who have experienced a heart attack are more likely to quit smoking than are smokers who have not experienced a heart attack.
3. Smokers with higher levels of education are more likely to quit smoking than are smokers with lower levels of education following the experience of a heart attack.

Additional secondary hypotheses test six possible explanations for an education or education–heart attack effect on smoking cessation. Two hypotheses test whether psychological factors associated with education affect smoking behavior.

4. Smokers with higher levels of cognitive ability are more likely to quit smoking than are smokers with lower levels of cognitive ability.
5. Smokers who are more future oriented are more likely to quit smoking than are smokers who are less future oriented.

Similarly, two hypotheses test whether social-environment factors associated with education influence smoking behavior.

6. Smokers who are not married to other smokers are more likely to quit smoking than are smokers married to other smokers.
7. Smokers who do/did not work as a machine operator or laborer are more likely to quit smoking than are smokers who worked as a machine operator or laborer.

Finally, two hypotheses test the effects of resources factors associated with education on smoking behavior.

8. Smokers who report greater net worth are more likely to quit smoking than are smokers who report lower net worth.
9. Smokers who are covered by employer-provided health insurance are more likely to quit smoking than are smokers without employer-provided health insurance.

Samples

Although a large body of past research has consistently supported the strong negative association between higher levels of education and smoking, less conclusive evidence exists on a causal relationship between years of education and quitting smoking, particularly among middle-aged or older smokers (U.S. Department of Health and Human Services 1989, 1990). In order to isolate the effect of education on the process of modifying smoking behavior, we tracked the effects of education on smoking cessation following the experience of a heart attack between 1992 and 1994 (when the data for HRS waves 1 and 2 were collected) among smokers age fifty-one to sixty-one in 1992.[2] Heart attack was chosen as an example of a major smoking-related health event that, if diagnosed, can be reported with reasonable precision in surveys.

Two primary respondent groups were drawn for this study. First, a full sample included the 8,656 age-eligible respondents for whom we have unambiguous smoking history data in both 1992 and 1994 interviews. Among those respondents, 3,216 reported they had never smoked cigarettes or had smoked less than 100 cigarettes in their lives prior to 1992; 3,049 reported they had smoked in the past but had quit by 1992; and 2,391 reported they were current smokers in 1992 who had either continued to smoke or had quit smoking by 1994. The full sample provided us with data on the relationships between smoking history and various social, physical health, psychological, and economic characteristics and helped us to refine our major analytic models on smoking cessation. The second respondent group, which included the 2,391 people who reported they were current smokers in 1992 for whom we had matching 1994 data on smoking status, was the basis for our major analytic models.

Analysis Plan

We tested multivariate models using various subgroups of the full and smoking samples. First, exploratory models tested the effects of education and other hypothesized predictors on three dichotomous outcomes: never smoking among all middle-aged adults, quitting prior to 1992 among middle-aged adults who had smoked in the past but were not current smokers in 1992, and having experienced a heart attack between 1992 and 1994.[3] Findings from these analyses informed the design of our analyses on smoking cessation.

Second, the models that focused on our major analytic interest — smoking cessation between 1992 and 1994 — were tested on the smokers sample only. Given the dichotomous outcome measure for this set of analyses as well, the models were tested using logistic regression.[4] In these primary analyses, we regressed smoking cessation between 1992 and 1994 on sequentially entered blocks of variables that test the relative contributions of selected variables proposed to measure the education–smoking behavior relationships and controlling for documented correlates of smoking cessation and heart attack.

The independent variables in our models of smoking cessation were restricted to

1. the measures of major analytic interest: education, incident heart attack, and an interaction term for education by heart attack;
2. potential predictors that may explain the education–heart attack effect on smoking cessation, including selected psychological, social-environment, and resources factors;
3. the primary correlates of smoking cessation: gender and measures of depressed or addictive personalities; and

4. additional correlates of heart attack: race/ethnicity and specific measures of heart-related health.

Among the independent variables of major analytic interest, education is measured as the number of years of education completed by 1992 (zero to seventeen years, with seventeen representing postbaccalaureate education), centered on twelve years of education. The measure of incident heart attack indicates whether or not the respondent reports having experienced a heart attack between 1992 and 1994 (0 = no; 1 = yes). The interaction term, representing the dependency of education on heart attack, is measured as years of education multiplied by the experience of an incident heart attack (Jaccard, Turrisi, and Wan 1990).

The independent variables include six psychological, social-environment, and resources factors that may explain the effects of the interaction term on smoking cessation. These factors were also measured at baseline in 1992. Among the psychological factors, cognitive ability is a measure that combines the standardized total scores (Z-scores) from two cognitive performance tests available in the HRS—the immediate and delayed word recall tests as well as the WAIS-R word similarities test (0 to 54).[5] Future orientation is measured by whether or not the respondent reports a short-term financial planning horizon (a few months to one year) or a medium-term financial planning horizon (a few years), with a long-term planning horizon (more than five years) being the reference category.

The social-environment factors include whether the respondent's spouse smokes (0 = no; 1 = yes) and whether the respondent worked as a machine operator or laborer (0 = yes; 1 = no). The resources factors include a measure of logged net worth (centered on the mean) and a dichotomous measure of whether the respondent is covered by employer-provided health insurance (0 = no; 1 = yes).

Finally, we include documented correlates of smoking cessation measured at baseline in 1992: gender (0 = male; 1 = female); heavy smoking measured as current cigarette dosage of greater than twenty-five per day (0 = no; 1 = yes); heavy drinking measured as currently drinking more than two alcoholic drinks per day (0 = no; 1 = yes); and the number of Center for Epidemiologic Studies Depression scale (CES-D) depressive symptoms experienced most or all of the time in the past week (0 to 8), centered on the mean number of CES-D symptoms. Similarly, we include documented correlates of heart attack measured at baseline: two measures of race/ethnicity (1 = African American or 1 = Latino; 0 = white or other race/ethnicity as the reference category); diagnosis of high blood pressure in the past (0 = no; 1 = yes); obesity measured as greater than the third quartile of body mass index for the HRS respondents (0 = no; 1 = yes); irregular exercise measured as light exercise less than once a week (0 = no; 1 = yes); and two measures of self-assessed health status (1 = good or 1 = fair/poor health; 0 = excellent/very good as the reference category).

Results

Correlates of Smoking History

Table 1 describes the characteristics of four subgroups of Americans age fifty-one to sixty-one in 1992, arrayed according to their smoking history in 1992 and 1994: (1) respondents who reported in both 1992 and 1994 that they had never smoked cigarettes; (2) those who reported in 1992 that they had smoked in the past but had quit prior to 1992; (3) those who reported they were current smokers in 1992 but were not smokers in 1994; and (4) respondents who reported they were current smokers in both 1992 and 1994. As expected, in general, middle-aged adults without any smoking history had fewer risk factors for heart disease and more characteristics associated with higher education than did smokers in 1992 or 1994. For example, never smokers are disproportionately female with higher levels of education and cognitive ability compared with their counterparts who report a smoking history. Never smokers also experienced significantly fewer heart attacks prior to 1992 and fewer heart attacks between 1992 and 1994, have a lower history of high blood pressure, drink less heavily, and report better self-assessed health as well as fewer CES-D depressive symptoms than do smokers in 1992 or 1994. Never smokers are also less likely to be married to smokers or to work as machine operators or laborers and are more likely to report higher net worth than are recent smokers. Past smokers — smokers who quit smoking prior to 1992 — are statistically similar to never smokers on many characteristics, including education, depressive symptoms, self-assessed health, cognitive ability, spousal smoking, employer-provided health insurance, and net worth. Three significant differences between those groups are worth noting. Compared with never smokers, past smokers are disproportionately men, people who experienced a heart attack before 1992, and people who reported they drink heavily. These differences are significant at the $p < .05$ level.

In contrast, current smokers in 1992 and 1994 are less well educated, heavier drinkers, report higher levels of depressive symptoms, and test lower in cognitive ability than do never or past smokers in those

TABLE 1. Frequencies, Means, and Medians on Selected Characteristics of U.S. Adults Age 51–61, by Smoking History

Characteristics[a]	Never Smoked	Smoker Prior to 1992	Smoker in 1992/ Quit by 1994	Smoker in 1992 and 1994
Psychosocial Risk Factors				
Female[b]	66.0	41.0	51.9	50.8
Race/ethnicity[b]				
White	81.2	85.3	78.7	82.4
African American	9.4	8.4	12.8	10.4
Latino	6.4	4.9	5.8	5.3
Other	3.0	1.4	2.7	1.9
Father's education (mean, 0–17)[b,c]	9.3	9.5	9.3	8.9
	3.8	3.9	3.8	3.8
Education (mean, 0–17)[b,c]	12.7	12.6	12.0	11.8
	3.0	3.0	2.8	2.9
Heart attack prior to 1992[b]	3.0	7.3	6.5	5.7
Heart attack 1992–94[b]	.9	2.5	9.4	2.2
High blood pressure[b]	35.7	42.9	40.3	33.8
Heavy smoker in 1992[b]	—	—	19.8	30.1
Heavy smoker prior to 1992	—	39.6	—	—
Heavy drinker[b]	1.5	5.3	6.6	10.2
Irregular exerciser[b]	46.4	42.4	50.3	51.4
Obese[b]	24.0	27.4	25.4	16.6
Self-reported health[b]				
Excellent/very good	59.9	56.3	43.2	45.8
Good	24.8	26.2	28.7	28.4
Fair/poor	15.3	17.6	28.1	25.8
CES-D symptoms (mean, 0–8)[b,c]	.7	.7	1.0	1.0
	1.3	1.3	1.6	1.6
Psychological Factors				
Cognitive ability (mean, 0–54)[b,c]	20.4	19.9	18.6	18.8
	6.7	6.6	6.3	6.8
Future orientation[b]				
Short-term planner	25.7	25.4	27.7	32.1
Medium-term planner	35.6	33.7	38.5	31.5
Long-term planner	38.7	41.0	33.8	36.4
Social-Environment Factors				
Spouse smokes[b]	11.1	12.9	28.5	31.1
Blue collar worker[b]	17.2	25.8	26.8	31.2
Resources Factors				
Net worth (median)[b]	124,000	120,000	72,000	70,000
Employee health insurance[b]	74.6	76.4	71.6	64.9
N	3,216	3,049	402	1,989

Source: Authors' calculations using data from HRS Waves 1 and 2.

[a]Values for all characteristics except "heart attack 1992–94" are those reported at baseline in 1992.
[b]Values are significantly different across smoking history categories.
[c]Standard deviations are presented below means.

years. Smokers in 1992 and 1994 are more likely to be married to other smokers and to report lower net worth than never or past smokers. Importantly, people who quit smoking between 1992 and 1994 also disproportionately report having experienced a heart attack during that same period.

Predictors of Never Smoking and Quitting among Past Smokers

Tables 2 and 3 present results of exploratory analyses focusing on two of the smoking states illustrated in columns 1 and 2 of tables 1 — never smoking and having quit smoking prior to 1992. The goal of each of these analyses is to gain some understanding of the role of education on pre-1992 smoking behavior while controlling on selected correlates of smoking in order to better design our major analytic models concerning smoking cessation between 1992 and 1994. As shown in models 1 through 4 in each table, blocks of variables were entered sequentially: (1) demographic and status origin characteristics; (2) years of education; (3) measures of health behaviors and lifestyle as well as physical and emotional health that may be associated with education; and (4) selected psychological, social-environment, and resources consequences of education. For ease of interpretation, the tables present parameter estimates and *t*-statistics as well as odds ratios.

As shown in table 2, certain enduring characteristics of individuals that may be seen as precursors to education are consistently associated with whether or not middle-aged adults ever smoked. For example, being female or Latino significantly increases the odds of never smoking in model 1. These factors remain significant in models 2–4 as well, even after education, health, lifestyle, and education consequences are introduced. Most central to our interest is that education is highly significant across models 2–4, increasing the odds of never smoking by 5–8 percent for every additional year of education beyond high school. In other words, more highly educated people are less likely to have ever started smoking. In model 4, other behavioral, social-environment, and health factors such as being a heavy drinker, being married to a smoker, or having experienced a heart attack prior to 1992 are also significantly associated with never smoking. Interestingly, greater numbers of CES-D depressive symptoms contribute significantly to decreased odds of never smoking. Model 4 also shows that working as a machine operator or laborer decreases the odds of never smoking while greater net worth increases the odds.

Table 3 presents data for middle-aged adults who ever smoked and

TABLE 2. Logit Equations Showing Never Smoking Regressed on Education, Incident Heart Attack, and Selected Predictors among U.S. Smokers Age 51–61, 1992 and 1994

Characteristics[a]	Model 1 Parameter Estimate	Model 1 Odds Ratio	Model 2 Parameter Estimate	Model 2 Odds Ratio	Model 3 Parameter Estimate	Model 3 Odds Ratio	Model 4 Parameter Estimate	Model 4 Odds Ratio
Intercept	−1.003*** (24.811)		−1.150*** (25.372)		−1.285*** (15.934)		−1.102*** (12.391)	
Female	.865*** (17.93)	2.375	.899*** (18.446)	2.457	.878*** (15.478)	2.405	.810*** (13.899)	2.247
African American[b]	−.020 (.227)	.980	.020 (.226)	1.020	.265* (2.535)	1.304	.214* (2.01)	1.239
Latino[b]	.280** (2.585)	1.323	.471*** (4.208)	1.601	.520*** (3.948)	1.682	.501** (3.749)	1.651
Father's education	.011 (1.668)	1.011	−.012 (1.703)	.988	−.021*** (2.618)	.980	−.020* (2.551)	.980
Education			.074*** (7.663)	1.077	.061** (4.895)	1.063	.051*** (4.04)	1.052
Cognitive ability					.005 (.264)	1.005	.000 (.010)	1.000
Short-term planner[c]					−.027 (.398)	.973	.003 (.048)	1.003
Medium-term planner[c]					.070 (1.160)	1.072	.084 (1.381)	1.088
Blue collar worker					−.244** (3.189)	.783	−.225** (2.897)	.799
Net worth					.111*** (7.527)	1.117	.104*** (6.958)	1.109

Characteristics[a]	Model 1 Parameter Estimate	Odds Ratio	Model 2 Parameter Estimate	Odds Ratio	Model 3 Parameter Estimate	Odds Ratio	Model 4 Parameter Estimate	Odds Ratio
Employee health insurance					.047 (.732)	1.048	.040 (.618)	1.041
Obese							.100 (1.557)	1.105
Irregular exercise							.009 (.169)	1.009
Heavy drinker							−1.279*** (6.945)	.278
Spouse smokes							−.709*** (9.157)	.492
Heart attack 1992–94							−.541*** (3.683)	.582
High blood pressure							−.011 (.196)	.989
CES-D symptoms							−.044* (1.990)	.957
Log-likelihood ratio	373.857		398.487		453.522		642.876	
df	3		5		11		18	
p	.0001		.0001		.0001		.0001	
N	7,783		7,783		6,647		6,647	

Source: Authors' calculations using data from HRS Waves 1 and 2.

Note: T-statistics are in parentheses.

*p < .05. **p < .01. ***p < .001.

[a]Values for all characteristics except "Heart attack 1992–94" are those reported at baseline in 1992.

[b]Reference category is white and other non–African American or Latino ethnicity.

[c]Reference category is long-term planner.

TABLE 3. Logit Equations Showing Smoking Cessation Prior to 1992 Regressed on Education, Incident Heart Attack, and Selected Predictors among U.S. Adults Age 51–61, 1992

Characteristics[a]	Model 1 Parameter Estimate	Model 1 Odds Ratio	Model 2 Parameter Estimate	Model 2 Odds Ratio	Model 3 Parameter Estimate	Model 3 Odds Ratio	Model 4 Parameter Estimate	Model 4 Odds Ratio
Intercept	.653*** (14.39)		.502*** (10.247)		.457*** (4.985)		.617*** (5.848)	
Female	-.401*** (6.903)	.670	-.382*** (6.539)	.682	-.467*** (6.758)	.627	-.478*** (6.467)	.620
African American[b]	-.229* (2.185)	.796	-.185 (1.756)	.831	.086 (.664)	1.089	-.073 (.541)	.930
Latino[b]	.016 (.115)	1.016	.242 (1.685)	1.273	.308 (1.861)	1.361	.332 (1.943)	1.394
Father's education	.034*** (4.379)	1.034	.003 (.388)	1.003	-.004 (.442)	.996	-.006 (.584)	.994
Education			.096*** (8.146)	1.101	.037* (2.434)	1.037	.024 (1.518)	1.024
Cognitive ability					.052* (2.187)	1.053	.049* (1.986)	1.050
Short-term planner[c]					-.057 (.691)	.945	-.029 (.331)	.972
Medium-term planner[c]					.050 (.667)	1.051	.088 (1.126)	1.092
Blue collar worker					-.177* (2.127)	.838	-.129 (1.475)	.879
Net worth					.123*** (7.450)	1.131	.126*** (7.371)	1.134

Characteristics[a]	Model 1		Model 2		Model 3		Model 4	
	Parameter Estimate	Odds Ratio	Parameter Estimate	Odds Ratio	Parameter Estimate	Odds Ratio	Parameter Estimate	Odds Ratio
Employee health insurance					.170* (2.228)	1.186	.029* (2.187)	1.192
Obese							.528*** (6.281)	1.695
Irregular exercise							-.305*** (4.533)	.737
Heavy drinker							-.603*** (4.589)	.547
Spouse smokes							-1.184*** (14.567)	.306
Heart attack 1992–94							.345* (2.357)	1.412
High blood pressure							.332*** (4.614)	1.394
CES-D symptoms							-.109*** (4.13)	.897
Log-likelihood ratio	75.700		143.501		213.286		583.502	
df	4		5		11		18	
p	.0001		.0001		.0001		.0001	
N	4,902		4,902		4,180		4,180	

Source: Authors' calculations using data from HRS Waves 1 and 2.

Note: T-statistics are in parentheses.

*p < .05.

**p < .01.

***p < .001.

[a]Values for all characteristics except "Heart attack 1992–94" are those reported at baseline in 1992.

[b]Reference category is white and other non–African American or Latino ethnicity.

[c]Reference category is long-term planner.

contrasts those who quit prior to 1992 with those still smoking in 1992. Among the precursors of education shown in model 1, being female or African American reduces the odds of past quitting. In contrast, higher levels of father's education (our measure of status origins) are positively associated with prior quitting. When education is introduced in models 2–4, only being female remains consistently significant among the pre-precursors. Education itself is significantly linked to past quitting as expected — those who are more highly educated are more likely to have quit smoking before 1992 — but only in models 2 and 3. Once the consequences of education are entered into model 4, education itself loses significance. All of our health and lifestyle measures plus cognitive ability, net worth, and employee health insurance are also significantly associated with prior quitting and all in the direction we would expect from the literature. That is, higher levels of cognitive ability and net worth, having employer-provided health insurance coverage, or having been diagnosed with a previous heart attack or high blood pressure contribute positively to having quit smoking prior to 1992. In contrast, detrimental health behaviors such as irregular exercise or heavy drinking are negatively associated with prior quitting.

Predictors of Incident Heart Attack

Finally, table 4 presents results of exploratory analyses focusing on the experience of an incident heart attack. In addition to trying to understand how education contributed to smoking behavior prior to 1992 (when the HRS started), we also wanted to understand how education might have influenced the experience of a heart attack between 1992 and 1994 (net of selected correlates of heart attack) in order to compare our findings on middle-aged adults with findings in the literature.

Surprisingly, neither education nor the consequences of education appear to play a role in the likelihood of an incident heat attack, counter to recent studies (Diez-Roux et al. 1995; Feinstein 1993; Feldman et al. 1989; Matthews et al. 1989). However, other findings shown in table 4 demonstrate support for other existing literature. For example, being female or a heavy drinker significantly decreases the odds of experiencing a heart attack. In contrast, being a smoker in 1992, having been diagnosed with high blood pressure, and reporting higher levels of CES-D depressive symptoms increase the odds.

In sum, the three sets of exploratory analyses indicate that education is importantly linked to never starting smoking but only indirectly to stopping prior to 1992 and to the experience of an incident heart attack. The consequences of education — represented here as lifestyle and health status as well as psychological, social-environment, and resources factors—suppress the association between education itself and prior stopping. Other factors that are influential to both past smoking states include gender and race/ethnicity. In general, all of the potential predictors in these exploratory models except father's education are consistently associated with past smoking behavior. Fewer of the potential predictors in our models are significantly related to incident heart attack, but those that are generally support the literature and also are associated with educational level. Although the findings from the exploratory analyses are associational rather than causal, they provide us with useful information on which to base and interpret our models of smoking cessation between 1992 and 1994. The major analytic models that are described in the following combine all of the potential predictors of past smoking behavior and incident heart attack except father's education.

Predictors of Smoking Cessation between 1992 and 1994

In this section, we describe the results of the multivariate analyses on those people we are most interested in, those represented in columns 3 and 4 of table 1 — the people who reported they were current smokers in 1992 and who had subsequently quit or continued smoking. The goal of these analyses is to discern the effects of education, heart attack, and the interaction of education and heart attack as well as selected psychological, social-environment, and resources factors on smoking cessation between 1992 and 1994.

The four simple models in table 5 demonstrate the effects of the following variables on smoking cessation by 1994: (1) heart attack alone; (2) education alone; (3) education and heart attack together; and, finally, (4) education, heart attack, and an interaction term for education with heart attack. Consistent with other studies, model 1 demonstrates that the experience of a heart attack is a significant predictor of smoking cessation by 1994. In contrast, model 2 shows that education alone is not. Heart attack's significant effects on quitting remain essentially the same when controlling for educational levels (model 3). In this model, incident heart attack strongly and positively predicts smoking cessation, quadrupling the odds of quitting.

In order to explore the relationship among education, heart attack, and smoking cessation further, model 4 introduces an interaction term for education and heart attack. Here, the interaction term is significant and positive, implying that for those who experienced a heart attack, each additional year of education beyond high school increases the odds

TABLE 4. Logit Equations Showing Experience of Heart Attack 1992–94 Regressed on Selected Risk Factors and Correlates of Education among U.S. Adults Age 51–61, 1992 and 1994

Characteristics[a]	Model 1 Parameter Estimate	Model 1 Odds Ratio	Model 2 Parameter Estimate	Model 2 Odds Ratio	Model 3 Parameter Estimate	Model 3 Odds Ratio	Model 4 Parameter Estimate	Model 4 Odds Ratio
Intercept	-3.801*** (29.377)		-3.610*** (26.903)		-3.779*** (13.804)		-5.161*** (11.827)	
Female	-1.223*** (6.181)	.294	-1.242*** (6.276)	.289	-1.225*** (4.981)	.294	-1.300*** (5.051)	.273
African American[b]	.112 (.381)	1.118	-.011 (.037)	.989	-.535 (1.291)	.586	-.511 (1.211)	.600
Latino[b]	-.284 (.717)	.753	-.696 (1.673)	.498	-.692 (1.369)	.500	-.402 (.798)	.669
Father's education	-.076*** (3.321)	.927	-.034 (1.318)	.967	-.018 (.584)	.983	-.020 (.635)	.981
Education			-.126*** (4.206)	.881	-.050 (1.142)	.951	-.037 (.810)	.964
Cognitive ability					-.028 (.372)	.972	.027 (.354)	1.028
Short-term planner[c]					.396 (1.531)	1.485	.275 (1.042)	1.316
Medium-term planner[c]					.210 (.844)	1.233	.209 (.826)	1.233
Blue collar worker					.283 (1.198)	1.327	.225 (.942)	1.252
Net worth					-.119** (3.104)	.888	-.041 (.978)	.960
Employee health insurance					-.192 (.801)	.825	.057 (.225)	1.058

Characteristics[a]	Model 1 Parameter Estimate	Model 1 Odds Ratio	Model 2 Parameter Estimate	Model 2 Odds Ratio	Model 3 Parameter Estimate	Model 3 Odds Ratio	Model 4 Parameter Estimate	Model 4 Odds Ratio
Past smoker							.633 (1.872)	1.884
Smoker in 1992							.972*** (3.733)	2.644
Heavy smoker							.157 (.508)	1.170
Obese							.362 (1.610)	1.437
Irregular exercise							.068 (.325)	1.070
Heavy drinker							−1.031* (2.000)	.357
Spouse smokes							−.473 (1.655)	.623
High blood pressure							.662** (3.108)	1.938
CES-D symptoms							.291*** (5.185)	1.338
Log-likelihood ratio	55.388		72.619		62.957		142.458	
df	4		5		11		20	
p	.0001		.0001		.0001		.0001	
N	7,771		7,771		6,637		6,637	

Source: Authors' calculations using data from HRS Waves 1 and 2.

Note: T-statistics are in parentheses.

*$p < .05$. **$p < .01$. ***$p < .001$.

[a]Values for all characteristics are those reported at baseline in 1992.

[b]Reference category is white and other non–African American or Latino ethnicity.

[c]Reference category is long-term planner.

TABLE 5.   Logit Equations Showing Smoking Cessation by 1994 Regressed on Education and Incident Heart Attack between 1992 and 1994 among U.S. Smokers Age 51–61 (N = 1,924)

	Model 1		Model 2		Model 3		Model 4	
Characteristics[a]	Parameter Estimate	Odds Ratio	Parameter Estimate	Odds Ratio	Parameter Estimate	Odds Ratio	Parameter Estimate	Odds Ratio
Intercept	−1.702***		−1.635***		−1.706***		−1.703***	
	(26.793)		(26.946)		(26.772)		(26.783)	
Heart attack 1992–94	1.590*** (5.821)	4.903			1.615*** (5.885)	5.027	1.827*** (5.995)	6.218
Education			.016 (.703)	1.016	.025 (1.084)	1.026	.007 (.281)	1.007
Heart attack × education							.362** (2.632)	1.436
Log-likelihood ratio	30.491		30.497		31.679		41.635	
df	1		1		2		3	
p	.0001		.0001		.0001		.0001	

Source: Authors' calculations using data from HRS Waves 1 and 2.

Note: T-statistics are in parentheses.

*p < .05.   **p < .01.   ***p < .001.

[a]Values for all characteristics except "Heart attack 1992–94" are those reported at baseline in 1992.

of quitting smoking by 900 percent or more (from the exponentiated sum of the parameter estimates of the main effect for heart attack and the interaction effect for heart attack by education). In contrast, each additional year of education beyond high school increases the odds of quitting by less than 1 percent among those who did not experience a heart attack. Thus, education moderates the well-known heart attack and smoking cessation link, a finding illustrated graphically in figure 1.

In this figure, we plot probability values and show that a high school or college education dramatically increases the probability of quitting smoking among people who experienced an incident heart attack compared with those who did not. As illustrated in the bottom curve, the probability of quitting smoking is remarkably low among those without an incident heart attack, with higher levels of education increasing that probability only very modestly (from 14 to 16 percent). In stark contrast, among individuals who did experience a heart attack (top curve), higher levels of educational attainment clearly play a role in smoking cessation. Middle-aged adults with at least some high school education had a 30 percent probability of quitting if they had a heart attack, compared to a 53 percent probability for those who completed high school, 83 percent

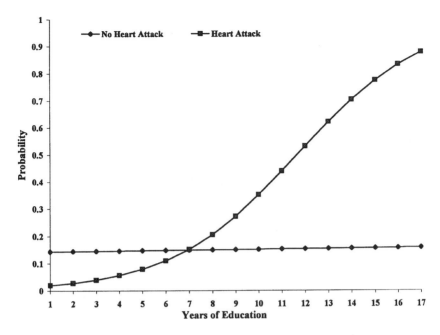

Fig. 1. Probability of quitting smoking by 1994, given the experience of a heart attack 1992–94 in U.S. adults ages 51–61 (table 5, model 4)

for those with a college education, and 88 percent for those with a postbaccalaureate education. People who never attended any high school and also experienced an incident heart attack were about as likely to quit smoking as those who did not experience a heart attack between 1992 and 1994.

Table 6 shows that introducing additional predictors of smoking cessation to model 4 of table 5 changes the story only slightly. In general, the additional predictors do not modify the powerful effect of education on the impact of heart attack on smoking cessation. Model 5 includes not only education, heart attack, and the interaction of education and heart attack but also the primary correlates of smoking cessation and heart attack. In model 6, we add the potential explanations for an education and heart attack interaction. In those two models, heart attack remains a significant (and somewhat stronger) predictor of quitting, compared with model 4. Education as a main effect continues to be nonsignificant. However, the effect of the interaction between education and heart attack remains significant and virtually unchanged in strength from its effect in the previous model without the primary correlates.

TABLE 6. Logit Equations Showing Smoking Cessation Regressed on Education, Incident Heart Attack, Selected Predictors, and Interaction Terms among U.S. Smokers Age 51–61, 1992 and 1994 (*N* = 1,924)

Characteristics[a]	Model 5		Model 6		Model 7	
	Parameter Estimate	Odds Ratio	Parameter Estimate	Odds Ratio	Parameter Estimate	Odds Ratio
Psychosocial Risk Factors						
Intercept	−1.676***		−2.280***		−2.231***	
	(11.669)		(6.515)		(6.219)	
Heart attack 1992–94	1.901***	6.692	1.900***	6.689	1.230	3.422
	(5.979)		(5.908)		(1.438)	
Education	.017	1.017	.007	1.007	.009	1.009
	(.658)		(.254)		(.317)	
Female	.021	1.021	−.004	.996	−.006	.994
	(.157)		(.028)		(.040)	
African American[b]	.120	1.128	.199	1.220	.194	1.214
	(.584)		(.911)		(.885)	
Latino[b]	.333	1.396	.445	1.561	.449	1.567
	(1.213)		(1.591)		(1.597)	
Heavy smoker	−.677***	.508	−.657***	.518	−.678***	.507
	(4.104)		(3.952)		(4.037)	
Heavy drinker	−.198	.820	−1.195	.823	−.188	.829
	(.799)		(.780)		(.749)	
CES-D symptoms	.002	1.002	.014	1.014	.016	1.016
	(.036)		(.307)		(.361)	
High blood pressure	.168	1.183	.163	1.177	.155	1.167
	(1.205)		(1.166)		(1.101)	
Obese	.443**	1.557	.463**	1.589	.483**	1.620
	(2.844)		(2.953)		(3.072)	
Irregular exercise	−.065	.937	−.088	.915	−.083	.920
	(.511)		(.691)		(.647)	
Good health[c]	−.009	.999	.016	1.016	.011	1.011
	(.000)		(.101)		(.070)	
Fair/poor health[c]	−.064	.938	.027	1.027	.030	1.031
	(.355)		(.146)		(.165)	
Explanations						
Cognitive ability			−.056	.946	−.063	.939
			(1.201)		(1.328)	
Short-term planner[d]			−.130	.878	−.164	.848
			(.766)		(.951)	
Medium-term planner[d]			.341*	1.406	.299*	1.349
			(2.288)		(1.969)	
Spouse smokes			−.134	.875	−.124	.883
			(.951)		(.863)	

TABLE 6. (*cont.*)

Characteristics[a]	Model 5 Parameter Estimate	Model 5 Odds Ratio	Model 6 Parameter Estimate	Model 6 Odds Ratio	Model 7 Parameter Estimate	Model 7 Odds Ratio
Explanations						
Blue collar worker			−.162	.850	−.175	.840
			(.996)		(1.042)	
Net worth			.036	1.036	.033	1.034
			(1.351)		(1.210)	
Employee health insurance			.247	1.280	.246	1.278
			(1.608)		(1.554)	
Interactions						
Heart attack × education	.364**	1.439	.371**	1.449	.352*	1.422
	(2.671)		(2.672)		(2.182)	
Heart attack × cognitive ability					.154	1.167
					(.682)	
Heart attack × short-term planner					1.029	2.799
					(1.113)	
Heart attack × medium-term planner					1.213	3.363
					(1.449)	
Heart attack × spouse smokes					−.450	.638
					(.513)	
Heart attack × blue collar worker					−.155	.857
					(.208)	
Heart attack × net worth					.054	1.055
					(.561)	
Heart attack × employee health insurance					.259	1.296
					(.369)	
Log-likelihood ratio	77.741		96.515		99.717	
df	14.000		21.000		28.000	
p	.0001		.0001		.0001	

Source: Authors' calculations using data from HRS Waves 1 and 2.

Note: T-statistics are in parentheses.

*p < .05.   **p < .01.   ***p < .001.

[a]Values for all characteristics except "Heart attack 1992–94" are those reported at baseline in 1992.

[b]Reference category is white and other non–African American or Latino ethnicity.

[c]Reference category is excellent health.

[d]Reference category is long-term planner.

Among the correlates of smoking cessation, only being a heavy smoker, obesity, and the experience of heart attack are significant predictors; heavy smoking decreases the odds of quitting and being overweight or having a heart attack increases the odds, while all other factors are held constant. In addition, among the explanatory factors added in model 6, medium- versus long-term financial planning significantly predicts smoking cessation, strongly and unexpectedly increasing the odds of smoking cessation.

Finally, in model 7, we add to our previous model a set of interaction terms representing the product of heart attack by each of the psychological, social-environment, and resources factors. We do this for two primary reasons. First, because each of these factors represents consequences of education, we wanted to test the relative effects of education and its consequences both separately and as interaction terms.[6] Second, we also wanted to test the effect of the heart attack–education interaction term after including all other education-related interaction terms. Model 7 indicates that, even with all of the interaction terms entered into the model, the results are scarcely altered, with one exception. Heart attack by education holds as the only significant interaction term, but the main effect for heart attack loses significance as well as considerable strength. Heavy cigarette dosage, obesity, and midterm planning remain solid as other significant predictors.

Discussion

This study's analyses of the effect of education on smoking cessation among middle-aged adults led to both expected and unexpected results, providing at least partial support for our primary and secondary hypotheses. Surprisingly, and counter to previous research (Douglas 1998; U.S. Department of Health and Human Services 1989) as well as one of our primary hypotheses, education alone was not a significant predictor of smoking cessation in middle-aged adults. In contrast, heart attack was significant, supporting both literature and one primary hypothesis. More importantly, the interaction of education and heart attack was a powerful and significant predictor of smoking cessation: among smokers who experienced a heart attack, higher levels of education played a protective role by increasing the likelihood that they would quit smoking. Absent a heart attack, higher levels of education had virtually no effect on whether or not a person quit. Although this may seem contrary to the expectation that increasing levels of formal education should lead to participating in more protective health behaviors (Fuchs 1982; Kenkel

1991), it may also reflect the fact that education had already exerted a major effect on smoking behavior before 1992 in our middle-aged adults by reducing the likelihood that a more highly educated person would have ever started smoking or would have remained a smoker until 1992.

The dramatic influence of higher levels of education following the experience of a heart attack suggests that more highly educated older smokers "learn" from their heart attacks and quit smoking. This result is particularly striking given the selection effect on smokers. As reported by other studies and our exploratory analyses, many people with higher levels of education had never smoked or, if they had smoked, had already quit by 1992, quite possibly in response to three decades worth of surgeon general's reports, smoking-related health events, and family or workplace pressures. The highly educated people who were still smokers in 1992 may have been longer-term smokers or more heavily addicted to cigarettes than were their counterparts who quit and, thus, may have found quitting under most circumstances to be especially difficult. Alternatively, they may have been exposed to other life events and risks or had different personality characteristics that impeded their quitting previously. Whatever their initial barriers to quitting, education apparently prevailed over addiction and other factors to impel the better-educated middle-aged individuals to quit smoking once faced with a heart attack.

Second, we found partial support for only one of our six secondary hypotheses testing possible psychological, social-environment, and resources explanations for an education or education–heart attack effect on smoking cessation. In particular, one of the psychological factors, future orientation, helped us disentangle the effect of the heart attack–education interaction. Being a medium- versus long-term planner unexpectedly increased the odds of quitting smoking, counter to the idea that people who are more future oriented should participate in more healthful and less addictive behaviors (Becker, Grossman, and Murphy 1991, 1994; Fuchs 1982). Preliminary analyses not presented here indicated that long-term planners were generally more highly educated and less likely to be smokers in the first place, compared with medium-term planners. However, long-term planners who were smokers in 1992 were also disproportionately heavy smokers, compared with short- and medium-term planners. It may be that the current smokers whose behaviors were analyzed in this study were affected by their future orientation differently than were past smokers. Their heavier cigarette dosage may have raised the "cost" of quitting to such an extent that their higher education or degree of future orientation became less protective. Alternatively, medium- versus long-term planning may reflect a more "realistic" tally of the costs and benefits associated with smoking cessation in older age. For example, middle-aged smokers may surmise that even though quitting considerably reduces the risks of heart attack, lung cancer, and other diseases within five to fifteen years, the fact that these diseases are generally associated with older age may promote the belief that there is little eventual health benefit in stopping a presumably pleasurable habit in later life (Douglas 1998; U.S. Department of Health and Human Services 1990).

No evidence was found in our analyses to support the effects of cognitive ability or the social-environment or resources factors associated with education that we posited might play a role in smoking cessation among middle-aged adults and help us to explain the heart attack by education interaction effect. Despite their nonsignificance, the inclusion of education consequences in our models — particularly in interaction terms — did lessen both significance and strength of the heart attack by education interaction. Perhaps other measures of psychological orientation, social environment, or resources would have proved more informative.

Finally, among the primary correlates of smoking cessation, heavy cigarette smoking in 1992 negatively influenced quitting by 1994. Since some people with higher levels of education continued to smoke despite widely available information in the community on the dangers of cigarette smoking (Kenkel 1991), factors other than health information must have driven decisions to quit or continue smoking. Our analyses pointed toward one such factor: the odds of smoking cessation decreased strongly among heavy smokers, demonstrating that the cost of quitting may be greater for more strongly addicted smokers, even after controlling for education and the experience of a heart attack. These results support other recent research (e.g., Marbella, Layde, and Remington 1995) also finding heavy smokers to be less likely to quit smoking.

In addition, being overweight strongly predicted smoking cessation, although physical activity did not, lending partial support to the notion that participation in some beneficial health behaviors should increase the likelihood of participating in other such behaviors (Matthews et al. 1989; Wagenknecht et al. 1990; Winkleby et al. 1992). In particular, middle-aged adults who are overweight may recognize the need to eliminate or control one risk factor for heart-related disease (smoking) but not others (exercise or weight management), reasoning that smoking cessation may be a more critical predictor of enhanced health than either of the other health behaviors.

Additional factors identified in the literature as associated with education, heart attack, and smoking cessation (e.g., gender, race/ethnicity, heavy drinking, history of high blood pressure, self-assessed health status, and depressive symptoms) failed to reach significance in our models, whether or not we controlled for additional education–heart attack "explanations." Certain attributes of the study's data set may have limited our ability to identify these or other potential predictors of smoking cessation. First, the HRS collects disease and health-condition data by self-report. Although experience with heart attack in the past two years is likely to be remembered reasonably well by respondents and the HRS does ask what year the heart attack occurred, the data are only as good as the respondent's recall. Second, our measure of smoking cessation is static and indirect in that it is based on reports of current or past smoking behavior in 1992 and 1994. If a respondent stopped smoking between 1992 and 1994, the HRS does not ask when he or she quit. Thus, we cannot know whether a report of no longer smoking in 1994 means the person has quit for a day, a month, a year, or permanently. Neither can we know for certain that smoking cessation followed the heart attack in the case of those smokers who experienced incident heart attacks. Finally, we did not consider the influence of other long-term or more recent health problems other than high blood pressure on the decision to quit smoking. Clearly, smoking cessation is a complicated decision-making process that defies simple analysis or interpretation in our cohort of middle-aged adults.

Conclusion

This essay started by acknowledging the well-established positive association between higher levels of education and enhanced health, including protective health behaviors. Ultimately, our study results augmented the wealth of evidence from various academic disciplines in confirming that association. Higher levels of education do, in fact, play a role in one health-enhancing behavior, at least under some circumstances among preretirement-aged Americans. Our study also supported the documented connection between heart attack and smoking cessation. In addition, our study provided a surprising twist on those links: the move to quit smoking following the experience of a heart attack among middle-aged adults was significantly and dramatically moderated by their level of educational attainment. Among older smokers without an incident heart attack, the probability of quitting smoking was less than one in six. However, among older smokers who experienced a heart attack, only those with an education of at least high school or beyond changed their smoking behavior. Each additional year of educational attainment beyond high school dramatically raised the probability of quitting—from one in two for those with a high-school education to near certainty for those with postbaccalaureate education.

Although this study's focus on change in one health behavior following the experience of a potentially life-threatening health event was intentionally narrow, our analyses shed some light on the association between education and health. Our probe of education's effects on smoking cessation demonstrated that education alone did not always provide sufficient incentive to quit smoking among our group of older adults. As noted, these smokers may be different from younger smokers in many ways, resulting in their being more resistant to decades of public health messages about the dangers of cigarette smoking. The higher levels of knowledge, skills, and abilities proxied by educational attainment furnished the necessary justification for quitting in such individuals only when they suffered the shock of a life-threatening health event. Future research could add to our understanding in this area by exploring education's effects on a wider range of health and economic outcomes at different points across the life course, incorporating different moderating life events as well as other potential mediators of those outcomes.

NOTES

A preliminary version of this essay was presented at the F. Thomas Juster Symposium held on December 13–14, 1996, at the University of Michigan, Ann Arbor, Michigan. Support for this research was provided by NIA Grant No. P20-AG12846, NIA Grant No. U01-AG09740, and NIA Grant. No. T32-AG00117. This essay also appeared in the *Journal of Health and Social Behavior* (December 1998). Reprinted by permission. The authors thank Duane Alwin, John Bound, and Dick Campbell for their insightful comments on earlier drafts. The authors also thank John Mirowsky, editor of the *Journal of Health and Social Behavior,* and other anonymous reviewers for their helpful comments. Correspondence should be addressed to: Linda A. Wray, Institute for Social Research, University of Michigan, Ann Arbor, MI 48106–1248.

1. The public release data set for wave 3 of the HRS is expected to be available in early 1999.

2. In order to retain as many of the cases of incident heart attack as possible, all heart attacks between 1992 and 1994 were counted among respondents for whom these heart attacks represented first heart attacks as well as respondents for whom the heart attacks represented subsequent heart attacks.

3. The exploratory models focused on three dichotomous outcomes: never having smoked, quitting prior to 1992, and experiencing a heart attack between 1992 and 1994. These models were tested on four sequentially entered blocks of vari-

ables: (1) demographic and status origin characteristics; (2) level of education; (3) health status, health behaviors, and lifestyle variables; and (4) selected psychological, social-environment, and resource factors. All of the variables except the measure of status origins — father's educational attainment — reached significance in most of the exploratory models. These variables were included in the final models predicting smoking cessation and are described in detail in the essay's text. Father's educational attainment was measured as the number of years the respondent reports his or her father completed, centered on twelve years of education.

4. Smoking cessation has been documented to be a dynamic process with alternating periods of quitting and relapse before permanent abstinence (U.S. Department of Health and Human Services 1990). While acknowledging that dynamic process, we are constrained in our analyses to using a static measure based on changes in self-reported smoking status at two points in time, 1992 and 1994.

5. We combine these scores in order to tap two dimensions of cognitive ability — fluid and crystallized abilities — that may influence a person's capacity for making informed decisions. Fluid ability measures processing capabilities that affect the ability to acquire new information. Often used in standardized cognitive screens for older adults, the word recall tests primarily (although not exclusively) assess fluid ability, which may decline somewhat with aging. In contrast, crystallized ability measures the actual acquisition of that information in the form of knowledge-based abilities (e.g., verbal and abstract reasoning) that are closely tied to educational attainment, remaining stable or even increasing throughout the life course. Word similarities tests primarily measure crystallized ability.

6. Preliminary analyses that are not presented here demonstrated that a heart attack by cognitive ability interaction term (as a substitution for a heart attack by education interaction term) was a significant predictor of smoking cessation. That seemed a logical finding given that education and cognitive ability are often perceived as two sides of the same coin, that is, tapping into a similar concept. However, their moderate correlation ($r = 0.44$) suggests that they are still measuring different traits. Similar analyses were conducted substituting interaction terms comprised of heart attack by each of the other psychological, social-environment, and resources factors believed to be consequences of education. However, none of these other interaction terms proved to be significant predictors in the preliminary analyses.

REFERENCES

Adler, Nancy, Thomas Boyce, Margaret A. Chesney, Sheldon Cohen, Susan Folkman, Robert L. Kahn, and S. Leonard Syme. 1994. "Socioeconomic Status and Health: The Challenge of the Gradient." *American Psychologist* 48:15–24.
Anda, Robert F., David F. Williamson, and Luis G. Escobedo. 1990. "Depression and the Dynamics of Smoking: A National Perspective." *Journal of the American Medical Association* 264:1541–45.

Antonovsky, Aaron. 1967. "Social Class, Life Expectancy, and Overall Mortality." *Milbank Memorial Fund Quarterly* 45:31–73.

Baile, Walter F., George E. Bigelow, Sidney H. Gottlieb, Maxine L. Stitzer, and J. D. Sacktor. 1982. "Rapid Resumption of Cigarette Smoking following Myocardial Infarction: Inverse Relation to MI Severity." *Addictive Behaviors* 7:373–80.

Becker, Gary S., Michael Grossman, and Kevin M. Murphy. 1991. "Rational Addiction and the Effect of Price on Consumption." *American Economic Review* 81:237–41.

———. 1994. "An Empirical Analysis of Cigarette Addiction." *American Economic Review* 84:396–418.

Becker, Gary S., and Kevin M. Murphy. 1988. "A Theory of Rational Addiction." *Journal of Political Economy* 96:675–700.

Behrman, Jere R. 1997. "Conceptual and Measurement Issues." In *Social Benefits,* edited by Jere R. Behrman and N. Stacey, 17–67. Ann Arbor: University of Michigan Press.

Breslau, Naomi, Edward Peterson, Lonni Schultz, Patricia Andreski, and Howard Chilcoat. 1996. "Are Smokers with Alcohol Disorders Less Likely to Quit?" *American Journal of Public Health* 86:985–90.

Brownson, Ross C., Carol A. Smith, Michael Pratt, Nilsa E. Mack, Jeannette Jackson-Thompson, Cynthia G. Dean, Sue Dabney, and Joan C. Wilkerson. 1996. "Preventing Cardiovascular Disease through Community-Based Risk Reduction: The Bootheel Heart Health Project." *American Journal of Public Health* 86:206–13.

Bucher, Heiner E., and David R. Ragland. 1995. "Socioeconomic Indicators and Mortality from Coronary Heart Disease and Cancer: A Twenty-two-Year Follow-up of Middle-Aged Men." *American Journal of Public Health* 85:1231–36.

Centers for Disease Control. 1987. *Smoking, Tobacco, and Health: A Fact Book.* Rockville, MD: U.S. Department of Health and Human Services.

Coburn, David, and Clyde R. Pope. 1974. "Socioeconomic Status and Preventive Health Behaviour." *Journal of Health and Social Behavior* 15:67–78.

Diez-Roux, Ana V., F. Javier Nieto, Herman A. Tyroler, Larry D. Crum, and Moyses Szklo. 1995. "Social Inequalities and Atherosclerosis." *American Journal of Epidemiology* 141 (10): 960–72.

Douglas, Stratford. 1998. "The Duration of the Smoking Habit." *Economic Inquiry* 36:49–64.

Escobedo, Luis G., and John P. Peddicord. 1996. "Smoking Prevalence in US Birth Cohorts: The Influence of Gender and Education." *American Journal of Public Health* 86:231–36.

Ettner, Susan L. 1996. "New Evidence on the Relationship between Income and Health." *Journal of Health Economics* 15:67–85.

Farrell, Phillip, and Victor R. Fuchs. 1982. "Schooling and Health: The Cigarette Connection." *Journal of Health Economics* 1:217–30.

Feinstein, Jonathan S. 1993. "The Relationship between Socioeconomic Status and Health: A Review of the Literature." *Milbank Memorial Fund Quarterly* 71:279–322.

Feldman, Jacob J., Diane M. Makuc, Joel C. Kleinman, and Joan Cornoni-Huntley. 1989. "National Trends in Educational Differentials in Mortality." *American Journal of Epidemiology* 133:1246–55.

Fuchs, Victor R. 1982. "Time Preferences and Health: An Exploratory Study." In *Economic Aspects of Health,* edited by Victor Fuchs, 93–120. Chicago: University of Chicago Press.

Glassman, Alexander H., John E. Helzer, and Lirio S. Covey. 1990. "Smoking, Smoking Cessation, and Major Depression." *Journal of the American Medical Association* 264:1546–49.

Grossman, Michael, and Robert Kaestner. 1997. "The Effects of Education on Health." In *Social Benefits,* edited by Jere R. Behrman and N. Stacey, 69–123. Ann Arbor: University of Michigan Press.

Hamilton, James L. 1972. "The Demand for Cigarettes: Advertising, the Health Scare, and the Cigarette Advertising Ban." *Review of Economics and Statistics* 54:401–11.

Ippolito, Richard A. 1979. *Staff Report on Consumer Responses to Cigarette Health Information.* Washington, DC: Government Printing Office.

Jaccard, James, Richard Turrisi, and Choi K. Wan. 1990. *Interaction Effects in Multiple Regression.* Paper no. 07–072, Sage University Paper series on Quantitative Applications in the Social Sciences. Newbury Park, CA.

Jarvis, M. J. 1995. "Gender Differences in Smoking Cessation: Real or Myth?" *Tobacco Control* 3:324–28.

Kenkel, Donald S. 1991. "Health Behavior, Health Knowledge, and Schooling." *Journal of Political Economy* 99:287–305.

Kitagawa, Evelyn, and Philip M. Hauser. 1973. *Differential Mortality in the U.S.* Cambridge, MA: Harvard University Press.

Lewit, Eugene M., Douglas Coate, and Michael Grossman. 1981. "The Effects of Government Regulation on Teenage Smoking." *Journal of Law and Economics* 24:545–69.

Marbella, Anne M., Peter M. Layde, and Patrick Remington. 1995. "Desire and Efforts to Quit Smoking among Cigarette Smokers in Wisconsin." *Wisconsin Medical Journal* (November): 617–20.

Matthews, Karen A., Sheryl F. Kelsey, Elaine N. Meilahn, Lewis H. Kuller, and Rena R. Wing. 1989. "Educational Attainment and Behavioral and Biologic Risk Factors for Coronary Heart Disease in Middle-Aged Women." *American Journal of Epidemiology* 129:1132–44.

Nevid, J. S., R. A. Javier, and J. L. Moulton. 1996. "Factors Predicting Participant Attrition in a Community-Based, Culturally-Specific Smoking-Cessation Program for Hispanic Smokers." *Health Psychology* 15 (3): 226–29.

O'Loughlin, J., G. Paradis, L. Renaud, G. Meshefedjian, and T. Barnett. 1997. "The Yes, I Can Quit Smoking Course — Does It Help Women in a Low-Income Community Quit?" *Journal of Community Health* 22 (6): 451–68.

Patterson, Ruth E., Alan R. Kristal, and Emily White. 1996. "Do Beliefs,

Knowledge, and Perceived Norms about Diet and Cancer Predict Dietary Change?" *American Journal of Public Health* 86:1394–1400.

Perlmutter, Marion. 1986. "A Life-Span View of Memory." In *Life-Span Development and Behavior,* edited by P. B. Baltes, D. L. Featherman, and R. M. Lerner, 272–307. Hillsdale, NJ: Lawrence Erlbaum.

Rakowski, William, M. Julius, Thomas Hickey, Lois Verbrugge, and Jeffrey Halter. 1987. "Correlates of Preventive Health Behavior in Late Life." *Research in Aging* 9:331–55.

Ransford, A. Edward. 1986. "Race, Heart Disease Worry, and Health Protective Behavior." *Social Science and Medicine* 22 (12): 1355–62.

Rogers, Richard G., Charles B. Nam, and Robert A. Hummer. 1995. "Demographic and Socioeconomic Links to Cigarette Smoking." *Social Biology* 42:1–21.

Ross, Catherine E,. and Chia-ling Wu. 1995. "The Links between Education and Health." *American Sociological Review* 60:719–45.

———. 1996. "Education, Age, and the Cumulative Advantage of Health." *Journal of Health and Social Behavior* 37:104–20.

Salthouse, Timothy A. 1991. *Theoretical Perspectives on Cognitive Aging.* Hillsdale, NJ: Lawrence Erlbaum.

Salthouse, Timothy A. 1996. "The Processing-Speed Theory of Adult Age Differences in Cognition." *Psychological Review* 103:403–48.

Samet, Jonathan M. 1992. "The Health Benefits of Smoking Cessation." *Medical Clinics of North America* 76 (2): 399–414.

Schneider, Lynne, Benjamin Klein, and Kevin M. Murphy. 1981. "Governmental Regulation of Cigarette Health Information." *Journal of Law and Economics* 24:575–612.

Schultz, Theodore W. 1975. "The Value of the Ability to Deal with Disequilibria." *Journal of Economic Literature* 13 (3): 827–46.

Strecher, V. J., M. W. Kreuter, and S. C. Kobrin. 1995. "Do Cigarette Smokers Have Unrealistic Perceptions of Their Heart Attack, Cancer, and Stroke Risks?" *Journal of Behavioral Medicine* 18 (1): 45–54.

Syme, S. Leonard, and Lisa F. Berkman. 1976. "Social Class, Susceptibility, and Sickness." *American Journal of Epidemiology* 104:1–8.

Umberson, Debra. 1987. "Family Status and Health Behaviors: Social Control as a Dimension of Social Integration." *Journal of Health and Social Behavior* 28:306–19.

U.S. Department of Health and Human Services. 1989. *Reducing the Health Consequences of Smoking: Twenty-five Years of Progress—A Report of the Surgeon General.* Paper no. CDC-89:8411. Washington, DC: U.S. Department of Health and Human Services.

———. 1990. *The Health Benefits of Smoking Cessation—A Report of the Surgeon General.* Paper no. CDC-90:8416. Washington, DC: U.S. Department of Health and Human Services.

———. 1994. *National Household Survey on Drug Abuse: Population Estimates, 1993.* Paper no. (SMA) 94-3017. Rockville, MD: U.S. Department of Health and Human Services.

Wagenknecht, Lynne E., Laura L. Perkins, Gary R. Cutler, Stephen Sidney, Gregory L. Burke, Teri A. Manolia, David R. Jacobs, Kiang Liu, Gary D. Friedman, Glenn H. Hughes, and Stephen B. Hulley. 1990. "Cigarette Smoking Is Strongly Related to Education Status: The CARDIA Study." *Preventive Medicine* 19:158–69.

Welch, Finis. 1970. "Education and Production." *Journal of Political Economy* 78:35–59.

Wenger, N. K. 1995. "Hypertension and Other Cardiovascular Factors in Women." *American Journal of Hypertension* 8 (12): S94–99.

Winkleby, Marilyn A., Darius E. Jatulis, Erica Frank, and Stephen P. Fortmann. 1992. "Socioeconomic Status and Health: How Education, Income, and Occupation Contribute to Risk Factors for Cardiovascular Disease." *American Journal of Public Health* 82:816–20.

Winkleby, Marilyn A., C. Barr Taylor, Darius E. Jatulis, and Stephen P. Fortmann. 1996. "The Long-Term Effects of a Cardiovascular Disease Prevention Trial: The Stanford Five-City Project." *American Journal of Public Health* 86:1773–79.

Wister, Andrew V. 1996. "The Effects of Socioeconomic Status on Exercise and Smoking." *Journal of Aging and Health* 8:467–88.

Wray, Linda A., A. Regula Herzog, Robert J. Willis, and Robert B. Wallace. 1996. "Cognitive Ability, Incident Health Events, and Other Life Changes." Paper presented at the F. Thomas Juster Symposium, December 13–14, Ann Arbor, MI.

The Association of Influenza Vaccine Receipt with Health and Economic Expectations among Elders: The AHEAD Study

Robert B. Wallace, Sara Nichols,
and Michael D. Hurd

Preventive interventions take many forms. They may be environmental modifications in which no personal behavior is necessary to enjoy the benefits, such as the pasteurization of milk. Other interventions are largely or solely determined by individual behavior and preferences, including smoking cigarettes, exercise habits, dietary intake, and personal risk-taking activities. However, social, cultural, and educational factors bear on these behaviors in substantial ways. Another type of preventive intervention is the clinical intervention, discretionary preventive maneuvers that are administered by or under the aegis of health professionals, such as immunizations, disease screening, and professional counseling. The determinants of utilizing these interventions are also complex, as they may be requested or suggested by both providers and patients or even administratively mandated in certain situations. One particular clinical preventive intervention, the receipt of influenza immunization, is the subject of this essay.

With respect to older adults, there is a broad range of clinical interventions recommended by various expert groups. In brief, influenza vaccine is one of several vaccines recommended for adults (Plichta 1996; Centers for Disease Control and Prevention 1994). It is particularly indicated for adults with chronic conditions that predispose to poor health outcomes when viral influenza occurs and for all persons over sixty-five years of age. It decreases the frequency and severity of viral influenza as well as some of the secondary bacterial infections and excess mortality that are particularly prominent among older adults during influenza outbreaks, both in the community and within chronic care institutions.

The Assets and Health Dynamics among the Oldest Old (AHEAD) study, a multiwave, representative sample of Americans seventy years and older, offers the opportunity to study the determinants and correlates of receipt of certain discretionary preventive interventions in national context. AHEAD is an interdisciplinary study of the dynamics of health, social, and economic transitions in the oldest old and the interactions among them. It provides longitudinal data through biennial surveys on transitions in health status and other life domains such as economic well-being, employment, marital and family status, and reliance on public and private support systems (Soldo et al. 1997). Among the health measures available, AHEAD wave 2 specifically sought self-reports of receipt of influenza immunization as well as several other preventive interventions. This, along with a variety of demographic, health, and related factors (see the following) allows a detailed exploration of the correlates of influenza vaccine use in the United States.

In addition to these health and health-related factors, the inclusion of economic variables in AHEAD allowed an additional approach to understanding the factors associated with the receipt of influenza vaccine. Many economic models are based on forward-looking behavior by individuals. The basic premise is that, in a population, predicting future economic or other behaviors in the face of uncertainty, such as consumption or saving of personal resources, can be approximated by querying individuals about their expectations of future events related to the outcome(s) of interest (Hurd and McGarry 1995). In this study we applied two of these personal expectations to our analytic models in order to explore whether they added explanatory power to vaccine receipt.

Methods

The data used in this analysis were derived from the wave 2 interview of AHEAD, conducted in 1995 and 1996. At the time of analysis, data were only partially edited and were not yet available for public release. Therefore, the findings reported here must be regarded as preliminary and subject to some alteration when further refined data releases occur. All variables were specified in advance of the analysis. Only noninstitutionalized persons were included as influenza vaccine may be administered to those in long-term care settings as a matter of policy. After determining the bivariate distributions of the study variables, we used logistic regression, with receipt of influenza vaccine in the year prior to survey as the dependent variable, to determine the relation between this receipt and several social, demographic, and health measures as well as two personal expectations variables derived from the economics section of the instrument. Those variables with a bivariate significance level of $p < 0.10$ were entered into multivariate logistic regression models; the final models are presented subsequently. There was relatively little missing data for most variables with the exception of the expectations items themselves, where up to 10 percent of the respondents did not answer these items. Those who did not respond to these items were excluded from the models, as were individuals with proxy interviews. Also, since individuals with any missing study variables are eliminated from multivariate models and no imputations were included, the final models had a somewhat reduced sample size, from 5,776 to 4,825. Thus, findings may not be fully representative of the sampled population. Logistic models were screened for first and second order interactions among independent variables; none was found. The models were performed without adjustment for sample weights.

The analytical framework used is one that has been commonly used to explore the predictors of access to medical care (Aday and Andersen 1974). In this construct, sets of predisposing, enabling, and need factors were explored as predictors of vaccine receipt, followed by the personal expectations. *Predisposing* variables included age (years); educational attainment (years); gender; marital status (married/not married); and ethnic group (white, African American, and other); *Resources and other enabling variables* included net economic worth (in dollars, $\log_{10}$ transformed) and two measures of medical care utilization: number of annual physician visits in the past year and any prior nursing home admission (yes/no). *Need-related factors* included overall self-perceived health status (excellent, very good, good, fair, poor); a history of any of seven major medical conditions (cancer, lung conditions, heart conditions, stroke, diabetes mellitus, arthritis, and high blood pressure); two measures of physical disability (use of any equipment or device to walk or difficulty walking up several flights of stairs); one hygienic behavior (currently smoking cigarettes); and a high depressive symptom scale score (upper quartile of the Center for Epidemiologic Studies Depression scale).

In addition, two personal expectations relevant to health were chosen from several available. Subjects were queried, using an analog scale, to denote the probability that they would be alive in five years and the probability that an illness would occur in the future that would deplete savings. Because of digit preference and the tendency to note a probability of 0.5, these two variables were defined categorically, based on examination of the distributions, as highest vs. lowest quartile and highest vs. lowest tertile of responses, respectively.

Results

Table 1 shows a list and a summary of a bivariate relations between the independent variables noted here and the odds of having received influenza vaccine. Among the predisposing variables, age, educational attainment, and ethnic group status were not associated with vaccine receipt. In contrast, men and those currently married were more likely to report receipt of influenza immunization. Among the resources and enabling characteristics, having a higher net economic worth and a higher number of physician visits were associated with increased likelihood of vaccine receipt. Having been in a nursing home was not associated with receipt of vaccine, but the number of persons was relatively small compared to the other analytic categories. Among the need-related variables, having a good vs. excellent health status was associated with greater vaccine receipt, as was a history of heart and lung conditions, arthritis, and high blood pressure, while no association was found for cancer, stroke, and diabetes. One of the two measures of disability, having difficulty walking up several flights of stairs, was positively associated with vaccine receipt, while those who currently smoked cigarettes were negatively associated. In the case of the two personal expectations, those who placed themselves in the highest quartile of expecting to live five or more years and those in the highest tertile of expectation of a savings-depleting illness were both less likely to report receiving vaccine.

Table 2 shows the final logistic regression models for estimating the odds of influenza vaccine receipt. The two models were run the same way except that each contained only one of the expectation variables, since some collinearity was expected. In addition, for the regression models we created a variable that counted the number of diseases reported from the list of seven shown in table 1. In model 1 (including the self-reported probability of surviving five years), women were less likely to receive vaccine, and there were positive associations with net worth, number of physician visits, and number of diseases. Those who smoked cigarettes or who expressed a high likelihood of surviving for the next five years were less likely to have received the vaccine. In model 2, the findings were basically the same. Those specifying a high probability of having an illness that would deplete savings were less likely to report receiving the vaccine.

TABLE 1. Initial Variables Explored as Predictor Variables for Receipt of Influenza Vaccine[a]

	Bivariate Significance ($p < 0.10$)
Predisposing Variables	
1. Age	NS
2. Educational attainment	NS
3. Gender (M/F)	+
4. Marital status	+
5. Ethnic group	NS
Resources and Enabling Characteristics	
6. Log of net worth	+
7. Number of annual physician visits	+
8. Prior nursing home admission	NS
Need-Related Factors	
9. Self-perceived health status	
VG* vs. Exc	NS
G vs. Exc	+
F vs. Exc	NS
P vs. Exc	NS
10. History of various illnesses	
Cancer	NS
Lung condition	+
Heart condition	+
Stroke	NS
Diabetes	NS
Arthritis	+
High blood pressure	+
11. Physical disability	
Use of equipment to walk	NS
Difficulty walking up several flights	+
12. Currently smoking cigarettes	−
13. Depressive symptom scale	NS
Personal Expectations	
14. Expect to live more than five years (probability of highest vs. lowest quartile)	−
15. Expect illness to deplete savings (probability of highest vs. lowest tertile)	−

Source: Authors' calculations from AHEAD Wave 2.

[a]See text for definition of variables.

+ = positive association ($p < 0.0$) with receipt of intervention.

− = negative association ($p < 0.1$) with receipt of intervention.

NS = no association.

*Exc = excellent, VG = very good, G = good, F = fair, and P = poor.

TABLE 2. Final Logistic Regression Models for Receipt of Influenza Vaccine in the Year Prior to Survey

1. Model with probability of survival variable

Variables	Odds Ratio	Significance
Female gender	0.74	0.003
Number of physician visits	1.04	0.001
Log_{10} net worth	1.42	0.001
Current smoker	0.55	0.001
Number of diseases	1.13	0.001
Probability of surviving 5 yrs. (high vs. low quartile)	0.76	0.055

2. Model with probability of illness depleting savings

Variables	Odds Ratio	Significance
Female gender	0.73	0.005
Number of physician visits	1.02	0.001
Log_{10} net worth	1.43	0.001
Current smoker	0.46	0.001
Number of diseases	1.13	0.001
Probability of illness depletion of savings (high vs. low tertile)	0.76	0.021

Source: Authors' calculations from AHEAD Wave 2.

Discussion

Our findings offer, to our knowledge, a new approach to understanding preventive behavior among older persons. Influenza vaccine is of proven efficacy and is recommended for all persons over sixty-five years of age (Centers for Disease Control and Prevention 1994). Yet, there is substantial underutilization of this and other vaccines recommended for adults (American College of Physicians 1994). The reasons for such underutilization are complex and not fully understood. Suggestions have included lack of access to immunization services, underappreciation of the clinical and public health impact of the infections, lack of reimbursement for vaccine administration, and ambiguity over vaccine efficacy (Fedson 1994). With respect to immunization practices relevant to older persons, substantial variation in practice patterns has been demonstrated among physicians (Majeroni et al. 1993), and varying beliefs on susceptibility to influenza among elders have been reported (Gianino et al. 1996), factors that may help less than complete utilization.

This study did not explore personal beliefs about influenza susceptibility per se but explored economic expectations relevant to the issue. We found, after controlling for a variety of vaccine utilization factors, that the two expectations studied both related to concurrent vaccine receipt. Those who had a high expectation of living five years or more were 25 percent less likely to have been vaccinated, even after controlling for several health status indicators. One apparent explanation is that this reflects an attitude of less vulnerability to health threats in general and possibly a lesser motivation to seek vaccine. Another possibility is that longer expected survivorship was associated with a need to conserve personal resources, causing an economic disincentive to seek immunization even after controlling for a detailed measure of economic means — net worth. This disincentive, if correct, may be operating despite the availability of free vaccine through Medicare since 1993 ("Race-specific" 1995).

This economic interpretation is also consistent with the finding that those with a high expectation of having an illness that would deplete savings were also 25 percent less likely to have received vaccine. Fear of depleting resources might be a powerful incentive to avoid discretionary medical spending, and even though the vaccine may be available without cost, this may not have been widely known or the co-payment costs of a medical visit may have been additionally anticipated. Among other possible explanations for the observed effect of expecting a savings-depleting illness is an abiding pessimism that preventives will be of no substantial value. However, whether this reflects pessimism or not, it is also possible that this taps some dimension of health status and prognosis not tapped in the variety of other health items. None of these explanations can be established from this study.

Other factors explored in relation to vaccine receipt were of interest, and these will be contrasted with the Current Beneficiary Survey (CBS), which was conducted on Medicare recipients in 1992, before influenza vaccine was a specific Medicare benefit ($N \sim 9{,}000$) (Mark and Paramore 1996). Older age was associated with higher vaccine receipt in the CBS but not in AHEAD. In AHEAD, men were more likely to have received vaccine, but there were no gender differences in the CBS. In both surveys, at least in bivariate analyses, those married were more likely to receive vaccine. In the CBS, Hispanics were less likely to have received vaccine, but no ethnic group effect was found in AHEAD.

When considering resources and other enabling characteristics, CBS participants with incomes over $10,000 reported increased vaccine use. In AHEAD, personal net worth, perhaps a more complete assessment of economic resources, was the analytic variable, but the result was similar — higher net worth levels were associated with higher vaccine receipt. This highlights the fact that even when vaccine is available without cost, economic factors continue to be a determinant of vaccine receipt, and this suggests that further investigation of economic factors would be of value. Also, in the CBS, having a regular source of medical care was associated with increased vaccine receipt, and in AHEAD a similar but not identical measure, annual number of physician visits, showed a similar association. In AHEAD, prior nursing home admission was not associated with vaccine receipt; this was not explored in the CBS. This finding was perhaps unexpected, as most long-term-care institutions have policies favoring immunization.

Among the need-related factors, both studies showed evidence that less than excellent health status was associated with higher vaccine use, in keeping with the recommendation to apply influenza vaccine to those with chronic illnesses (American College of Physicians 1994). With respect to specific conditions, AHEAD found increased vaccine receipt among those with heart, lung, hypertensive, and arthritic conditions, and in multivariate analysis, the number of conditions among seven was associated with increased receipt. The CBS analyzed cancer history only, and as with AHEAD, no significant association was found. In keeping with the general health status findings, one measure of physical disability, difficulty in climbing several flights of stairs, was also associated in bivariate but not multivariate analyses with increased vaccine use.

Two additional health status factors were explored in AHEAD but not in the CBS. Current cigarette smoking was associated in multivariate analyses with decreased receipt of vaccine, particularly unfortunate because of the increased risk of untoward health consequences of influenza among those with smoking-related conditions. Cigarette smoking may reflect resistance to participating in preventive measures, leading to lesser use of available clinical preventive services. It may also reflect a perception that the smoker will be treated differently in the health care system. In any case, current smoking may serve as an empirical risk factor for decreased vaccine use and of increased targeting by immunization programs. We also explored a depressive symptom score to assess the possibility that negative affect may be a sign of reduced prevention-seeking behavior; however, no association was found.

Many of the factors studied in both AHEAD and the CBS had similar findings, but some differences did occur. This was not unexpected, since the CBS was done three years earlier and took place before Medicare began to pay for influenza vaccine. Also, there were often substantial differences in item content and structure. For example, the CBS explored whether the respondent was enrolled in a Medicare HMO, while AHEAD had more health and function status items and more detailed personal and family economic data. Many other possible correlates of vaccine receipt were not studied by either survey, such as type of transportation availability, perceived susceptibility to influenza infection, and medical contraindications to influenza immunization.

The determinants of use of discretionary clinical preventive maneuvers, those that require health professional administration, are complex and relate both to the patient and professional behavior as well as to the organizational, fiscal, and social settings wherein preventive care takes place. Nevertheless, from the perspective of the community-dwelling elder, it appears that examining personal economic expectations may lead to a greater understanding of reasons for failure to receive an intervention that might reduce discomfort and even be lifesaving.

REFERENCES

Aday L. A., and R. M. Andersen. 1974. A framework for the study of access to medical care. *Health Service Research* 9:208–20.

American College of Physicians. 1994. Task Force on Adult Immunization/ Infectious Disease Society of America. In *Guide for Adult Immunization.* 3d ed. Philadelphia: American College of Physicians.

Centers for Disease Control and Prevention. 1994. Prevention and control of influenza. Part 1: Vaccines — Recommendations of the Advisory Committee on Immunization Practices. *Morbidity and Mortality Weekly Report* 43: (no. RR-9).

Fedson, D. 1994. Adult immunization: Summary of the National Vaccine Advisory Committee report. *Journal of the American Medical Association* 272:1133–37.

Gianino, C. A., K. Corazzini, W. T. Tseng, and J. P. Richardson. 1996. Factors affecting influenza vaccination among attendees at a senior center. *Maryland Medical Journal* 45:27–42.

Hurd, M. D., and K. McGarry. 1995. Evaluation of the subjective probabilities of survival in the Health and Retirement Study. *Journal of Human Resources* 30:S268–91.

Majeroni, B. A., J. Karuza, C. Wade, M. McCreadie, and E. Calkins. 1993. Gender of physicians and preventive care for community-based adults. *Journal of the American Board of Family Practice* 6:359–65.

Mark, T. L., and L. C. Paramore. 1996. Pneumococcal pneumonia and influenza vaccination: Access to and use by US Hispanic Medicare beneficiaries. *American Journal of Public Health* 86:1545–50.

Plichta, A. M. 1996. Immunization: Protecting older adults from infectious disease. *Geriatrics* 51:47–52.

Race-specific differences in influenza vaccination levels among Medicare beneficiaries — United States, 1993. 1995. *Morbidity and Mortality Weekly Report* 44:24–27.

Soldo, Beth J., Michael D. Hurd, Willard L. Rodgers, and Robert B. Wallace. 1997. "Asset and Health Dynamics Among the Oldest Old: An Overview of the AHEAD Study." *Journals of Gerontology: Social Sciences* 52B(special issue): 1–20.

Intergenerational Transfers: Blood, Marriage, and Gender Effects on Household Decisions

Beth J. Soldo, Douglas A. Wolf,
and John C. Henretta

In the United States the co-residence of an adult child with elderly parents is relatively rare, even at ages eighty-five and over (U.S. Bureau of the Census 1996). Norms supporting the residential independence of single-generation families remain strong in spite of seemingly countervailing forces (Macunovich et al. 1995). Improvements in old age survivorship (Manton and Stallard 1996), low levels of wealth, especially for minorities (Smith 1997), and high out-of-pocket health care costs for the elderly (Moon and Mulvey 1995) might be expected to encourage house sharing of elderly parents and their middle-aged children. Yet recent cross-sectional estimates indicate that only about 7 percent of adult children with a surviving parent co-reside while only one in five elderly parents lives with an adult child (Freedman et al. 1991).

Despite the low prevalence of multigenerational living arrangements, monitoring trends in household structure yields insights into the imprint of demographic processes on family structures (Wolf 1994) and the rhythms of the life-cycle dependency (Marks 1996). For sociologists, shared living arrangements also suggest family function and cohesion (Goldscheider and Goldscheider 1989; Goldscheider and Waite 1991) as well as the social isolation of the elderly (Crimmins and Ingegneri 1990). Co-residence with adult kin is a distinctively private sector response to old age dependency (Michael, Fuchs, and Scott 1980; Kotlikoff and Morris 1990) that may substitute for financial assistance (Rosenzweig and Wolpin 1993) or presage caregiving (Stern 1995).

This chapter considers co-residence in the broad context of intergenerational transfers (Soldo and Hill 1993; Couch, Daly, and Wolf 1995). From this perspective, co-residence is understood as an exchange of resources — in this case, residential space — across generations of kin, linked by blood and marriage. Models of intergenerational transfers typically assume that these behaviors result from explicit consideration of all possible options. Each potential choice is characterized by a distinctive profile of household goods including, among other things, consumption, domestic services, personal care, companionship, recreation, security, privacy, autonomy, power, and authority (Burch and Matthews 1987). Choosing an option from the available set involves weighing trade-offs across alternative levels of these household goods. Independent living, which affords the most privacy and autonomy, is assumed to be the preferred arrangement but entails foregone economies of scale, a possible loss of companionship, and limited access of services. Choices are constrained by opportunities available for co-residence — the composition of the set of possible living arrangements — and by the preferences and resources of each individual child and his or her older parents as they evaluate alternatives (see, e.g., Schwartz, Danziger, and Smolensky 1984). The outcome observed is assumed to result from choices in which each party to the decision achieves the highest possible level of well-being, given the options available. When a possible donor of residential space is married, the decision-making process also involves consideration of the potential costs and benefits for other kin, including the spouse's surviving parents who also may be at risk for living with the couple. Unlike the decision to allocate time or financial resources to family members, the decision to share space with a relative is unambiguously a joint decision of the husband and wife.[1]

Estimating behavioral models of intergenerational transfers requires extensive microdata on affinal and consanguineal kin. Most surveys contain far more detail about the respondent than about his or her immediate family and even less about the respondent's older and younger kin living elsewhere. Surveys of the elderly, for example, usually measure the health status and economic resources of older parents but largely neglect competing claims on the resources of their adult children. Surveys of younger age groups provide information on the economic circumstances or transitional situations of adult children, while characteristics of their parents as potential providers of housing or other services are largely unavailable or poorly measured (DaVanzo and Goldscheider 1987).

Extensive data on ascending and descending generations within both the husband's and the wife's families are required to fully account for claims on the resources of middle-aged adults. The Health and Retirement Study (Juster and Suzman 1995) provides many of these needed data elements for a large representative panel of the birth cohorts of 1931–41. At a point in the life cycle when the prevalence of the four-generation family peaks (Soldo 1996), detailed family rosters in HRS provide individual-level data on key sociodemographic attributes of children, siblings, and elderly parents of respondents and their spouses (Soldo and Hill 1995).

This study examines co-residence between married adult children and their elderly unmarried mothers. By focusing on this type of dyad, we mirror prior research, examining the living arrangements of older unmarried women who are at greatest risk for co-residing with adult offspring (Chevan and Korson 1972; Michael, Fuchs, and Scott 1980; Cooney 1989; Wolf and Soldo 1988). We extend the existing literature by explicitly representing the "competition" for residential space between the wife's and the husband's unmarried mothers.

Correlates of Shared Living Arrangements

Because we conceptualize shared living arrangements as a choice resulting from a joint decision involving all potential co-resident kin, we require data representing the decision criteria of each family member to model those choices. Theory and past research on the living arrangements of the elderly suggest a number of such criteria. From the perspective of an older parent, the most important of these may be functional capacity. Personal care compensates for limitations in self-care capacity and is typically within the purview of younger kin. Earlier research indicate that older parents with functional limitations are far more likely to live with kin than functionally independent elderly (Wolf 1984, 1990; Bishop 1986; Soldo, Wolf, and Agree 1990).

The overall size and composition of the family group shape the set of potential outcomes, having a structural effect on residential arrangements. From the older person's perspective, the larger the family size, the more opportunities there are for co-residence. From a child's vantage point, however, additional siblings are likely to lower any single child's probability of co-residing, depending on the characteristics of the siblings. Analyses that depict each child within a family as a potential donor demonstrate the effects of sisters on the allocation of responsibility for elderly parents across the sibship. Having younger sisters, for example, reduces a given child's probability of co-residing with a parent (Wolf and Soldo 1988). Individuals with more sisters are less likely to provide care to a parent and contribute fewer hours of active caregiving (Wolf, Freedman, and Soldo 1997). Observed racial and ethnic differences in family size, as well as in education, also may account for higher proportions of multigenerational households among blacks and Hispanics (Aquilino 1990; Burr and Mutchler 1992; Zsembik 1993).

A middle-aged couple has potentially up to four opportunities for co-residing with an unmarried elderly parent.[2] Each spouse's unmarried parent(s) may require assistance, and each may have one or more other children — including other married children — with whom he or she could potentially co-reside. The matrix of interlocking family network theoretically relevant to the choice of a living arrangement may be quite extensive, including siblings, spouses of siblings, and their children. Such complexities have rarely been addressed, although they are the subject of several studies of living arrangements in Japan (Hirosima 1987, 1988), where it is common for a middle-aged couple to live with the son's mother. Kojima (1990) also has modeled the married couple's decision to co-reside with either spouse's mother. His results indicate that characteristics of both the husband and wife (birth order, family size), along with those of the elderly mothers (marital and health status), are important predictors of co-residence.

Of particular interest in this essay are the ways in which gender and familial ties based on blood rather than marriage mediate decisions about living with an elderly parent. The effect of being female has such a marked effect on the probability of assisting kin of any age that Hagestad (1986) and others have described women as the "kin keepers" of the U.S. family. The process by which women are recruited to this important social function may be self-sustaining to the extent that intergenerational transfers engender reciprocity (Henretta et al. 1997) and, through the demonstration of familial obligation and caring (Stark 1995), instill a stronger sense of family responsibility in daughters.

A married woman typically is responsible for maintaining contact not only with her own family but also with her husband's. Her more intimate knowledge of the lives and needs of elderly kin on both sides of the family may give wives a greater voice in directing flows of support across her and her husband's extended families. The mother-daughter axis is generally recognized as being far more important than a married woman's bond with her mother-in-law (Rossi and Rossi 1990; Merrill 1993). No doubt there are psychological reasons for this, including, perhaps, inherent competition between a husband's wife and his mother. But the mother-daughter bond also may be stronger by virtue of the longer and more varied life history an adult daughter has in common with her own mother. Simply because of the care and intimacies they shared when the mother was caring for her young daughter, the reduced privacy of multigenerational households may be more tolerable for an adult daughter than for a daughter-in-law. Finally, the biologic linkage of mother to daughter is enduring, while the linkage of daughter-in-law to mother-in-law is conditional on the continuation of the son's marriage. Other things being equal, we would expect the mother-daughter bond to be more heartfelt and durable, and, thus, deciding whether to live with the wife's or the husband's mother would be resolved in favor of the wife's mother.

Data and Methods

Identifying Adult Children at Risk for Co-residence

The Health and Retirement Study (HRS) is a panel survey of the U.S. noninstitutionalized population born between 1931 and 1941. Respondents were screened from an area sample of approximately 70,000 households (Heeringa and Connor 1995). Wave 1 data were collected in 1992, wave 2 data in 1994. This research utilized the most recent versions then available: the wave 1 public release file and the wave 2 beta file. The HRS design includes interviews with respondents and their spouses or partners, regardless of age. In wave 1, interviews were completed with 12,652 respondents from 7,702 households. The wave 2 beta release includes 11,596 individual interviews: 10,692 self-interviews, 175 proxies for deceased sample members, 658 proxies for living panel members, 66 interviews with respondents not included in wave 1, and 5 that are unclassified in the beta release of the data. Excluding the new and unclassified interviews, 91 percent of wave 1 respondents are included in the wave 2 beta version.

Data for the analysis presented here are drawn from both waves of HRS though the sample is defined as a wave 2 cross-sectional sample. In the final analysis we include only wave 2 married (or partnered) households in which the sampled couple had one or more unmarried mothers (our rationale for this restriction is described subsequently). We exclude single HRS respondents because of our interest in understanding the potential *intra*generational competition between the husband's and the wife's parents for co-residence with their married middle-aged adult children. In wave 2 there are 3,011 married and opposite-sex partnered households with one to four living parents, married or unmarried.[3] Each of these couples is theoretically at risk for living with an older parent.

Table 1 shows the distribution of couples with one or more living parents by the marital status of the wife's and husband's parents. Shown in the last column is the count of parents observed in wave 2 as living with their HRS offspring and the relative number of HRS couples co-residing with that type of parent. The topology of parental types in table 1 is not a mutually exclusive classification. It is common, for example, for the wife's parents to be alive and married to each other, while her slightly older husband has already lost his father and only his unmarried mother survives.

Very few middle-aged children have both biologic parents alive and married to each other (465 of the wives and 264 husbands). All but 3 of these 729 married adult children are residentially independent of their married parents. The remarriage of a previously divorced or widowed parent is relatively rare,[4] but a second marriage virtually precludes co-residence with adult children of the earlier marriage (only one case is observed in the sample represented in table 1).[5] Because the odds of co-residing with married or remarried parents approximate zero, couples are deleted from the analytic sample if *all* of their surviving parents are married or remarried (651 of the 3,011 couples observed in table 1).

There is an appreciable risk of a middle-aged couple co-residing with a parent only if one or the other spouse has an unmarried parent. Reflecting gender differentials in mortality and the average difference in age between husbands and wives, the 3,011 couples with surviving parents have far fewer unmarried fathers (389) than unmarried mothers (2,502). Without taking into account the competition from the other spouse's parent(s), it appears that middle-aged couples are more likely

TABLE 1. Number and Co-Residence Status of Living Parents, Married Couples:[a] HRS, Wave 2 (n = 3,011)

	Number[b]	Number (%) Co-Residing
Wife's Parents		
Both alive, married to each other	465	2 (0.4%)
Mother alive		
Unmarried	1,327	70 (5.3%)
Remarried	133	1 (0.8%)
Father alive		
Unmarried	224	11 (4.9%)
Remarried	161	0 (0.0%)
Husband's Parents		
Both alive, married to each other	264	1 (0.4%)
Mother alive		
Unmarried	1,175	23 (2.0%)
Remarried	89	0 (0.0%)
Father alive		
Unmarried	165	5 (3.0%)
Remarried	118	0 (0.0%)

Source: From HRS Wave 2.
[a]Includes opposite-sex partners.
[b]Counts are not mutually exclusive.

to co-reside with an unmarried mother (rather than an unmarried father) and with the wife's (rather than the husband's) unmarried parent. At its highest, the proportion of couples co-residing with a parent is only slightly more than 5 percent (5.3 percent of couples co-reside with the wife's unmarried mother).

Table 2 shows the implications of alternative definitions of couples at risk for living with an unmarried parent. All couples with at least one unmarried parent are included in the first row. In this subset, living with either the wife's or the husband's father is too rare to be modeled. Only 11 fathers of the wife and but 5 fathers of the husband co-reside. Even further restricting the at-risk definition to couples with one or more unmarried mothers (as shown in row 2) does not eliminate the need to estimate coefficients for the rare residential competition between the divorced parents of one spouse or between the one spouse's unmarried mother and the other's unmarried father.

Row 3 of table 2 shows the at-risk sample analyzed below. This sample is defined as those couples with at least one living unmarried mother *and* no unmarried fathers. Excluded are the 148 couples who would be subject to residential pressures from an unmarried mother *and* from a divorced or widowed father. Of the remaining 1,960 couples whose co-residential risks are analyzed subsequently, 875 (or 44.6 percent) are at risk for living only with the wife's unmarried mother and 732 (or 37.3 percent) for living only with the husband's unmarried mother. Three hundred fifty-three couples (or 18.0 percent of the analysis sample) are potentially at risk for living with the unmarried mother of either the husband or his wife. This group is of particular interest because of

TABLE 2.   Co-Residence Status for Alternative Definitions of "Risk" Set

	Number (%) with Co-Resident Unmarried Parent			
	Wife's Mother	Wife's Father	Husband's Mother	Husband's Father
Couples with 1+ unmarried parents ($n = 2,360$)	69 (2.9%)	11 (0.5%)	22 (0.9%)	5 (0.2%)
Couples with 1+ unmarried mother ($n = 2,126$)	69 (3.2%)	6 (0.3%)	22 (1.0%)	2 (0.1%)
Couples with 1+ unmarried mothers, no unmarried fathers ($n = 1,960$)	66 (3.3%)	—	22 (1.1%)	—
Only wife's mother ($n = 875$)	50 (5.7%)	—	—	—
Only husband's mother ($n = 732$)	—	—	13 (1.8%)	—
Both mothers ($n = 353$)	15 (4.2%)	—	8 (2.3%)	—

Source: From HRS Wave 2.

the potential competition between the two mothers-in-law for space in the household of their married adult children.

Variable Definitions

We model co-residence with an unmarried mother of the husband or the wife as a function of a limited set of variables describing the potential donor couple and the characteristics of their unmarried mothers. Our model allows for two types of generational competition. The couple's own children have a strong *inter*generational claim on their parents' resources. Presumably the larger a couple's family size, the more likely it is that the youngest child may still be living at home or that an older child has returned to his or her parent's home (Heer, Hodge, and Felson 1985; DaVanzo and Goldscheider 1987; Rosenzweig and Wolpin 1993). We measure potential demands on the resources of the HRS couple simply in terms of the count of the couple's children (own, step-, and adopted offspring of both spouses). We anticipate that the number of children will have a negative effect on the couple's probability of living with the husband's or the wife's unmarried mother.

To index *intra*generational competition, we include variables indicating whether the spouse's mother also is unmarried and her attributes. Among the 353 married couples in which both spouses' mothers are alive, these variables represent a direct measure of competition between the two mothers for co-residence with the couple. Another form of intragenerational competition is represented by a variable indicating whether the unmarried mother's former spouse (i.e., the wife's or husband's father) also is alive and therefore, by virtue of our sample selection criteria, remarried; that is, our analysis sample excludes couples in which either spouse's father is alive and *un*married. Thus, while some of the unmarried older mothers in our sample face competition from their son- or daughter-in-law's unmarried mother, none of them face competition from their own unmarried former spouse. The fact that their former spouse has remarried, however, may influence their child's willingness to provide co-residence. Finally, we include an indicator of whether the "other" spouse has married parents. Other things being equal, having married in-laws should increase the odds that the HRS couple will live with the other spouse's unmarried mother.

The couple's economic circumstances are represented in our analysis by two variables. The first is net wealth, calculated as the sum of reported current-market values of investment real estate, vehicles, farms or businesses, IRA accounts, equities, cash, CDs or bonds, and other real assets, minus outstanding debt. The second, the wife's years of schooling, is included as an indirect measure of the value of her time in market work.

Four variables measure attributes of unmarried elderly mothers. The mother's chronological age adjusts for the increasing risk of dependency with advanced age and is expected to have a positive effect on the probability of co-residing with her married HRS child. Whether the unmarried mother needs "help with basic personal needs like dressing, eating, or bathing" was assessed by her daughter or daughter-in-law.[6] This measure of personal care problems was coded as a dummy variable. Another binary variable indicates whether the unmarried mother's former husband is alive and remarried. In the cohorts of HRS parents, divorce was less likely than it is in successive cohorts; if a couple divorced, however, mothers typically were granted sole custody of their children. As adults these children are likely to have a stronger attachment to the parent who raised them (Goldscheider and Waite 1991). This bond may be even stronger if the noncustodial parent (usually the father) remarries and implicitly absolves children from the earlier marriage of responsibility for his well-being (Amato, Rezac, and Booth 1995).

Finally we include a simple count of each unmarried mother's number of surviving children other than the married HRS reference child. We expect that this measure of the potential substitution of other children as residential partners will reduce the odds that the unmarried mother will live with her married HRS offspring. In instances where both the husband and the wife have unmarried parents, two family structure variables are part of the model—one indicates the number of the husband's siblings and the other the count of the wife's. In combination, the two variables yield insight into the extent to which a couple considers differences in the size of their respective family networks in allocating scarce resources between their unmarried mothers.

The parental attributes just described enter our model in two forms. First, the set of mother's attributes is allowed to have "direct" or "own" effects on the log-odds of co-residence with their married son or daughter. Parental attributes also are allowed to have cross effects, that is, the existence, age, health, and other characteristics of a *husband*'s mother are allowed to influence the log-odds of co-residence with the *wife*'s mother, and vice versa. These cross effects only operate when both husband and wife have a living parent, at least one of whom is an unmarried mother.

The mean values of these predictor variables are shown in table 3. These summary statistics are shown separately for two overlapping groups, the 1,228 couples among which the wife's mother is alive and unmarried and the 1,085 couples in which the husband's mother is alive and unmarried (the 353 couples doubly at risk are found in both groups). The HRS couples used in our analysis have an average of 3.4 children and mean net worth in excess of $200,000. The wives have, on average, slightly more than twelve years of schooling.

Gender differences in age at marriage and age at death create circumstances that would seem to cancel each other in advantaging the unmarried mother of the husband or the wife. Somewhat more husbands than wives with an unmarried mother have unmarried mothers-in-law as well, creating circumstances of *intra*generational competition for co-residential space. Such circumstances would seem to favor the unmarried mother of the wife because of the strength of the mother-daughter bond. On the other hand, the husband's mother would seem to be favored in the 18.4 percent of couples in which both spouses have surviv-

TABLE 3.   Mean Value of Variables Describing Couples at Risk for Co-Residing with an Unmarried Mother: HRS Wave 2

Summary Statistics[a]	Couples at Risk for Co-Residence with	
	Wife's Mother	Husband's Mother
Characteristics of Couple		
Number of children	3.4	3.4
Wife's education (years)	12.5	12.4
Net wealth	$218,076	$206,102
Characteristics of Mother		
Personal care needs	22.3%	26.2%
Age	79.7	81.9
Former husband alive	2.9%	2.3%
Number of other children		
(husband's or wife's siblings)	3.0	2.8
Characteristics of Other Parent(s)		
Mother is alive, unmarried	28.7%	32.5%
Parent(s) are alive, married	12.1%	18.4%
Mother has personal care needs[b]	22.2%	16.2%
Mother's age[b]	80.7	77.4
Number of other children[b]	2.6	2.9
n	1,228	1,085

Source: From HRS Wave 2.

[a]Means for continuous variables, percentages for dummy variables. Means shown are conditional on reference mother being alive.

[b]Conditional means (percentages), including only cases where *other* mother is alive.

ing mothers but only the husband's mother is unmarried while the wife's mother is still married.

Because the middle-aged husband is typically older on average than his wife, his mother also is older on average than his unmarried mother-in-law (81.9 years versus 79.7 years); his mother also is somewhat more likely to have personal care needs (26.2 percent versus 22.3 percent). On average, the husband's unmarried mother has somewhat fewer children who could substitute for their married brother as a residential partner for their mother. If co-residence with an elderly parent were strictly a utilitarian decision, the smaller families and higher risk of the husband's unmarried mother having personal care limitations would give his mother the edge in claiming residential space in the household of her son and his wife.

The variables shown under the heading "Characteristics of other parent[s]" are the variables representing potential cross effects. Note that parental characteristics among the set of couples in which both spouses' mothers are alive differ from the corresponding characteristics in the overall sample. For example, while the average age of unmarried mothers of HRS husbands is 81.9, the average age of those same mothers in the subsample where both mothers are alive is slightly lower, 80.7. Compared with all mothers in the sample, the mothers of couples in which *both* mothers are alive are younger, healthier, and have fewer children.

Model Estimates

We use a trinomial logit framework, modified to account for whether the couple is at risk for living with the unmarried mother of only the husband, only the wife, or both. The probability of co-residence with mother j ($j = 1$ indicates the husband's mother, and $j = 2$ indicates the wife's mother) is given by equation (1), in which R_j is a dummy variable indicating that the couple is at risk of co-residence with the jth mother. The outcome $Y = 0$ corresponds to co-residence with

$$\Pr[Y = j] = \frac{R_j e^{\beta_j X}}{1 + R_1 e^{\beta_1 X} + R_2 e^{\beta_2 X}} \tag{1}$$

neither mother, with implicit parameter vector $\beta_0 = 0$. If only one of the spouse's mothers is at risk according to our criteria, equation (1) collapses to a binary logit expression. The dependent variable therefore represents three mutually exclusive categories: co-residence with neither mother, with only the wife's mother, or with only the husband's mother.[7] If, given the existence of both spouses' unmarried mothers, the null hypothesis $\beta_1 = \beta_2$ cannot be rejected, then the model is "symmetric": the effect of some attribute of the wife's mother on the log-odds of co-residence with the wife's mother is no different than the effect of the same characteristic of the husband's mother on the log-odds of co-residence with her. The presence in each array of alternative-specific attributes of variables representing the other parent(s)' existence and attributes makes our model a variant of "universal" or "mother" logit (McFadden 1981).

Results

The logistic regression coefficients for couples at risk for co-residing with either the wife's or the husband's unmarried parent are shown in table 4.[8] Our indicator of intergenerational competition — number of children — is found to significantly reduce only the odds of living with the wife's mother. Although we expected that having an unmarried mother-in-law would reduce the odds of living with one's own mother, the variable indicating the potential for intragenerational competition is not significant in either equation. Neither is the effect of one's spouse having married parents significant in either equation. The couple's wealth has a significant and negative effect only on the odds of living with the wife's mother, suggesting that co-residence is an acceptable substitute for a couple's financial transfers only to the wife's mother. A true transfer stream of the magnitude necessary to purchase residential independence for an elderly unmarried mother is likely to have a positive correlation with couple wealth.

Attributes of the at-risk mother are selectively significant and in the expected direction for both residential outcomes. Unmarried mothers with personal care problems have an increasing risk of living with their married son or daughter. The effect of having an unmarried mother with care problems is considerably stronger in predicting co-residence with the wife's unmarried mother and is significant only in the equation for co-residing with the wife's mother. Having other children as possible residential substitutes is negative and significant in both equations, although the difference between these coefficients in the two equations is not significant.

Predicted probabilities, based on the coefficients shown in table 4, can be used to display gradations in the risk of living with the husband's or the wife's unmarried mother when both mothers are at risk for co-residence. Predicted probabilities are shown for a baseline scenario in the first row of table 5. In this baseline scenario, the age of the unmarried mother of the husband is fixed at age eighty-two, the age of the wife's unmarried mother at age eighty, and the couple has three children. All other variables in this baseline scenario are fixed at zero, that is, neither

TABLE 4.   Estimated Model of Coresidence between Couples and Elderly Unmarried Mothers

Explanatory Variables	Wife's Mother	Husband's Mother	χ^{2a}
	Coefficients for Co-Residence with		
Intercept	−3.082	−9.647	2.605
	(1.835)[b]	(3.633)	
Number of children	−0.126	0.076	2.273
	(0.074)	(0.113)	
Wife's education	0.054	0.097	0.144
	(0.058)	(0.095)	
Net worth (in $100,000s)	−0.221	−0.171	0.091
	(0.095)**	(0.138)	
Characteristics of Potential Co-Resident Parent			
Personal care needs	0.548	0.433	0.039
	(0.296)*	(0.495)	
Age	0.007	0.061	1.382
	(0.021)	(0.040)	
Number of other children	−0.159	−0.384	2.019
	(0.066)**	(0.144)***	
Former husband is alive	0.885		
	(0.581)		
Characteristics of Other Parent(s)			
Mother is alive, unmarried	0.472	0.256	0.015
	(0.987)	(1.462)	
Parent(s) alive, married	0.006	−0.205	0.021
	(0.765)	(1.235)	
Mother's personal care needs	0.561	0.075	0.244
	(0.531)	(0.829)	
Mother's age	−0.012	−0.008	0.030
	(0.012)	(0.018)	
Number of other children	−0.018	0.155	1.133
	(0.107)	(0.122)	

*$p < 0.10$.   **$p < 0.05$.   ***$p < 0.01$.

[a]The χ^2 statistic permits a test of the hypothesis that the effects of the indicated variable on the log-odds of co-residence with the wife's mother and with the husband's mother are equal.

[b]Standard errors shown in parentheses.

mother has personal care problems and both the husband and the wife are only children. Under this condition where neither mother requires personal help, the unmarried mother of the wife is twice as likely to live with the HRS couple as the husband's mother (.038 versus .018).

In the next panel, we consider hypothetical couples where the unmarried mother of only the husband, only the wife, or both have personal care needs. If only one mother has personal care limitations, the odds of living with her married offspring are approximately the same as her odds in the baseline scenario. Conditional on the wife's unmarried mother having self-care problems, the odds of living with the functionally independent unmarried mother of the husband are reduced slightly relative to her odds in the baseline scenario. The odds for a disabled mother of the husband living with the reference couple never equal those of the nondisabled mother of the wife in the baseline. In the simulated event that both mothers have self-care problems, the wife's mother is nearly four times as likely as the husband's disabled mother to live with the couple. Indeed, when only the husband's mother is simulated to have self-care problems, the odds of living with the wife's healthy mother increase relative to the baseline, rather than decrease as we would expect if multigenerational living arrangements were strictly a caregiving solution.

TABLE 5. Predicted Probabilities of Co-Residence between HRS Couple and Unmarried Mothers, by Mother's Personal Care Needs and Sibling Structure of Husband and Wife

	Probability of Co-Residence with	
	Wife's Mother	Husband's Mother
Baseline[a]	.038	.018
Personal Care Needs[b]		
Only wife's mother	.064	.019
Only husband's mother	.064	.027
Both	.105	.027
Sibling Structure[c]		
Husband and wife each have two siblings	.077	.018
Wife is only child and husband has two siblings	.103	.013
Husband is only child and wife has two siblings	.078	.038

Source: From HRS Wave 2.

[a]Baseline scenario: husband's mother is 82; wife's mother is 80; couple has three children; wife's education is 12.5 years; couple's net worth is $218,076; all other variables = 0.

[b]Baseline scenario but varying personal care needs (activities of daily living [ADLs]) of mothers as indicated.

[c]Baseline scenario but varying number of siblings of husband and wife as indicated. Both husband's and wife's mothers have personal care needs (ADLs).

In the bottom panel of table 5, we consider the implications of each spouse having siblings who could possibly substitute for them in living with their unmarried and disabled mother. In the first scenario, the unmarried mothers of both the husband and the wife are functionally limited and both spouses are assumed to have two siblings. Comparing these probabilities (.077 for the wife's mother and .018 for the husband's) with the predicted probabilities when both mothers are disabled but both spouses are only children (.105 and .027) illustrates the substitution effect of having siblings. While the chance of living with the husband's impaired mother is reduced by one-third when the husband is simulated to have two siblings, the chance of living with the wife's mother is reduced by only one-quarter. It appears that having siblings does not curtail a married daughter's filial commitment as much as it does a married son's.

The scenarios shown in the last two rows illustrate the ways in which the husband and wife trade off maternal obligations with their siblings in order to reconcile competition between their respective unmarried mothers. In these simulated couples, both mothers have self-care problems, one spouse is an only child, and the other has two siblings. As we would expect, the odds for living with the unmarried mother who has but one child (the HRS child) are higher than those under the scenario where both disabled mothers have three children (the HRS child and 2 others). More remarkable, however, is the consistent preference for the wife's mother. Even when the wife's mother has other options for living with an adult child and husband is an only child (last row), the couple has a .078 predicted chance of living with her frail mother but only a .038 chance of living with the husband's disabled mother. The odds for co-residing with the husband's mother under this extreme case only equal those of the baseline odds of living with the wife's functionally independent mother. Under none of the simulated scenarios shown in table 5 is the couple more likely to live with the husband's mother than the wife's.

Finally it is important to note that under no circumstances is the couple more likely to live with an unmarried mother than to live alone. Even when the unmarried mothers of both spouses are disabled and have no other children, co-residence between married midlife children and their widowed or divorced mothers is unusual, according to our model.

Discussion

Our analysis provides additional evidence that characteristics of both unmarried mothers and their adult children and children-in-law affect the probability of an elderly mother and adult child living together. We confirm the findings of prior studies that show that co-residence of elderly divorced or widowed mothers and their married adult children is largely reserved for mothers with self-care problems. But our analysis also extends existing research by expressly allowing for competition between the husband's and the wife's unmarried mothers in claiming space in the household of a married child.

Our major finding can be easily summarized: the mother-daughter bond appears to overwhelm other factors in influencing the couple's decision whether to live with the husband's or the wife's unmarried mother. Even in cases where the husband's mother is disabled and lacks other residential alternatives while the wife's mother is independent and has other children, the odds still favor the wife's mother. Although we have described maternal competition for residential space in the language of the "wife's versus the husband's mother," it may be more useful to describe this as a competition between the wife's mother and her mother-in-law. While the number of co-residential arrangements in our sample of HRS couples in wave 2 is small, the wife's report of who benefits from this arrangement provides some insights into the dynamics of multigenerational households. The vast majority of HRS wives who live with their mothers or mothers-in-law report that the arrangement primarily yields benefits for the co-residing mother. This is particularly the case for co-residing mothers-in-law, 82 percent of whom are reported to be the sole beneficiary. Daughters are far more likely to report that the co-residential arrangement conveys benefits for both them and their own mothers.[9] Ingersoll-Dayton, Starrels, and Dowler (1996) similarly report that a co-residing mother-in-law provides less help with housework and child care to her daughter-in-law than do own mothers in comparable households. Choosing to share a home with the wife's unmarried mother may be motivated by stronger kin bonds, but the arrangement may be sustained by a cumulative reciprocity between the mother and daughter.

Our results have implications not only for understanding the joint decision-making process by which husbands and their wives allocate resources to their respective families of origin but also for anticipating how the smaller families of the "baby boom" generation may respond to more complex allocation problems across fragmented family networks. Wachter (1997) has recently argued that declines in the sheer number of biologically linked kin in descending generations of a family will be offset by claims on more distant kin, including stepchildren. Our analysis suggests a limited potential for this pattern of substitution. Relative to stepchildren, biologic children are likely to have a greater commitment to their own mothers' well-being. Yet even the claim of a husband's biologic mother on joint residential space is substantially weaker than that of the wife's biologic mother, suggesting that even own children are not interchangeable resources for parents. It is reasonable to expect that a stepmother's, especially the husband's stepmother's, claim would be weaker still—implying a very limited role for distant kin.

Because of limitations in sample size we have not been able to include all the variables that other researchers, including ourselves (Wolf and Soldo 1988; Soldo, Wolf, and Agree 1990), have shown to affect the risk of residing with an older frail mother. Among the more important of these factors may be differences between the income and assets of adult children and their elderly parents that persist despite the intergenerational correlation of wealth. Finally, we have not taken into account the potential endogeneity of maternal co-residence and the selection of a primary caregiver described by Stern (1995) and Pezzin, Kemper, and Reschovsky (1996). Further research also needs to consider how race and ethnicity specify the residential competition between the husband's and wife's unmarried mothers (Wolf and Soldo 1988; Burr and Mutchler 1992; Zsembik 1993).

NOTES

This research was supported in part by the National Institute on Aging Grant No. UO1 AG09740. John Henretta was a visiting professor at Age Concern Institute of Gerontology, King's College, London, at the time this research was conducted. Chiara Capoferro provided research assistance at Georgetown University. The authors also would like to acknowledge their intellectual debt to F. Thomas Juster, whose strong commitment to interdisciplinary collaboration in all things HRS encouraged the research reported in this essay.

1. In contrast, transfers in the currencies of time or money may be unilaterally decided by one spouse or another. A wife may decide to allocate some of her time to help care for a grandchild or assist her mother while a husband may opt to provide financial help to a child from an earlier marriage.

2. The rare situation in which all biologic parents of the husband and wife are alive and unmarried occurs only if both sets of parents were previously divorced and never remarried or subsequent marriages ended in divorce or death of partner.

3. The sample of couple households at risk for co-residence with a parent(s) was constructed as follows. The 11,596 individual observations were formed into 7,193 households after eliminating 68 observations (34 potential households) whose household indicator variables showed they lived in a household with

another respondent but in which only one of the pair said they were married or partnered. We were uncertain whether the household indicator or the marital status information was in error. From the 7,193 households, we eliminated six same-sex couples, yielding a household count of 7,187. There were a total of 6,903 family respondents in these 7,193 households; that is, 284, or 4 percent, lacked the wife's detailed report of her own and her husband's extended families (secer = 1). One additional household was eliminated because of problems with the wave 1 sib data. Of these 6,902 households, 1,379 unmarried respondents and 1,544 married respondents did not have surviving parents; 968 unmarried respondents and 3,011 married respondents had at least one surviving parent.

4. Hagestad (1986) observes that remarriage in mid- and late life is a "disproportionately male experience" (p 132). There is no instance of an HRS couple at wave 2 having an elderly remarried mother and an unmarried father.

5. Amato, Rezac, and Booth (1995) similarly report that remarried parents, even mothers, receive less help from their adult children than do parents whose marriages are intact.

6. Wives provided all the details on the status of their own and their spouses' parents; they also enumerated both their own and their spouses' siblings.

7. One case was eliminated in which the HRS couple lived with both unmarried mothers.

8. Our most complex model (when both mothers are unmarried) includes only fifteen terms, two of which are intercepts. Limitations in the number of couples living with either the wife's unmarried mother ($n = 66$) or the husband's unmarried mother ($n = 22$) preclude estimation of models with anything but the most basic terms.

9. Determining whose needs are served by an intergenerational transfer becomes more complex if the flow of resources is viewed dynamically. A transfer flowing in one direction (between parent and child) at one point in the life cycle may indicate an exchange balanced by an offsetting flow earlier in the life cycle or an anticipated one in the future (Henretta et al. 1997).

REFERENCES

Amato, Paul R., Sandra J. Rezac, and Alan Booth. 1995. "Helping between Parents and Young Adult Offspring: The Role of Parental Marital Quality, Divorce, and Remarriage." *Journal of Marriage and the Family* 57:363–74.

Aquilino, William S. 1990. "The Likelihood of Parent-Adult Child Co-residence: Effects of Family Structure and Parental Characteristics." *Journal of Marriage and the Family* 52:405–19.

Bishop, Christine E. 1986. "Living Arrangement Choices of Elderly Singles: Effects of Income and Disability." *Health Care Financing Review* 7:65–73.

Burch, Thomas K., and Beverly J. Matthews. 1987. "Household Formation in Developed Societies." *Population and Development Review* 13:495–512.

Burr, Jeffrey A., and Jan E. Mutchler. 1992. "The Living Arrangements of Unmarried Elderly Hispanic Females." *Demography* 29 (1): 93–112.

Chevan, Albert J., and J. Henry Korson. 1972. "The Widowed Who Live Alone: An Examination of Social and Demographic Factors." *Social Forces* 51:45–53.

Cooney, Teresa M. 1989. "Co-residence with Adult Children: A Comparison of Divorced and Widowed Women." *Gerontologist* 29:779–84.

Couch, Kenneth, Mary C. Daly, and Douglas A. Wolf. 1995. "Time? Money? Both? The Allocation of Resources to Older Parents." Paper presented at the annual meeting of the Population Association of America, San Francisco.

Crimmins, Eileen M., and Dominique G. Ingegneri. 1990. "Interaction and Living Arrangements of Older Parents and Their Children." *Research on Aging* 12:3–35.

DaVanzo, Julie, and Frances K. Goldscheider. 1987. "Coming Home Again: Returns to the Nest in Young Adulthood." *Population Studies* 44:241–55.

Freedman, Vicki, Douglas A. Wolf, Beth J. Soldo, and Elizabeth H. Stephen. 1991. "Intergenerational Transfers: A Question of Perspective." *Gerontologist* 31:640–47.

Goldscheider, Frances K., and Calvin Goldscheider, eds. 1989. *Ethnicity and the New Family Economy.* Boulder, CO: Westview Press.

Goldscheider, Frances K., and Linda J. Waite, 1991. *New Families, No Families: The Transformation of the American Home.* Berkeley, CA: University of California Press.

Hagestad, Gunhild O. 1986. "The Aging Society as a Context for Family Life." *Daedalus* 115 (1): 119–69.

Heer, David M., Robert W. Hodge, and Marcus Felson. 1985. "The Cluttered Nest: Evidence That Young Adults are More Likely to Live at Home Now Than in the Past." *Sociology and Social Research* 69:436–41.

Heeringa, Steven G., and Judith H. Connor. 1995. "Technical Description of the Health and Retirement Study Sample Design." Survey Design and Sampling Unit, Institute for Social Research, University of Michigan, Ann Arbor, MI.

Henretta, John, Martha S. Hill, Wei Li, Beth J. Soldo, and Douglas A. Wolf. 1997. "Selection of Children to Provide Care: The Effects of Earlier Parental Transfers." *Journal of Gerontology: Psychological and Social Sciences* (Special Issue) 52B:110–19.

Hirosima, Kiyosi. 1987. "Recent Change in Prevalence of Parent-Child Co-residence in Japan." *Jinkōgaku Kenkyū* [Journal of population studies] 10:33–41.

———. 1988. "A Model of Parent/Child Coresidability Taking Account of Post-nuptial Competition." *Jinkō Mondai Kenkyū* [Journal of Population Problems] 186:14–34.

Juster, F. Thomas, and Richard Suzman. 1995. "An Overview of the Health and Retirement Study." *Journal of Human Resources* 30 (Special Issue): S7–56.

Ingersoll-Dayton, Berit, Marjorie E. Starrels, and David Dowler. 1996. "Caregiving for Parents and Parents-in-laws: Is Gender Important?" *Gerontologist* 36:483–91.

Kojima, Hiroshi. 1990. "Determinants of Co-residence of Married Couples with an Older Mother in Japan." Paper presented at the annual meeting of the Gerontological Society of America, Boston, MA.

Kotlikoff, Laurence, and John Morris. 1990. "Why Don't the Elderly Live with Their Children?: A New Look." In David Wise, ed., *Issues in the Economics of Aging.* Chicago: University of Chicago Press.

Macunovich, Diane J., Richard A. Easterlin, Christine M. Schaeffer, and Eileen M. Crimmins. 1995. "Echoes of the Baby Boom and Bust: Recent and Prospective Changes in Living Alone among Elderly Widows in the United States." *Demography* 32:17–28.

Manton, Kenneth G., and Eric Stallard. 1996. "Longevity in the United States: Age and Sex-Specific Evidence on Life Span Limits from Mortality Patterns, 1960–1990." *Journal of Gerontology: Social Sciences* 51A:B362–75.

Marks, Nadine F. 1996. "Caregiving across the Lifespan: National Prevalence and Predictors." *Family Relations* 45:27–36.

McFadden, Daniel L. 1981. "Econometric Models of Probabilistic Choice." In C. Manski and Daniel L. McFadden, eds., *Structural Analysis of Discrete Data,* 198–272. Cambridge: MIT Press.

Merrill, Deborah M. 1993. "Daughters-in-Law as Caregivers to the Elderly: Defining the In-Law Relationship." *Research on Aging* 15:70–91.

Michael, Robert T., Victor R. Fuchs, and Sharon R. Scott. 1980. "Changes in the Propensity to Live Alone: 1950–1976." *Demography* 17:39–56.

Moon, Marilyn, and Janemarie Mulvey. 1995. *Entitlements and the Elderly.* Washington, DC: Urban Institute Press.

Pezzin, Liliana E., Peter Kemper, and James Reschovsky. 1996. "Does Public Care Substitute for Family Care? Experimental Evidence with Endogenous Living Arrangements." *Journal of Human Resources* 31:650–76.

Rosenzweig, Mark R., and Kenneth J. Wolpin. 1993. "Intergenerational Support and the Life-Cycle Incomes of Young Men and Their Parents: Human Capital Investments, Coresidence, and Intergenerational Financial Transfers." *Journal of Labor Economics* 11:84–112.

Rossi, Alice S., and Peter H. Rossi. 1990. *Of Human Bondage: Parent-Child Relations across the Life Course.* New York: Adine de Gruyter.

Schwartz, Saul, Sheldon Danziger, and Eugene Smolensky. 1984. "The Choice of Living Arrangements by the Elderly." In Henry J. Aaron and Gary Burtless, eds., *Retirement and Economic Behavior,* 229–53. Washington, DC: Brookings Institution.

Smith, James P. 1997. "Wealth Inequality among Older Americans." *Journal of Gerontology: Psychological and Social Sciences* (Special Issue) 52B:74–81.

Soldo, Beth J. 1996. "Cross Pressures in Middle-Aged Adults: A Broader View." Guest editorial in *Journal of Gerontology: Social Sciences* 51B: S271–73.

Soldo, Beth J., and Martha S. Hill. 1993. "Intergenerational Transfers: Economic, Demographic, and Social Perspectives." In George L. Maddox and M. Powell Lawton, eds., *Annual Review of Gerontology and Geriatrics,* 13:187–216. New York: Spring.

———. 1995. "Family Structure and Transfer Measures in the Health and Retirement Study: Background and Overview." *Journal of Human Resources* 30 (Special Issue): S138–57.

Soldo, Beth, J., Douglas A. Wolf, and Emily M. Agree. 1990. "Family, Households, and Care Arrangements of Frail Older Women: A Structural Analysis." *Journals of Gerontology: Social Sciences* 45:S238–49.

Stark, Oded. 1995. *Altruism and Beyond: An Economic Analysis of Transfers and Exchanges within Families and Groups.* Cambridge: Cambridge University Press.

Stern, Steven. 1995. "Estimating Family Long-Term Care Decisions in the Presence of Endogenous Child Characteristics." *Journal of Human Resources* 30:551–80.

U.S. Bureau of the Census. 1996. "65+ in the United States." *Current Population Reports, Special Studies,* no. P23–190. Washington, DC: U.S. Government Printing Office.

Wachter, Kenneth W. 1997. "Kinship Resources for the Elderly." *Philosophical Transactions of the Royal Society: Biological Sciences,* series B, 352:1811–18.

Wolf, Douglas A. 1984. "Kin Availability and the Living Arrangements of Older Women." *Social Science Research* 13:72–89.

———. 1990. "Household Patterns of Older Women: Some International Comparisons." *Research on Aging* 12:463–86.

———. 1994. "The Elderly and Their Kin: Patterns of Availability and Access." In Linda G. Martin and Samuel H. Preston, eds., *Demography of Aging.* Washington, DC: National Academy Press.

Wolf, Douglas A., Vicki Freedman, and Beth J. Soldo. 1997. "The Division of Family Labor: Care for Elderly Parents." *Journal of Gerontology: Psychological and Social Sciences* (Special Issue) 52B:102–9.

Wolf, Douglas A., and Beth J. Soldo. 1988. "Household Composition Choices of Older Unmarried Women." *Demography* 25:387–403.

Zsembik, Barbara A. 1993. "Determinants of Living Alone among Older Hispanics." *Research on Aging* 15 (4): 449–64.

Contributors

Richard V. Burkhauser	Cornell University
Jeff Dominitz	Senior Economist, Resolution Economics, LLC
Debra Dwyer	State University of New York at Stony Brook
Alan L. Gustman	Dartmouth College
John C. Henretta	Department of Sociology, University of Florida
A. Regula Herzog	Institute for Social Research, University of Michigan
Daniel Hill	Institute for Social Research, University of Michigan
Michael D. Hurd	The RAND Corporation, Department of Economics, State University of New York, NBER
N. Anders Klevmarken	Department of Economics, Uppsala University
Maarten Lindeboom	Free University of Amsterdam and Tilberg University, the Netherlands
Charles F. Manski	Department of Economics, Northwestern University
Olivia S. Mitchell	Department of Risk Management and Insurance, University of Pennsylvania
Sara Nichols	Department of Demography, Georgetown University
Andrew A. Samwick	Dartmouth College
James P. Smith	The RAND Corporation

Beth J. Soldo	Department of Demography, Georgetown University
Frank P. Stafford	Department of Economics, Institute for Social Research, University of Michigan
Thomas L. Steinmeier	Texas Technical University
Jules Theeuwes	University of Amsterdam, the Netherlands
Steven F. Venti	Department of Economics, Dartmouth College
Robert B. Wallace	College of Medicine, University of Iowa
Robert J. Willis	Institute for Social Research, University of Michigan
David A. Wise	National Bureau of Economic Research, Cambridge, MA
Isolde Woittiez	University of Leiden, the Netherlands
Douglas A. Wolf	Center for Policy Research, Syracuse University
Edward N. Wolff	New York University
Linda A. Wray	Institute for Social Research, University of Michigan